Diversity in the Workforce

Diversity in the Workforce is a comprehensive, integrated teaching resource providing students with the tools and methodologies they need to negotiate effectively the multicultural workplace, and to counter issues of discrimination and privilege.

Written from an American perspective, the book not only covers the traditional topics of race, gender, ethnicity, and social class, but moves beyond this to explore emerging trends around 'isms' (racism, sexism) as well as transgender issues, spirituality, intergenerational workforce tensions, cross-cultural teams, physical appearance stigmatizing, visible and invisible disabilities, and racial harassment. The book:

- Presents theoretical models to help students think critically about the issues that emerge from workforce diversity;
- Includes a historical perspective that explains the roots of the issues in the workplace today;
- Covers potential legal and ethical issues;
- Introduces a social justice paradigm to encourage social action;
- Illustrates strategies organizations are using to leverage diversity effectively.

With end-of-chapter questions encouraging students to engage in difficult conversations and case studies to stimulate students' awareness of the real problems and issues that emerge from diversity, this book will help students develop the critical, analytical, problem-solving, and decision-making skills they need to mediate or resolve diversity issues as future professionals.

Marilyn Y. Byrd is an assistant professor at the University of Mary Hardin-Baylor, USA. She teaches undergraduate and graduate courses in human resource management, organizational behavior, managerial communications, and business ethics. She is also on the steering committee for the Culture and Diversity Special Interest Group at the Academy of Human Resource Development.

Chaunda L. Scott is an associate professor and the coordinator of the Master of Training and Development Program at Oakland University, USA. She teaches a number of HRD classes at undergraduate and master's levels. She received a Cutting Edge Research Award from the Academy of Human Resource Development in 2009, and in 2013 she was named one of the top 25 Education Professors in Michigan by Online Schools Michigan.

Diversity in the Workforce

Current Issues and Emerging Trends

Edited by Marilyn Y. Byrd & Chaunda L. Scott

Routledge
Taylor & Francis Group

NEW YORK AND LONDON

3-11-15
LN
$66.45

First published 2014
by Routledge
711 Third Avenue, New York, NY 10017

and by Routledge
2 Park Square, Milton Park, Abingdon, Oxon OX14 4RN

Routledge is an imprint of the Taylor & Francis Group, an informa business

Library of Congress Cataloging-in-Publication Data

Diversity in the workforce : current issues and emerging trends/
    edited by Marilyn Y. Byrd & Chaunda L. Scott.
        pages cm
    Includes bibliographical references and index.
    1. Diversity in the workplace.   I. Byrd, Marilyn Y.   II. Scott, Chaunda L.
    HF5549.5.M5D5694 2014
    331.13′3—dc23
    2013026917

ISBN: 978-0-415-85902-8 (hbk)
ISBN: 978-0-415-85903-5 (pbk)
ISBN: 978-0-203-79777-8 (ebk)

Typeset in Caslon
by Apex CoVantage, LLC

Acknowledgments

Dr. Marilyn Y. Byrd: I would like to recognize my family, who has been a source of love, inspiration, guidance, support, and encouragement throughout my lifetime: father, the late Luby L. Smither; mother, the late Dorothy M. Smither; son, Shannon Kyle Byrd; and sisters, the late Carolyn A. Moore, and the late Vickie J. Williams. I would also like to recognize my nephews, Blanton D. Moore, Jason L. Williams, and Jarred B. Williams; and my niece, Jessica Y. Williams-Horn. Finally, I recognize my best friend, Larry D. Piggee, who helps me to stay focused. To the contributing authors, thank you for the endless amount of time you spent working on this textbook. Your contributions are immeasurable. Above all, I acknowledge and give thanks to my Father, in heaven, who continues to bless me in abundant ways.

Dr. Chaunda L. Scott: First, I want to thank all of the contributing authors (subject matter experts) for being a part of this timely and important project. Second, I want to thank the reviewers of this textbook for their helpful feedback. Third, I want to thank my Oakland University Master of Training and Development graduate assistants, Stephanie Johnson and Sherita Jackson, for the outstanding support they provided to this project. I want to also acknowledge the following individuals: my late parents, Walter R. Scott and Margaret A. Scott, and grandparents, George Smith and Addie Smith, for helping me keep my eyes focused on achieving personal and professional goals; my wonderful brothers, Anthony R. Scott, Sr., Walter R. Scott, Jr., and George J. Scott; and my amazing nephews, Anthony R. Scott, II, and Bryson G. Scott, for their passionate support of this project. And last, but not least, I want to recognize my phenomenal mentors, Dr. Charles V. Willie; Dr. Cornel West; my pastor, Dr. Carlyle Fielding Stewart, III; Dr. Terrence E. Maltbia; Dr. Victoria J. Marsick; Dr. Lyle Yorks; Dr. Barbara Mabee; and Dr. Robert Homant for their continuous encouragement and heartfelt support of this critical publication.

Special Acknowledgments

Drs. Byrd and Scott would like to recognize and thank Sharon Golan, Manjula Raman, and the supporting staff from Routledge for their guidance from the conception to the final publication of this textbook. The opportunity to work with Routledge has been a rewarding experience. We trust that this textbook will become a valuable addition to Routledge's resources on diversity in the workforce.

Special Tribute

The editors and authors of this textbook pay tribute to the life of Dr. Roosevelt R. Thomas (May 24, 1944–May 17, 2013) pioneer, thought leader, and guru of managing diversity. We stand on the shoulders of trailblazers like Dr. Thomas as we continue down the road he paved.

Contents

Foreword by Charles V. Willie, Ph.D.

Charles W. Eliot Professor of Education Emeritus
Harvard University

This book discusses some of the supporters of workforce diversity such as government legislation, executive orders, grassroots movements, and educational institutions. Also, the chapters commissioned for this book recognize the value of using specific models, frameworks, and other analytic methods that reveal good, better, and best ways of attaining workforce diversity. Another value of this book is the diversity of intellectual capital and experiences of the chapter authors. They reside in East and West, North and South regions of the United States. It is appropriate that a book on diversity in the workforce should be prepared by a diversified group of scholars. The diversity of scholars has also contributed to the variety of cases used. This is a book that deals with multiple categories of humanity: Women as well as men; Black, Brown, and White people; blue-collar and white-collar workers; and so on.

The emphasis on diversity in this book is aligned with modern and ancient history. In modern history, there is the U.S. Supreme Court's majority opinion in *Grutter vs. Bollinger* (2003). Justice Sandra Day O'Connor repeatedly mentioned "the educational benefits of a diverse student body." Moreover, she said that "the [University of Michigan] Law School's educational judgment that such diversity is essential to its mission is one to which we defer." A story in ancient history tells us that Noah built an ark to save his family from the Great Flood. He also made space onboard to accommodate several couples of nonhuman animals who represented all animals on earth. This was done to guarantee continuity for all after the water receded. Assuming that diversity is a "public good," the authors in this book tell us about alternative ways of achieving it.

Preface

Marilyn Y. Byrd and
Chaunda L. Scott

The purpose of this textbook is to bring to light current issues in diversity that have not been adequately addressed and recognize emerging trends that are having an impact on diversity in the workforce. The need for this textbook stems from our roles as professors in the fields of Human Resource Management (HRM) and Human Resource Development (HRD). We have become increasingly aware of our students' curiosity to: (1) know more about the history of diversity and the issues associated with it in order to better understand its significance in the workplace; and (2) learn what specific knowledge and skills they will need to respond to complex human diversity issues and tensions in the 21st century workplace (Thomas, 2005).

This textbook is intended as a primary resource for upper-level undergraduate and graduate diversity courses across the disciplines of HRD, HRM, Adult Education, Business Administration, Communication, Counseling, Educational Leadership, Human Relations Organizational Leadership, Public Administration, Training and

Development, Teacher Education, and Workforce Education and Development, to name a few. It can also be used as a reference resource for practitioners who are involved in the work of diversity education and diversity training.

The goal of this textbook is to provide students (future business professionals, practitioners, educators, managers, counselors, etc.) with a more informed perspective of diversity by presenting historical, social, and contextual accounts of diversity. Our ultimate goal is to stimulate thinking that recaptures the original essence of recognizing diversity in the workforce and take action-oriented steps towards social justice and social change.

Key Features

This textbook contains several key features that set it apart from similar textbooks on diversity:

1. Students are provided with definitions of historical, current, and emerging terms, theories, and concepts that relate to diversity in the workforce.
2. Real-world examples are provided that illustrate tensions that emerge from diversity.
3. A list of website links to organizations that support diversity initiatives and efforts are provided to enhance students' learning experiences.
4. End-of-chapter critical-thinking discussion questions offer an opportunity for students to engage in difficult conversations in an instructor-facilitated environment. Students will apply critical-thinking skills in order to make an informed decision about the problem or situation that is encountered.
5. End-of-chapter legal, actual, and/or simulated cases reinforce concepts presented in the chapter, which allow students to experience and apply what has been learned to realistic situations. Using a case study pedagogy, students will have the opportunity to test diversity models and frameworks. The case study pedagogy is not designed to come up with a "right" answer, but rather to engage students in conversation about the choices they make.

How to Analyze Case Studies

To make informed decisions and choices, students should use an appropriate method for analyzing cases. Students should begin the analysis by reading the cases thoroughly in order to gather the pertinent facts. The following questions are essential to this process:

• What is the situation? • What is my role in the situation? • What more do I need to know about the situation? • What are the relevant facts? • What supporting evidence do I have?

After the fact-finding part of the process, students consider the options for making an informed decision, and then take the appropriate action. According to McDade (1995), a powerful element of the case study pedagogy is the instructor-facilitated discussion process that follows the analysis—a process that helps students to make important connections and links to the real world. Therefore, instructors play an important part in this part of the process by encouraging student participation, guiding the exploration of the issues from different perspectives, and engaging students in critical debate. The diversity of thought that emerges offers an opportunity for students to learn in a collaborative environment and to consider workforce diversity problems and situations in a variety of ways.

McDade, S.A. (1995). Case study pedagogy to advance critical-thinking. *Teaching of Psychology, 22*(1), 9–10.

Thomas, R. (2005). *Building on the promise of diversity: How we can move to the next level in our workplaces, our communities, and our society.* New York: Amacom.

Instructor Resources

Accompanying this textbook are PowerPoint slides for each chapter, a resource list of supporting organizational websites, and a comprehensive test bank of essay questions.

PART I
ESTABLISHING FOUNDATIONS OF DIVERSITY IN THE WORKFORCE

1

Historical Perspectives for Studying Diversity in the Workforce

Chaunda L. Scott

Chapter Overview

This chapter begins by presenting the learning objectives, the meaning of diversity in the workforce/workforce diversity, diversity, human diversity and a definition of what workforce diversity is not. The importance of knowing the history of human diversity and workforce diversity in the United States will also be discussed, followed by a summary of five key government legislations that have helped to shape and govern the field of workforce diversity. Next, a brief history of human diversity and workforce diversity in the United States will be highlighted, trailed by a summation of the types of organizations in the United States that have emerged as they relate to managing a diverse workforce. Several examples will be shared underscoring the impact that Affirmative Action and Civil Rights laws have had on advancing equal opportunities for minorities and women in the United States. Table 1.1, The Trends in Mandating, Managing, and Leveraging Diversity in the Workforce Framework 1954–2014 by Scott (2014), will also be introduced alongside the reasons why workforce diversity should be studied. Chapter 1 concludes by highlighting the chapter summary, definitions of key terms, and critical-thinking discussion questions. Note: the terms diversity in the workforce and workforce diversity will be used interchangeably throughout this chapter.

Learning Objectives

After reading this chapter, along with completing the chapter summary questions and the case discussion questions, you will be able to:

- Define diversity in the workforce/workforce diversity, diversity, human diversity, and what workforce diversity is not
- Explain the reasons why it is important to know the history of human diversity and workforce diversity in the United States
- Describe key historical government legislations that have helped shape the practice of workforce diversity and direct related human resource development and human resource management decision making and policy
- Explain how the histories of human diversity and workforce diversity have influenced the practice of workforce diversity to date
- Describe the dynamics and dimensions of monolithic, plural, and multicultural organizations
- Explain the ways in which equal opportunities for minorities and women have improved, remained unchanged, or declined in the Unites States since the Affirmative Action and Civil Rights eras
- Describe The Trends in the Mandating, Managing, and Leveraging Diversity in the Workforce Framework 1954–2014 by Scott (2014)
- Explain why students and practitioners in the 21st century should study the practice of workforce diversity

Diversity in Workforce

In the United States, what do the terms **diversity in the workforce** and **workforce diversity** suggest? Do they just mean hiring qualified men and women in the workplace who represent different races, ages, ethnicities and, sexual orientations? Well the answer to this questions is *no*, because workforce diversity is not just about the above-mentioned physical characteristics and individualities in the workplace. It is much more than this. However, unfortunately, this is what many people believe workforce diversity represents.

To provide a clearer understanding of what diversity in the workforce in the United States symbolizes, this chapter describes workforce diversity as valuing the myriad of ways that leaders, business partners, employees, consultants, student workers, volunteers, customers, and visitor groups are commonly viewed as being similar and dissimilar to one another in work environments (Scott, 2012). For example, these characteristics include but are not restricted to gender; race; skin color; age; ethnicity; sexual orientation; marital status; partner status; parental status; maternal status; socioeconomic status; dialect; disability; spiritual beliefs; religious beliefs; ancestry; cultural customs, norms, and traditions; choices of cuisine; eye color; hair color and texture; style of dress; professional appearance; height and weight; educational level; professional work experience; military experience; world view; personality; knowledge, skills, and abilities; work ethic; creative talents; demeanor; mannerisms; professionalism; adaptability to change; handling stress; managing conflict; dealing with emotions; leadership style; followership style; occupation titles; occupation responsibilities; weekly schedules; seniority level; salary level; functioning in teams; functioning autonomously; cultivating a welcoming work environment; level of personal commitment; degree of professional loyalty; providing feedback; receiving feedback; delivering customer service; receiving customer service; expressing appreciation; conveying disapproval; professional interest; personal interests; life experiences; where one lives; birth place; style of living; and political views (Scott, 2012).

As shown by the extensive, and yet evolving, list of similar and dissimilar characteristics presented above, the construct of workforce diversity is one that is wide-ranging in its approach in that it acknowledges not only numerous human ways of being in work environments, but also numerous human ways of knowing, behaving, and communicating in the workforce simultaneously. The descriptive terms similar and dissimilar also play an instrumental role in the definitions of workforce diversity in that they shift the focus from just being on individual differences to include the variety of ways individuals are alike in work settings. The definitions of diversity and human diversity likewise follow the same format in that they too focus on "the countless ways human beings are similar as well as dissimilar from one another throughout the world" (Scott, 2012).

Moreover, by distinguishing the individuals in the workforce by their occupational and nonoccupational roles in the definition of workforce rather than just by the single term "individuals" more clearly helps us to better understand the types of roles that individuals from a variety of diverse backgrounds perform in the workforce. Thus, relieving the readers of this chapter in speculating what these roles are.

According to ASME Professional Practice Curriculum (n.d.), workforce diversity is not: (1) an "affirmative action" strategy; (2) a "quota" system aimed at hiring a certain number of qualified minorities and women in organization; or (3) a lack of professional standards in the workforce because qualified minorities and women are represented at all levels of the organization. Therefore, by having a clearer understanding of what workforce diversity is, and is not, in both theory and practice, new insights are offered for advancing workforce diversity in the 21st century, specifically in the areas of "leadership, research and measurement, education, alignment of management systems, and follow-up" (Cox, 2001, p. 19).

The Reasons Why It Is Important to Know the History of Human Diversity and Workforce Diversity in the United States

At present, the relatively young and evolving field of workforce diversity in the United States is a popular area of study in a variety of professional disciplines, which include human resource development, training and development, human resource management, organizational leadership, workforce education and development, entrepreneurship, counseling, military education, adult education, and educational leadership, to name a few. It is also an area of study that continues to prosper and be recognized as one of the core guiding principles in many types of organizational settings, e.g., fortune 500 corporations, for-profit and nonprofit agencies, mid-size companies, small businesses, institutions of higher education, and K–12 academies.

Yet, in spite of these affirmations, less emphasis has been placed on connecting it to the history of diversity and workforce diversity in the United States. This is mainly because much of the literature available on human diversity and workforce diversity (e.g., in textbooks, mainstream books, films, and articles) is being presented from a modern-day perspective, with little or no mention of their connection to their historical beginnings.

It is also important to connect the historical aspects of human diversity to the current state of diversity in the workforce so that current and future research and practice initiatives may be centered around our understanding the following questions:

- How will we know and understand what past events in the United States have or have not helped to shape the current state of human diversity and workforce diversity developments?
- How are we going to determine what current efforts in the United States will or will not help to shape our understanding of the future of human diversity and workforce diversity developments?
- How will we know if we are not duplicating past human diversity and workforce diversity behaviors, practices, and events that have been harmful in both theory and practice to individuals and organizations without being knowledgeable of the history of human diversity and its current relationship to workforce diversity in the United States?

It is further interesting to point out a few little known historical diversity and workforce diversity facts that are critical to understanding and applying these concepts in practice. For example, did you know that:

- the term "diversity includes everyone" (Thomas, 1991, p. 10)?
- the United States has been "culturally diverse for several hundred years" (McMillian-Capehart, 2003, p.1)?
- the earlier terms used to describe different groups of people by race were "Mongolian, Caucasian, [and] Negro" (McMillian-Capehart, 2003, p. 2)?
- diversity issues were not mentioned in the "organizational literature" in the United States "until the civil rights movement of the 1960s brought about an awareness of African Americans in the workforce" (McMillian-Capehart, 2003, p.1) ?
- (according to McMillian-Capehart, 2003) the idea of human diversity in the workforce was mainly disregarded by corporations as an important issue until Johnston and Packer's (1987)

groundbreaking research titled *Workforce 2000: Work and Workers for the Twenty-First Century* raised awareness of its importance?

Given these astonishing facts, there is a need for individuals studying the topic of diversity in the workforce and practitioners working in professional fields to be familiar with the history of diversity and workforce diversity in the United States in order to better understand its importance as it relates to valuing and leveraging the current and emerging dynamics of workforce diversity in the 21st century. In the next section, five key government directives will be presented as an introduction to the brief history of human diversity and workforce diversity in the United States that follows.

Historical Government Legislations That Have Helped to Shape the History and Practice of Workforce Diversity

Brown versus the Board of Education *1954 (United States Supreme Court Ruling)*

In 1950, Oliver Brown, an African American man and father attempting to enroll his seven-year-old daughter Linda Brown into a White elementary school located in Topeka, Kansas, along with other African Americans who were doing the same thing (Oracle Education Foundation, 2013). They were doing this because the White school was closer to their home and it had much better educational resources than the African American school that his daughter was currently attending (Oracle Education Foundation, 2013). During this same year, all of the African American children were denied admission into the White school because of their race (Oracle Education Foundation, 2013). In 1951, Oliver Brown, along with other African American parents who were dissatisfied with the White school's decision to deny their children admission, decided to sue the state of Kansas over this issue. However, later in 1951, they lost their case because of their race (Oracle Education Foundation, 2013). Then in 1952, Oliver Brown, along with the National Association for the Advancement of Colored People (NAACP), other African American parents and supporters who were also very dissatisfied with the current state of educational opportunities for African American children, took this case to the United States Supreme Court (Oracle Education Foundation, 2013).

On "May 17, 1954 the United States Supreme Court issued a unanimous decision that it was unconstitutional [and a violation of] the 14th amendment to separate children in public schools for no other reasons than their race" (Congress of Racial Equality, 2013). Even though this ruling passed, schools in the United States moved very slowly in integrating African Americans students along with treating them fairly. This is mainly because a lot of individuals during this time period "were still prejudice against Blacks" (Oracle Education Foundation, 2013). Nonetheless, the *Brown vs. the Board of Education*'s triumph was successful in reforming educational enrollment practices and policies as we know them today for all students and by bringing "this country one step closer to living up to its democratic ideas" (Congress of Racial Equality, 2013).

Governmental Mandate—10925—First Stage of Affirmative Action

This government directive was distributed by President John F. Kennedy in 1961 (Brunner, 2013). The objective of this directive was to ensure that all employment-related procedures funded by the United States government are culturally nondiscriminatory.

Governmental Mandate—Title VII Civil Rights Act of 1964
(Amended in 1972 and 1991)

Signed by President Lyndon B. Johnson in 1964, this act forbids acts of unfairness and inequality in all forms as it relates to "race, color, religion, and national origin" (Brunner, 2013, p. 1). In 1965, the Civil Rights Act of 1964 was enforced and regarded as a defining moment in the history of the United States by moving "from 346 years of treating blacks as inferior in every way to treating them as equals in education, housing, employment, public accommodations and receipt of federal funds" (Bennett-Alexander & Hartman, 2007, p. 182). During this same time period in 1965 in the United States, the "Beatles" rock and roll band was growing in popularity and fame ((Bennett-Alexander & Hartman, 2007).

Governmental Mandate—11246—Affirmative
Action—The Implementation Stage

This government mandate was distributed by President Johnson in 1965 for the purpose of ordering all "government contractors" (e.g., service providers, freelancers, consultants, and suppliers) "take affirmative action" as it relates to employing [qualified] minorities that have been historically excluded because of their "race, color, religion, sex, and national origin" (Brunner, 2013, p. 1). This mandate further required that all government employers take measures such as the following: (a) establish procedures to confirm that fair hiring practices were followed, (b) keep records that document their hiring practices, and (c) create a timeline to show when objectives were met (Brunner, 2013). Roughly two years later, in 1967, this mandate was modified to include gender for the purpose of addressing and monitoring gender inequality issues in employment (Brunner, 2013).

Governmental Mandate—Philadelphia Order

Then in 1969 President Richard Nixon created the Philadelphia Order, which required "government contractors" to use unprejudiced employment procedures and show that "affirmative action" was used in increasing the numbers of minorities and women hired in construction jobs (Brunner, 2013). According to Brunner, the city of Philadelphia was selected because it was identified by the United States government as an offensive lawbreaker of the equal opportunity regulation for being intimidating and unreceptive to hiring African Americans.

A Brief History of Human Diversity and Workforce Diversity

As noted previously by McMillian-Capehart (2003), the United States has a long history of being humanly diverse. It is also a society that consists of both U.S.-born minorities (Schafer, 2010) and immigrants. Apart from the Native Americans, also known as the first Americans (Schaefer, 2010), the entire populace of the United States has immigrant roots (McMillian-Capehart, 2003). According to Gossett (1963, as cited in McMillian-Capehart, 2003), the early immigrant groups of the 16th and 17th centuries served mainly as the manual [slave] workforce in the United States, which included individuals of "African descent, Spanish descent, and European descent" as well as "Italians, [the] Irish, Russians, Germans, Scandinavians, Norwegians and [individuals of] Native American descent" (p. 3). During this same time period and continuing through the 19th century, the established views by the early "English" settlers specifically towards "African and Indian" slaves was that they would conform to the American way of knowing and being by becoming "Christians" (p. 3). According to Newman (as cited in Schaefer, 2010), what this idea suggests is that the immigrant groups would ultimately take on "a new cultural identity" and become a part of the "melting pot" (p. 23) in the United States.

After slavery ended in the United States in the mid-19th century and through the early 20th century, there were U.S.-born minorities and immigrant groups (e.g., African Americans, African immigrants, Chinese Americans, Chinese immigrants, Mexican Americans, and Mexican immigrants) that were not allowed to fully participate in American society because of racism, prejudice, and discrimination (Schaefer, 2010). Jim Crow segregation racial separation laws were as well enforced during this time period (Parrillo, 2005). Examples of Jim Crow separation laws include but are not limited to the following: "separate hospitals for Blacks, separate prisons for Blacks, separate public and private schools for Blacks, separate cemeteries for Blacks, separate restrooms for Blacks, and separate public accommodations for Blacks," to name a few (Pilgrim, 2012). Moreover, during this timeframe, specifically in 1920, women were finally granted the right to vote (The Fight for Women's Suffrage, 2013).

By the 1960s, the U.S. government under the direction of President Kennedy and his Committee on Equal Opportunity began validating the idea of workforce diversity to end acts of "discrimination by the government and its contractors" (ASME Professional Practice Curriculum, n.d.). Beginning in 1961, President John F. Kennedy created Governmental Mandate 10925—First Stage of Affirmative Action to eliminate cultural prejudice in employment financed by the United States government (Brunner, 2013). In 1964, President Lyndon B. Johnson passed the Title VII Civil Rights Act, which forbids "discrimination of all kinds based on race, color, religion and national origin" (p. 1). Also in 1964, President Johnson delivered a powerful lecture to the graduates of Howard University, a historically Black university, where he endorsed the need for a government mandate like affirmative action in the United States (Brunner, 2013). In this lecture, President Johnson noted that the civil rights directives by themselves could not eradicate acts of inequality the United States (Brunner, 2013). He further stated that:

> You cannot wipe away the scars of centuries [e.g., slavery, lynching, racism, sexism, inequality, discrimination, unfairness, and prejudice] by saying: now, you are free to go where you want, do as you desire, and choose the leaders you please. You do not take a man [and woman] who for [hundreds of] years has been hobbled by chains, liberate [them] bring [them] to the starting line of a race, saying 'you are free to compete with all the others,' and still justly believe you have been completely fair. . . . This is the next and more profound stage of the battle for civil rights. We seek not just freedom but opportunity—not just legal equity but human ability—not just equality as a right and theory, but equality as a fact and result. (Brunner, 2013, p. 1)

To further expand and promote equal employment opportunity, President Johnson enforced Governmental Mandate 11246—also recognized as Affirmative Action—The Implementation Stage (Brunner, 2013). As previously stated, the purpose of this mandate was to require that government contractors take affirmative action steps toward hiring qualified minorities that had been historically excluded from employment opportunities. This was a critical move during this time period because it shifted the practice and conversation on affirmative action from just focusing on racial issues to focusing on fair employment policies and procedures. In 1967, this order was modified to include gender for the purpose of addressing and monitoring gender inequality issues (Brunner, 2013).

President Richard Nixon introduced the Philadelphia Order in 1969 to ensure more equitable and fair hiring practices in the construction industry. The city of Philadelphia was selected because the government identified certain employers there as being offensive lawbreakers of the equal opportunity regulation; specifically by being intimidating and unreceptive to hiring African Americans. President

Nixon also made it known (1) that "quotas" would not be used; and (2) that state workers would need to prove that "affirmative action" efforts were being enforced by keeping records to validate that the objectives and target dates provided by the government were utilized in enlarging the numbers of qualified minorities and women hired in construction jobs (Brunner, 2013). Note: the Philadelphia Order was the most authoritative government mandate in assuring "fair hiring practices in construction jobs" (p. 1).

According to Workforce Diversity History (ASME Professional Practice Curriculum, n.d.), although government directives and strategies of the 60s and 70s did not have a vast impact on eliminating covert biases, eradicating disguised acts of inequity in business settings, and on changing the viewpoints of employers and employees regarding the need for workforce diversity efforts, "human resource" strategies in business settings "improved" as a result of the changes issued by the Affirmative Action and Civil Rights laws. Examples of these improvements according to Glazer (1975, as cited in McMillian-Capehart, 2003) include: (1) a demand for organizations to be free of prejudice and unfairness; (2) a demand for organizations to treat minorities and women applicants and workers fairly; and (3) an increase in qualified minorities and women applying for jobs and being employed by organizations. However, aside from these positive developments, many organizations recognized that just employing diverse employees did not provide them with the anticipated advantages of workforce diversity (ASME Professional Practice Curriculum, n.d.). There were also signs that declared organizations would have to create a cadre of new practices and policies to truly reap the advantages of a workforce that is diverse (ASME Professional Practice Curriculum, n.d.).

By the 1980s, many organizations began to realize that diversity should be regarded as a core business strategy rather than just viewed as an authorized and legalized methodology sponsored by the United States government with which they must comply (ASME Professional Practice Curriculum, n.d.). Additionally in the 80s, the concept of "managing workforce diversity" was viewed as a useful effort that would help workplaces begin to create diverse and inclusive work settings (Thomas, 2006). Diversity training also emerged during this time period in the workplace and continued to blossom in the 90s in business settings (ASME Professional Practice Curriculum, n.d.) as an approach used to assist employees in understanding their own beliefs, actions, and biases as it relates to working with diverse employee groups (Noe, 2010). Noe further asserts that diversity training assists employees and in gaining the competencies needed to work in multicultural and multiethnic work setting. According to Diversity Training University International (2013), diversity training is one of the most popular and well-known initiatives being used by organizations.

Presently, in the 21st century, workforce diversity frameworks and approaches such as diversity management (Thomas, 1991, 2006), strategic diversity management (Thomas, 2006), and world-class diversity management (Thomas, 2010) are being utilized by many organizations along with a variety strategies in the forms of organizational policies and practices, i.e., vision and mission statements, cultural and climate audits, and strategic planning to assist organizations in achieving their diversity goals (Thomas, 1991, 2006, 2010). Organizational initiatives in the areas of recruitment and retention, education and training, mentoring, and career development are also being utilized by organizations to meet modern-day diversity objectives (Cox, 1993, 2001).

Yet, in spite of the progress being made by many organizations that welcome, value, and reap the benefits of workforce that is diverse, there is still a need for more organizations in the United States to fully embrace the concepts of diversity and workforce diversity beyond just having written diversity mission and vision statements (Scott, 2012). There is also a need for more organizations to draw upon effective and well-known workforce diversity strategies for guidance to create constructive diverse and inclusive work settings (Scott, 2012). For example, the diversity management frameworks previously mentioned by Thomas (1991, 2006, 2010) are invaluable resources that organizations can draw upon to begin crafting constructive diverse and inclusive work settings (Scott, 2012). Note: a description of the above frameworks by Thomas (1991, 2006, 2010) can be found in The Trends in Mandating, Managing, and Leveraging Diversity in the Workforce Framework 1954–2014 by Scott (2014) on pages 20–26.

Types of Organizations in the United States

According to Cox (1993), there have been three kinds of organizations in the United States that have highlighted the specific aspects of human diversity enlargement and change. The first type is called the "monolithic organization" and is described as being a "homogeneous" workforce made up of mainly White men in upper management positions with a few females and people of color employed in low ranking positions, e.g., typists, cooks, and janitors. Cox further states that monolithic organizations were "designed by" and for homogeneous individuals. Therefore, according to Cox, in a monolithic organization, attention is not focused on creating workplaces that are diverse. As a result, Cox asserts that minorities and women employed in monolithic organizations encounter acts of unfairness and prejudice that were rooted in the "policies and practices of the organization" (p. 227). Finally, monolithic organizations are characterized by low levels of conflict due to its largely homogeneous composition (Cox, 1993).

The second type of organization type is the plural organization. The plural organization according to Cox (1993) is more liberal in its approach to creating and cultivating a diverse organization because it is more "heterogeneous" (diverse) than the monolithic organization. The reason for this is that it seeks out human diversity and uses supportive practices to do so (Cox, 1993). The practices used include but are not limited to hiring and promotion efforts. Various types of diversity training sessions are also used to educate individuals in plural organizations about diversity (Cox, 1993). For example, these types of organizations may offer manager training on equal opportunity such as civil rights laws, ADA [the American Disabilities Act], and sexual harassment (Cox, 1993). Yet, according to Cox "the plural organization tends to be diverse in phenotype, but genuine cultural diversity in these organizations may be limited" (p. 228). One reason for this, as noted by Cox, is that plural organizations rely on standard integration efforts over innovative diversity efforts to foster diversity inclusion. Last, Cox notes that diversity management guidelines and procedures in plural organizations are often viewed by some White men as a form of affirmative action that provides advantages to minorities and women while limiting opportunities for White men.

The third type of organization submitted by Cox (1993) is called the multicultural organization. The central features of this type of organization, according to Cox, include welcoming human diversity; hiring qualified minorities and women at all ranks; utilizing and appreciating the diverse talents and perspectives that minorities and women bring to the organization; the absence of racism, sexism, prejudice, and discrimination in personnel and higher administration-related procedures; and effective diversity management strategies that assist with reducing human diversity-related hostilities (e.g., clashes, disputes, and potential lawsuits) amongst diverse employee groups and the organization. To assist organizations who are seeking to become multicultural organizations, Cox and Blake (1991, as cited in Cox, 1993), offer a framework for driving change in work settings as it relates to managing and appreciating diversity in the workforce. The component of their five-stage framework examines the areas of "leadership, research and measurement, education, changes in culture and management systems, and follow-up" (p. 229–241). In Chapter 2, this framework will be discussed in more detail to highlight its theoretical underpinnings and utility as it relates to the construction of multicultural organizations.

Given the evolving history of human diversity and workforce diversity to date, the question now becomes how have issues related to human diversity equality improved in the workplace and society since the affirmative action and civil rights eras? According to a panel of consultants from the Crossroads Anti-Racism Organizing and Training Organization (1996) many issues related to human diversity equality in society and the workplace have greatly improved, while other issues have remained unchanged, or declined. Below, several examples are highlighted by the Crossroads Anti-Racism Organizing and Training (1996) panel of consultants along with other sources on the aforementioned three areas.

Affirmative Action and the Civil Rights Eras: A Progress Report

Examples of How Human Diversity Equality Issues Have Improved in the United States since the Affirmative Action and Civil Rights Eras

- The disassembling of segregation laws (e.g., African Americans and minorities were permitted to drink from any public water fountains, use any public rest rooms, and sit on any seats of the bus).

- Increased educational opportunities for people of color and women (e.g., as a result of the *Brown vs. the Board of Education* Supreme Court ruling in 1954 ending race-based school segregation and the dismantling of other segregation laws in general).

- More qualified people of color and women employed in the workplace (e.g., as a result of the civil rights and affirmative action legislation and improved educational opportunities).

- Increased employment opportunities available for people of color and women in a variety of fields and positions (e.g., health care, business, science, education, criminal justice, government, technology, and human service fields).

- A growing middle class of people of color and women (e.g., due to improve educational and employment opportunities for these groups).

- More multicultural and human diversity educational resources are available (e.g., books, films, courses, educational trips to different countries, seminars, webcasts, and conferences).

- Open housing (e.g., people of color can choose where they want to live).

- An increased acceptance of inclusivity of human diversity (e.g., more diverse leaders, business partnerships, employees, consultants, student workers, volunteers, customers, and visitor groups in the workforce [Scott, 2012]; more diverse friendships, relationships, marriages, multicultural adoptions, and church memberships; and greater acceptance of homosexuality, same-sex marriages, bisexuality, and the transgendered lifestyle. However, this does not take into account the culture and climate of an organization as being one that is welcoming and supportive or non-welcoming and unsupportive of a diverse workforce (Scott, 2012).

- More dialogue in organizations, K–12 schools, universities, government agencies, and religious settings on issues related to human diversity (e.g., racism, gender inequality, sexual orientation, ageism, disability issues and concerns, ethnic bullying, religion and spirituality immigration, multiculturalism, and diversity and inclusion policies and practices).

- More people of color and women have been elected as government officials, (e.g., the election of Barack Hussein Obama in 2008 and re-election in 2012 as the 44th and the first two-term African American President of the United States. Note: President Barak Hussein Obama identifies himself as African American (Washington, 2008) even though his cultural background is biracial. And in 2003 and 2007, Jennifer Mulhern Granholm was elected as the 47th governor of Michigan, Michigan's first two-term white female governor. Note: Jennifer Mulhern Granholm is a Canadian-born American citizen (Bell, 2012).

Examples of How Human Diversity Equality Issues Have Remained Unchanged in the United States Since the Affirmative Action and Civil Rights Eras

- Unemployment gap remains higher for people of color than Whites with the same level of education and work experience.
- Financial support by the government is less in urban communities as compared to suburban communities.
- The poverty gap is unchanged for people of color.

Examples of How Human Diversity Equality Issues Have Declined in the United States Since the Affirmative Action and Civil Rights Eras

- Affirmative action laws have been disassembled in several states, (e.g., in California, Texas, and Michigan). The question that now remains to be answered is how has the elimination of these laws in several states helped or hindered the progress in the United States in achieving equality for all people (Scott, 2012)?
- Racism along with various modern forms of discrimination are functioning at the institutional level in the United States and internationally and are imbedded within the climate and culture of society (e.g., inadequate work standards and conditions for certain ethnic groups and their children, unfair financial business transactions and practices, racial hate crimes, racial profiling, linguistic profiling, obesity profiling, age profiling, sexual orientation profiling, and bullying and ethnic bullying to name a few).

Rapidly changing demographics in the United States is also another important workforce diversity issue that has emerged since the Affirmative Action and Civil Rights movements. For example, according to Schafer (2010), the immigrant population in the United States has remained steady since the country attained its independence. Nevertheless, "in the last thirty years the numbers of legal immigrants has exceeded the numbers of the early 1900s."

A second demographic forecast noted by Camarota (as cited in DeSimone, Werner, & Harris, 2002, p. 621) is that the United States workforce will reflect the following population patterns by the year 2020.

- The percentage of women will enlarge beyond its current range of "60%."
- African Americans will make up "11%" of the labor force "through 2020."
- "Hispanics" will make up "14%" of the labor force "by 2020."
- "Asians" will make up "6%" of the labor force "by 2020."

According to Schafer (2010), even though the population trends above highlight that the United States is becoming more diverse, the social ills of "prejudice, discrimination and mistrust" will more than likely continue to persist.

Given the profound history of workforce diversity to date, where do we go from here as it relates to addressing current and emerging workforce diversity issues? To answer this question, Table 1.1 introduces The Trends in Mandating, Managing, and Leveraging Diversity in the Workforce Framework—1954–2014 by Scott (2014), which provides an overview of the government-ordered directives and voluntary organizational strategies used in the United States over the past 60 years to integrate human diversity into the workforce. This framework also provides an opportunity for students and practitioners to critically reflect on the current strengths and limitations of existing workforce diversity efforts as well as consider what new workforce diversity policies and practices will be needed in the future to further leverage workforce diversity.

Table 1.1 The Trends in Mandating, Managing, and Leveraging Diversity in the Workforce Framework, 1954–2014 (Scott, 2014)

	TREND ONE	TREND TWO	TREND THREE
Eras	Affirmative Action Era—reactive mandated government stances	Diversity Management and Strategic Diversity Management Eras—voluntary progressive stances adopted by organizations that support workforce diversity practices	World-Class Diversity Management Era—a voluntary, proactive, and progressive stance adopted by organizations that support this workforce diversity approach
Timeframe	1954–2014	1980–2014	2010–2014
Definitions	Affirmative Action Efforts Highlighted in the Era:	Diversity Management is an administrative procedure for creating work settings that support the entire workforce (Thomas, 1991, p. 10).	World-Class Diversity Management offers a strategic process to advance the current state of diversity management in organizations worldwide.
	Brown vs. the Board of Education, Executive Order 10925—Affirmative Action Stage One, The Civil Rights Act, Governmental Mandate 11246—Affirmative Action Implementation Stage, and the Philadelphia Order stances.	In 1984–1996 Diversity Management was defined as creating work settings "that work for all employees" (Thomas, 2006, p. 93).	World Class Diversity Management is a strategic process aimed at developing premier policies and practices to deal with "any" diversity concern worldwide in the workplace (Thomas, 2010, p. 3).
	Affirmative Action programs "are meant to break down barriers, both visible and invisible, to level the playing field, and to make sure everyone is given an equal break" (Civil Rights 101, 2013). Affirmative Action is also a "temporary measure" (2013).	In 1984, the American Institute of Managing Diversity was created by Dr. Roosevelt Thomas to offer an accompaniment "to Affirmative Action," a new viewpoint on "racial issues within the workforce," build literature on this topic, and "facilitate" organizational "change" associated with the management of diversity in the workforce (Thomas, 2006, p. 87).	
	After the Civil War ended along with slavery in the late 19th century, Jim Crow segregation laws in the early 20th century enforced racial separation along with the support of racism and discrimination (Parrillo, 2005, p. 99).		
	The 1954 *Brown vs. the Board of Education* United States Supreme Court ruling legalized "that it was unconstitutional [and a violation of the 14th amendment] to have separate schools for children for no other reasons than their race" (Congress for Racial Equality, 2013).		

(Definitions continued)		
	Governmental Mandate—10925 First Stage of Affirmative Action.

This government directive was distributed by President John F. Kennedy in 1961 (Brunner, 2013, p. 1). The objective of this directive was to ensure that all "hiring and employment" efforts funded by the United States government are culturally nondiscriminatory (p. 1).

In 1964, President Lyndon B. Johnson approved the Civil Right Acts which outlaws acts of unfairness and inequality in all forms as it relates to "race, color, religion, and national origin" (Brunner, 2013, p. 1). In 1965, the Civil Rights Act of 1964 was enforced (Bennett-Alexander & Hartman, 2007, p. 182).

Governmental Mandate—11246 Affirmative Action is Implemented.

This government mandate was distributed by President Johnson in 1965 for the purpose of ordering all "government contractors" (e.g., service providers, freelancers, consultants, and suppliers) "take affirmative action" as it relates to employing [qualified] minorities that have been historically excluded because of their "race, color, religion, sex, and national origin" (Brunner, 2013, p. 1). This mandate further required that all government employers take measures such as the following: (a) establish procedures to confirm that fair hiring practices were followed, (b) keep records that document their hiring practices (p. 1), and (c) create a timeline to show when objectives were met (p. 1). Roughly two years later, in 1967, this mandate was modified to include gender for the purpose of addressing and monitoring gender inequality issues in employment (p. 1).

In 1969, the Philadelphia Order was presented by President Nixon to "guarantee fair hiring practices in construction jobs" (Brunner, 2013, p. 1). According to Brunner (2013), the city of Philadelphia was chosen because they were identified by the government as aggressive lawbreakers of the "equal opportunity" regulations because of their reluctance to work with African Americans (p.1). It was also required that state workers keep records to validate that they were meeting the government objectives and target dates regarding enlarging the numbers of qualified minorities and women hired (p. 1). | In 1996–2000 Diversity Management was defined by Thomas (as cited in Thomas, 2006, p. 89) as "any mixture of items characterized by differences and similarities."

"Diversity Management [is] the practice of addressing and supporting multiple lifestyles and personal characteristics within a defined group. Management activities include educating the group and providing support for the acceptance of and respect for various racial, cultural, societal, geographic, economic and political backgrounds" (Diversity Management, 2013).

In 2001–2005 Strategic Diversity Management was defined as the art of "making quality decisions amid differences, similarities and tensions" in the workforce (Thomas, 2006, p. 93). |

(Continued)

Table 1.1 *(Continued)*

	TREND ONE	TREND TWO	TREND THREE
Focus	The focus of Affirmative Action is on recruiting "qualified" females and diverse groups that have historically been denied access to employment opportunities so they can be a part of the larger talent pool that all workers are selected from (Bennett-Alexander & Hartman, 2007, p. 184).	Diversity Management is an organizational strategy that expands the focus of workforce diversity "beyond race and gender" to include other human diversities, e.g., ethnicity, sexual orientation, social class, disability, and religion, to name a few (Thomas, 1991, p.12). Diversity Management permits individuals from all diverse back grounds to thrive in work settings as they meet organizational goals. (Thomas, 1991, p.167). Strategic Diversity Management is focused on rendering quality assessments "amid differences, similarities and tensions" in the workforce (Thomas, 2006, p. 93)	Prerequisites needed to attain World-Class Diversity Management standing in the workplace, according to Thomas (2010. p. 4) includes the following: Creating respected theoretical models, policies, and practices that can be used to deal with varying humans diversity matters worldwide in work settings. Creating procedures and practices that can communicate across global borders effectively about matters of diversity. Creating procedures and practices that promote knowledge of the entire field of diversity, not just matters related to the dimensions of diversity, e.g., ethnicity, age, and sexual orientation, to name a few. Establishing procedures that can be modified worldwide to deal with diversity matters. Creating coalitions to develop diversity criteria to guide the practice of World-Class Diversity Management.

Advantages	A benefit of "Affirmative Action" is that it has been the chief, often the exclusive, strategy for including and assimilating minorities and women into the corporate world" (Thomas, 1999, p. 17).	A benefit of Strategic Diversity Management is that it must be utilized by professionals that have high levels of "diversity management skills and diversity maturity" (Thomas, 2006, p. 154-161) Another benefit of Strategic Diversity Management is that it is a well-thought-out process to address diversity concerns and conflicts in the workplace and to make informed judgments in the area of diversity management. It also provides "time for reflection" to prevent diversity matters form escalating (Thomas, 2006. p. 150). An additional benefit of Strategic Diversity Management is that it can assist with the handling of "tensions" in the workplace, e.g., "racism and sexism" (Thomas, 2006, p. 166).	The benefits of World-Class Diversity Management according to Thomas (2010, p. 9-12) include: Building worldwide organizational relationships that foster cooperation Creating "world" diversity theoretical models, policies, and procedures that can be used by companies globally Moving organizations away from just focusing on "race, gender, and ethnicity" Enhancing "global talent management" in organizations Creating "world-wide best practices in diversity management" Enhancing overall organizational "professionalism" and "readiness" to manage World-Class diversity

(Continued)

Table 1.1 *(Continued)*

	TREND ONE	TREND TWO	TREND THREE
Challenges	A challenge surrounding Affirmative Action is the incorrect belief that its purpose is to legally employ "unqualified women and minorities" over "qualified white males" (Bennett-Alexander & Hartman, 2007, p. 181).

A second misguided belief about Affirmative Action is that it is just a preference effort designed specifically for "unqualified women and minorities" to purposely take employments opportunities away from Whites who are qualified (Bennett-Alexander & Hartman, 2007, p. 181).

A third inaccurate belief about Affirmative Action is that it only provides advantages to unqualified Blacks, when in fact White women are the main beneficiaries of Affirmative Action as it relates to their inclusion in the workforce (Bennett-Alexander & Hartman, 2007, p. 181). | A misconception surrounding the idea of managing diversity is that its focus is on "white males managing women and minorities" rather than a management strategy that encourages and enables all workers in work settings (Thomas, 1999, p. 11).

Another misconception surrounding the idea of managing diversity offered by Thomas (as cited in Thomas, 2006, p.87) is that it is focused on monitoring or restricting diverse workers in the workforce, instead of being known as a concept that encourages all workers to prosper in the workforce.

A challenge surrounding Strategic Diversity Management is that must be utilized by professionals that have high levels of "diversity management skills and diversity maturity" (Thomas, 2006, p. 154–161). | Challenges surrounding World-Class Diversity Management according to Thomas (2010, p. 6-8) include:

The absence of expertise by leaders, supervisors, and professionals to effectively manage diversity in the workplace along with their support for it

A limited view of what diversity represents

A lack of attention given to respected theoretical models and practices that would be useful to the discipline of diversity

Diversity is not fully perceived as a valued-added organizational strategy. Therefore, the need for diversity in organizations is weakening

Diversity is viewed as a problem for organizations to address rather than a value added opportunity for organizations to invest in

"Leaders" rely on their personal understanding of diversity to manage diverse work environments and to address specific diversity matters |

Goals	A goal of "Affirmative Action programs [is to] break down barriers, both visible and invisible, to level the playing field, and to make sure everyone is given an equal break" (Civil Rights 101, 2013) Affirmative Action is also a "temporary measure" (2013). Another goal of Affirmative Action is to recruit "qualified" females and diverse groups that have historically been denied access to employment opportunities so they can be a part of the larger talent pool that all workers are selected from (Bennett-Alexander & Hartman, 2007, p. 184).	The goal of Diversity Management as an administrative procedure is to create work settings that support the entire workforce (Thomas, 1991, p. 10). A goal of Diversity Management is "addressing and supporting multiple lifestyles and personal characteristics within a defined group. Management activities includes educating the group and providing support for the acceptance of and respect for various racial, cultural, societal, geographic, economic and political backgrounds" (Diversity Management, 2013). The goal of Strategic Diversity Management is to offer "quality decisions amid differences, similarities and tensions" in the workforce (Thomas, 2006, p. 93)	The goal of the World-Class Diversity Management concept "is to demonstrate that it is possible to establish and pursue World-Class Diversity Management standards" (Thomas, 2010, p. 13).

(Continued)

Table 1.1 (Continued)

	TREND ONE	TREND TWO	TREND THREE
Implications For Additional Research and Practice Efforts in the Field of Workforce Diversity	More research is needed in the field of workforce diversity to dismantle the inaccurate belief that Affirmative Action's purpose is to legally employ "unqualified women and minorities" over "qualified white males" (Bennett-Alexander & Hartman, 2007, p. 181); More research is needed in the field of workforce diversity to dismantle the inaccurate belief that Affirmative Action is a preference initiative designed specifically for "unqualified women and minorities" to purposely take employment opportunities away from whites that are qualified (Bennett-Alexander & Hartman, 2007, p. 181); and More research is needed in the field of workforce diversity to dismantle the inaccurate belief that Affirmative Action only provides advantages to unqualified African Americans, when in fact White women are the main beneficiaries of Affirmative Action (Bennett-Alexander & Hartman, 2007, p. 181). More research is needed in the field of workforce diversity to determine if future workforce diversity equality action strategies will be needed to monitor minority and women employment practices in the workforce beyond the 21st century.	More research is needed in the field of workforce diversity to clarify that managing diversity "is not about white males managing women and minorities" (Thomas, 1991, p. 11). More research is needed in the field of workforce diversity to clarify that managing diversity is not focused on monitoring or restricting diverse groups in the workforce, Thomas (as cited in Thomas, 2006, p. 87). More academic strategic diversity management focused courses and certificate programs are needed to assist current and future diversity professionals in attaining a high level of "diversity management skills and diversity maturity" in order to make quality diversity-related assessments and handle diversity-related conflicts in the work settings (Thomas, 2006, p. 161–162).	More research is needed in the field of workforce diversity to support the benefits of the World-Class Diversity Management framework (Thomas, 2010, p. 8). More research is needed in the field of workforce diversity on examining the challenges surrounding the World-Class Diversity Management concept (Thomas, 2010, p. 6–8). More research is needed in the field of workforce diversity on how the concept of diversity integration (Scott, 2012) could be used as a specific process to integrate new and recently hired persons from similar and dissimilar backgrounds worldwide into "World-Class" diverse organizations (Thomas, 2010, p. 3). Note: integration is defined as: "The act or process or an instance of [incorporating] equals into society or an organization of individuals of different groups [such as] races" (Integration, n.d.). A re-visioning of the goals for creating diverse and inclusive World-Class workplaces worldwide is needed that returns the focus to organizational social justice. Organizational social justice is the "ideology that organizations, through a representing agent, seek to achieve a state wherein all individuals feel included, accepted, and respected and human dignity and equality are practiced and upheld" (Byrd, 2012, p. 120).

Why Study Workforce Diversity?

Workforce diversity should be studied to track and measure the progress it is making toward achieving its organizational mission, vision, and objectives (Scott, 2012). In the 21st century, diversity in the workforce has been a key practice in advancing a variety of organizational goals and practices as demonstrated by DiversityInc's Top 50 Companies for Diversity list in 2013 (DiversityInc, 2013).

Kerby and Burns (2012) asserted that diversity is currently playing an essential strategic function in advancing the economic future of the United States as an increasing number of qualified minorities and women become employed. To recognize some of the economic advantages of diversity in the workforce, Kerby and Burns introduced 10 economic benefits of a diverse workforce:

- drives economic growth,
- captures a greater share of the consumer market,
- ensures that recruiting from a more [qualified] diverse candidate pool will result in a more qualified workforce,
- helps to prevent employee turnover,
- fosters creativity and innovation,
- assists businesses in adapting to a dynamic nation to become competitive in the economic market,
- encourages entrepreneurialism,
- promotes diversity in business ownership, particularly among women of color,
- creates a competitive economy in a globalized world, and
- contributes to diversity in the boardroom.

Based on the economic benefits of diversity in the workforce, there is a need for students and practitioners today to be familiar with as well as understand the: (1) impact that historical, current, and emerging workforce diversity economic trends had, have, or are project to have in the workforce; and (2) how to develop, implement, and leverage current and emerging economic workforce diversity economic policies and practices. By studying the diversity in the workforce from a historical and modern day perspective, students and practitioners in professional fields will be better equipped with the specific knowledge, skills, and abilities needed to handle economic-related developments and issues that relate to diversity in the workforce.

Chapter Summary

In this chapter, workforce diversity, diversity, human diversity, and what workforce diversity is not were defined and discussed, along with the importance of knowing the history of human diversity and workforce diversity in the United States. A summary of five key government legislations were also presented that assisted in advancing the practice of workforce diversity as we know them today, alongside a brief history of diversity and workforce diversity in the United States. Next, a summation of the types of organizations in the United States that have emerged as they relate to managing a diverse workforce were highlighted, trailed by several examples that underscored the impact that Affirmative Action and Civil Rights laws have had on advancing equal opportunities for minorities and women in the United States.

Table 1.1 also introduced The Trends in Mandating, Managing, and Leveraging Diversity in the Workforce Framework 1954–2014 to emphasize the evolution of the practice of workforce diversity and assist the readers of this chapter in critically reflecting on what future strategies could be used to advance the field of workforce diversity beyond its current state. Several reasons were shared as well explaining why students and practitioners should study workforce diversity in the 21st century. Chapter 1 concludes by highlighting the definitions of key terms and critical-thinking discussion questions.

Definition of Key Terms

Discrimination—"The denial of opportunities and equal rights to individuals and groups [in society and in the workplace] because of prejudice or for other arbitrary reasons" (Schafer, 2010, p. 36).

Diverse—The countless ways human beings are viewed by themselves and other individuals as being similar or dissimilar to other individuals throughout the world (Scott, 2012).

Diversity (or human diversity)—The countless ways human beings are similar as well as dissimilar to one another throughout the world (Scott, 2012).

Fourteenth Amendment—Accepted by the United States Constitution in 1868, this regulation declares "that no state could deprive any person of life, liberty, or property, without due process of law; nor deny to any person within its jurisdiction the equal production of the law" (Fourteenth Amendment, n.d.).

Human diversity (or diversity)—The countless ways human beings are similar as well as dissimilar to one another throughout the world (Scott, 2012).

Inclusion—"Inclusion is the act of creating environments in which any individual or group can be and feel welcomed, respected, supported, and valued to fully participate. An inclusive and welcoming climate embraces differences and offers respect in words and actions for all people" (Clayton-Pedersen, O'Neil, & Musil, 2007).

Inequality—The condition of "being unequal or uneven." The unfair "distribution" of "opportunity" (Inequality, n.d.).

Prejudice—"A negative attitude towards an entire category of people," e.g., prejudging racial and ethnic groups without just cause (Schaefer, 2010, p. 36).

Racism—"A doctrine that one race is superior" (Schaefer, 2010, p. 13).

Sexism—"The ideology that one sex is superior to all others" (Schaefer, 2010, p. 356).

Stereotypes—"Unreliable, exaggerated generalizations about all members of a group that do not take individuals differences into account" (Schaefer, 2010, p. 17).

Workforce diversity (and diversity in the workforce)—Terms that refer to valuing the myriad of ways that leaders, business partners, employees, consultants, student workers, volunteers, customers, and visitors groups are similar as well as dissimilar to one another in work environments. For example, these categories include, but are not limited to, gender; race; skin color; age; ethnicity; sexual orientation; marital status; partner status; parental status; maternal status; socioeconomic status; dialect; disability; spiritual beliefs; religious beliefs; ancestry; cultural customs, norms, and traditions; choices of cuisine; eye color; hair color and texture; style of dress; professional appearance; height and weight; educational level; professional work experience; military experience; world view; personality; knowledge, skills and abilities; work ethic; creative talents; demeanor; mannerisms; professionalism; adaptability to change; handling stress; managing conflict; dealing with emotions; leadership style; followership style; occupation titles; occupation responsibilities; weekly schedules; seniority level; salary level; functioning in teams; functioning autonomously; cultivating a welcoming work environment; level of personal commitment; degree of professional loyalty; providing feedback; receiving feedback; delivering customer service; receiving customer service; expressing appreciation; conveying disapproval; professional interest; personal interests; life experiences; where one lives; birth place; style of living; and political views (Scott, 2012).

Workforce diversity is not—An "affirmative action" strategy, a quota system aimed at hiring certain number of qualified minorities and women in organizations, a lack of professional standards in the workforce because qualified minorities and women are represented at all levels of the organization (ASME Professional Practice Curriculum, n.d.).

Critical-Thinking Discussion Questions

1. Explain how the *Brown versus the Board of Education's* decision has influenced the current state of education as we know it today?

2. Why was President Kennedy's role so important in addressing racial equality?

3. What impact did President Johnson's speech on affirmative action at Howard University in 1964 have on you?

4. What strategies do you recommend to address acts of inequality in the workplace?

5. What strategies do you recommend to address acts of racism and discrimination in the workplace?

6. If you were a manager in a homogeneous organization, how would you go about creating a multicultural organization?

7. How are the terms diversity and workforce diversity similar and different?

8. In your opinion, why is workforce diversity so important in the 21st century?

9. In what way has Affirmative Action been effective in promoting diversity and inclusion in organizations and society?

10. In what way has the Title VII Civil Rights Act of 1964 been effective in promoting diversity and inclusion in organizations and society?

11. Explain what diversity does not represent.

12. Name six specific differences between eras one and two highlighted in Scott's (2014) The Trends in Mandating, Managing, and Leveraging Diversity in the Workplace Framework 1954–2014.

13. Name six specific differences between eras two and era three highlighted in Scott's (2014) Trends in Mandating, Managing, and Leveraging Workforce Diversity 1954–2014 Framework.

14. Explain what workforce diversity represents.

References

ASME Professional Practice Curriculum (n.d.). Workforce diversity history. Retrieved from http://professionalpractice.asme.org/MgmtLeadership/Diversity/History.cfm

Bell, B. (2012, September 27). Five questions "this week": Jennifer Granholm. *ABCNEWS.com/Politics.* Retrieved from http://abcnews.go.com/blogs/politics/2012/09/five-questions-this-week-jennifer-granholm/

Bennett-Alexander, D.D., & Hartman, L.P. (2007). *Employment law for business.* New York: McGraw-Hill/Irwin.

Brunner, B. (2013). Timeline of affirmative action milestones. Retrieved from www.infoplease.com/spot/affirmative timeline1.html

Byrd, M. (2012). Theorizing leadership of demographically diverse leaders. In M. Paludi (Ed.), *Managing diversity in today's workplace: Strategies for employees and employers (Women and careers in management)* (pp. 103–124). Santa Barbara, CA: Praeger (ABC-CLIO).

Camarota, S.A. (2001) A book review: Legal U.S. immigration: influences on gender, age and skill composition. *Industrial and Legal Relation Review, 34*(2), January, 319–392.

Civil Rights 101 (2013). Affirmative action. Retrieved from www.civilrights.org/resources/civilrights101/affirmaction.html

Clayton-Pedersen, O'Neil, & Musil (2007). Equity, inclusion, and diversity. Glossary. University of California Berkley. Retrieved from http://diversity.berkley.edu/sp_glossary_of_terms

Congress of Racial Equality (2013). *Brown vs. the Board of Education.* One of the most important decisions in the civil rights movement. Retrieved May 18, 2013, from www.core-online.org/History/brown_vs_board.htm#summary

Cox, T., Jr. (1993). *Cultural diversity in organizations: Theory, research and practice.* San Francisco: Berrett-Koehler Publishers.

Cox, T., Jr. (2001). *Creating the multicultural organization: A strategy for capturing the power of diversity.* San Francisco: Jossey-Bass.

Cox, T.H., & Blake, S. (1991). Managing cultural diversity: Implications for organizational competitiveness. *The Executive, 5*(5): 45–56.

Crossroads Anti-Racism Organizing and Training (Producer and Director) (1996). *Ending racism: For a racism-free 21st century* [Film]. Plainfield, NY: The First Unitarian Society.

DeSimone, R.L., Werner, J. M., & Harris, D.M. (2002). *Human resource development.* (3rd ed.). Orlando, FL: Harcourt College Publishers.

Diversity Management (2013). In Businessdictionary.com. Retrieved January 3, 2013, from www.businessdictionary.com/definition/diversity-management.html#ixzz2UnupqBnN

Diversity Training University International (2013). Retrieved from www.dtui.com/

DiversityInc (2013). DiversityInc Top 50 Companies for Diversity 2013. Retrieved April 8, 2013, from www.diversityinc.com/the-diversityinc-top-50-companies-for-diversity-2013/

Fourteenth Amendment (n.d.). Dictionary.com Unabridged. Retrieved from http://dictionary.reference.com/browse/fourteenth amendment

Glaser, N. (1975). *Affirmative action: Ethics, inequality and public policy.* New York: Basic Books, Inc.

Inequality (n.d.). Merriam-Webster's.com Dictionary. Retrieved from www.merriam-webster.com/dictionary/inequality

Integration (n.d.). Merriam-Webster's.com Dictionary. Retrieved from www.merriam-webster.com/dictionary/integration

Johnston, W.B., & Packer, A.E. (1987). *Workforce 2000: Work and workers for the twenty-first century.* Indianapolis, IN: Hudson Institute.

Judy, R.W., & D'Amico, C. (1997). *Workforce 2020: Work and workers in the 21st century.* Indianapolis, IN: Hudson Institute.

Kerby, S., & Burns, C. (2012). The top ten economic facts of diversity in the workplace: A diverse workforce is integral to a strong economy. Washington D.C.: Center for American Progress. Retrieved May 11, 2013, from www.scribd.com/doc/99905188/the-top-10-economic-facts-of-diversity-in-the-workplace

McMillian-Capehart, A. (2003). Hundreds of years of diversity: What took so long? *Equal Opportunity International, 22*(8).

Noe, R.A. (2010). *Employee training & development.* (5th ed.). New York: McGraw-Hill Higher Education.

Oracle Education Foundation (2013). *Brown v. the Board of Education.* Retrieved from http://library.thinkquest.org/J0112391/brown_v__board_of_education.htm

Parrillo, V.N. (2005). *Diversity in America.* (2nd ed.) Thousand Oaks, CA: Pine Forge Press.

Pilgrim, D. (2012). Jim Crow Museum of Racist Memorabilia. Using objects of intolerance to teach tolerance and promote social justice website. Ferris State University. Big Rapids: MI. Retrieved from www.ferris.edu/htmls/news/jimcrow/location.htm

Schaefer, R. (2010). *Racial and ethnic groups.* Upper Saddle River, NJ: Prentice Hall.

Scott, C.L. (2012). Winter semester. Cultural diversity in the workplace course: Human resource development 367. Class lecture topic: Workforce diversity: Past, present and future. Oakland University, Rochester, Michigan.

The Fight for Women's Suffrage (2013). The History Channel website. Retrieved from www.history.com/topics/the-fight-for-womens-suffrage

Thomas, R. R., Jr. (1991). *Beyond race and gender: Unleashing the power of your total work force by managing diversity.* New York, NY: American Management Association.

Thomas, R. R., Jr. (2006). *Building on the promise of diversity: How can we move to the next level in our workplaces, our communities and our society.* New York, NY: American Management Association.

Thomas, R. R., Jr., & Associates, Inc. (2010). *World-class diversity management: A strategic approach.* San Francisco, CA: Berrett-Koehler Publishers.

Washington, J. (2008, December 14). AP: Many insisting that Obama is not black. The Huffington Post. Retrieved from www.huffingtonpost.com/2008/12/14/ap-many-insisting-that-ob_n_150846.html

2

SUGGESTED THEORIES, MODELS, AND FRAMEWORKS USED TO ADDRESS EMERGING DIVERSITY ISSUES IN THE WORKFORCE

Chaunda L. Scott

Chapter Overview

A fundamental question that students and practitioners often ponder and ask is, what exactly are theories, models, and frameworks and what are they used for? To clarify these terms, I offer the following definitions. First, a theory or theories represent a group of expectations or realities that seek to offer a credible or practical justification "of cause-and-effect relationships among a group of observed phenomenon," e.g., facts, experiences, occurrences, events, or trends (Theory, 2013.). A model or models are best understood as being a visual, condensed, and reader-friendly descriptions of realities in the form of ideas or endeavors in society that serve to offer a meaning by: (1) removing needless factors; (2) creating hypothetical situations to question possible outcomes; and (3) clarifying activities or actions based on earlier explanations (Model, 2013). Last, a framework or frameworks offer a general synopsis of inter-connected components that link to a certain process that has explicit goals and act as a "guide" in making revisions or in the redevelopment of an idea (Framework, 2013). Therefore, according to Agar and Kottke (2004, as cited Stockdale & Crosby, 2004), when we draw upon reliable "theories, models [and frameworks] to guide our research and practices," (p. 56) we are able to build and expand knowledge on organizational diversity topics that contribute new insights towards furthering the practice of workforce diversity beyond its current state. The seven theoretical and practice-based paradigms highlighted in this chapter aim to introduce students and practitioners to the range of current and emerging diversity in the workforce trends, issues, and concerns by providing: (1) a variety of explanations regarding why various current and emerging workforce diversity issues and concerns subsist; (2) an opportunity to reflect on the role of managing current and emerging workforce diversity trends, issues, and concerns; (3) an opportunity to reflect on what additional workforce diversity factors and trends may need to be further explored; and (4) an opportunity to engage in critical reflection by drawing upon the critical theories, models, and frameworks in this chapter to respond to the critical-thinking discussion questions and case questions in chapters 4 through 16.

Learning Objectives

After reading this chapter, along with completing the chapter summary questions and the case discussion questions, you will be able to:

- Describe current and emerging workforce diversity trends, issues, and concerns
- Describe practical strategies that can be used to effectively manage and leverage these workplace organizational ills
- Describe the circumstances and ways in which current and emerging workforce diversity trends, issues, and concerns should to be addressed by organizations
- Describe the characteristics of organizations that are equipped to embrace and manage current and emerging workforce diversity trends, issues, and concerns
- Think critically and strategically about current and emerging workforce diversity trends, issues, and concerns and their role in managing and leveraging them in the 21st century

Critical Racism Pedagogy—A Conceptual Discussion Model

Derived from the critical theory school of thought, Byrd and Scott (2010) introduced the four-step Critical Racism Pedagogy Model to highlight its utility in guiding constructive dialogue on various forms of racism (i.e., individual, institutional, and cultural). This model is long overdue considering that in a variety of professional fields (e.g., human resource development and human resource management), discussions on racism as well as other types of inequities (e.g., sexism, classism, ageism, and homophobia), often seem to present challenges for many instructors to facilitate meaningful and constructive discussion (Byrd & Scott, 2010). These problems regularly exist due to: (1) instructors being ill-prepared to facilitate discussions on racism and other types of "isms" because they lack knowledge of these content areas; (2) the sensitive and complex nature of these topics is challenging in and of itself to facilitate; and (3) insufficient literature and resources that exist on racism and other parallel inequitable acts within professional disciplines for instructional purposes (Byrd & Scott, 2010).

Since diversity-centered courses are generally where discussions of race and racism take place, it has been our experience in facilitating diversity courses that many of our students have been resistant and reluctant to participate when racism is introduced under the topics of race, ethnicity, and inequity (Byrd & Scott, 2010). This resistance might stem from the instructors' and students' lack of understanding of how racism historically was deeply rooted in the fabric of this country, along with how it still lingers today in many contemporary forms in the workplace and the general society.

The resulting lack of constructive classroom discussion on the roots and contemporary forms of racism suggests that students will not graduate with the skills needed for de-racialized thinking in workplace settings and in the broader society (Byrd & Scott, 2010). For example, Byrd and Scott noted that in their academic and professional classroom experiences, students have asked questions such as:

1. What is the definition of racial groups and is White a racial group?
2. What exactly is racism?
3. Why is racism being discussed in diversity courses?
4. What indicators suggest that racism has affected individuals and institutions?
5. How does racism continue to affect individuals and institutions?
6. Can all cultural and ethnic groups be racists, too?
7. What can be done to end racism?

These types of questions indicate that students need to become critically conscious of racism and its impact on individuals and institutions before they can participate in discussions and make meaning of the resulting dialogue. As a result, the challenge for educators is to find and develop the appropriate strategies for guiding constructive discussions on racism in classroom and boardroom settings.

Situating Racism Within the Critical Theory School of Thought

According to Merriam, Caffarella, and Baumgartner (2007), "the identification of systems of power and oppression as a lens through which to analyze society is a key component of critical theory" (p. 250). Critical philosophies are also welcomed additions to several academic subject areas that seek to address issues of authority and domination in society. For example, these subject areas include "history, law, literature and the social sciences" (Critical Theory, 2013), African American studies, sociology, multicultural education, higher education, human resource development, human resource management, queer studies, women's studies, White privilege, and workforce diversity, to name a few. As highlighted by the previous subjects mentioned, critical philosophies are as well rooted in both historical and contemporary real-world contexts with their common goals focused on societal change (Questia, n.d.). Given the common focus and aims of critical philosophies, they are deemed best suited for understanding and examining issues of racism in society. Examples of the specific critical philosophies that are useful in exploring issues of racism in organizations and educational settings include critical theory, critical pedagogy, and critical race pedagogy. In familiarizing the readers of this chapter with these critical concepts, brief definitions of these theories are provided, beginning with critical theory.

Critical theory in general is a concept that seeks to assist individuals and groups in rising above the societal forces that govern and oppress them (Critical Theory, 2013). As a socio-political instrument, critical theory investigates how and in what ways authoritative and oppressive acts in society affect individual groups (Creswell, 1998). The goal of critical theory is "human emancipation" (Critical Theory, 2013). Critical pedagogy is a teaching and learning concept aimed at raising students' awareness of "freedom, recognizing authoritarian tendencies, connecting knowledge to power and taking constructive action" that lead to "social justice" (Questia, n.d.). Shor (1996) defines critical pedagogy as an educational tool that assists learners in inquiring about the guidelines and procedures that rule over them and about examining their role and place in society so they can better understand their life situations and circumstance in society. Shor (1996) also views critical pedagogy as an instructional method that is devoted to learners because it allows them an opportunity to take control of their learning.

Last, critical race pedagogy (CRP), which originated from critical pedagogy (Lynn, 2004) is a concept that investigates issues related to and resulting from "racial, ethnic and gender subordination" through the life "experiences of educators of color" (p. 154). According to Lynn, CRP also provides opportunities for dialogue to occur among "educators on color" (p. 154) that have had encounters with racism and sexism. CRP as well provides an opportunity for faculty of color to develop constructive educational approaches and methods that can be used to address these matters. Because CRP views issues of race and racism as serious universal and persistent social ills, as noted by Solorzano and Yosso (2005), CRP's central aim, according to Bernal (2002, as cited in Byrd & Scott, 2010), is to expose discriminatory guidelines and procedures in organizations so they can be dismantled.

To date, many educators that teach about race and racism in our global society have relied on viewpoints like the colorblind and reverse discrimination concepts to explain race and racism in society, when in reality they are suppressing the true meanings and negative challenges surrounding race and racism to sustain the existing social order of power and privilege for certain groups in society. With this being said, critical race instruction aims to uncover policies and practices in institutions that have been utilized to dominate and devalue individuals unjustly as well to enable and liberate individuals at the same time (Solorzano & Yosso, 2005). CRP is also grounded in the real world experiences of educators of color that have encountered racism and thus, their experiences serve as the foundation for being able to recognize it, understand it, examine it, evaluate it, discuss it, and teach about it in courses like workforce diversity and related curricula (Lynn, 2004).

In drawing upon the common themes of critical theory, critical pedagogy, and critical race pedagogy and our own experiences with racism in society as African American professional women, we constructed the Critical Racism Pedagogy Model as a facilitation instrument for use in educational and organizational settings to: (1) lead and guide structured, thought-provoking, and beneficial dialogue on racism in its various forms, e.g., individual racism, institutional racism, and cultural racism (Jones, 1997); (2) give voice to and discuss with students and professionals how racism persists and promotes prejudice, discrimination, stereotyping, unfairness, and injustices; and (3) engage students and professionals in a discourse that stimulates an exchange of ideas on how racism in its various forms (Jones, 1997) can be eradicated for the purpose of promoting organizational justice, a form of social justice, that "seeks to achieve a state wherein all individuals feel included and respected and human dignity and equality and practiced and upheld" (Byrd, 2012, p. 120).

Figure 2.1 describes the four phases of the critical racism pedagogy discourse model that offers utility in both educational and organizational settings.

Applying the Four-Step Process Using the African and African American Culture as an Example

As we will discuss in Chapter 3, the principle of social justice refers to the active quest for equality and fairness in reaction to behaviors and attitudes that can contribute to a non-inclusive organizational culture. However, there is a need to first educate individuals so that social justice is the desired outcome. Using the African and African American culture as an example, instructors and facilitators would apply the CRP framework by first introducing the concepts of individual and institutional racism and educating participants on ways that these systems have emerged from a historical perspective. For example, in Step 1, to demonstrate individual racism, participants could be shown a video clip of a movie such as Alex Haley's *Roots* that portrays the captivity of African people from their homeland who were forced to work in this country without wages. The enslavement of African people (and later African Americans that were born in the United States) for more than 200 years against their will demonstrates institutional racism.

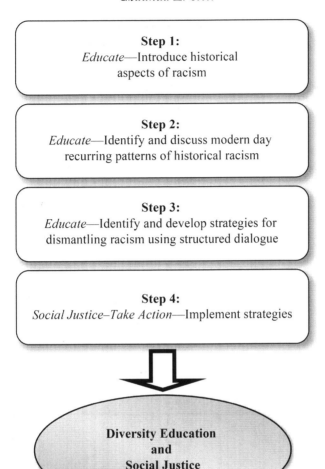

Figure 2.1 Critical Racism Pedagogy Four-Step Conceptual Model
Critical Racism Pedagogy Four-Step Conceptual Model for Integrating Dialogue on Racism in HRD Diversity Courses in A Framework Integrating Dialogue on Forms of Racism within Human Resource Development Workplace Diversity Courses and Workplace Settings: Implications for HRD. Proceedings of the 2010 Academy of Human Resource Development Conference (pp. 1315–1336). Knoxville: University of Tennessee–Knoxville. © Byrd & Scott 2010

In Step 2, participants are educated and enlightened on the recurrence and ongoing systems of individual and institutional racism. For example, the Coca-Cola discrimination lawsuit could be used as a case study to illustrate how race discrimination persisted in a major U.S. beverage industry. In 2001, Coca-Cola settled a race discrimination lawsuit for $192.5 million and was forced to make sweeping reforms in key human resource development and human resource management practices relating to discriminatory pay, promotions, and evaluations occurring in 1997 (Wade, 2002). Despite these reforms, the company continued to face race discrimination allegations as evidenced in a 2008 race discrimination lawsuit.

In Step 3, structured dialogue is used to identify and develop strategies for dismantling racism in workplace situations. Structured dialogue is a critical process of the CRP framework. The process of structured dialogue involves moving beyond awareness of diversity to discussing the destructive nature of racists' actions and practices that continues to pervade organizations and institutions (Kormanik & Apperson, 2002). For example, continuing with the Coca-Cola case, the following questions could be discussed:

1. What indicators of individual racism are apparent in the case?
2. What indicators of institutional racism are apparent in the case?
3. Comment on Coca-Cola's management responsibility for the persistence of discriminatory human resource practices in wake of the 2001 lawsuit.
4. Where does the problem exist in allowing these practices to persist?
5. Who is accountable?
6. What strategies could have been be used and developed to address the problems in the Coca-Cola case before the lawsuit?

Finally, in Step 4 and continuing with the Coca-Cola example, participants are made aware of strategies that were implemented by Coca-Cola in response to the court ruling in 2001. Coca-Cola's Three Pillars of Diversity Education, which combines the *Breaking Down the Barriers* training program, invited speakers, and a diversity library, are action strategies that the company implemented to address race discrimination. Finally, the strategies implemented by Coca-Cola exemplify a quest for social justice aimed to promote a culture of fairness, equity, and inclusion.

The outcome of applying the four-step CRP framework is responsive diversity education that results in social justice. The CRP framework presents a focused technique regarding how academic instructors and practitioners in organizations can guide safe and critical discussions on racism, utilizing the vehicle of diversity education to eradicate acts of racism and promote social justice in work settings simultaneously (Byrd & Scott, 2010).

Social Justice Critical Reflection Model (SJCRM)

Parallel to Byrd & Scott's (2010) Critical Racism Pedagogy (CRP) conceptual model that offers utility in both academic and organizational boardrooms, Ingram and Walters (2007) developed the Social Justice Critical Reflection Model (SJCRM) as a call for social justice education and training in school settings in general, but especially the teacher education discipline "to encourage active intellectual processes for cultivating diversity understanding and social justice" (p. 24). The SJCRM consists of five unified concepts: (1) descriptive thinking; (2) dialogic thinking; (3) critical reflection; (4) critical conscious; and (5) praxis. Figure 2.2 provides and illustration of the SJCRM.

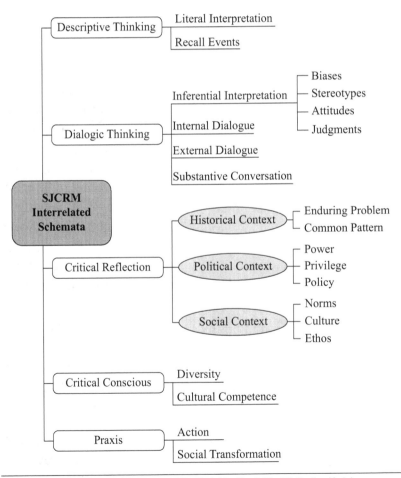

Figure 2.2 The Interrelated Schemata of the Social Justice Critical Reflection Model
© Ingram and Walters, 2006

- **Descriptive thinking (DT)** is an outcome of reading written materials and then reiterating what was read. DT lacks giving reasons for circumstances and does not value historical perspectives and is therefore deemed inadequate for promoting learning and perceived learning derived from DT (Ingram & Walters, 2007).
- **Dialogic thinking (DIT)** occurs when an individual engages in discourses "with self and others" (p. 28) as they relate to "patterns" of preconception such as prejudices, opinions, injustices, morals, and values. Although DIT and DT might seem to be ranked by preference, they can be utilized in any order. DIT discussions may also take place within the school setting or outside of the school. Examples of discussions could include "family, community, faith, schooling, culture, gender, socialization patterns, and ethnicity" (p. 28).
- **Critical reflection (CR)**, a concept grounded in the earlier work of John Dewey (1933), is a process of self-analysis that encourages an individual to reframe or situate solutions in a cultural, ethnic, or governmental context. Therefore, CR challenges as well as stimulates contextual ways of knowing.
- **Cultural conscious (CC)** is a concept that describes how one develops a deeper understanding of personal beliefs and how this belief system can be enacted in everyday practices. CC is viewed as respecting human diversity in ways that embrace and promote diverse ways of knowing as it relates education, equity, access, (sponsorship) and opportunities for people whose racial, cultural, religious, and ethnic identities subject them to "discrimination and marginalization" (p. 31).
- **Praxis (PX)** is an educational strategy that requires giving thoughtful attention to the various types of information and facts that have been gathered and reflected upon and placing that information into practice. The ultimate goal and expected outcome is social justice and organizational change.

Ingram and Walters's (2007) Social Justice Critical Reflection Model provides another precise approach regarding how academic and professional settings can utilize the social school of thought to promote diversity understanding and social change that results in social justice.

Giving Voice to Polyrhythmic Realities—A Framework

Sheared's (1999) Polyrhythmic Realities Framework was introduced in the discipline of adult education to emphasize the adversities related to students' life encounters as they relate to the "intersection of race, gender, and class" (p. 36). In using the Polyrhythmic Realities Framework as a diagnostic tool, Sheared assessed the perceptions of African American students enrolled in adult basic education (ABE) programs and found that they were more inclined to be involved in learning if they felt more associated with the educators, their peers, and the curriculum objectives.

Sheared (1999) further uncovered that if African American students' polyrhythmic realities and life encounters were recognized by their Adult Basic Education (ABE) "staff, teachers, and administrators" (p. 38), they stayed in the program. However, when African American students felt unsupported by their ABE programs, Sheared noted that they quit the program based on not having their learning concerns dealt with satisfactorily.

According to Sheared (1999), the concept of polyrhythmic realities signifies how the constructs of "race, class, gender, and language" as well as other less visible individualities influence the ways pupils view themselves along with the ways pupils or educators want to be viewed in educational settings.

Grounded in an Afrocentric epistemological perspective, the Polyrhythmic Realities Framework according to Sheared (1999) makes a conscious effort to provide a way through which an individual's actions and thoughts are understood from being rooted in their life encounters as it relates to their "history, culture, economics, race, gender, language, sexual orientation, and religion," (p. 40) to name a few.

Sheared (1999) also acknowledged that utilizing the Polyrhythmic Realities Framework to guide culturally centered educational practices and policies allows learners, such as adult students, to develop the confidence they need to give voice to issues of concern, and most importantly, persist and succeed in a variety of settings where learning takes place (e.g., profit and nonprofit agencies) that are often intolerant of diverse ways of knowing and being.

According to Sheared (1999), in order for all educators to appreciate completely the polyrhythmic realities of African-Americans, as well as all other diverse groups, the uniqueness of human diversity must be recognized in educational settings. Sheared further asserted that allowing students to have an opportunity to give voice to their polyrhythmic realities and their life encounters in learning environments can assist them in gaining the knowledge and skills they need to succeed in society and confront unsupportive governing practices and policies. Sheared's cultural framework offers utility in that it helps us to understand how educators and students in a variety of educational settings as well as practitioners and employees in a variety of organizational settings can learn from their intersecting polyrhythmic realities and life encounters.

The Diverse Voices Conference Model

"I built it . . . and they came." Dr. Chaunda L. Scott

According to Ukpokoud (2010), today's higher education students need cultural knowledge, skills, and abilities in order to be successful in life and society in our evolving diverse world. Shorter-Gooden (2013), too, notes that today's corporations must aggressively strive to promote "diversity" for the purpose of acting in response "to an unequal playing field and shifting demographics" (p. 207). Shorter-Gooden (2013) further acknowledges that one way a corporation, including educational academies and universities, can begin to develop human diversity knowledge is when they "infuse diverse perspectives throughout the substantive work of the organization, for example, in educational curricular programming" (p. 207).

In 1999, as a response to the above and similar kinds of educational and organizational needs identified over the past 15 years, I created the Diverse Voices Conference at Oakland University (OU) in Rochester, Michigan, a predominantly white university. The aims of this higher education conference are twofold:

1) To create a safe environment for intergenerational dialogue on topics of diversity and inclusion by engaging students, faculty, staff, business leaders, professionals, and community members in critical discussions on these current issues. Examples of these issues include persisting societal inequities, such as racism, sexual orientation harassment, and bullying, to name a few (Scott, Greer, Willard-Traub, & Johnson, 2003; Scott, 2005, 2011).

2) To encourage the development of solutions that can be used by the individuals in attendance to address human diversity concern and issues in education, organizations, and society (Scott et al., 2003; Scott, 2005, 2011).

The Diverse Voices Conference is a grant-funded higher education initiative that serves as an extension of diversity education beyond the classroom as a way to broaden diversity and inclusion discussions by including the groups named above who are interested in and concerned about human diversity issues and dismantling inequities in society (Scott, 2011). The Diverse Voices Conference also supports one of OU's core values and mission which is "diversity and inclusion" (Oakland University, 2013).

The outcomes of the Diverse Voices Conference focus on expanding all conference participants' and attendees' knowledge of:

1) Their own cultural, racial, and social identity and the divergent perspectives of others who are different from themselves;
2) Theories and proven practices that support and value human diversity and address inequalities such as how to reduce prejudice, discrimination, and stereotyping; and
3) The effective strategies corporate and civic leaders are using, have used, or could use to enhance their organizations and communities by addressing human diversity issues as a critical success factor (Scott, 2005, 2011).

The Diverse Voices Conference also assists in the development of students' oral and presentation skills, and their overall professionalism as they relate to speaking out publically in support of valuing all aspects of human diversity. There is also a strong need today in higher education and organizational settings to have a public diversity and inclusion forum like the Diverse Voices Conference, where students' participation and comments are not based on grades, where professionals aren't required to attend, and where scholarly and practical teaching and learning on diversity and inclusion takes place in a supportive environment free of charge (Scott et al., 2003; Scott, 2005, 2011). The Diverse Voices Conference meets this need (Scott, 2005, 2011).

The planning for Diverse Voices begins approximately ten months prior to the conference date (Scott, 2011). Students pursuing degrees in higher education at OU and other Michigan universities are identified and invited to attend the conference (Scott, 2005; 2011). The student and faculty presenters are selected via abstracts vetted by the Diverse Voices Faculty Advisory Board (Scott, 2011). The presenters are selected based solely upon the quality of their abstracts. Also, during the planning period, a keynote speaker (local, national, or renowned) is identified, contacted, and confirmed. Air travel and accommodations are secured for the keynote speaker if need be, supplies are purchased; entertainment and food service providers are contacted (Scott, 2011).

As the conference grew from 1999 to the present, the venue moved from a lecture hall to an auditorium to accommodate a growing number of attendees who come to listen to speakers, and to actively engage in critical diversity discussions. The most recent Diverse Voices Conference drew just over 400 participants (Scott, 2011).

The Diverse Voices Conference is held annually in March and always on a Saturday from 11:00 am-3:00 pm (Scott et al., 2003; Scott, 2005; 2011). Past themes include Diversity Matters, Race Matters, What Does Diversity Look Like, Diversity at Work, Working Diversity, and the Relationship between Equity and Excellence, to name a few. Previous keynote speakers such as Marianne Williamson, renowned author and speaker; Dr. Juanita Johnson Bailey, professor and scholar from the University of Georgia; Dr. Elizabeth Tisdale, professor and scholar from Penn State University; and Dr. Carlyle Fielding Stewart, III, pastor, teacher, scholar, and author from Michigan represent the types of distinguished orators who have shared their diverse perspectives at a Diverse Voices Conference. At the conclusion of the presentations, the audience and presenters engage in a question and answer period followed by a fellowship period at the reception (Scott, 2005, 2011).

Prior to the end of the conference, all participants are encouraged to complete a survey, provide suggestions, and evaluate the conference. Surveys are collected and analyzed for improving future conferences by the Diverse Voices Advisory Board. Of the surveys collected to date, (approximately 3,500) over 98% of all evaluations rate the conference as "excellent" and participants overwhelmingly request additional conferences on the topic of diversity and inclusion (Scott, 2005, 2011). Table 2.1, provides an overview of the planning process of the Diverse

Table 2.1   The Diverse Voices Conference Model

THE PLANNING PROCESS

Planning Begins 10 Months Prior to the Diverse Voices Conference Date

Select and Confirm Conference Theme
Diverse Voices Advisory Board
Founder and President of the Diverse Voices Conference
[The First Month]

Confirm and Reserve Date, Time Period, and Location
Where the Conference and Reception will be Held
Diverse Voices Advisory Board
Founder and President of the Diverse Voices Conference
[The First Month]

Compile a List of Internal University Courses to Invite and External Universities to Invite
Diverse Voices Advisory Board
Founder and President of the Diverse Voices Conference
[The Second Month]

Create an E-Flyer and Application to Invite Students to
Apply to Speak at the Upcoming Conference
Send the E-Flyer and Application Out Monthly by E-mail to the Host University List Serve and to
    External Universities
Diverse Voices Advisory Board
Founder and President of the Diverse Voices Conference
[The First Five Months]

Select and Confirm Renowned Keynote Speaker
Along with Lodging and Travel Itinerary if Needed
Diverse Voices Advisory Board
Founder and President of the Diverse Voices Conference
[The Sixth Month]

Select and Confirm Faculty Presenter
Diverse Voices Advisory Board
Founder and President of the Diverse Voices Conference
[The Sixth Month]

Select and Confirm Diverse Voices Conference Student Ambassador
Diverse Voices Advisory Board
Founder and President of the Diverse Voices Conference
[The Sixth Month]

Select and Confirm Diverse Voices Conference Student Speakers
Diverse Voices Advisory Board
Founder and President of the Diverse Voices Conference
[The Sixth Month]

Select and Confirm Entertainment, Student Organization Helpers, Order Supplies and
    Certificates
Diverse Voices Advisory Board
Founder and President of the Diverse Voices Conference
[The Seventh Month]

Confirm Time Allotted for the Question and Answer Period
Founder and President of the Diverse Voices Conference
[The Seventh Month]

(Continued)

Table 2.1 *(continued)*

THE PLANNING PROCESS

Confirm Time Allotted for the Final Thoughts and Thank You Period
Founder and President of the Diverse Voices Conference
[The Seventh Month]

Confirm Time Allotted for the Evaluation Period
Founder and President of the Diverse Voices Conference
[The Seventh Month]

Confirm Refreshment Options and Confirm Time Allotted for the Reception
Diverse Voices Advisory Board
Founder and President of the Diverse Voices Conference
[The Seventh Month]

Print Diverse Voices Conference Programs and Evaluation Forms
Founder and President of the Diverse Voices Conference
[The Seventh Month]

Complete and Finalize All Remaining Diverse Voices Conference Tasks
Diverse Voices Advisory Board
Founder and President of the Diverse Voices Conference
[Seventh–Ninth Month]

The Diverse Voices Conference Takes Place
[Tenth Month]

Send Thank You Notes
to the Keynote Speaker, Faculty Presenter, All Student Speakers, Entertainers,
and All Other Individuals and Groups that Assisted with the Diverse Voices Conference Tasks
Founder and President of the Diverse Voices Conference
[Tenth Month–One Week After the Diverse Voices Conference]

Scott, C. L., (2011). The Diverse Voices Conference model: An extension of diversity education beyond the classroom. Conference presentation/abstract. Eleventh Annual Lilly Conference on College and University Teaching and Learning, Traverse City, Michigan, September 22–25, 2011.

Voices Conference model, which offers utility in both higher education and organizational settings.

Out of the 407 conference attendees at the last Diverse Voices Conference, 350 are Caucasian undergraduate and graduate students from Oakland University and other Michigan universities. Thirty participants reported ethnicities including African American, Asian American, Arab American, Hispanic, and Latino. The remaining 27 conference attendees represent faculty, community and business leaders, and parents. With over 99% of attendees reporting their ethnicity as Caucasian, Diverse Voices provides the ideal forum for reaching all who come, but especially the majority who has never participated in an educational conference focused on diversity and inclusion. Future plans include expanding the Diverse Voices

Conference within the United States, South Africa, and other international countries.

As a human resource development educator, scholar, and diversity and inclusion specialist, my commitment to human diversity inclusion and eradicating racism is sincere and passionate. I am also honored to have the opportunity to engage my students, other students, national scholars, business leaders, professionals, and community members in an open dialogue on diversity issues in my classroom, in a conference setting, and within an institution of higher education. Moreover, it has been most rewarding to see that my students along with the public enjoy the Diverse Voices Conference as much as I do. I want to as well thank Oakland University publically for their continued support of my Diverse Voices work. Given the success of the Diverse Voices Conference to date, I invite educational institutions and organizations alike to consider replicating the Diverse Voices Conference for the purpose of promoting human diversity inclusion through the use constructive and critical dialogue in your own settings, and to assist in the development of strategies to eradicate all forms of human inequalities in society.

The Diverse Voices Conference is another unique model that provides a fresh approach to engage students, business professionals, and the general public in dialogues on issues related diversity and inclusion and social inequities.

Model for Creating Diversity—A Theoretical Framework

Another theoretical model that is useful for managing and leveraging current and emerging workforce diversity issues is Allen and Montgomery's (2001) Model for Creating Diversity (MCD). Based on the earlier work of Kurt Lewin (1951), the MCD serves as a welcomed addition to the focused area of diversity management because of its ability to guide organizational development and change strategies that promote and advance diversity inclusion. Lewin's (1951) Organizational Development and Change Model is based on three main components:

1. *Unfreezing* a current organizational position, for example, current organizational objectives, efforts, guidelines, and procedures.

2. *Moving* forward to create an innovative organizational position, for example, disassembling, amending, or crafting innovative objectives, initiatives, strategies, and procedures.
3. *Refreezing* an innovative organizational position to meet their current and future objectives, for example, original innovative objectives, efforts strategies, and procedures.

The MCD builds on Lewin's (1951) model by directing diversity management change in work environments and emphasizing the outcome of the change strategy. The components of the Allen and Montgomery's (2001) MCD are described as follows:

1. *Unfreezing* top management's current commitment, vision, and mission toward diversity management in workplace settings. This also includes unfreezing leaders' stated efforts as well as diversity-related objectives.
2. *Moving* or developing new diversity management initiatives, policies, practices, and goals in workplace settings. For instance, develop a variety of workplace diversity-focused training and education programs (e.g., sexual orientation harassment, racial profiling, ethnic profiling, bullying, and disability awareness), mentoring and coaching programs, recruitment and outreach programs, and co-op and internship programs, along with new diversity management goals, a time line, and a detailed strategic plan to achieve these objectives.
3. *Refreezing* newly developed workplace diversity management initiatives, policies, practices, and goals. For example, sponsor— on an ongoing basis—diversity-centered training and education programs in the workplace (e.g., sexual orientation harassment, racial profiling, ethnic profiling, bullying, and disability aware- ness), mentoring and coaching programs, recruitment and outreach programs, and co-op and internship programs. Also, management should regularly communicate with the workplace community by newsletter, e-mail, and annual reports regard- ing what the new diversity management goals are, their level of attainment, and their lack of success.

4. *Competitive advantage* is the outcome of refreezing newly developed workplace diversity management initiatives, policies, practices, and goals previously highlighted in phases 1–3.

The uniqueness of Allen and Montgomery's (2001) MCD is that it offers a simple and pragmatic approach to guide developmental and change strategies that are focused on promoting and advancing the practice of diversity management in work settings globally in the 21st century and beyond.

The Multicultural Organization Theoretical Framework

According to Cox (1993, 2001), a multicultural organization is one that seeks to assist all of its workers, regardless of their varying backgrounds, in reaching their personal and professional goals, while contributing to the success of the organization. The exclusive characteristics of multicultural organizations offered by Cox (1993) consist of the following:

> a culture that fosters and values cultural differences pluralism as an acculturation process full structural integration full integration of the informal networks an absence of institutionalized cultural bias in human resource management systems and practices a minimum of intergroup conflict due to the proactive management of diversity. (p. 229)

A multicultural organization consists of five components: leadership, research and measurement, education, a culture and management system audit, and follow-up. First, effective leaders are needed at all levels of an organization to act as change agents and to provide the necessary management strategies and practices that support an inclusive work environment. Second, organizations need to conduct relevant research that identifies their diversity needs as well as updating those currently in place. According to Cox (1993) data collection and analysis are needed on related organizational matters such as "equal opportunity, the analysis of attitudes and perceptions of employees, and data that highlights differential career experiences of members from different cultural groups" (p. 235). Third, education efforts should extend beyond awareness and sensitivity training. Training efforts should include helping all organizational members (including leaders) to acquire the skills they need to help their organization transform itself into a multicultural organization based on the needs determined in the research and measurement process. Fourth, a cultural and management systems audit should be viewed as "a comprehensive assessment on the organizational cultural and human resource management system of the organization" (p. 237). The goal of a cultural and management systems audit is to expose acts of unfairness towards diverse groups, expose organizational actions that are questionable in meeting the needs of diverse groups, and eliminate barriers that may hinder the success of every individual in the organization. Finally, follow-up is needed to evaluate and ensure that organizations are able to demonstrate a "zero correlation of socio-cultural identity with opportunity, motivation, and achievement as well as full capitalization on the potential benefits of workforce diversity" (p. 239).

Embedded Intergroup Relations Theory—A Framework

Another theoretical framework that is useful for analyzing current and emerging workforce diversity issues and concerns is Clayton Alderfer's (1987) Embedded Intergroup Relations Theory (EIRT). EIRT explains the effects of diversity in relation to one's group identity in organizational settings. Identity groups are characterized by sharing common biological traits, sharing historical background and experiences, and sharing similar worldviews (Nkomo & Cox, 1996.) The dynamics that emerge from diverse groups is characterized by the notion of embeddedness. Embeddedness means that groups exist inside other groups. Diverse groups and organizations are both open systems that influence and are influenced by the environments in which they are embedded (Alderfer & Tucker, 1996). EIRT supports Wagley and Harris's (1964) description of diverse groups:

1. Diverse groups receive unequal and differential treatment compared to other individuals with dissimilar characteristics.
2. Diverse groups are easily recognizable because of distinguishing physical and/or cultural characteristics that are not highly regarded by the dominant group.

3. Diverse groups share a sense of community and common bond.
4. Group membership is assigned or socially constructed.
5. Group members generally tend to affiliate themselves with like individuals because of their social isolation.

EIRT brings to light the common experiences of diverse groups within the workplace. Experiences are more easily recognized and understood by individuals who belong to the same identity group. When these experiences are perceived as adverse, unjust, or unfair, individuals belonging to diverse groups in workplace settings are most likely to make meaning and find support from group membership. Therefore, the usefulness of the EIRT model is that it highlights the need for organizations of the 21st century to strengthen intergroup relations among all employees for the purpose of creating a more inclusive, supportive, and productive workplace.

Note: Please see Table 1.1 The Trends in Mandating, Managing, and Leveraging Diversity in the Workforce Framework 1954–2014 by Scott (2014) on pages 20–26 of the previous chapter for an overview of the diversity management framework (Thomas, 1991), the strategic diversity management framework (Thomas, 2006) and the world-class diversity management approach (Thomas, 2010). These additional paradigms by Dr. Roosevelt Thomas R., Jr., are also instrumental resources that educators and practitioners can use to craft constructive diverse and inclusive work settings (Scott, 2012).

Chapter Summary

This chapter introduced several theories, models, and frameworks that can be used to enhance workforce diversity initiatives, policies, and goals as they relate to: (1) respecting and valuing human diversity in work settings and (2) managing current and emerging workforce diversity developments. This chapter also provided a variety of explanations regarding why various workforce diversity practices exist. Moreover, it provided an opportunity to reflect on what additional workforce diversity issues and concerns may need to be addressed.

Lastly, this chapter encouraged you to think critically about how current and emerging workforce diversity trends can be used to advance the practice of workforce diversity.

___

Definition of Key Terms

Framework—A framework or frameworks offers a general synopsis of interconnected components that links to a certain process that has explicit goals and acts as a "guide" in making revisions or in the re-development of an idea (Framework, 2013).

Model—A model or models are best understood as being a visual, condensed, and reader-friendly descriptions of realities in the form of ideas or endeavors in society that serve to offer a meaning by: (1) removing needless factors; (2) creating hypothetical situations to question possible outcomes; and (3) clarifying activities or actions based on earlier explanations (Model, 2013).

Theory—A theory or theories represent a group of expectations or realities that seek to offer a credible or practical justification "of cause-and-effect relationships among a group of observed phenomenon," e.g., facts, experiences, occurrences, events, or trends (Theory, 2013).

___

Critical-Thinking Discussion Questions

1. In general, what is the purpose of a theory, model, and framework?
2. In what three ways could the Critical Racism Pedagogy Model be useful in the classroom and the boardroom?
3. In what three ways could the Social Justice Critical Reflection Model be useful in the university?
4. What are three purposes of Sheared's (1999) Polyrhythmic Realities Model?
5. Name five discussion themes that could be discussed at a Diverse Voices Conference along with the reasons why you selected each theme.
6. Name four strengths of the Multicultural Organization Model.
7. What are three strengths of the Embedded Intergroup Relations Theory (EIRT) theory?
8. What are four strengths of the Model for Creating Diversity?

References

Agar, M.D., & Kottke, J.L. (2004). Models and practice of diversity management: A historical review and presentation of a new integration theory. In M.S. Stockdale & F.J. Crosby (Eds.), *The psychology and management of workplace diversity* (pp. 55–77). Malden, MA: Blackwell Publishing.

Alderfer, C. P. (1987). An intergroup perspective on group dynamics. In J. Lorsch (Ed.), *Handbook of organizational behavior,* (pp. 190-222). Englewood Cliffs, NJ: Prentice-Hall.

Alderfer, C.G., & Tucker, R.C. (1996). A field experiment for studying race relations embedded in organizations. *Journal of Organizational Behavior, 17,* 43–57.

Allen, R.S., & Montgomery, K.A. (2001). Applying an organizational developmental approach to creating diversity. *Organizational Dynamics, 30*(2), 149–161.

Bernal, D.D. (2002). Critical race theory, Latino critical theory, and critical raced-gendered epistemologies: Recognizing students of color as holders and creators of knowledge. *Qualitative Inquiry, 8*(1), 105–126.

Byrd, M. (2012). Theorizing leadership of demographically diverse leaders. In M. Paludi (Ed.), *Managing diversity in today's workplace: Strategies for employees and employers (Women and careers in management)* (pp. 103–124). Santa Barbara, CA: Praeger (ABC-CLIO).

Byrd, M., & Scott, C.L. (2010). *A framework integrating dialogue on forms of racism within Human Resource Development workforce diversity courses and workplace settings: Implications for HRD.* Proceedings of the 2010 Academy of Human Resource Development Conference (pp. 1315–1336). Knoxville: University of Tennessee–Knoxville.

Cox, T., Jr. (1993). *Cultural diversity in organizations: Theory research and practice.* San Francisco, CA: Berrett-Koehler Publishers.

Cox, T., Jr. (2001). *Creating the multicultural organization: A strategy for capturing the power of diversity.* San Francisco, CA: Jossey-Bass.

Critical Pedagogy (2013). In the free online encyclopedia.com. Retrieved April, 6, 2013, from http://encyclopedia.thefreedictionary.com/Critical+pedagogy

Critical Theory (2013). In the free online dictionary.com. Retrieved April 6, 2013, from http: http://encyclopedia.thefreedictionary.com/Critical+theory

Creswell, J.W. (1998). *Qualitative inquiry and research design: Choosing among five traditions.* Thousand Oaks, CA: Sage.

Framework (2013). In businessdictionary.com. Retrieved April 6, 2013, from www.businessdictionary.com/definition/framework.html

Ingram, I.L., & Walters, T.S. (2007). A critical reflection model to teach diversity and social justice. *Journal of Praxis in Multicultural Education, 2*(1), 23–41.

Jones, J.M. (1997). *Prejudice and racism.* (2nd ed.). New York: McGraw-Hill.

King, J.E. (1991). Dysconscious racism: Ideology, identity, and the miseducation of teachers. *Journal of Negro Education, 60*(2), 133–146.

Kormanik, M.B., & Apperson, K.S. (2002). Diversity dialogues in the workplace: A study of implementation issues. In T.M. Egan & S.A. Lynham (Eds.), *Proceedings of the Academy of Human Resource Development* (pp. 19–26). Bowling Green, OH.

Lewin, K. (1951). *Field theory in social science.* New York: Harper Row.

Lynn, M. (2004). Inserting the race into critical pedagogy: An analysis of race-based epistemologies. *The Journal of Educational Philosophy and Theory, 37*(2), 153–165.

Merriam, S.B., Caffarella, R.S., & Baumgartner, L.M. (2007). *Learning in adulthood: A comprehensive guide* (3rd ed.). San Francisco: Jossey Bass.

Model (2013). In businessdictionary.com Retrieved April 6, 2013, from www .businessdictionary.com/definition/model.html

Nkomo, S.M., & Cox, T., Jr. (1996). Diverse identities in organizations. In S.R. Clegg, C. Hardy, & W.R. Nord (Eds.), *Handbook of organization studies* (pp. 338–356). Thousand Oaks, CA: Sage.

Oakland University Role and Mission Statement (2013). Retrieved June 24, 2013, from www.oakland.edu/2020/

Questia (n.d.). Critical Pedagogy. Retrieved from www.questia.com/library/ education/curriculum-and-instruction/critical-pedagogy

Scott, C.L. (2005). The Diverse Voices Conference: A framework promoting multicultural education. Conference Presentation. National Association of Multicultural Education (NAME) Fifteenth Annual International Conference. Atlanta, Georgia.

Scott, C.L. (2011). The Diverse Voices Conference model: An extension of diversity education beyond the classroom. Conference Presentation/ Abstract. Eleventh Annual Lilly Conference on College and University Teaching and Learning, Traverse City, Michigan, September 22–25, 2011.

Scott, C.L. (2012). Winter semester. Cultural diversity in the workplace course: Human Resource Development 367. Class lecture topic: Workforce diversity. Past, present and future. Oakland University, Rochester, Michigan.

Scott, C.L., Greer, B.M., Willard-Traub, M., & Johnson, R. (2003). The Diverse Voices program, a best practice in higher education: A collaborative approach. Conference Presentation. First Annual Alumni of Color Conference. Harvard Graduate School of Education, Cambridge Massachusetts.

Sheared, V. (1999). Giving voice: Inclusion of African American students' polyrhythmic realities in adult basic education. In T.C. Guy (Ed.), *Providing culturally relevant adult education: A challenge for the twenty-first century. New Directions for Adult Education, 82,* 33–48.

Shor, I. (1996). *When students have power: Negotiating authority in a critical pedagogy.* Chicago: University of Chicago Press.

Shorter-Gooden, K. (2013). Culturally competent organization. *Library Quarterly: Information, Community, Policy, 83*(3), 207–211.

Solorzano, D., & Yosso, T. (2005). Maintaining social justice hopes within academic realities: A Freirean approach to critical race/LatCrit pedagogy.

In Z. Leonardo (Ed.), *Critical pedagogy and race* (pp. 69–92). London: Wiley-Blackwell.

Stockdale, M.S., & Crosby, F.J. (Eds.) (2004). *The psychology and management of workplace diversity.* Malden, MA: Blackwell Publishing.

Theory (2013). In businessdictionary.com. Retrieved April 6, 2013, from www.businessdictionary.com/definition/theory.html

Thomas, R. R., Jr. (1991). *Beyond race and gender: Unleashing the power of your total work force by managing diversity.* New York, NY: American Management Association.

Thomas, R.R., Jr. (2006). *Building on the promise of diversity: How can we move to the next level in our workplaces, our communities and our society.* New York, NY: American Management Association.

Thomas, R.R., Jr., & Associates, Inc. (2010). *World-class diversity management: A strategic approach.* San Francisco, CA: Berrett-Koehler Publishers.

Ukpokoud, O.N. (2010). How a sustainable campus-wide diversity curriculum fosters academic success. *Multicultural Education, 17*(2), pp. 27–36.

Wade, C.L. (2002). Racial discrimination and the relationship between the directorial duty or care and corporate disclosure. *The University of Pittsburgh Law Review, 63*, pp. 389–440.

Wagley, C., & Harris, M. (1964). *Minorities in the new world.* New York: Columbia University Press.

3

EXPLORING THE RELATIONSHIP BETWEEN THE ORGANIZATIONAL CULTURE AND DIVERSITY IN THE WORKFORCE

Marilyn Y. Byrd

Chapter Overview

This chapter links organizational social justice as a necessary outcome of an organizational culture that practices inclusive diversity principles. In this chapter, the varying perspectives of organizational culture will be considered. Second, the ways that an organization's culture can convey a message of exclusion in today's multi-diverse workplace will be discussed. Third, the affective reactions and consequences of a non-inclusive organizational culture will be examined. Fourth, leadership and management commitment to an inclusive organizational culture will be addressed. Finally, emerging perspectives advocating organizational social justice will be explored.

Learning Objectives

After reading this chapter, along with completing the chapter summary questions and the case discussion questions, you will be able to:

- Recognize the varying perspectives of organizational culture
- Explain how the organization's culture can convey a message of exclusion

- Explain the affective nature of exclusion in the workplace
- Explain leadership and management's role in ensuring a culture that is inclusive
- Identify emerging trends and perspectives in organizational culture

Organizational culture is shared assumptions, values, and beliefs of members within an organization (Schein, 1992). **Culture** is the organization's customary way of doing things with the philosophies and assumptions underlying these distinct customs (Burack, 1991). An organization's culture should be a nurturing environment that welcomes all forms of human difference. An organization's culture is represented in a number of ways: storytelling, ceremonies, artifacts, and so on. The concept of an organization's culture has roots in anthropology and sociology. From this viewpoint, culture can be considered a way of life within a group that is transferred from one generation to another. Within the culture, individuals share basic assumptions that are passed down, using these assumptions to teach newcomers ways to perceive, think, and feel, and the correct way to apply those perceptions in relation to problems of external adaptation and internal integration (Schein, 1992).

Individuals within the culture usually share common cultural characteristics, uniting them in a way that makes it relatively easy to transfer attitudes and beliefs. Applied to the workplace, culture is the way of life of an organization. The culture plays an integral role in individual, group, and overall organization behavior. The organization's behavior establishes the climate of the organization. The climate is the emotions and attitudes by which members interact with each other and react and accept members from outside.

Embedded within the topic of an organization's culture is perceived notions of difference based on biases and prejudices of individuals within an organization. When individuals act upon their biases and prejudices, a hostile environment may occur.

Varying Perspectives of Organizational Culture

There are varying perspectives on how organizational culture exists in the workplace. Traditionally, organizational culture has been addressed in terms of normative beliefs, which focus on expected behavior and conduct in organizations (Cooke & Szumal, 1993).

Sandra E. Spataro (2005) has introduced three forms of organizational culture to better understand diversity in terms of group membership: culture of differentiation, culture of unity, and culture of integration. These dimensions of organizational culture place emphasis on the characteristics that are salient in group membership.

In a culture of differentiation, positive or negative values are placed on salient forms of difference. For example, an individual having a postgraduate degree places that person in a positive, preferred state of being different. A person who has a handicap, such as a speech impediment, is placed in a negative, lesser-preferred state of difference. Therefore, in this type of culture, some people may experience a preferred status and therefore could enjoy greater privilege and respect than those in a lesser-preferred status. Because the performance of those in a lesser-preferred status may be negatively affected, managers are challenged to create a culture where negative reactions are reduced or eliminated.

In a culture of unity, the salient feature is based on a common identity. While this type of culture is intended to unite members under a common bond and purpose, it could have the opposite effect in some professions. For example, the fire department is a profession that White males traditionally dominate. While this trend is slowly changing, the culture of this profession is responding much more slowly.

In a culture of integration, the salient feature is highlighting difference. Businesses and organizations embrace this type of culture when making a business case for diversity. Gaining new perspectives and ideas are thought to add value to the overall mission and success of the organization.

Spataro (2005) points out that diversity is any dimension or characteristic by which individuals are perceived as different. Individuals are now defining themselves around varying forms of workplace diversity such as physical or mental disabilities, marital status, and so on. In addition, organizations are being challenged to recognize not only emerging forms of diversity in the workforce, but individual situations that can place individuals into noninclusive situations such as physical appearance (beautyism, obesity, etc.). Emerging forms of difference will continue to influence and challenge cultures to change.

Creating an Organization's Culture

Discrimination, prejudice, and stereotypes refer to unfair social behaviors, attitudes, or beliefs. These types of behaviors, attitudes, and beliefs involve denying certain "individuals or groups of people equality of treatment which they may wish" (Allport, 1954, p. 51). In the workplace, unfair social behaviors can contribute to a culture of oppression for individuals and groups from diverse groups. A culture of oppression is counter to the idea of a workplace that embraces and celebrates diversity. From this perspective, the organizational culture can be viewed as a system that can alter or deny rites of passage to newcomers based or bias or prejudice against individuals and groups.

A culture of oppression is maintained through the **organizational social culture**. An organization's social culture is represented through social networking systems, such as the "good ol' boy network." The good ol' boy network is a social system within workplaces that allows biases to linger and endure, and as a result creates a social stratification of exclusion. Hence, the good ol' boy network is one way that the culture maintains exclusion. The organization's social culture determines who is accepted and who remains an outsider.

Organizations with a positive attitude for diversity will ensure a climate is maintained that welcomes and supports all individuals. As with many organizations that are embracing and celebrating diversity, the primary goal is to emphasize a culture that is embracing and celebrating diversity to make a case for diversity for business success, using terms such as embracing diversity, celebrating diversity, enhancing diversity, and so on. An organization's statement or commitment to diversity is often representative of the culture. It is a way to gain trust and demonstrate a concern for a socially safe place to work. There is a general sense that diversity has been adequately addressed by organizations given the various legislation that has been passed. However, the point that is being overlooked is that legislation cannot force behaviors to change. Indeed, legislation does address equality; however, it is not reasonable to expect that legislation can change or control attitudes.

Google is representative of a company with a positive organizational social culture. Google's statement of diversity listed on the company's website reflects a culture that is based on inclusion and respect (www. google.com/diversity/culture.html):

> We strive to cultivate a wholly inclusive workplace everywhere we operate in the world. We want all Googlers to love coming to work every day, not just for their projects and the great perks, but for the inclusive culture where they can feel free to be themselves and thrive. . . .
>
> At Google, we are committed to a supportive work environment, where employees have the opportunity to reach their fullest potential. Each Googler is expected to do his or her utmost to create a respectful workplace culture that is free of harassment, intimidation, bias and unlawful discrimination of any kind.

Companies like Google that market their cultures not only on the basis of inclusion, but based on one of respect, are demonstrating a culture of integration as described by Spataro (2005). Regardless of one's difference, these types of cultures demonstrate a responsibility to creating a climate where one can expect to be received into a culture that is respectful and hostile-free.

The Affective Nature of a Noninclusive Organizational Culture

Changing the culture means targeting levels of the organization that are influential in moving beyond awareness toward transforming the culture into one that is more open and receptive to the multiple forms of diversity that are emerging in the workplace. Executives and managers are responsible for conveying the message and *operationalizing the practice of* inclusion throughout the organization. Human resource training specialists play a critical role by designing curriculum that is aimed at educating and preparing executives and managers to create inclusive environments where individuals from diverse groups have the opportunity to thrive and perform at an optimum level.

While commonly recognized forms of diversity in the workforce (race, gender, and age) are still critical areas for organizational culture change, issues stemming from physical appearance (obesity, attractiveness, disabilities, etc.) are also placing individuals in categories of difference that create bias and as such are emerging as new areas where the organization's culture can be unwelcoming and nonreceptive.

An unwelcoming culture toward diverse members can produce adverse psychological and physiological outcomes. Members of diverse groups often react by trying to prove themselves equal or worthy of inclusion. For example, in response to racism, a coping strategy known as John Henryism has been associated with African Americans who expend high levels of performance resulting in high levels of stress and causing poor physical and mental health (James, 1994).

In addition, members from diverse work groups that perceive an unwelcoming culture often react toward their work environment. Examples include:

- Having physical reactions when entering the workplace
- Associating certain individuals with a specific behavior
- Feelings of frustration experiencing the issue but being unable to articulate it so that it has meaning to someone not having the experience
- Feelings of embarrassment, anguish, and pain
- Feelings of rage

Considering how an unwelcoming culture can trigger these types of emotional responses, which in turn can impact personal performance, teamwork, and overall organizational well-being, raises concerns for leadership and management.

Implications for Leaders and Managers

Developing an organizational culture that embraces diversity and inclusion requires executives who are willing to set a vision and managers who are willing to accept the responsibility for placing initiatives into action. Cox's (1993) widely recognized diversity framework places leadership and education among the top components needed to transform an organization's culture into one that welcomes diversity. First, leadership in an organization must understand the implications of how all forms of diversity can positively or negatively impact the organization's culture. Second, leadership must realize that education is broader than training and should support underutilized educational tools such as facilitated dialogue, cases analyses, and personal coaching to guide the process of changing the culture.

Organizations that are concerned with building a socially just organization will have a two-fold concern in training approaches. People of color or minorities will have opportunities to bring issues into open dialogue. Whites, or those from a majority or dominant group, will be held accountable for realizing that their position of privilege allows oppression to remain alive and well.

Furthermore, leadership in an organization that is committed to social justice will encourage and support open discussions that relate to issues of power and oppression. Organizations address diversity, but rarely is social justice and conflicts that stem from a diverse workforce discussed under the heading of diversity. Instead, the emphasis of diversity is that the workplace is representative of all types of people and backgrounds. The topic has been generalized to the point where issues stemming from the fact that differences exist become embedded. Action-oriented leadership is willing to advocate a social justice mission into the organization's culture.

Emerging Trends and Perspectives of Organizational Culture

Viewing organizational culture within a social justice framework gives a different perspective of organizational culture. The principle of social justice refers to the quest for equality and rights in reaction to the mindset of power and privilege, which can contribute to a noninclusive culture.

Organizational justice is the concern for fairness and equality within an organization or workplace as practiced by its human resources (Colquitt, Greenberg, & Zapata-Phelan, 2005). Organizational justice has been studied according to equity theory: procedural, distributive, and interactional justice (Cropanzano, Rupp, Mohler, & Schminke, 2001). *Procedural* justice relates to implementing processes in a fair and unbiased way. *Distributive* refers to the allocation of resources or rewards in a fair and unbiased way. *Interactional* refers to interacting with and treating people in a fair and unbiased way.

However, a shift toward organizational social justice is needed. **Organizational social justice** is the "ideology that organizations operating through a representing agent seek to achieve a state whereby all individuals feel included, accepted, and respected, and whereby human dignity as well as equality are practiced and upheld" (Byrd, 2012, p. 120). Organizational social justice is not based on perception; rather, this idea is based on how social justice is applied to diversity. Central to organizational social justice is nontolerance for behaviors, attitudes, situations, and issues that target diverse work groups or a discourteous and hostile culture that can be unwelcoming to individuals of diverse work groups.

Examples of attitudes and behaviors that create a negative impact on diverse individuals or groups include unfriendly gestures, unwillingness to communicate, unwillingness to offer information, unwillingness to acknowledge, name calling, slurs, degrading treatment, and the display of suggestive signs and symbols. Focusing on ways that behaviors, attitudes, and assumptions can contribute to noninclusive culture is a management concern. Therefore, a proactive approach is to implement cultural audits. **Cultural audits**, the process of periodically and consistently assessing the tone and attitudes of all organizational members toward more inclusive workforce practices and beliefs, should be implemented to ensure organizational justice. The fact that the Equal Employment Opportunity Commission (2010) continues to successfully bring suit against organizations and businesses that practice hostile environments based on discrimination under Title VII of 1964 is evidence that hostile work environments continue to exist in the workforce.

Although legislation such as Title VII of the Civil Rights Act of 1964 and 1991 prohibit discrimination against protected groups, adverse behaviors against these groups persist, as evidenced through the increasing number of complaints that is handled by the Equal Employment Opportunity Commission (EEOC). Twenty-first century organizations should advocate more socially just environments and seek strategies for transforming organizations into more open and welcoming environments so that all individuals can experience greater job satisfaction and personal well-being.

Chapter Summary

This chapter presented a social perspective of organizational culture. Traditionally, organizational culture has been studied as the beliefs, symbols, artifacts, and basic assumptions of an organization—the personality of the organization. By viewing organizational culture at the individual level, the focus is centered on the stereotypes and social attitudes of employees. Stereotypes and social attitudes that are directed toward diverse work groups can create a hostile work environment, which compromises an inclusive organizational culture. Shifting focus to the individual level of an organization's culture highlights the need for organizational social justice. Organizational social justice was introduced in this chapter as an ideology that seeks social change within organizations and institutions where diverse groups coexist.

Definition of Key Terms

Cultural audits—Process of periodically and consistently assessing the tone and attitudes of all organizational members toward more inclusive workforce practices and beliefs.

Culture—The organization's customary way of doing things and the philosophies and assumptions underlying these distinct customs.

Organizational culture—Shared assumptions, values, and beliefs of members within an organization.

Organizational justice—Concern for fairness and equality within an organization or workplace as practiced by its human resources.

Organizational social culture—Social networking system; an organization's social systems gatekeeper; good ol' boy network.

Organizational social justice—Ideology that organizations operating through a representing agent seek to achieve a state whereby all individuals feel included, accepted, and respected and whereby human dignity as well as equality is practiced and upheld.

Critical-Thinking Discussion Questions

1. Discuss the ethical implications of a noninclusive organizational culture.

2. Research companies on *Fortune's* Best Places to Work list. Provide examples of two organizations that have statements of diversity that convey organizational social justice. Discuss initiatives these organizations use to practice organizational social justice.

3. Interview a manager or someone with leadership authority in a business or organization for their insight on the meaning of inclusion in the workplace. Ask them to provide specific examples of ways their business or organization practices inclusion.

4. Assume your organization has conducted a cultural audit and the findings indicate the need for a culture change that is more supportive of the varying types of diverse work groups. What type of diversity initiative would you implement?

Case Study: Leadership and Organizational Culture at the Rosebud Fire Department

The Rosebud Fire Department (RFD) is an all-White organization located in southeast Texas. Rosebud is the most racially and ethnically diverse county in this region of the state. RFD employees, as are all city employees, are provided with an employee handbook that explicitly prohibits discrimination in any form, including ridiculing, mocking, or belittling any person. Employees are prohibited from making offensive or derogatory comments to any person, either directly or indirectly, based on race, color, sex, religion, age, disability, sexual orientation, or national origin, and from creating or contributing to an offensive or intimidating work environment.

When Fire Chief Wright met with firefighter Harper for the purpose of Harper's annual review, the chief digressed into a conversation about his church, saying. "*I can't believe those n—— have started coming to my church looking for handouts.*" This statement made firefighter Harper uncomfortable for the remainder of the meeting. A few days later, Chief Wright along with two of his subordinates, Robb and Peters, were gathered in the break room. When the morning's news reported the recent termination of a local community college president, a Black male, for a first-time offense of driving under the influence, the chief commented, "*I'll bet there was more to that story. You never can tell about n——.*" Robb and Peters were shocked. Shortly after that incident, Chief Wright entered the office of firefighter R. Lewis to discuss fire inspection codes. Before getting down to business, Wright engaged Lewis in small talk then suddenly began talking about the free meal program at his church. Lewis was surprised, but also offended when Wright complained, "*It was a good program until the n—— started showing up for handouts.*" When Wright repeated the racial slur during that same conversation, Lewis felt compelled to issue a complaint to his immediate supervisor, Lieutenant Terrell. When Terrell reported Lewis's complaint to Captain Martin, second in command at RFD, Martin had already learned about the incidents involving Harper, Robb, and Peters. The biggest surprise came when Martin revealed that the chief had used the "n" word during a conversation with him. However, Martin was not prepared to take the matter further. Since an employee had reported a situation of an offensive nature directly to him, Terrell knew he had to approach the chief. When Terrell contacted the chief, the chief indicated he would not only meet with Lewis but with Harper, Robb, and Peters (who had not issued formal complaints) and apologize for his behavior. In the subsequent meeting, the chief apologized for his comments but attempted to justify his comments with, "*I guess I just got caught up in fire station off the record kind of talk.*" He tried to rationalize his comments by saying he had been meaning to address the issue of offensive language with his staff because he had recently overheard a fireman using this type of language.

Eventually the union became involved and charged Wright with intentionally and repeatedly using racist language during the course of his official work day, and expressing a racist attitude in the presence of subordinates, thereby compromising his ability to effectively command and supervise the RFD as well as represent the community of Rosebud. Initially the Chief was placed on three-day suspension without pay pending an investigation by the Police and Fire Commission. He was eventually suspended for three months without pay after the investigation was completed.

Discussion Questions

1. Research the history and tradition of the fire department profession for insight on the culture of this industry.
2. Given the demographics, is it questionable why the Rosebud Fire Department is still all White?
3. Do you believe that the chief's racist behavior calls into question his ability to effectively advocate for hiring minorities, particularly Black men to the all-White fire department? Why or why not?
4. Due to his racist comments and attitude, comment on Wright's ability to enforce the city's antidiscrimination work rules, do you believe Wright has lost the respect of his subordinates? Explain.
5. Given there are employees within RFD that do not share the chief's racist attitudes, is this indicative there are tensions within the culture? Explain.
6. Based on his behavior, comment on the chief's ability to enforce the city's antidiscrimination policy. Do you believe the chief compromised the city's policy against a hostile work environment given there were no Blacks or other protected classes of people employed at RFD? Why or why not?

7. Deliberate change in an organization happens from the top down. But what if the problem is at the top? What about the captain's attitude?
8. Do you believe the chief received a just or too severe punishment? Explain.
9. What needs to happen at RFD—diversity training or diversity education? Justify your conclusion.

Legal Perspectives

EEOC vs. Nordstrom, Inc.

In April 2009, Nordstrom settled an EEOC lawsuit alleging a hostile work environment was permitted despite complaints by Hispanic and Black employees about a department manager who said she "hated Hispanics" and that they were "lazy" and "ignorant" and that she didn't like Blacks and told one employee, "You're Black, you stink." Under the terms of the settlement, Nordstrom will pay $292,000, distribute copies of its antidiscrimination policy to its employees, and provide antiharassment training.

EEOC vs. E&D Services, Inc.

In August 2009, a Mississippi-based drilling company agreed to pay $50,000 to settle a Title VII lawsuit alleging that four employees, three White and one Black, experienced a hostile work environment from racial harassment and retaliation while assigned to a remote drilling rig in Texas. The harassment included being subjected to racial taunts and mistreatment from Hispanic employees and supervisors and having their safety threatened because the supervisors conducted safety meetings in Spanish only and refused to interpret for them in English. Told that they needed to learn Spanish because they were in South Texas, the employees said that instead of addressing their complaints of discrimination, they were fired. The company agreed to establish an effective antidiscrimination policy and to provide antidiscrimination training to its employees.

(Source: www.eeoc.gov/eeoc/initiatives/e-race/caselist.cfm)

References

Allport, G. W. (1954). *The nature of prejudice.* Reading, MA: Addison-Wesley.
Burack, E. (1991). Changing the company culture: The role of human resource development. *Long Range Planning, 24*(1), 88–95.
Byrd, M. (2012). Theorizing leadership of demographically diverse leaders. In M. Paludi (Ed.), *Managing diversity in today's workplace: Strategies for*

employees and employers (Women and careers in management) (pp. 103–124). Santa Barbara, CA: Praeger (ABC-CLIO).

Colquitt, J., Greenberg, J., & Zapata-Phelan, C. P. (2005). What is organizational justice? A historical overview. In J. Greenberg & J. Colquitt (Eds.), *Handbook of organizational justice* (pp. 3–56). Mahwah, NJ: Lawrence Erlbaum Associates.

Cooke, R. A., & Szumal, J. L. (1993). The impact of group interaction styles on problem-solving effectiveness. *Journal of Applied Behavioral Science, 30,* 415–437.

Cox, T., Jr. (1993). *Cultural diversity in organizations: Theory, research and practice.* San Francisco: Berrett-Koehler.

Cropanzano, R., Rupp, D. E., Mohler, C. J., & Schminke, M. (2001). Three roads to organizational justice. In J. Ferris (Ed.), *Research in personnel and human resource management* (pp. 1–113). New York: JAI.

Equal Employment Opportunity Commission (2010). Retrieved from www.eeoc.gov/eeoc/initiatives/e-race/caselist.cfm

Google (2013). Google diversity and inclusion. Retrieved from www.google.com/diversity/culture.html

James, S. A. (1994). John Henryism and the health of African Americans. *Culture, Medicine, and Psychiatry, 18,* 163–182.

Schein, E. (1992). *Organizational culture and leadership* (2nd ed.). San Francisco: Jossey-Bass.

Spataro, S. E. (2005). Diversity in context: How organizational culture shapes reactions to workers with disabilities and others who are demographically different. *Behavioral Sciences and the Law, 23,* 21–38.

Thomas, R. R. (1991). *Beyond race and gender: Unleashing the power of your total workforce by managing diversity.* New York: AMACOM.

PART II
DIVERSITY IN THE WORKFORCE: CURRENT ISSUES

4

RACE AND DIVERSITY IN THE WORKFORCE

Marilyn Y. Byrd

Chapter Overview

Race is represented under Title VII as a protected category of diversity in the workforce. However, limited discussion takes places on racism as a lingering social justice issue that persists as an outcome of race diversity in the contemporary workplace. This chapter will offer a historical perspective of race and will introduce sociological theoretical perspectives for studying racism as a consequence of race diversity in the workforce.

Learning Objectives

After reading this chapter, along with completing the chapter summary questions and the case discussion questions, you will be able to:

- Explain the distinctions between race and ethnicity
- Provide sociological theoretical perspectives of race
- Provide historical perspectives of racism in the United States
- Provide a social justice advocacy for studying racism

Race is a socially constructed category that denotes differences among people. The term is politically sustained to categorize people according to a specific group (Banton, 2000). Skin color is the most salient representation of how a person is judged based on race.

According to Banton (2000), new ways of explaining human difference have emerged but historical perspectives continue to influence racial thinking. This position is based on the variety of new ways that the word "race" is used, although the historical ones exist simultaneously. Historically, the word has been used to identify humans in terms of descent, biological type, and subspecies.

A racialized way of thinking has become popularized by a socialized application and through administration and political uses that "support old style racial explanations" (Banton, 2000, p. 53). The "conception of race as subspecies is not easily grasped by man . . . whereas race as type is much simpler and can be easily twisted to deal with conflicting evidence" (p. 58). Older concepts of race were grounded in notions based upon an individual's descent and then later to Darwin's controversial theory of evolution. The contemporary concepts of race generally have been that of "race as type," although this conception was rendered invalid by Darwin's theory of evolution. Since the conception of race as descent was not earlier conceptions are still considered legitimate.

Ethnicity is a term that has emerged and in many cases has been used as an interchangeable term for race. The term *ethnicity* is a more contemporary way to denote different cultures and origins. But the term does not hold the historical implications for other cultures and origins that are associated with individuals of African descent. Another contemporary term being used is **people of color**. *People of color* is a term that is used to designate groups that are non-White and as such maintains a racial divide among groups (Zack, 2005).

However, the Black/White binary has been central to the discussion of race for several reasons. First, a divided country based on a system of slavery gave way to a state of physical freedom, but a segregated country still existed. Second, the struggle continued and led to the Civil Rights Movement, a historic period in the United States advocating for social justice by protesting the segregated practices that prevented Blacks from equal access and equal opportunity. Finally, the early 1960s was a period of civil unrest in the United States and further highlighted the racial divide between Black and White racial groups and brought about a huge movement for civil rights.

Civil rights are enforceable rights or privileges that if interfered with by another gives rise to an action for injury (Cornell University Law School, 2010). During this period of time in society, the Black/

White binary persisted from the lingering effects of slavery and continues to be the major cause of racism.

Sociological Theoretical Perspectives for Studying Race

A number of social science theorists have sought to offer theories that will lend a better understanding of race and ethnicity. Constructionist and structural theories both acknowledge that race and ethnicity are social constructs that shape how people are situated within the larger society. Further, both approaches are concerned with resolving the dilemma of what race and ethnicity mean and how society in general perceives these socially constructed notions. Both approaches recognize group identity and the categorization of a group or population of people. Table 4.1 identifies some major differences between structural and constructionist approaches to race and ethnicity (Bonilla-Silva, 1997; Loveman, 1997).

The constructionist perspective has been the prevailing notion for studying race and ethnicity in the social sciences. However, we need a deeper understanding of race that explains the system of racism. The structural approaches to race and ethnicity seek to study how power and privilege continue to sustain a racial structure.

Table 4.1 Contrasts of Constructionist and Structural Approaches to Race and Ethnicity

CONSTRUCTIONIST	STRUCTURAL
Focus on group characteristics	Focus on antagonisms created by group difference
Narrow view of racism	Broad view of racism
Focus on culture, ideology, and identity	Focus on power
By-product of economic, political, and social forces	Product of economic, political, and social forces
Groups contribute in the making and creating of their identities	Groups categorized
Static	Changing
Free-floating ideology	Structural and embedded
Psychological and irrational	Systemic and rational
Historicity	Contemporary structure
Overt behavior	Overt and covert behavior

According to the constructionist approach, race and ethnicity are categories, and specific identities of human beings "trying to solve problems, defend or enhance their positions, justify their actions, establish meanings, achieve understanding, or otherwise negotiate their way through the world in which they live" (Cornell & Hartmann, 1998, p. xviii). Constructionists emphasize ideological and cultural processes for understanding race and ethnicity. Structuralists will say that constructionist approaches have a narrow view of racism. As a result, the constructionist approach does not adequately address the problem of racism, which is deeply embedded within institutionalized practices within society. Structural approaches challenge systems that allow antagonisms stemming from racism to exist—systems that block mobility for marginalized people who encounter a hierarchy in which Whites have political and economic power (Waters, 1999). Structural approaches to understanding race and ethnicity suggest that power structures are responsible for the gaps in economic disparity, unemployment, poverty, and access to resources that sustain life. Thinking of race in terms of structure means that we are acknowledging the privilege of some and thus giving credence to racial hierarchy.

The constructionists believe that racial and ethnic groups are socially constructed and are by-products of economic, political, or social forces. As those forces change, so do their racial and ethnic products (Cornell & Hartmann, 1998). Structuralists would add that the creation of racism is a by-product of economic, political, and social forces' actions upon race and ethnicity.

Constructionists believe in a free-floating ideology—that groups contribute to the making and sustaining of their identities. Therefore, constructionists are concerned with how groups form and construct identity, and how people within groups conceptualize themselves and others (Cornell & Hartmann, 1998). Theorists that speak from the constructionist paradigm believe that as certain groups contend with situations that arise within their social arenas, identities are constructed as people try to make sense of their world. Racial categories then "become socially significant to the extent they are used to organize and interpret experience, to form social relations, and to organize individual and collective action" (p. 24). Structuralists would add that as time passes, categories are subject to change, particularly as people struggle to assign other people to them. As products of social change, circumstance, human interpretation, and social action, race and ethnicity are not static, but rather variable, diverse, and contingent upon social arenas such as politics, labor markets, residential space, social institutions, culture, and daily experience (Cornell & Hartmann, 1998). Furthermore, racial categories are used as a foundation for government action and other practices where justification to distinguish people is presumed necessary.

Some constructionists' approaches to race and ethnicity are grounded in historical conceptions that slavery is responsible for an irrational, rigid, and overt form of racism (Bonilla-Silva, 1997). Structuralist approaches will say that racism today is more covert and subtle in nature due to its embedded position within institutionalized practices that are controlled by Whites. Theorists that are advancing the structural approach to race maintain racial discrimination is no longer one of inequality but rather one of racial mistreatment within the structures of society. The inequality that is taking place now occurs behind closed doors. Those who hold the power are making decisions that affect people of color. In the United States, that power typically belongs to Whites.

Selected Theories From the Constructionist and Structural Approaches

The constructionist and structural approaches to race and ethnicity represent the worldviews that generally agree upon basic assumptions. However some theorists, while speaking from these paradigms, advance their own interpretations in an effort to render a deeper understanding of how race and ethnicity shape our lives. Table 4.2 represents six selected theories or interpretations to identify how the different worldviews or paradigms represent the study of race.

Table 4.2 Selected Constructionist and Structural Theories

CONSTRUCTIONIST	STRUCTURAL
Omi & Winant (racial formation)	Feagin (systemic racism: theory of oppression)
Murji & Solomos (racialization)	Lewis (Whiteness)
Nagel (ethnic identity)	Bonilla-Silva (racialized social systems)

Racial Formation

The racial formation theory suggested by Omi and Winant (1994) suggests that to some extent we all learn some technique to categorize people whether we are consciously aware of it or not. This satisfies a need to comprehend, explain, and determine social actions. But to understand how to combat racial discrimination that might occur through social action and how to dismantle the systems that tolerate and perpetuate racial discrimination, we should consider the socio-historical contexts of race. The racial formation theory seeks to address the topics of historicity, group identity, and social comprehensiveness as well as account for the way individuals and groups have to manage conflictual racial meanings in everyday experiences (Winant, 2000) that is lacking in structural approaches. Racial formation is produced as the meaning of race changes through the practice of societal groups. Racial formation theory suggest that in the United States race and ethnicity should be understood as constructs of social organization that are politically determined by the state.

Racialization

Bonilla-Silva (1997) presents a strong argument from a structural per-spective for a theorization of race and ethnicity that uses the concept of racialization. Revisiting the notion of racialization, an idea advanced by Banton (1979), Murji and Solomos (2005) find this idea is useful in "describing the processes by which racial meanings are attached to particular issues and the manner in which race appears to be a key factor in the ways they are defined and understood" (p. 3). However, Murji and Solomos do not offer a theoretical perspective. Rather, they incite dialogue concerning the multiple uses of racialization—as "a problematic, a framework, or as a process" (p. 4). This brings to light the question: If we cannot be clear about what the process of racial-ization is, we cannot be clear as to whether racialization captures the purpose and essence for which it is intended at a given point in time.

Ethnic Identity

Nagel's (1994) study of ethnic identity is a constructionist approach that addresses how ethnic groups are "negotiated, defined and produced through social interaction inside and outside ethnic communities" (p. 152). Nagel does not emphasize race and ethnicity, but rather ethnicity and culture. In doing so, the element of historicity is taken away but the dimension of boundaries is added. Nagel's approach is useful for accommodating the issue of immigration. "Boundaries determine who is a member and who is not and designates which ethnic categories are available for individual identification at any point in time" (p. 154). But if this is the case, then Nagel's approach has structural implications as well, because designating categories then becomes a process that is regulated by the state.

Theory of Oppression

Feagin (2006) advances a structural approach based on a theory of oppression. Feagin points out that while discrimination has been made illegal, institutionalized practices such as employment, education, and other practices within the public domain still allow racism. These structures dominate society because "white officials at all levels of the government who rarely take aggressive action to significantly reduce racial discrimination in the U.S." (p. 24) typically control them.

Feagin's (2006) approach challenges constructionists to broaden their perspective of historicity and see the reality that oppression experienced during slavery lingers on in a more contemporary form of oppression embedded within structural systems. This oppression is being fed by the large-scale wealth-generating resources of White Americans and through the resources that grant privilege to some while continuing to marginalize others. Feagin's approach departs from the constructionist view in that he seeks to give voice to the "experiences, views, understandings, and interests of those oppressed as well as the experiences, views, and understanding, and interests of their oppressors" (p. 9). Structural systems such as economic, political, educational, media, and public institutions in the United States continue to oppress because these systems decide who have the power and how groups are situated within these systems and institutions.

Study of Whiteness

Lewis (2004) suggests that all people within society are racialized, including Whites. Lewis (2004) acknowledges the structure of racial

hierarchy, but questions, "How can race be structural and embedded, yet superficial, arbitrary and whimsical, shifting with times
and circumstances. Here, Lewis is challenging both the structural
and constructionist approaches. Studies of race and ethnicity do not
adequately account for Whiteness, or how Whites are a part of the
structure that have created and sustained a racialized society. "Understanding the relationship between the daily performance of race and
larger racial structure is key to our understanding of how race works
more generally and to how it shapes the lives of whites" (p. 629). The
literature on race and ethnicity tends to focus on understanding these
constructs from the perspectives of the marginalized groups, leaving
us with limited insight on the construct of "Whiteness."

Structural Theory

Bonilla-Silva (1997) argues, "the central problem of the various
approaches to the study of racial phenomena is their lack of a structural theory of racism" (p. 465). Bonilla-Silva contends that in order to
explain the social construction of race, we must understand the structural notion of race. Bonilla-Silva's position is that when race emerged
as a social construct, this racialized system resulted in privileging
some groups over others. In the case of U.S. society, Whites assume a
privilege over Blacks and other people of color. From Bonilla-Silva's
perspective, Whites are the major actors in sustaining a racial social
system because, in doing so, they reap the benefits of a racial order,
whereas members defined as belonging to subordinate groups struggle
to challenge and change the racial status quo.

Bonilla-Silva (2003) challenges a **color-blind** ideology that difference is seen, but not acknowledged as being different. According to
Bonilla-Silva, a color-blind ideology:

- Operates on the idea of sameness, with Whiteness being the
  norm
- Defines experiences and sets standards according to the norm
- Results in an avoidance of the topic of racism

As a result, a color-blind ideology curtails the topic of racism and
accusations of racial discrimination, acting as a curtain for racists to

hide their racial views. Furthermore, this ideology serves as a tool in challenging and attacking legal rights that have been gained by minority groups. Bonilla-Silva (2003) suggests rather than attempting to sell the idea of nonracism, we should adopt the notion of antiracism.

The structural theory developed by Bonilla-Silva (1997) comes close to presenting a coherent framework for studying race and ethnicity. The theory is based on "concepts elaborated by the institutionalist, the internal colonial, and the racial formation perspectives" (p. 467), contending that race be studied from the viewpoint of racism. While Bonilla-Silva's theory does not aim to give a universal explanation of race and ethnicity, the intention is to provoke dialogue that should direct theorization toward that goal.

Racism in the United States

Racism is a process whereby socialized racist notions become integrated with actions and practices in such a way that these actions and practices become actualized and reinforced through routine situations (Essed, 1991). In the workplace, these situations can occur through individual actions or institutional practices. Although there has been progress, racism continues to persist, and for the most part, people of color are perceived as unequal by White America.

Racism is racial prejudice sustained by power, privilege, and resources (Feagin & Sikes, 1994). This prejudice perpetuates racism and is rationalized by the belief that a group's abilities, values, and culture are attributed to physical features such as skin color. Modern-day racism encompasses subtle as well as covert acts of White bigots and is "inescapable in the everyday worlds of African Americans. Almost any encounter with Whites, in workplaces, schools, neighborhoods, and public places can mean a confrontation with racism" (p. 4). Essed (1991) theorized racism as a process that has become routine in ordinary, everyday actions and practices. The term *racism* is also related to concepts such as discrimination, prejudice, and stereotypes (Dovidio, Brigham, Johnson, & Gaertner, 1996), but it is more encompassing than any of these. Dovidio et al. further stated that the actions of discrimination, prejudice, and stereotypes can also be viewed as unjust social behaviors, attitudes, or beliefs. In its very essence, racism involves not only negative attitudes and beliefs but also the social power to disadvantage some groups of people and at the same time it offers advantages to other groups.

Jones (1997) offered the perspective that there are two types of racism at the social levels. The first type is individual racism, which relates to the interplay of stereotypes, prejudices, and discrimination that manifest and support unequal treatment and practices between members of diverse groups. The second is institutional racism, which refers to the undeliberate handling or acceptance of institutional procedures (e.g., qualifying for a home mortgage, unfair hiring practices, inequitable admissions criteria) that have unjustly limited the opportunities of certain groups of people.

Individual Racism

According to Brigham (1993), individual racism can be expressed both overtly and covertly. Overt racism is intentional and the perpetrator's racist motives are clearly expressed (Ridley, 2005). On the other hand, covert racism is more subtle or hidden and the perpetrator's motives are difficult to detect. Many contemporary approaches to individual racism acknowledge the persistence of overt, intentional forms of racism but also consider the automatic or unconscious processes and indirect expressions of bias as represented by covert racism.

In contrast to overt and covert racism, Dovidio and Gaertner (1998) identified aversive racism, which represents a subtle, often unintentional, form of bias. This bias projects itself through harsh racial feelings and beliefs that are developed unconsciously. Dovidio and Gaertner further asserted that, because of these unconscious biases, aversive racism suggests that individuals may often participate in acts of discrimination while maintaining a positive opinion of one's self.

McConahay (1986) conceptualized a theory of modern racism that provides a tool to measure the dimensions of cognitive racial attitudes. The theory is based on the notion that negative attitudes formed by Whites regarding African Americans are affective and are acquired early in life. Modern racism posits four assumptions. First, people with racist attitudes maintain the position that racism no longer exists. Second, people with racist attitudes believe that minorities use tactics such as affirmative action to gain access to opportunities that would be otherwise unattainable. Third, people with racist attitudes maintain that Blacks are too aggressive in using laws such as affirmative action to their advantage. Finally, people with racist attitudes believe that Blacks who utilize policies such as affirmative action are undeserving. Racism in overt and covert forms can contribute to social policies that form the basis of institutional racism.

Institutional Racism

According to Klinker and Smith (1999), institutional racism reflects the differential effects of policies, practices, and laws on members of certain racial groups. Historically, institutional racism developed from intentional racism, such as limiting immigration and the voting rights of certain racial groups. Another historical example highlights how the majority group created and justified laws that enabled them to enslave Africans and African Americans and confiscate property from indigenous tribes (Klinker & Smith, 1999). While Fields (1990) suggested that institutional racism is: (1) independent of individual racism and (2) requires the active support of individuals that have an awareness or intention to discriminate, Feagin and Vera (1995) stated that the concept of institutional racism is not recognized as racially unfair because it is ingrained into policies and laws, which suggests that it is morally right. However, what is seen as fair and just can and does vary according to one's perspective.

Persistence of Racism in the Workplace

According to Bonilla-Silva (2003), avoiding discussions of racism allows individuals to hide their true racial viewpoints, which is another way that the majority viewpoint remains. Avoiding or ignoring the topic of racism suggests that the topic is either too volatile or that it is not serious enough to engage in conversations.

A popular misconception is that post–**civil rights** laws and legislation have eradicated racism. Post–civil rights laws and legislation mandating equal opportunity have created a color-blind ideology that operates on the notion of sameness (Bonilla-Silva, 2003). However this notion is a mechanism for avoiding discussions of racism and conceals the individual and institutional levels in which racism is still prevalent. Acknowledging racism is necessary not only for those subjected to the experience (individual level) but also for those involved in policymaking practices and procedures (institutional level).

Another misconception is that the election of the first African American president in 2008 is an indicator that racism no longer exists (Reed & Louis, 2009). However, incidents of alleged racism in the workplace persist. In July 2009, the *Houston Chronicle* reported two female firefighters recently returned to their living quarters to find racial and sexual graffiti in their personal spaces. KTVT in Dallas/Fort Worth reported March 12, 2009, that Confederate flags, racist graffiti, and a hangman's noose were discovered in various parts of Turner Industries, a pipe factory in Paris, Texas. On July 29, 2009, the *State Journal-Register* in Springfield, Illinois, reported a noose that was discovered hanging in a workspace at the City Water, Light, and Power. To African American people, these symbols are connected to a period of time in this country when African American people were subjected to inhumane and egregious acts of hate. Therefore, the recurrence of these symbols in contemporary times conveys a subtle meaning of racism.

DiversityInc, reported that during the 2012 election, the growing popularity of social media helped to spread racial hatred before and after the re-election of President Obama. Because of the multiple modes of social media available, it is likely that stereotypical images pervade the workplace and threaten the goal of an inclusive workplace to make all people feel welcomed and respected. According to DiversityInc, derogatory depictions of the President as a monkey or with exaggerated physical features along with other demeaning attacks on the President and Michelle Obama targeted their identity as African Americans rather than targeting their political views or affiliation. Attacking the President of the United States in such a blatant, stereotypical, racist, and disrespectful way casts a shadow on the prevalence of racism in society.

Uncovering Racism in Diversity

Generally, companies, businesses, and organizations recognize and acknowledge their commitments and efforts in promoting diversity in the workplace. In fact, diversity initiatives are recognized as one indicator of success for companies appearing on *Fortune's* Best Companies to Work For list. Rarely discussed or acknowledged, however, are the issues that emerge from a diverse workforce. The nature of diversity among groups and the perceptions and assumptions about certain racial groups can produce negative attitudes and behaviors. To truly appreciate, value, and embrace diversity requires changes in negative attitudes and behaviors that result in the persistence of racism in institutional and organizational settings (Thomas, 1991, 2005). Therefore, moving organizations toward a state of valuing and appreciating diversity is counterproductive if acts of racism continue to persist.

Bernier and Rocco (2003) argued that rarely have the effects of race and racism been used to study diversity and the issues that emerge from diversity in the workplace. Consequently, diversity, in terms of race, within organizations cannot be leveraged unless there is an understanding of the historical and contemporary causes of racism. Although organizations are making strides to be viewed as diversity-focused, the state of being diverse often places individuals into categories that leave them open to being labeled, stigmatized, and vulnerable to actions and perceptions based on that category. Deitch et al. (2003) reported that modern acts of racism such as unwelcoming attitudes, unwillingness or refusal to cooperate, and avoidance or refusal to acknowledge have replaced the more blatant and outward displays of racism; however, this statement is being challenged in wake of the reappearance of blatant acts like nooses, racial graffiti, and displaying of the Confederate flag. These adverse actions and perceptions are discriminatory, prejudicial, and stereotypical and can all permeate from racism.

Emerging Perspectives on Racism as a Social Justice Issue

Racism is a social justice issue that served as a historical root of workforce diversity and training in the United States (Cox, 1993). However, Jane Elliott, a noted diversity trainer, says (PBS, 2010):

. . . we are still conditioning people in this country and, indeed, all over
the globe to the myth of white superiority. We are constantly being told
that we don't have racism in this country anymore, but most of the people
who are saying that are white.

Furthermore, as long as we continue to use certain language (such
as race and ethnicity) certain groups in society will continue to be
viewed in terms of a specific category. Racialized language feeds the
system of racism and allows it to persist through political categorization and institutionalized practices within our society.

Realistically speaking, changing large systems that control the public domain from racialized thinking would be a slow and arduous act.
Assigning people to a "race" has been engrained in this society for
years. We are categorized (racialized) immediately from birth, and the
birth document becomes an immediate identifier as to who we are. To
contest this categorization would still remain a government-controlled
process, which means how a person experiences race remains under
the power and control of the state. Shifting this power from the state
is a matter for social advocacy and perhaps a new social movement.

Chapter Summary

The word *race* has had various historical meanings. However, the word
has emerged in more contemporary terms to categorize individuals
according to groups. In doing so, certain groups maintain a marginalized status in society based on group affiliation. Although legislation
was passed to protect individuals based on race as well as other diverse
categories, attitudes and behaviors formed from nonacceptance of
individuals continue. In the workplace, these attitudes play out in form
of verbal or physical actions that communicate the practice of racism.
Leadership within organizations is responsible for ensuring socially
just organizations whereby all individuals feel safe and welcomed.

Definition of Key Terms

Civil rights—A civil right is an enforceable right or privilege that if interfered
with by another gives rise to an action for injury.

Civil Rights Movement—A social justice movement in the United States in the early 1960s advocating equal access and equal opportunity for Black Americans.

Color-blind—Difference is seen but not acknowledged as being different; attempting to promote a nonracist policy.

Constructionist theory—Explains racial and ethnic groups as socially constructed based on by-products of economic, political, or social forces. As those forces change, so do the racial and ethnic by-products.

Ethnicity—Ethnicity is a more contemporary way to denote different cultures and origins, including people of color.

Individual racism—Interplay of stereotypes, prejudices, and discrimination that manifest and support unequal treatment and practices between members of diverse groups.

Institutional racism—Differential effects of policies, practices, and laws on members of certain racial groups; deliberate or undeliberate handling or acceptance of institutional procedures (e.g., qualifying for a home mortgage, unfair hiring practices, inequitable admissions criteria) that have unjustly limited the opportunities of certain groups of people.

People of color—A term used to designate groups that are non-White.

Race—Socially constructed category that denotes differences among people and is politically sustained to assign people to categories.

Racialization—Processes by which racial meanings are attached to particular issues and the manner in which race appears to be a key factor in the ways they are defined and understood.

Racism—Process whereby socialized racist notions become integrated with actions and practices in such a way that these actions and practices become actualized and reinforced through routine situations.

Structural theory—Explains racism as a by-product of economic, political, and social forces' actions upon race and ethnicity.

Critical-Thinking Discussion Questions

1. Discuss how the historical development of racial groups contributes to sustaining racism in the United States.

2. Compare and contrast the constructionist and structural theories of race.

3. Discuss ways that institutional racism could exist in the workforce. Give specific examples.

4. Discuss ways that individual racism could exist in the workforce. Give specific examples.

Legal Perspectives

In June 2013, allegations of systemic racism were filed against Paula Deen, a world-renowned chef, for using the "N" word. Employees also reported to the Rainbow/PUSH Coalition, a social change organization, that Blacks were paid disproportionately from Whites and received fewer opportunities for advancement.

In September 2012, the Equal Employment Opportunity Commission (EEOC) obtained a settlement of $630,000 filed against a California trucking firm and its successor on the behalf of African American, Latino, and East Indian workers. The workers alleged discrimination on the basis of race, national origin, and religion. In the original complaint, management and employees were alleged to have subjected drivers to racial slurs, such as using the "N" word when referring to Black drivers, calling East Indian drivers "Taliban" or "camel drivers," and using the word "spic" when referring to a Latino manager. White workers were also alleged to be given more favorable job assignments than non-Whites.

In May 2008, the Equal Employment Opportunity Commission (EEOC) obtained a settlement of $1.65 million in a racial harassment case filed against a general contractor and its subsidiaries on behalf of a class of African American employees who were subjected to egregious racial harassment at a construction site in Bethlehem, Pennsylvania. The harassment included a life-size noose made of heavy rope hung from a beam in a class member's work area for at least 10 days before it was removed; the regular use of the "N" word; and racially offensive comments made to Black individuals, including "I think everybody should own one," "Black people are no good and you can't trust them," and "Black people can't read or write." Additionally, racist graffiti was written in portable toilets, with terms such as "coon," "if u not white u not right," "white power," "KKK," and "I love the Ku Klux Klan." Additional remedies were injunctive relief enjoining each defendant from engaging in racial harassment or retaliation, antidiscrimination training, the posting of a notice about the settlement, and reporting complaints of racial harassment to the EEOC for monitoring. (*Source:* www.eeoc.gov/eeoc/initiatives/e-race/caselist.cfm)

References

Banton, M. (1979). Analytical and folk concepts of race and ethnicity. *Ethnic & Racial Studies, 2*(2), 127–138.
Banton, M. (2000). The idiom of race: A critique of presentation. In L. Back & J. Solomos (Eds.), *Theories of race and racism* (pp. 53–63). London: Routledge.

Bernier, J. D., & Rocco, T. S. (2003). Working in the margins of Critical Race Theory and HRD. *Proceedings of the 2003 Midwest Research to Practice Conference in Adult, Continuing, and Community Education* (pp. 13–18). Columbus: The Ohio State University.

Bonilla-Silva, E. (1997). Rethinking racism. *American Sociological Review, 62,* 465–79.

Bonilla-Silva, E. (2003). *Racism without racists: Color blind racism and the persistence of racial inequality in the United States.* New York: Rowman & Littlefield.

Brigham, J. C. (1993). College students' racial attitudes. *Journal of Applied Social Psychology, 23,* 1933–1967.

Cornell, S. E., & Hartmann, D. (1998). *Ethnicity and race: Making identities in a changing world.* Thousand Oaks, CA: Pine Forge Press.

Cornell University Law School (2010). Retrieved from http://topics.law.cornell.edu/wex/Civil_rights

Cox, T., Jr. (1993). *Cultural diversity in organizations: Theory, research and practice.* San Francisco: Berrett-Koehler.

Deitch, E. A., Barsky, A., Butz, R. M., Chan, S., Brief, A. P., & Bradley, J. C. (2003). Subtle yet significant: The existence and impact of everyday racial discrimination in the workplace. *Human Relations, 56*(11), 1299–1324.

DiversityInc (2012). Racist Obama Facebook pages & your office: What do you need to know? Retrieved June 26, 2013, from: www.diversityinc.com/diversity-management/racist-obama-facebook-pages-your-office-what-do-you-need-to-know/

Dovidio, J. F., Brigham, J. C., Johnson, B. T., & Gaertner, S. L. (1996). Stereotyping, prejudice, and discrimination: Another look. In N. Macrae, M. Hewstone, & C. Stangor (Eds.), *Confronting racism: The problem and the response* (pp. 3–32). Newbury Park, CA: Sage.

Dovidio, J. F., & Gaertner, S. L. (1998). On the nature of contemporary prejudice: The causes, consequences, and challenges of aversive racism. In J. Eberhardt & S. T. Fiske (Eds.), *Confronting racism: The problem and the response* (pp. 3–32). Newbury Park, CA: Sage.

Essed, P. (1991). *Understanding everyday racism: An interdisciplinary theory.* Newbury Park, CA: Sage.

Feagin, J. (2006). *Systemic racism: A theory of oppression.* London: Routledge.

Feagin, J. R., & Sikes, M. P. (1994). *Living with racism: The Black middle-class experience.* Boston: Beacon Press.

Feagin, J. R., & Vera, H. (1995). *White racism.* New York: Routledge.

Fields, B. (1990). Slavery, race and ideology in the United States of America. *New Left Review, 181.*

Jones, J. M. (1997). *Prejudice and racism* (2nd ed.). New York: McGraw-Hill.

Klinker, P. A., & Smith, R. M. (1999). *The unsteady march: The rise and decline of American commitments to racial equality.* New York: Free Press.

Lewis, A. (2004). What group?: Studying whites and whiteness in the era of color blindness. *Sociological Theory, (22)*4, 623–464.

Loveman, M. (1997). Is race essential? A comment on Bonilla-Silva. *American Sociological Review, 64*(6), 891–898.

McConahay, J. B. (1986). Modern racism and ambivalence, and the modern racism scale. In J. F. Dovidio & S. L. Gaertner (Eds.), *Prejudice, discrimination, and racism* (pp. 91–125). Orlando, FL: Academic Press.

Murji, K., & Solomos, J. (Eds.) (2005). *Racialization: Studies in theory and practice.* Oxford: Oxford University Press.

Nagel, J. (1994). Constructing ethnicity: Creating and recreating ethnic identity and culture. *Social Problems, 41*(1), 152–176.

Omi, M., & Winant, H. (1994). *Racial formation in the United States: From the 1960s to the 1990s.* London: Routledge.

PBS (2010). A class divided. Retrieved from www.pbs.org/wgbh/pages/frontline/shows/divided/etc/crusade.html

Reed, W. L., & Louis, B. M. (2009). No more excuses: Problematic responses to Barack Obama's election. *Journal of Africana Studies, 13*(2), 97–109. doi:10.1007/s12111–009–9088–3

Ridley, C. R. (2005). *Overcoming unintentional racism in counseling and therapy.* Thousand Oaks, CA: Sage.

Thomas, R. R. (1991). *Beyond race and gender.* New York: AMACOM.

Thomas, R. R. (2005). *Building on the promise of diversity: How can we move to the next level in our workplaces, our communities, and our society?* New York: AMACOM.

Waters, M. C. (1999). Explaining the comfort factor: West Indian Immigrants confront American race relations. In M. Lamont (Ed.), *Cultural territories of race: Black and White boundaries* (pp. 63–96). Chicago: University of Chicago Press.

Winant, H. (2000). The theoretical status of the concept of race. In L. Back & J. Solomos (Eds.), *Theories of race and racism* (pp. 181–190). London: Routledge.

Zack, N. (2005). *Thinking about race.* Florence, KY: Wadsworth Publishing, Cengage Learning.

5

GENDER AND DIVERSITY IN THE WORKFORCE

Brenda Lloyd-Jones, Lisa Bass,
and Gaetane Jean-Marie

Chapter Overview

In the 21st century, gender issues are becoming more prominent as women increasingly enter the workforce. This demographic shift has attracted the interest of corporate and government sectors, prompting policy considerations and implications regarding these new workers (Powell & Greenhaus, 2010). Like race and ethnicity, gender is pivotal to initiatives seeking to recognize and embrace diversity under the auspices of globalization and the need for marketplace innovation (Kurowski, 2002; Soni, 2000). Dolan (2004) notes that a diverse public sector is important for symbolic reasons and should reflect a pluralistic nation. As such, the public will be more responsive to bureaucratic decisions when the workforce "looks like America" (Dolan, 2004).

Women are now an integral part of the diverse workforce, not only supplementing family income but also pursuing careers in formerly predominantly male professions. Men are also exploring new work-related options and rethinking conventional gender-role stereotypes. Thus, some gender issues that primarily mattered to women are now concerns of men as well (DeLaat, 2007). While the increased presence of women in the professional and business world suggests that the struggle for gender equality is over, women and men continue to confront gender inequality due to persistent gender bias in areas including advancement, compensation, benefits, and family obligations (Meyerson & Fletcher, 2000; Reece & Brandt, 2008).

Gender-related issues in the workforce attract considerable attention from researchers and practitioners in an effort to understand the complex issues impacting working women and men. Much of the research literature on the subject of gender focuses on issues related to women (Stewart, Bing, Gruys, & Helford, 2007).

Learning Objectives

After reading this chapter, along with completing the chapter summary questions and the case discussion questions, you will be able to:

- Apply a social role framework to conceptualize gender and diversity in the workforce
- Chronicle a historical overview of the role of gender and diversity in the earliest periods of the U.S. workforce
- Explain how gender discrimination in the workplace occurs
- Describe the myth of equality and distinguish the glass ceiling from the glass escalator
- Understand contemporary issues facing women and men in the workplace and the implications for policy and practice

Conceptualizing Gender and Diversity in the Workforce: A Social Role Perspective

In the scholarship on diversity and inequality within organizations, gender issues (e.g., sex differences and similarities, division of labor, stereotypes, discrimination, and wage gap inequality) merit considerable attention in framing discussions on diversity in the workforce. Women and men in the workforce confront a number of gender-related issues that manifest in tacit or expressed practices and are steeped in traditional beliefs and values.

Whereas the study of diversity in the workforce draws from sociology and psychology, it has primarily been examined in the management literature (DiTomaso, Post, & Parks-Yancy, 2007). Similarly, the study of gender draws on psychology including but not limited to social role theory, providing a linkage between gender and diversity in the workforce. Social role theory seeks to explain the cause of differences and similarities in social behavior (Eagly, 1987; Eagly,

Wood, & Diekman, 2000). Based on meta-analytic methods to aggregate differences between women and men, research suggests that they behave similarly more than 98% of the time (Eagly, 1987; Eagly et al., 2000). However, when differences occur, research also suggests that these differences become stereotypes between the sexes. Furthermore, as Vogel, Wester, Heesacker, and Madon (2003) observe, "these differences, although small, are important because they may emerge more strongly under some conditions and less strongly under others" (p. 519). The body of literature underscores the perspective that the differences between men and women reinforce gender stereotypes in the workplace, benefitting men as women gain more access to opportunities that were previously denied to them.

In considering the experiences of both women and men in the workforce, it is important to distinguish between the terms *sex* and *gender*. **Sex** indicates the binary categories of female and male (Powell & Greenhaus, 2010, p. 2). **Gender** refers to the social construction of differences between women and men and the social attributes and opportunities associated with being female and male (E-Mine Electronic Mine Information Network, 2009; Marini, 1990). From a Western perspective, gender is rooted in societal beliefs that females and males are naturally distinct and more or less opposed social beings (Amott & Matthaei, 2007). Central to the distinction between sex and gender are **gender roles**, which are traditional beliefs about what functions are appropriate for women and men (Perrone, Wright, & Jackson, 2009; Powell & Greenhaus, 2010), and **gender stereotypes**, which are deeply embedded assumptions and beliefs about the gender attributes and differences of individuals and/or groups (Fiske-Rusciano & Cyrus, 2005). Hence, gender, race, and class historically constitute fundamental categories that shape the American workforce as basic conduits for social inequalities between women and men (Dovidio, Kawakami, & Gaertner, 2002; Portes & Rumbaut, 1996). Through the development of capitalism, for instance, men's work included activities such as hunting, farming, and other forms of rigorous manual labor, while women spent much of their time occupied with domestic work such as cooking, cleaning, and making or mending clothes for the family (Lewis, 1999). These role distinctions between women and men existed from the earliest times of U.S. history.

Historical Overview of Gender and Diversity in the Workforce

During the pre-industrialization era, the diversity of the American workforce included African slaves, immigrant workers, and convicts who were primarily men, and they were the cornerstone of the agricultural labor market. The influence of sex and gender roles and stereotypes in the workforce impacted women's participation in the agricultural labor market. As the United States became industrialized, the need for labor increased, and the market consisted not only of immigrants but also rural Americans and very young women (Fullerton, 1993; Johnston & Packer, 1987; Kurowski, 2002). Management theorists, however, discounted the diversity of the workforce in the earlier periods and treated it as inconsequential assuming that a homogenous audience understood its role tacitly (Kurowski, 2002, p. 185). Several scholars argue that diversity in the workforce gained prominence because of the social, political, and economic changes that were occurring in the labor force (e.g., DiTomaso et al., 2007; Friedman & DiTomaso, 1996; Johnston & Packer, 1987).

The gradual presence of women in the diverse workforce, beginning as early as the 1900s, reveals that women desired **gender equality**—a social order in which women and men would share the same opportunities and the same constraints concerning full participation in both the economic and the domestic realms (Bailyn, 2006). In 1909, the first significant strike by working women, called "The Uprising of 20,000" (see Figures 5.1 and 5.2), was conducted by shirt-waist makers in New York who protested low wages and long working hours (Goodman, 1990).

Beginning some 30 years later, from 1940 to 1960, the number of working women and the proportion of working wives doubled. During World War II, large numbers of women entered the workforce, with Rosie the Riveter (see Figure 5.3) becoming a national symbol (Goodman, 1990). The earlier attempts to ignore diversity in the workforce in the management literature could not prevail, given the social transformation occurring in society. Although women workers were met with resistance, caution, and struggle, the workforce progressively began to reflect all people of diverse ethnicity and race.

Figure 5.1   The Uprising of 20,000 Slogan: "We'd rather starve quick than starve slow."
Source: Library of Congress Print and Photographs Online Catalog

The notion of diversity in the workforce gained momentum in the 1960s during the Civil Rights Movement as more African Americans entered the workforce (Kurowski, 2002; Soni, 2000). The surge of African American workers meant that their increased presence and visibility could no longer be overlooked and that there was a need to study and understand the experiences and attitudes of culturally diverse workers (e.g., Ford, 1985; Fullerton, 1993). In the 1980s, the report Workforce 2000 concluded that by the year 2000, "non-whites" would constitute 15% of the workforce as compared to 11% in 1970 (Johnston & Packer, 1987; Kurowski, 2002). According to the Bureau of Labor Statistics, the non-Whites constituted 19% of the U.S. workforce in 2011 (Solis & Galvin, 2012).

It was not, however, until the late 1980s that diversity models emerged to respond to changing workplace needs (Soni, 2000). In fact, diversity models act as interventions and are a proactive approach to fully and equitably utilizing, integrating, and rewarding workers of

Figure 5.2   The Uprising of 20,000, International Ladies Garment Workers Union
Source: Library of Congress Print and Photographs Online Catalog

different racial/ethnic and gender backgrounds (Cox, 1993; Loden & Rosener, 1991; Sims & Dennehy, 1993; Soni, 2000). According to Soni (2000), "American workplaces appear to be more receptive to diversity in the workforce as they enter the 21st century, though its merits are being debated everywhere" (p. 395). Diversifying the workforce is an

Figure 5.3 Rosie the Riveter: American Women Working During World War II
Source: Library of Congress Print and Photographs Online Catalog

Figure 5.3 *(Continued)*

effort to address inequities between women and men; however, women overwhelmingly continue to face discrimination in the workplace.

Gender Discrimination in the Workplace

Sipe, Johnson, and Fisher (2009) define **gender discrimination** as "gendered-based behaviors, policies, and actions that adversely affect a person's work by leading to unequal treatment or the creation of an intimidating environment because of one's gender" (p. 342). Gender discrimination is also referred to as sexism (Heckman, 1998; Powell & Greenhaus, 2010) and "occurs when employers make decisions such as selection, evaluation, promotion, or reward allocation on the basis of an individual's gender" (Sipe et al., 2009, p. 342). Prior to the enactment of Title VII of the Civil Rights Act of 1964, there was no legislation that prohibited gender discrimination. The U.S. government enacted both the Civil Rights Act of 1964 and the Equal Pay Act of 1963 to eradicate deeply entrenched patterns of discrimination in employment because of race, religion, sex, or national origin. The Pregnancy Discrimination Act of 1978 amended the Civil Rights Act of 1964 for the protection of pregnant females in the workforce.

Men confront gender issues (e.g., gender stereotypes and gender discrimination) in the workplace; however, research indicates that women face barriers far more often than do men (DeLaat, 2007). In a review of empirical studies, Ngo, Foley, Wong, and Loi (2003) identified four indicators of gender discrimination in the workplace: (a) women lag behind men in salary and salary advancement; (b) women's rewards and work conditions (i.e., pay, autonomy, authority) are commonly less favorable than men's; (c) women tend to work in dead-end jobs, resulting in lack of advancement; and (d) women are less likely than are men to use authority in the workplace (as cited in Sipe et al., 2009, p. 342). Gender discrimination can occur in various settings, but it happens much of the time in employment (e.g., gender wage gap and occupational sex segregation) (Ngo et al., 2003).

The **gender wage gap** is defined as the difference in earnings received by women and men for performing similar duties or tasks (Peterson & Morgan, 1995; Weichselbaumer & Winter-Ebmer, 2005). Historically, the pay gap between female and male workers was distinguished by level of education and physical prowess, which earned men more income than women (Fry, 2009). M. J. Williams, Paluck, and Spencer-Rodgers (2010) attribute this early perspective, which is prevalent even today, to the stereotypical view of men as higher-wage earners than women. Men, in the early periods of American history, acquired more education than women, and their physical strength was viewed as superior (Fry, 2009; Peterson & Morgan, 1995; Weichselbaumer & Winter-Ebmer, 2005).

In addressing the wage gap disparities, in 1963, Congress passed the Equal Pay Act to bridge the gender wage gap between women and men (Gibelman, 2003; Weichselbaumer & Winter-Ebmer, 2005). Additionally, the educational attainment of women beyond common schooling (i.e., K–12 level) has caused a realignment of the educational qualifications between women and men. Women now attend college at rates surpassing that of men (Fry, 2009; Peterson & Morgan, 1995; Weichselbaumer & Winter-Ebmer, 2005). The ratio of men attending college in October 2008 was 37%, while women's attendance was 42.5% during that same period (Fry, 2009). Women today have more access to higher education, which increases their opportunities for earning higher income.

Although significant strides toward closing the gender wage gap have been achieved, pay inequality persists (Blau & Kahn, 2007) (see Figure 5.4).

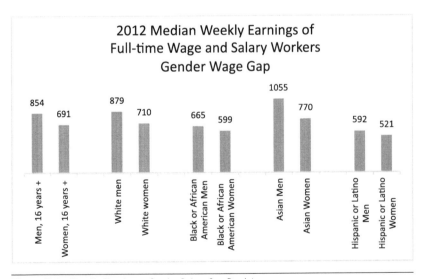

Figure 5.4   Despite New Laws, Gender Salary Gap Persists
Data Source: Bureau of Labor Statistics

Several factors account for the pay differences between the sexes. First, the number of women in lucrative, upper-level positions within organizations is few, and women tend to be concentrated in lower-echelon positions having limited opportunities for upward mobility (Alkadry & Tower, 2006). Similar gaps occur at lower-end wage and salary jobs. In a U.S. Census Report (2003), women who worked hourly had median hourly earnings of $9.89, while men earned $11.63 (p. 2). Second, women's average salaries are only a fraction of what is earned by men at all levels (Bayard, Hellerstein, Neumark, & Troske, 2003). Gaps in earnings between race and gender persist in contemporary statistics and in current analysis. The Bureau of Labor Statistics reports that in 2011, the median usual weekly earnings of full-time wage and salary workers were $549 for Hispanics, $615 for Blacks, $775 for Whites, and $866 for Asians. Among men, the earnings of Whites ($856), Blacks ($653), and Hispanics ($571) were 88%, 67%, and 59%, respectively, of the earnings of Asians ($970). The median earnings of White women ($703), Black women ($595), and Hispanic women ($518) were 94, 79, and 69%, respectively, of the earnings of Asian women ($751) (Solis & Galvin, 2012).

Finally, the side effects of supply and demand factors further drive salary differentials between men and women (Blau & Kahn, 2007). According to Blau and Kahn, an increase in the demand for jobs that require the skills in which men have more experience than women increases wage inequality.

A recent Presidential Proclamation (see Figure 5.5) by President Barack Obama declares National Equal Pay Day, garnering support for gender wage equality.

Occupational sex segregation is also associated with perpetuating the gender wage gap and refers to the concentrating of women and men into particular occupations (Mora & Ruiz-Castillo, 2004). For example, women tend to work in certain occupations, firms, and industries with other women more often than with men. Traditionally, organizations are based on norms and beliefs that are more frequently accommodating and adhered to by men than by women (van Vianen & Fischer, 2002). Oftentimes, women are excluded from male occupations because of men's social closure around these jobs (Levine, 2009;

The White House
Office of the Press Secretary
Presidential Proclamation—National Equal Pay Day   **April 20, 2010**
A PROCLAMATION

Throughout our Nation's history, extraordinary women have broken barriers to achieve their dreams and blazed trails so their daughters would not face similar obstacles. Despite decades of progress, pay inequity still hinders women and their families across our country. National Equal Pay Day symbolizes the day when an average American woman's earnings finally match what an average American man earned in the past year. Today, we renew our commitment to end wage discrimination and celebrate the strength and vibrancy women add to our economy.

Our Nation's workforce includes more women than ever before. In households across the country, many women are the sole breadwinner, or share this role equally with their partner. However, wage discrimination still exists. Nearly half of all working Americans are women, yet they earn only about 80 cents for every dollar men earn. This gap increases among minority women and those with disabilities.

Pay inequity is not just an issue for women; American families, communities, and our entire economy suffer as a result of this disparity. We are still recovering from our economic crisis, and many hardworking Americans are still feeling its effects. Too many families are struggling to pay their bills or put food on the table, and this challenge should not be exacerbated by discrimination. I was proud that the first bill I signed into law, the Lilly Ledbetter Fair Pay Restoration Act, helps women achieve wage fairness. This law brings us closer to ending pay disparities based on gender, age, race, ethnicity, religion, or disability by allowing more individuals to challenge inequality.

To further highlight the challenges women face and to provide a coordinated Federal response, I established the White House Council on Women and Girls. My Administration also created a National Equal Pay Enforcement Task Force to bolster enforcement of pay discrimination laws, making sure women get equal pay for an equal day's work. And, because the importance of empowering women extends beyond our borders, my Administration created the first Office for Global Women's Issues at the Department of State.

We are all responsible for ensuring every American is treated equally. From reshaping attitudes to developing more comprehensive community-wide efforts, we are taking steps to eliminate the barriers women face in the workforce. Today, let us reaffirm our pledge to erase this injustice, bring our Nation closer to the liberty promised by our founding documents, and give our daughters and granddaughters the gift of true equality.

NOW, THEREFORE, I, BARACK OBAMA, President of the United States of America, by virtue of the authority vested in me by the Constitution and the laws of the United States, do hereby proclaim April 20, 2010, as National Equal Pay Day. I call upon all Americans to acknowledge the injustice of wage discrimination and join my Administration's efforts to achieve equal pay for equal work.

IN WITNESS WHEREOF, I have hereunto set my hand this twentieth day of April, in the year of our Lord two thousand ten, and of the Independence of the United States of America the two hundred and thirty-fourth.

BARACK OBAMA

Figure 5.5   Presidential Proclamation—National Equal Pay Day
Source: Retrieved from: www.whitehouse.gov/the-press-office/presidential-proclamation-national-equal-pay-day

Tomaskovic-Devey & Skaggs, 1999). The "good ol' boys" network, as an example of social closure, hinders women's access and entry to prominent positions occupied by men. Coupled with the male-dominated organizational culture is the leisurely progression of women in senior-level jobs. In 2009, only 13.5% or just 697 out of 5,161 Fortune 500 executive positions were held by women (Catalyst Inc., 2010; Healthfield, 2010). Fortune 500 corporate board seats held by women in 2009 were just 15.2%, the same as in 2008, and just slightly higher than the 13% held in 2007 (Catalyst Inc., 2010; Healthfield, 2010). The underrepresentation of women in senior-level positions is further evident in the law profession, where women make up 46.7% of law students, but only 34.4% of active lawyers and 18.7% of the law-firm partners (Catalyst Inc., 2010). Most recent projections by the U.S. Department of Labor Bureau of Labor Statistics (2005) indicate that by 2014, more than 50% of all U.S. workers will be women. This increase has the potential to provide a tipping point that will positively transform organizations to level the playing field for women (Kalev, 2009).

The Myth of Equality: Glass Ceiling vs. Glass Escalator

In further exploration of occupational sex segregation, an examination of the "glass ceiling" and "glass escalator" effects provides further understanding of the prevailing inequalities between women and men in the workforce. In particular, women's and men's career opportunities in sex-segregated occupational contexts continue to perpetuate the "glass ceiling" effect, while men benefit from the "glass escalator" effect.

The term *glass ceiling* symbolizes barriers that are based on attitudinal or organizational bias preventing qualified women from advancing higher in their organizations (Danziger & Eden, 2007; Powell, 1999; U.S. Department of Labor, 1991). Danziger and Eden (2007) posit, "the glass-ceiling barrier sustains and reproduces occupational inequality between the sexes, even when individuals possess similar education, skills, and competence levels" (p. 130). Schilt's (2006) synthesis of the scholarly literature concerning the pervasiveness of the glass ceiling depicts the disparities between women and men in white- and blue-collar workplaces in which women continue to trail behind in opportunities and advancement. In further support of the glass-ceiling effect, Davies-Netzley (1998) and Kalev (2009) contend that, in comparison to men, women continue to cluster near the bottom of organizational and professional hierarchies, receive lower wages, and have limited advancement opportunity in the workforce.

With the proliferation of women in the workforce in recent decades, women increasingly have acquired managerial and professional occupations in various sectors (Cotter, Hermsen, Ovadia, & Vanneman, 2001; Davies-Netzley, 1998). In 1999, Hewlett-Packard appointed Carleton Fiorina as CEO, the first female chief executive officer of a Fortune 500 company. Heralding the dismantling of the glass ceiling, Fiorina claimed that "women face no limits whatsoever. There is not a glass ceiling" (Meyer, 1999, p. 56). In the same year, Catalyst Inc. (1999), in a report on the experiences of women of color in corporate America, underscored the persistence of the glass ceiling and concluded that women of color suffer from greater underrepresentation than do majority-group women. While women like Carleton Fiorina have ascended to executive-level positions, they have "cracked" but not shattered the glass ceiling.

In recent work by Reece and Brandt (2008), they argue that, although a woman may hold a managerial and/or professional position, which "reflects a twenty-five year pattern of gain in education and job status," women in general continue to be underrepresented in high-ranking jobs (p. 385). While executive-level positions are visible to women in the workplace, the glass ceiling phenomenon blocks their advancement and promotion. Further, women working in male-dominated fields such as business, medicine, law enforcement, and engineering face unfavorable treatment and impediments within organizational career mobility (Hultin, 2003). Attitudinal and organizational biases that persist, whether overtly or covertly, have economic consequences, both in lost productivity and turnover costs (Ragins, 1998). Women who face barriers in terms of advancement often leave to work in another organization or start their own business. While acknowledging the remarkable progress made by women in the workforce, Meyerson and Fletcher (2000) also criticize the discouragingly slow pace of women's advancement to top-level positions in which "many women [are] jumping off, becoming frustrated, and disillusioned with the business world" (p. 127). Consequently, the maladaptive nature of organizations is inclusive of women but remain more accommodating to men (C. L. Williams, 2009).

Unlike women who bump up against the glass ceiling in the workforce, men ride the "glass escalator" to ascend the hierarchy specifically within female-dominated organizations. The term *glass escalator*, coined by the sociologist Christine Williams (1992, 1995) refers to the promotion of men over women into management in female-dominated positions such as nursing, social work, elementary school teaching, and librarianship (Hultin, 2003; C. L. Williams, 1992, 1995). C. L. Williams (1992) contends that throughout the 20th century, these fields have been identified as women's work. According to Hultin (2003), "men in these positions are able to ride a 'glass escalator' up the internal career ladders and at a speed that their female counterparts can hardly enjoy" (p. 31). In female-dominated lines of work, men escape negative consequences of tokenism and are treated advantageously by employers, employees, and coworkers (C.L. Williams, 1992). The cultural reproduction of men's advantages in the workforce is "not a function of simply one process but rather a complex interplay between many factors such as gender differences in workplace performance evaluation, gendered beliefs about men's and women's skills and abilities, and differences between family and child care obligations of women and men workers" (Schilt, 2006, p. 468).

While women are disadvantaged in male-dominated workplaces, men benefit from their status in female-dominated fields. In particular, the pay structure of men in female-dominated professions favors men (Budig, 2002). Cognard-Black (2004) asserts that "gender as a major structural stratification mechanism privileges men in various setting compositions" (p.134). Such is the case in female-dominated lines of work in which the glass-escalator hypothesis rests on notions of discriminatory processes in the workplace (Hultin, 2003). The glass escalator provides a dual benefit for men, a patriarchal dividend or the advantages men in general gain from the subordination of women in the workforce (Connell, 1995, p. 79). Whether in male-dominated or female-dominated fields, men are accorded prestige and outpace women in advancement to positions of authority and pay (Schilt, 2006).

A recent trend garnering scholarly interest is the large number of men entering female-dominated fields. Sally Lindsay (2007) has coined this as the **masculinization of women's work**, meaning the movement of men into women's occupations. An example of this is in the field of nurse anesthesia. According to Lindsay (2007), the nurse anesthesia field has "evolved from a low-status, women's specialty to a high-status profession where males comprise nearly half of all the employees" (p. 429). The masculinization of women's work is a process of gender transformation in which more men are present in such fields as nurse anesthesia, and the occupation comes to be viewed as men's work (Lindsay, 2007; Lupton, 2006). Through the transformation process, the female-dominated field goes through three stages: infiltration, invasion, and takeover (Bradley, 1993). While Bradley's typologies provide a descriptive process, Lindsay (2007) argues that they do not fully capture why the process evolves. Lindsay (2007) offers four key themes that explain what draws men into these professions:

1. First, during times of social and political change, men are inclined to enter women's work for security or because they have few other alternatives.
2. A second factor identified in the masculinization of work is pay and opportunity to move up the career ladder quickly.
3. Changes in work conditions are a third factor influencing the masculinization of an occupation.
4. A fourth and related factor in the movement of men into women's jobs is the technological change. . . . Once a job becomes more technically oriented, men tend to gain a foothold (pp. 431–432).

These four factors illuminate the gradual masculinization of women's work and have implications about the maintenance and reinforcement of the glass escalator. Furthermore, what is yet to be studied in this area of inquiry is the socializing influence female-dominated fields over time may have on men. The myth of equality (i.e., glass ceiling and glass escalator) suggests that discrimination does not exist; however, it coexists with sexual harassment in the workplace.

Contemporary Issues for Women and Men in the Workforce

Demographic shifts in the workforce have significantly changed how American women and men view their roles both inside and outside of the work environment. In recent years, women's employment has multiplied considerably, and sociologists attribute the increased proportion of women in the workforce to the need for two-paycheck households due to the decline in men's wages (England, 2005, p. 265). The exodus of women from the home and their entry into the workforce has caused a shift in the traditional role of women and men at work and home. These changes introduced different gender issues to the United States workforce, including an increase in dual-couple earners and female breadwinners. At the beginning of the 21st century, only a third of U.S. households were traditional in that the husband provided the primary income through paid work, and the wife managed the home and children (Chapman, 2004). While this percentage of U.S. households fit the sole-male-earner model, approximately a third more had a female as the primary or sole earner (U.S. Department of Labor Bureau of Labor Statistics, 2004, 2008). The presence of dual-couple earners, female breadwinners, and the younger generations X and Y in the workforce has fueled female and male workers' requests for more autonomy over their work responsibilities in order to better accommodate their personal lives (Powell & Greenhaus, 2010). The introduction of work–life balance initiatives was a response to employees' request.

Work–Life Balance

The term **work–life balance** refers to the equilibrium between the amount of time and effort individuals commit to work- and nonwork-related activities (Powell & Greenhaus, 2010). The way in which individuals balance their work and nonwork lives is a central issue in business practices and in academic inquiry, particularly in disciplines such as organizational studies, gender studies, and sociological perspectives (Mescher, Benschop, & Doorewaard, 2010; Powell & Greenhaus, 2010). In this country, the work–life field began in the late 1970s when Americans exhibited increased mental and physical stress based on limited job autonomy and lack of support for an overall quality of life (Kossek, Lewis, & Hammer, 2010). Such workplace findings signaled the need for the development of a mutually beneficial balance between organizations' expectations and employees' desires.

Although terms such as work–personal life integration, work–life articulation, and work–personal life harmonization (Crompton & Brockmann, 2007; Lewis & Cooper, 2005; Rapoport, Bailyn, Fletcher, & Pruitee, 2002) have emerged in recent research and take into account a broader range of nonwork activities, the term *work–family balance* is most commonly used in the literature. However, by concentrating on employees with family responsibilities, work–family balance programs in organizations have encountered criticism from some employees who do not have children and, thus, do not have parental commitments (Haar & Spell, 2003). Another criticism of the term work–life balance is the word "balance," which suggests the presence of a static equilibrium that is achievable between paid employment and a life outside the job.

Work–Life Balance Initiatives

One way in which organizations address contemporary issues is through work–life balance initiatives (see Figure 5.6). The fundamental aim of work–life balance practice and policies is to enable employees to manage work and caregiving (Kossek et al., 2010). Such initiatives consist primarily of flexible working practices and family-friendly policies, although good practice demonstrates flexibility as being considerate of all workers, including those without caregiver responsibilities.

   Caregiving Options: Finding adequate care for children while parents work is a problem faced by many employed women and men and is considered the primary reason employees need work–life balance

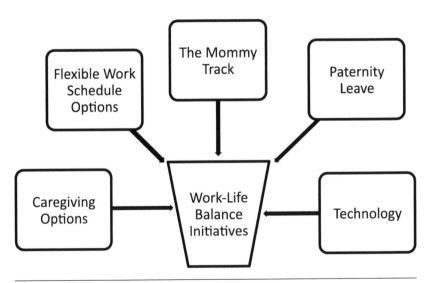

Figure 5.6   Work–Life Balance Initiatives

programs (Kossek et al., 2010; C. L. Williams, 2009). Employees who cannot balance the demands of work with available childcare are often disciplined or fired (Reese & Brandt, 2008). A salient role of work–life balance strategies is to focus on ways that working mothers and fathers can care for their children while maintaining employment. Some organizations provide subsidized on-site childcare centers for employees. Caring obligations extend beyond children and often include ageing parents and ailing family members. Employers increasingly recognize the difficulties of generational family problems.

A perspective considered less in the literature is that men are finding new opportunities to increase involvement with their families, thus shifting the narrow gender role of the male as primary wage earner (Perrone et al., 2009). Also changing is the increase in stay-at-home fathers. Responses of 70 interviewed fathers reveal that most of them worked part time, studied part time, or considered the time away from work as a way to create another form of work (Doucet, 2004). According to Perrone et al. (2009), as parents adapt to new careers and family roles, problems can occur. For instance, Brescoll and Uhlmann (2005) studied attitudes toward nontraditional parents and found that stay-at-home fathers and employed mothers were viewed more negatively than stay-at-home mothers and employed fathers. Additionally, for stay-at-home fathers, perceived social respect and regard was low. For employed mothers, however, perceived social respect and regard was just as high as for parents in traditional roles, which according to the researchers, may be attributed to women gaining social respect and regard by taking on the traditional male breadwinner role (Brescoll & Uhlmann, 2005).

Flexible Work Schedule Options: To assist employees with a balance between their personal and work lives, some companies make available flexiblework schedule arrangements, which include "flextime" options typically offering employees some choice on arrival and departure times (Reece & Brandt, 2008). The compressed work week is another flexible work choice and usually consists of four 10-hour days. Job-sharing arrangements involve two employees who share the responsibilities of one position. The benefit of this arrangement is that one employee might work during the mornings and the other during the afternoon.

Part-time jobs are another means of flexible scheduling. Many women with children secure part-time, rather than full-time, jobs (Cohen, 1999) because they often have the major responsibility for children and may not wish to or might be unable to work traditional, less flexible, and sometimes excessive work hours and schedules (Bailyn, 2006). Unfortunately, part-time jobs are customarily accompanied by "low pay, no benefits, no security, limited autonomy, and virtually no opportunities for advancement" (C. L. Williams, 2009, p. 290).

The Mommy Track: Some organizations have created the **mommy track** position with the idea of providing an opportunity for working mothers to devote time to both careers and families. However, critics of the initiative describe it as punitive because working mothers are forced to choose between developing a career or having a family and a career. If women select the latter choice, then they are relegated to a career path that is considered low status, excluding women from important projects. They also receive lower pay and generally feel ignored by their busier, career-oriented male or female counterparts. Further, studies reveal that mothers experience a per-child wage penalty of about 5% (England, 2005). Whereas the literature highlights work–life balance initiatives that address the needs of mothers in the workplace, better workplace accommodations are warranted.

Paternity Leave: **Paternity leave** is another work–life balance benefit and refers to a period of time that a father is legally allowed to be away from his job to spend time with his child. According to Halverson (2003), men use work–life balance initiatives much less than women do. He asserts that fathers who want to take paternity leave or time away from work to care for children often experience difficulty under the provisions of the Family and Medical Leave Act (FMLA). He argues that Congress had the best interests of women, rather than men, in mind when passing the Act. Such a claim reinforces "gender discrimination" in the workplace, which not only impacts women but men also. Additionally, some men fear workplace discrimination and work-related penalties should they rely on the FMLA for extended paternity leave. Like women who have battled maternity-related issues, men also must advocate for **family-friendly workplace** (FFW) policies, which

Hartin (1994) describes as procedures "designed to minimize the impact of work on family life" (p. 76). Important to the discourse on working men and women is the integration of work and family.

As the work–family literature suggests, a number of traditional gender role expectations persist despite the shift in who becomes the primary earner within the family. For example, research in the United States has found that when a husband is economically dependent on his wife, over time he actually does less housework than before (Brines, 1994). Similarly, Bittman, Thompson, and Hoffmann (2004) found that when wives in the United States earn 51% to 100% of household income, the couple tends to retain or return to the traditional gendered divisions of home labor. Managing the responsibilities associated with work and nonwork life continues to pose a challenge for many employed individuals.

Technology: The technology option is valuable to some women and men who want to strike a balance between family and work responsibilities. Telecommuting permits employees to work from home at a personal computer that is linked to their employer's computer system and includes other innovations to perform business away from the traditional office such as laptops, wireless phones, and Internet access to e-mail. Today's multigenerational workforce presents varied work styles and worker preferences. For instance, Generation X workers (born between 1960 and 1980) prefer to use technology when it offers them less stringent work hours to allow for greater work–life balance (Glass, 2007). In contrast, Generation Y workers (born between 1980 and 2000) are the first generation born into a technologically based world (Smola & Sutton, 2002) and generally favor instant messaging, text messaging, and e-mails rather than having a face-to-face conversation or using the telephone (Glass, 2007).

Limitations of Work–Life Balance Strategies

Although work–life balance strategies aim to improve the relationship between the work and personal lives of employees, they can make work intense and perpetuate stereotypes of ideal workers who are employees "unencumbered" by family or other nonworking responsibilities

(Kossek et al., 2010, p. 9). These researchers argue that organizations and scholars need to frame work–life balance initiatives as part of the "core employment systems to enhance organizational effectiveness," rather than strategies to support disadvantaged, nonideal workers such as those who use the system because they do not have an income to employ outside help. Additionally, women predominantly appear to use the option, which indicates that flexible working is implicitly seen as an issue of concern for mothers. In short, "[u]ntil work-life initiatives become more mainstream, a right and not a privilege limited to those individuals most in need of care giving assistance, they will continue to be marginalized" (Kossek et al., 2010). Stone (2007) concurs with Kossek's sociological argument and asserts:

> Until more men themselves take advantage of [workplace polices], or at least, as senior managers, permit and do not punish those who do, reduced-hour and flexible accommodations are likely to remain stigmatized and under-utilized, in a never-ending chase-the-tail scenario that rebounds to women's disadvantage. (p. 225)

Hewlett (2007) tempers both Kossek's and Stone's argument with an economic explanation, which asserts that corporations will implement flexible policies that accommodate working mothers only when they are convinced that such policies are in their economic interest to do so. Women and men continue to grapple with their work and personal demands. Although some progressive organizations are implementing work–life balance practices, additional accommodations are essential to better address the contemporary roles of women and men.

Chapter Summary

In the 21st century, women and men continue to experience inequality due to gender stereotypes and traditional gender roles in the workforce (Reece & Brandt, 2008). Specifically, these gender roles are in question because more women are educated and entering the workplace. Although women historically have struggled to ascend to senior-level positions, women are increasingly gaining access to professional and managerial positions in organizations. Accordingly, the gap between women and men in salary compensation appears to be narrowing; however, men still consistently out-earn women. Much of the literature identifies gender discrimination as the culprit for the persistent gender wage gap in addition to the masculinization of women's work.

Research studies indicate that women are disadvantaged in comparison with men on nearly every known economic indicator. Such instances of gender discrimination extend beyond wages and include underrepresentation of women in leadership positions and men performing traditional women's work, for example, nursing, elementary teaching, social work, and librarianship (Hultin, 2003). The disparity between women and men in management careers is often attributed to the glass ceiling, which blocks opportunities for women (Danziger & Eden, 2007). In contrast to women who push against the glass ceiling in the workforce, men cruise the glass escalator, which promotes them over women into management positions in female-dominated fields (Hultin, 2003; C. L. Williams, 1992, 1995).

Finally, research findings suggest that women and men in today's workforce seek successful careers in addition to a balanced personal life. Some employers have responded to employees' needs with initiatives featuring family-friendly policies that emphasize flexible work schedules, caregiving options, and technological arrangements. Some researchers (England, 2005; Kossek et al., 2010; Stone, 2007) contend that women and men who utilize work–life benefits are perceived to be less serious about their careers and therefore are often marginalized in the organization. In contrast, men and women who have a balanced professional and personal life are likely to be more productive in the workplace, which is a benefit for organizations.

The chapter calls attention to the importance of further examination of women's experience in the U.S. workforce given that they are disproportionately affected by gender inequality and discrimination in the workplace. Despite laws, such as the Civil Rights Act of 1964, as amended in 1991, and the Equal Pay Act of 1963 enacted to protect workers from overt discrimination, gender inequalities continue to exist in the workforce. Further, an understanding of the workplace culture as it affects the career development and retention of both women and men provides insight on the pervasive issues of gender discrimination. Minimizing the effect of gender discrimination may generate organizational benefits with regard to increased satisfaction, retention, and advancement of workers (Lloyd-Jones, 2009). Gender inequality and discrimination in the U.S. workforce will require unremitting attention at the individual, organizational, and federal levels.

Definition of Key Terms

Family-friendly workplace policies—Refers to procedures designed to minimize the impact of work on family life.

Flexible work schedule options—Includes flextime choices, typically offering employees some choice on arrival and departure times such as a *compressed work week* that usually consists of four 10-hour days and *job-sharing arrangements*, which involve two employees who share the responsibilities of one position.

Gender—The social construction of differences between women and men and the social attributes and opportunities associated with being female and male.

Gender discrimination—Connotes gender-based behaviors, policies, and actions that adversely affect a person's work by leading to unequal treatment or the creation of an intimidating environment because of one's gender.

Gender equality—Implies a social order in which women and men share the same opportunities and the same constraints concerning full participation in both the economic and the domestic realms.

Gender roles—Represent traditional beliefs about what functions are appropriate for women and men.

Gender stereotypes—Deeply embedded assumptions and beliefs about the gender attributes and differences of individuals and/or groups.

Gender wage gap—The difference in earnings received by women and men for performing similar duties or tasks.

Glass ceiling—Symbolizes barriers that are based on attitudinal or organizational biases preventing qualified women from advancing higher in their organizations.

Glass escalator—Symbolizes the promotion of men over women into management in female-dominated positions such as nursing, social work, elementary school teaching, and librarianship.

Good ol' boys network—An example of social closure, which can hinder women's access and entry to prominent positions occupied by men.

Masculinization of women's work—The movement of men into women's occupations.

Mommy track—Denotes a position that some organizations have created with the idea of providing an opportunity for working mothers to devote time to both careers and families.

Occupational sex segregation—The concentrating of women and men into particular occupations.

Paternity leave—A period of time that a father is legally allowed to be away from his job to spend time with his child.

Sex—The binary categories of female and male.

Title VII prohibits employment discrimination based on race, color, religion, sex, and national origins.

Work–life balance—The equilibrium between the amount of time and effort individuals commit to work- and nonwork-related activities.

Critical-Thinking Discussion Questions

1. In what ways do traditional gender roles perpetuate gender inequality and/or inhibit the quest toward equality in the workforce?

2. What kind of problems can occur as a result of the changing role of women and men in careers and family life?

3. What was the principal intent of the enactment of Title VII of Civil Rights Act of 1964 and Equal Pay Act of 1963?

4. What is your perspective on Sally Lindsay's concept of the masculinization of women's work? Does this concept represent progress toward equality in the workforce? What factors influence men's entry in female-dominated fields?

5. Compare and contrast glass escalator and glass ceiling.

6. In what ways do organizations develop and sustain norms and beliefs that are more accommodating to men than women?

7. How can employees sustain a healthy balance between their professional and personal lives?

Additional Assignments

1. As women and men grapple with deciphering their changing roles at work and at home, online resources may prove useful to them. Websites developed by professional organizations like the National Association of Female Executives (www.nafe.com), the Families and Work Institute (www.familiesandwork.org), and At-Home Dad (www.athomedad.com) offer sound support. Visit the site of your choice and write an analysis of how it might help individuals make an

educated decision about their personal and professional life choices. Share your findings with class members. (Adapted from Reece and Brandt, 2008.)

2. Identify an organization in your area and schedule an interview with someone in the Human Resources Department to learn about its family-friendly programs. Inquire about the benefits working mothers *and* fathers receive as a result of such initiatives. Write a 1- to 2-page paper describing your interview findings. Present your report to class members. (Adapted from Reese and Brandt, 2008.)

Case Study: Work–Life Balance

Marsha is a 34-year-old, highly competitive, technology-savvy single parent who works around the clock, taking work home from the office, reviewing global markets while preparing dinner, and reading to her six-year-old son before she finally goes to sleep. Further, when Marsha awakens each weekday morning, she commutes one hour each way from her home in a Chicago suburb to her downtown office in Chicago. Currently, Marsha is considering a position at a Fortune 500 health care company. Having experienced the fast pace, long hours, and frequent travel associated with a senior-level position, Marsha has reservations about accepting the recently offered executive-level position. Additionally, Marsha has recently established a serious goal of better balancing her personal and professional responsibilities. In anticipation of upcoming negotiations with the prospective employer, Marsha's executive coach has advised her to develop a list of questions that will assist Marsha in making a decision about the position.

Discussion Questions

1. What work–life balance initiatives might Marsha ask about during negotiations with her prospective employer?
2. What is the basic aim of work–life balance policies and practice?
3. Although Marsha is a parent and wants to divide her attention between work and nonwork commitments, why might she want to avoid the "mommy track?"

References

Alkadry, M., & Tower, L. (2006). Unequal pay: The role of gender. *Public Administration Review, 66*(6), 888–898.

Amott, T., & Matthaei, J. (2007). The structure of social institutions. In M. L. Andersen & P. H. Collins (Eds.), *Race, class and gender: An anthology* (pp. 283–291). Belmont, CA: Thomson Wadsworth.

Bailyn, L. (2006). Issues of work and family in different national contexts: How the United States, Britain, and Sweden respond. *Human Resource Management, 31*(3), 201–208.

Bayard, K., Hellerstein, J., Neumark, D., & Troske, K. (2003). New evidence on sex segregation and sex differences in wages from matched employee-employer data. *Journal of Labor Economics, 21*(4), 887–922.

Bittman, M., Thompson, S., & Hoffmann, S. (2004). Men's take-up of family-friendly employment provision. Policy research paper. Canberra: Department of Family and Community Services.

Blau, F. D., & Kahn, L. M. (2007). The gender pay gap: Have women gone as far as they can? *Academy of Management Perspectives, 21*(1), 7–23.

Bradley, H. (1993). Across the great divide. In C. Williams (Ed.), *Doing women's work: Men in nontraditional occupations*. Newbury Park, CA: Sage.

Brescoll, V. L., & Uhlmann, E. L. (2005). Attitudes toward traditional and nontraditional parents. *Psychology of Women Quarterly, 29*, 436–445.

Brines, J. (1994). Economic dependency, gender, and the division of labor at home. *American Journal of Sociology, 100*, 652–688.

Budig, M. J. (2002). Male advantage and the gender composition of jobs: Who rides the glass escalator? *Social Problems, 49*(2), 258–277.

Catalyst, Inc. (1999). Women of color in corporate management: Opportunities and barriers. Retrieved March 11, 2010, from www.catalyst.org/publication/57/women-of-color-in-corporate-management-opportunities-and-barriers

Catalyst, Inc. (2010). Statistical overview of women in the workplace. Retrieved from www.catalyst.org/publication/219/statistical-overview-of-women-in-the-workplace

Chapman, T. (2004). *Gender and domestic life*. New York: Palgrave MacMillan.

Civil Rights Act of 1964, 42 U.S.C. § 2000, P.L. 88–352 (1964).

Civil Rights Act of 1991, P.L. 102–166 (1991).

Cognard-Black, A. J. (2004). Will they stay, or will they go? Sex-atypical work among token men who teach. *The Sociological Quarterly, 45*(1), 113–139.

Cohen, J. L. (1999). Personal autonomy and the law: Sexual harassment and the dilemma of regulating "intimacy." *Constellations, 6*(4), 443–472.

Connell, R. (1995). *Masculinities*. Berkley: University of California Press.

Cotter, D. A., Hermsen, J. M., Ovadia, S., & Vanneman, R. (2001). The glass ceiling effect. *Social Forces, 80*(2), 655–681.

Cox, T., Jr. (1993). *Cultural diversity in organizations: Theory, research, and practice*. San Francisco: Barrett Koehler.

Crompton, R., & Brockmann, M. (2007). Class, gender and work-life articulation. In D. Perrons, C. Fagan, L. McDowell, K. Ray, & K. Ward (Eds.), *Gender divisions and working time in the new economy: Changing patterns of work, care and public policy in Europe and North America* (pp. 103–122). Cheltenham, United Kingdom: Edward Elgar.

Danziger, N., & Eden, Y. (2007). Gender-related differences in the occupational aspirations and career-style preferences of accounting students: A cross-sectional comparison between academic school years. *Career Development International, 12*(2), 129–149.

Davies-Netzley, S. A. (1998). Women above the glass ceiling: perceptions on corporate mobility and strategies for success. *Gender and Society, 12*(3), 339–355.

DeLaat, J. (2007). *Gender in the workplace: A case study approach.* Thousand Oaks, CA: Sage.

DiTomaso, N., Post, C., & Parks-Yancy, R. (2007). Workforce diversity and inequality: Power, status, and numbers. *Annual Review of Sociology, 33,* 473–502.

Dolan, J. (2004). Gender equity: Illusion or reality for women in the federal executive service? *Public Administration Review, 64*(3), 299–308.

Doucet, A. (2004). It's almost like I have a job, but I don't get paid: Fathers at home reconfiguring work, care, and masculinity. *Fathering: A Journal of Theory, Research, & Practice About Men as Fathers, 2*(3), 277–303.

Dovidio, J. F., Kawakami, K., & Gaertner, S. L. (2002). Implicit and explicit prejudice and interracial interaction. *Journal of Personality Social Psychology, 82,* 62–68.

Eagly, A. H. (1987). *Sex differences in social behavior: A social-role interpretation.* Hillsdale, NJ: Erlbaum.

Eagly, A. H., Wood, W., & Diekman, A. B. (2000). Social role theory of sex differences and similarities: A current appraisal. In T. Eckes & H. M. Trautner (Eds.), *The developmental social psychology of gender* (pp. 123–174). Mahwah, NJ: Erlbaum.

E-Mine Electronic Mine Information Network (2009). Gender and mine action: Key terms and definitions NEW. *Mine Action.* Retrieved December 28, 2009, from www.mineaction.org/overview.asp?0=1545

England, P. (2005). Gender inequality in labor markets: The role of motherhood and segregation. *Social Politics: International Studies in Gender, State and Society Online, 12,* 264–288.

Equal Pay Act of 1963. P.L. 88–38, 77 Stat. 56, 59 (1963).

Fiske-Rusciano, R., & Cyrus, V. (2005). *Experiencing race, class and gender in the United States* (4th ed.). Boston: McGraw-Hill.

Ford, D. L., Jr. (1985). Job-related stress of minority professional. In T. A. Beehr & R. S. Bhagat (Eds.), *Human stress and cognition in organizations: An integrated perspective* (pp. 287–323). New York: John Wiley & Sons.

Friedman, J. J., & DiTomaso, N. (1996). Myths about diversity: What managers need to know about changes in the U.S. labor force. *California Management Review, 38,* 54–77.

Fry, R. (2009). College enrollment hits all-time high, fueled by community college surge. *Pew Research Report: Pew Social Trends,* 1–5.

Fullerton, H. N., Jr. (1993). Another look at the work force. *Monthly Labor Review, 116*(11), 31–40.

Gibelman, M. (2003). So how far have we come? Pestilent and persistent gender gap in pay. *Social Work, 48*(1), 22–32.

Glass, A. (2007). Understanding generational differences for competitive success. *Industrial and Commercial Training, 39*(2), 98–103.

Goodman, D. (1990). Rediscovering American women: A chronology highlighting women's history in the United States and update—the process continues. In S. Ruth (Ed.), *Issues in feminism: An introduction to women's studies.* Mountain View, CA: Mayfield Publishing.

Haar, J., & Spell, C. S. (2003). Where is the justice? Examining work-family backlash in New Zealand: The potential for employee resentment. *New Zealand Journal of Industrial Relations, 28*(1), 59–75.

Halverson, C. (2003). From here to paternity: Why men are not taking paternity leave under the Family and Medical Leave Act. *Wisconsin Women's Law Journal, 18,* 257.

Hartin, W. (1994) Employment law. *Corporate Management, 46*(2), 75–76.

Healthfield, S. M. (2010). Women and work: Then, now and predicting the future for women in the workplace. Retrieved from http://humanresources .about.com/od/worklifebalance/a/business_women.htm

Heckman, J. J. (1998). Detecting discrimination. *Journal of Economic Perspectives, 12*(2), 101–116.

Hewlett, S. (2007). *Off-ramps and on-ramps: Keeping talented women on the road to success.* Boston: Harvard Business School Press.

Hultin, M. (2003). Some take the glass escalator, some hit the glass ceiling?: Career consequences of occupational sex segregation. *Work and Occupation, 30*(1), 30–61.

Johnston, W. B., & Packer, A. H. (1987). *Workforce 2000.* Indianapolis, IN: Hudson Institute.

Kalev, A. (2009). Cracking the glass cages? Restructuring and ascriptive inequality at work. *American Journal of Sociology, 114*(6), 1591–1643.

Kossek, E., Lewis, S., & Hammer, L. (2010). Work-life initiatives and organizational change: Overcoming mixed messages to move from the margin to the mainstream. *Human Relations, 63*(1), 3–19.

Kurowski, L. L. (2002). Cloaked culture and veiled diversity: Why theorists ignored early US workforce diversity. *Journal of Management History, 40*(2), 183–191.

Levine, J. A. (2009). It's a man's job, or so they say: The maintenance of sex segregation in a manufacturing plant. *The Sociological Quarterly, 50,* 257–282.

Lewis, J. J. (1999). Women and work in early America. Retrieved from http://womenshistory.about.com/od/worklaborunions/a/early_america .htm?p=1

Lewis, S., & Cooper, C. (2005). *Work-life integration: Case studies of organisational change.* Chichester, United Kingdom: John Wiley & Sons.

Lindsay, S. (2007). Gendering work: The maintenance of nurse anesthesia. *The Canadian Journal of Sociology, 32*(4), 429–448.

Lloyd-Jones, B. (2009). Implications of race and gender in higher education administration: An African American woman's perspective. *Advances in Developing Human Resources, 11*(5), 606–618.

Loden, M., & Rosener, J. (1991). *Workforce America: Managing diversity as vital resource.* Homewood: IL: Business One Irwin.

Lupton, B. (2006). Explaining men's entry into female-concentrated occupations: Issues of masculinity and social class. *Gender, Work and Organization, 13*(2), 103–128.

Marini, M. M. (1990). Sex and gender: What do we know? *Sociological Forum, 5*(1), 95–120.

Mescher, S., Benschop, Y., & Doorewaard, H. (2010). Representations of work-life balance support. *Human Relations, 63*(1), 21–39.

Meyer, M. (1999, August). In a league of her own. *Newsweek, 2,* 56.

Meyerson, D. E., & Fletcher, J. K. (2000). A modest manifesto for shattering the glass ceiling. *Harvard Business Review,* 127–136. Retrieved March 11, 2010, from www2.massgeneral.org/facultydevelopment/owc/pdf/Modest%20 Manifesto%20for%20Shattering%20the%20Glass%20Ceiling.pdf

Mora, R., & Ruiz-Castillo, J. (2004). Gender segregation by occupations in the public and the private sector. The case of Spain. *Investigaciones Economicas,* Vol. XXVIII (3).

Ngo, H., Foley, S., Wong, A., & Loi, R. (2003). Who gets more of the pie? Predictors of perceived gender inequity at work. *Journal of Business Ethics, 45,* 227–241.

Perrone, K., Wright, S., & Jackson, Z. V. (2009). Traditional and nontraditional gender roles and work-family interface for men and women. *Journal of Career Development OnlineFirst.* doi:10.1177/0894845308327736

Peterson, T., & Morgan, L. A. (1995). Separate and unequal: Occupation-establishment sex segregation and the gender wage gap. *American Journal of Sociology, 101*(2), 329–365.

Portes, A., & Rumbaut, R. G. (1996). *Immigrant America: A portrait.* Berkeley: University of California Press.

Powell, G. N. (1999). Examining the intersection of gender and work. In *Handbook of gender & work* (pp. ix–xx). Thousand Oaks, CA: Sage.

Powell, G. N., & Greenhaus, J. H. (2010). Sex, gender, and decisions at the family → Work interface. *Journal of Management.* Retrieved from http://jom .sagepub.com.ezproxy.lib.ou.edu/cgi/rapidpdf/0149206309350774v2

Pregnancy Discrimination Act of 1978, Amendment to the Civil Rights Act of 1964, 42 U.S.C. § 2000 *et seq.,* P.L. 88–352.

Ragins, B. R. (1998). Gender gap in the executive suite: CEOs and female executives report on breaking the glass ceiling, *Academy of Management, 12*(1), 28–42.

Rapoport, R., Bailyn, L., Fletcher, J. K., & Pruitee, B. (2002). *Beyond work-family balance: Advancing gender equity and workplace performance.* San Francisco: Jossey-Bass.

Reece, B. L., & Brandt, R. (2008). *Effective human relations: Personal and organizational applications.* Boston: Houghton Mifflin.

Schilt, K. (2006). Just one of the guys? How transmen make gender visible at work. *Gender & Society, 20*(4), 465–490.

Sims, R. R., & Dennehy, R. F. (1993). *Diversity and differences in organizations: An agenda for answers and questions.* Westport, CT: Quorum Books.

Sipe, S., Johnson, C. D., & Fisher, D. K. (2009). University students' perceptions of gender discrimination in the workplace: Reality versus fiction. *Journal of Education for Business, 28*(4), 339–349.

Smola, K. W., & Sutton, C. (2002). Generational differences: Revisiting generational work values for the new millennium. *Journal of Organizational Behavior, 23*, 363–382.

Solis, H. L., & Galvin, J. M. (2012). Labor force characteristics by race and ethnicity. Report 1036. Retrieved from http://stats.bls.gov/cps/cpsrace2011.pdf

Soni, V. (2000). A twenty-first century reception for diversity in the public sector: A case study. *Public Administration Review, 60*(5), 395–408.

Stewart, S. M., Bing, M. N., Gruys, M. L., & Helford, M. C. (2007). Men, women, and perceptions of work environments, organizational commitment, and turnover intentions. *Journal of Business and Public Affairs, 1*(1), 1–12.

Stone, P. (2007). *Opting out? Why women really quit careers and head home.* Berkeley: University of California Press.

Tomaskovic-Devey, D., & Skaggs, S. (1999). An establishment-level test of the statistical discrimination hypothesis. *Work and Occupation, 26*, 422–445.

U.S. Census Report. (2003). Washington, D.C.: U.S. Department of Commerce. Retrieved from www.census.gov/press-release/www/releases/archives/income_wealth/002484.htm

U.S. Department of Labor. (1991). *A report on the glass ceiling initiative.* Washington, D.C.: Author.

U.S. Department of Labor Bureau of Labor Statistics. (2004). Women in the labor force: A databook (Report 973). Retrieved from www.bls.gov/cps/wlf-databook.pdf

U.S. Department of Labor Bureau of Labor Statistics. (2005). *Employment outlook: 2004–2014.* Washington, D.C.: Government Printing Office.

U.S. Department of Labor Bureau of Labor Statistics. (2008). Women in the labor force: A databook (Report 1011). Retrieved from www.bls.gov/cps/wlf-databoodk-2008.pdf

U.S. Department of Labor Bureau of Labor Statistics. (2010). Quick stats on women workers. Retrieved from www.dol.gov/wb/stats/main.htm

van Vianen, A. E. M., & Fischer, A. H. (2002). Illuminating the glass ceiling: The role of organizational culture preferences. *Journal of Occupational and Organizational Psychology, 75*, 315–337.

Vogel, D. L., Wester, S. R, Heesacker, M., & Madon, S. (2003). Confirming gender stereotypes: A social role perspective. *Sex Roles, 11/12*, 519–528.

Weichselbaumer, D., & Winter-Ebmer, R. (2005). A meta-analysis of the international gender wage gap. *Journal of Economic Surveys, 19*(3), 479–511.

Western, B., & Pettit, B. (2005). Black-white wage inequality, employment rules, and incarceration. *American Journal of Sociology, 111*(2), 553–578.

Williams, C. L. (1992). The glass escalator: Hidden advantages for men in non-traditional occupations. *Social Problems, 39*, 253–267.

Williams, C. L. (1995). *Still a man's world: Men who do women's work.* London: University of California Press.

Williams, C. L. (2009). Talking 'bout my revolution: Opting-out and the end of feminism. *Sex Roles, 6,* 287–290. doi:10.1007/s11199–008–9496–1

Williams, M. J., Paluck, E. L., & Spencer-Rodgers, J. (2010). The masculinity of money: Automatic stereotypes predict gender differences in estimated salaries. *Psychology of Women Quarterly, 34,* 7–20.

6

ETHNICITY AND DIVERSITY IN THE WORKFORCE

Chaunda L. Scott and Terrance R. McClain

Chapter Overview

The complexity of the concept of identity confounds the interactions that we as humans have with one another. In reality, we are not one-dimensional, but multidimensional beings. Individual characteristics, family dynamics, historical factors, and social and political contexts all influence who we believe ourselves to be. In this chapter, we examine ethnicity as a separate construct from race, although related, along with how it impacts the workforce. Although there are other dimensions of our being that also blend with our race and ethnicity, making up our total being—gender, age, socioeconomic status, sexual orientation, abilities versus disabilities, and religious or spiritual beliefs—ethnicity is generally understood as a "fact or state of belonging to a social group that has a common or national tradition" (Ethnicity, 2013).

Chapter 6 will begin with a discussion of how ethnicity differs from race, followed by a discussion on how ethnicity is determined in the United States and how it is used to categorize ethnic groups. Next, will be a discussion on how ethnicity is used to discriminate against ethnic individuals or groups. Then, perspectives on ethnicity in the workforce will be presented, followed by issues surrounding ethnic expression. Chapter 6 concludes with a chapter summary, chapter questions, two case studies, and definitions of key terms.

Learning Objectives

After reading this chapter, along with completing the chapter summary questions and the case discussion questions, you will be able to:

- Discuss the differences and similarities between ethnicity and race
- Explain the various perspectives of ethnicity in American society
- Describe how ethnic characteristics are applied in the United States
- Identify and discuss the six characteristics that are criteria for determining a minority or subordinate group in the United States
- Understand discrimination based on ethnicity
- Discuss ethnicity as diversity in the workforce
- Understand the common issues related to workforce diversity

Ethnicity and Race

A discussion on ethnicity in the workforce cannot begin without a definition of ethnicity and how it differs from race. Kottak (2006) explains that **ethnicity** is "based on cultural similarities among members of the same ethnic group and the differences between that group and others" (p. 290).

Ethnic groups are identified in relation to the dominant culture. National origin and distinctive cultural patterns encompassing language, religious faith, shared traditions, values, symbols, and literature, music, and food habits are some of the distinctive characteristics that set groups apart. There are distinctions between ethnic groups expressed in language, religion, race, kinship, and geographical isolation. "Ethnicity is revealed when people claim a certain identity for themselves and are defined by others as having that identity" (Kottak, 2006, p. 290). Ethnicity is an expression of attachment to a group and its associated behaviors, which vary in intensity. Richard Jenkins (2007) points out that it is not only indicative of a collective identity, but that it matters greatly to the members of the ethnic group. Ethnicity is personal identity. And, although self-definition is important, it's not the only salient component of identity. It is argued that there is no such thing as "unilateral ethnicity," but a construct influenced by ethnic relations or the connections and contacts between those groups of people who appear to be the same with others who appear to be different. Therefore, it cannot be assumed that all people within any particular group are exactly the same as another. In other words, apparent cultural similarities do not influence ethnicity within group differentiation.

Jenkins further suggests that

> . . . ethnicity is not a matter of definable degrees or obvious kinds of cultural similarity or difference. There is no checklist with which to determine whether or not members of Group A are really ethnically different to members of Group B, or whether Group C is an ethnic group or some other kind of collectivity. Enumerating cultural traits or characteristics is not a useful way to understand or identify ethnic differences. Human beings are distinguished by their voices, and the baseline is always whether a group is seen by its members to be different. (p. 2)

Race, on the other hand, is a cultural category and not a biological category. Kottak (2006) suggests that "[o]nly cultural constructions of race are possible—even though the average person conceptualizes 'race' in biological terms" (p. 293). There is no scientific classification of race based on common genes (Kottak, 2006). In the United States, race is often confused with ethnicity because of a lack of a clear distinction between the two. Kottak gives the example of how in the United States, the term *Hispanic* "is an ethnic category that cross-cuts racial contrasts between black and white" (p. 293). In other words, a person who is Hispanic can be perceived as white or black depending on the hue of their skin tone. Race is also political. In the United States, **racial classification** "involves access to resources, including jobs, voting districts, and federal funding of programs aimed at minorities" (p. 296). This classification **ascribes status** onto people based on their perceived ethnic group affiliation. People of **mixed race** (e.g., Black and White) experience **hypodescent,** which automatically places them into the minority group regardless of physical appearance.

Ethnicity in the United States

Before discussing ethnicity in the United States, we must first understand American culture and how it affects ethnic identity. Kottak (2006) describes **culture** as a system of human behavior and thought that is not acquired by biological inheritance but by growing up in a particular society where exposure to specific cultural traditions (knowledge, beliefs, art, morals, laws, customs, habits, symbols) are learned and shared by individuals as members of a group. **Ethnic groups,** then, are "groups of people who share certain beliefs, values, habits, customs, and norms because of their common background" (p. 290). The common background in an ethnic group may include "a collective name, belief in common descent, a sense of solidarity, and an association with a specific territory, which the group may or may not hold" (as cited by Kottak, 2006, p. 290). In the United States, ethnicity can be treated as a subculture, minority group, or subordinate group based on different and shared learning experiences within the larger culture. For example, people may show loyalty to their neighborhood, school, and religion, and still participate in broader cultural activities such as voting in federal elections.

Before Christopher Columbus arrived, this country was already ethnically mixed. Native American tribes were societies of people with different languages, religions, and political systems. The arrival of Europeans, Africans, Chinese, and others only added to the ethnic variations already in existence. What sets ethnic groups apart is their national origin or distinctive cultural patterns. Over time, cultural patterns are introduced into other ethnic groups that cross perceived racial lines, making ethnic groups more difficult to classify. Schaefer (2004) gives the example of how Mexican, Puerto Rican, Cuban, and other Latin Americans are grouped together as Hispanic or Latino, although they cross perceived racial lines of Black or White. As an example, he illustrates the dilemma of a dark-skinned Puerto Rican who is perceived as Black in central Texas but viewed as Puerto Rican in New York City.

Other examples include:

- Irish, Polish, German, English, French, Scottish, Dutch, Swedish, Russian, Welsh, Portuguese, Armenian, and Norwegian are grouped together as White Americans.

- African (including its varieties of Black ancestry), Haitian, Jamaican, and depending on perceived racial features, those who are Hispanic or Latino are grouped together as Black Americans.
- Chinese, Filipino, Japanese, Indian, Korean, and Vietnamese are grouped together as Asian Americans.
- The 91 indigenous tribes which include the Cheyenne, Ojibway, Crow, and others are grouped together as Native or Indian Americans.

In American culture, White Americans are the dominant group sharing multiple ethnic identities.

Table 6.1 illustrates the diversity that exists in the United States according to the 2000 Census. Almost 18% of the population are members of racial minorities and 15.4% are Hispanic.

Table 6.1 Racial and Ethnic Groups in the United States, 2008*

CLASSIFICATION	NUMBER	PERCENTAGE OF TOTAL POPULATION
Racial groups		
Whites (includes 29.2 million White Hispanic)	228.2 million	75.0%
Blacks/African Americans	37.6 million	12.4%
Some other race alone	15.0 million	4.9%
Asian alone	13.4 million	4.4%
Two or more races	7.0 million	2.3%
Native Americans, Alaskan Native alone	2.4 million	0.8%
Native Hawaiian or other Pacific Islander alone	0.43 million	0.14%
Ethnic groups*		
White ancestry (single or mixed)	42.8 million	15.2%
Germans	30.5 million	10.8%
Irish	24.5 million	8.7%
English	15.6 million	5.6%
Italians	9.0 million	3.2%
Polish	8.3 million	3.0%
Hispanics (or Latinos)	47.0 million	

Note: Percentages do not total 100%, and subheads do not add up to figures in major heads because of overlap between groups (e.g., Polish American Jews or people of mixed ancestry, such as Irish and Italian). White ancestry data should be regarded as an approximation.
*From the 2000 Census
Source: U.S. Census Bureau, 2008

Table 6.2   Population Projections by a Census Bureau Report (2008)

	2008	2050
Non-Hispanic Whites	68%	46%
Hispanic (of any race)	15%	30%
Non-Hispanic Blacks	12%	15%
Asian American	5%	9%

The U.S. Census Bureau estimates population growth through 2050 to primarily include individuals of Hispanic or Latino decent. Table 6.2 suggests the non-Hispanic White population will decrease by 22% over the next 40 years while the Hispanic population will increase 15% to become 30% of the total population. Other ethnic minorities such as non-Hispanic Blacks (African Americans) will grow by only 3%, and the Asian population to increase by 5% in the same time frame.

Ethnic Classifications

America has often been referred to as a "melting pot," emphasizing the fact that we are a country that is made up of many races, ethnicities, and cultures. It is interesting to note that with migration, at various local levels, systems of racial and ethnic classification and consciousness are not congruent with general principles. The "melting pot" metaphor, ascribed to the United States as a refuge for all people who come to this country, is epitomized in the famous poem written by Emma Lazarus and engraved on a tablet within the pedestal on which the Statue of Liberty stands: "Give me your tired, your poor, Your huddled masses yearning to breathe free, The wretched refuse of your teeming shore. Send these, the homeless, tempest-tost to me, I lift my lamp beside the golden door!" This multicultural invitation and immigrant response to it has led to the melding of ethnic cultures. Kottak (2006) describes this melding as an **assimilationist model**, "the process of change a minority ethnic group may experience when moving to a country where another culture dominates" (p. 303). The assimilation model suggests that minority ethnic groups adopt the norms of the dominant culture as the dominant culture assimilates aspects of the minority cultures until certain aspects of both are no longer separate cultural units (Kottak, 2006).

One hypothesis is that ethnicity has aspects that are socially constructed, such as boundaries, identities, and cultures that are negotiated, redefined, and emerge as a result of social interaction within and without ethnic communities. The most salient issue of ethnic identity is the issue of boundaries, which are continuously negotiated by members of any ethnic group. Nagel (1994) suggests "ethnic identity is a composite of the view one has of oneself as well as the views held by others about one's ethnic identity" (p. 154). Ethnicity, therefore, is a socially constructed model that Nagel believes "stresses the fluid, situational, volitional, and dynamic character of ethnic identification, organization, and action" (p. 152). Therefore, ethnic identity is salient in various situations and with various audiences because every individual has a portfolio of ethnic identities to draw upon, which Nagel refers to as "layering" of ethnic identities. The U.S. Census not only demonstrates how people self-identify with a particular ethnic group, but it also demonstrates how self-identification changes through social interaction outside of the group. The following examples offered by Nagel (1994, p. 155–156) demonstrate different levels of ethnic identification in many ethnic communities in the United States.

- Of the various levels of ethnic identity available to Native Americans (*subtribal, tribal, regional, supra-tribal* or *pan-Indian*), the most salient identity is dependent on the nature of the interaction. For example, on the reservation, an American Indian might identify as "mixed-blood," or when speaking to someone from another reservation the person might identify as being from "Pine Ridge."
- Various levels of ethnic identity are available to Latino or Hispanic Americans. For example, an individual of Cuban ancestry may embrace varied identities based upon their interactions. The chosen ethnic identity is determined by the individual's perception of the audience, the social contexts, and the setting.
- For Asians, national origin (e.g., Japanese, Chinese, and Vietnamese) remains an important basis of identification rather than a pan ethnic identity.

- Among African Americans, the salience of a particular ethnic identification can be determined by context. At times it is advantageous for dark-skinned Caribbean immigrants to acknowledge and emphasize color and common ancestry with African Americans. There are other times, however, when people of the Caribbean highlight the distinctiveness between themselves and native-born Blacks.
- White Americans make ethnic distinctions as they negotiate their respective European ancestries, i.e., Italian, German, Polish, French, Irish, etc., or their Native American lineage may be more advantageous, based upon the audience and the perceived advantages of identifying as such.

Ethnic consciousness, like race consciousness, is informed by how aware members of the respective group and members of the larger society are of the ethnic differences that influence human interaction. Gold (2007) continues to acknowledge that there are both popular and social scientific understandings of classification and membership. In spite of the social basis for ethnicity, as it is with race, there are still powerful consequences with society at large, and within the workforce in particular. Race and ethnicity, as both group and individual identities, influence patterns of social conflict and the degree of opportunity available to various races and ethnicities.

Discrimination and Exclusion Based on Ethnicity

Kottak (2006) suggests that "ethnic differences can be the source of peaceful multiculturalism or in discrimination, or violent interethnic confrontation" (p. 306). The United States has experienced both peace and unrest because of ethnic differences. The Civil War and Civil Rights Movement are a few examples of conflict caused by ethnic difference. In particular, the Civil Rights Movement, a multiethnic effort, fought against **discrimination** in America's policies and practices against minority ethnic groups. In addition to discrimination, ethnic minority groups experience **prejudice** from the dominant culture, which devalues a group because of its assumed behavior, values, capabilities, or attributes (Kottak, 2006, p. 306). One of the results of discriminatory practices and prejudice against ethnic groups is **stereotyping** members of an ethnic group based on fixed ideas, often unfavorable, about what members of a group are like (p. 306). Another form of exclusion is **intrinsic racism,** "the belief that a (perceived) racial difference is sufficient reason to value one person less than another" (p. 297). Each of the examples causes individuals of minority ethnic groups to feel or become excluded for no other reason than their perceived differences from the dominant ethnic group.

The differentiation between ethnic groups in the United States, according to Schaefer (2004) is between racial groups, ethnic groups, and religious groups. Kottak (2006) suggests a broader list including politics, economy, religion, language, culture, and race as differences. These characteristics can be used to classify an individual into a minority ethnic status or subordinate group by the dominant group that results in discrimination, prejudice, and stereotyping. There are many negative effects on minority ethnic groups. For example, members of minority ethnic groups experience unequal treatment and have less power over their lives than members of a dominant group have over theirs. The physical or cultural characteristics of the minority ethnic group can distinguish them from the dominant group, such as skin color or language. Membership in a dominant or minority ethnic group is ascribed upon the bearer born involuntarily into the group. When a group is the object of long-term prejudice and discrimination, the feeling of "us versus them" often becomes intense, strengthening the solidarity of the members in the group. The solidarity encourages marriage within the group and discourages marriage to outsiders. Finally, new immigrants may be perceived as lacking knowledge about the ways of working, being, and knowing in American culture. This, therefore, hinders their ability to be more formally accepted in American culture. Prejudice, discrimination, segregation, and even extermination create social inequality experienced by minority ethnic groups around the world.

Ethnicity in the Workforce

How does ethnic diversity that encompasses visible and invisible differences between subordinate groups from the dominant culture complicate interactions in the workforce? One way is the assumption that members of a specific ethnic group will share common values, behaviors, and world views. While there are similarities within ethnic groups, there must also be an awareness of in-group differences that are not always apparent or acknowledged by those outside of the ethnic group. Additionally, while similarities are the fabric for weaving a sense of belonging within an ethnic group, they also nurture the perception of not belonging to the dominant group that causes exclusion. Studies on work groups have produced a myriad of theories with race and ethnicity as the central variable under investigation. There are a few assumptions that have evolved to explain behavior from an individual and/or within working group perspective (Shore et al., 2009).

- Humans judge each other on surface-level characteristics, such as race or gender, in the absence of additional information.
- Group membership based on these characteristics implies true similarities or differences between people, which then creates the formation of in-group and out-group distinctions.
- And, these judgments ultimately result in outcomes that may have negative effects for minority or out-group members (e.g., lack of mentors, stalled careers, and lower performance evaluations) or group productivity.

Another perspective is the "value in diversity" perspective, which focuses on positive predictions or positive outcomes of racial and ethnic diversity. The underlying assumptions of this perspective are:

- An increase in racial/ethnic diversity means that a work group will experience possible positive outcomes such as increased information, enhanced problem-solving ability, constructive conflict and debate, increased creativity, higher quality decisions, and increased understanding of different ethnicities/cultures.
- Surface-level diversity such as race is indicative of deeper-level differences, such as cognitive processes/schemas, differential knowledge base, different sets of experiences, and different views of the world (Shore et al., 2009, p. 118).

These are especially salient in reference to workforce diversity. Within the workforce, an understanding of the fluidity, variability, flexibility, and negotiability of the ethnicity and race as a construct must become a part of our collective consciousness. This means that, depending upon the cultural context and social situation, ethnicity may or may not be negotiable. When ethnicity does matter to people, it has the capacity to matter significantly, prompt them to action, and give birth to extremely powerful emotions. Successful workforce diversity encompassing multiple ethnic groups must work to avoid circumstances leading to discrimination, prejudice, and stereotyping through education focused on building a deeper level of knowledge of minority ethnic groups.

Common Issues Surrounding Ethnicity in the Workforce

Ethnic consciousness, like race consciousness, is informed by how aware members of the respective group and members of the larger society are of the ethnic differences that influence human interaction. Gold (2007) acknowledges that there are both popular and social scientific understandings of classification and membership. In spite of the social basis for ethnicity, as it is with race, there are still powerful consequences with society at large, and within the workforce in particular. Race and ethnicity, as both group and individual identities, influence patterns of social conflict and the degree of opportunity available to various races and ethnicities.

There are four common issues relevant to ethnic differences that have negative effects on ethnic minorities in the workforce. The first is language, which can hinder effective communication between management and employee group, management and consumer groups, employee groups in general, and employee and consumer groups. Perceived levels of social integration and communication skills can accelerate the frequency and intensity of conflict in the workplace. There is a growing insistence to require English as the official national language in the United States, which goes against the ideal that all races and ethnicities can come, and ideally be accepted on their own terms, and their cultures, traditions, and languages are accepted as part of their identity. For many of them, English is a second or third language, and for some in the workforce, this may lead to misunderstandings and mistakes. Additionally, these communication problems may create an atmosphere for stereotyping ethnic group members as lacking intelligence and being incompetent.

In the workplace, employees who speak a language other than English may be considered irritating to others outside of the ethnic group. The very same people who would adamantly refuse to use racial slurs are comfortable with expressing anger toward coworkers who don't speak English fluently. Supervisors and managers should take the initiative to provide support for minority members who struggle with the English language by making inquiries as to whether the employee is interested in improving their English speaking skills and providing information, services, and financial support if feasible to connect employees to available resources. If the employee expresses no desire to learn and speak the language more fluently, accept their decision and clearly explain any possible negative consequences that could affect potential advancement. Employers should be familiar with the EEOC guideline regarding the kind of nondiscriminatory working atmosphere that must be provided for all employees.

Another issue related to language is accents that effect communication in the workplace. Dictionary.com defines an **accent** as a mode of pronunciation, such as pitch or tone, emphasis pattern, or intonation and characteristic of speech by a particular person, group, or locality. Unfortunately, an accent has been used as a reason for lower scores on evaluations and performance reviews in the workplace (Esty, Griffin, & Hirsch, 1995). Accents have also been used as criteria for determining the intelligence of a speaker and have been the cause of hostility and ridicule directed toward those who speak with an accent. When an employee has an accent that inhibits his or her ability to effectively fulfill the requirements of the job description, then action must be taken. The first step is to communicate clearly to the employee how problems are arising as a result of his or her accent. At this juncture, several alternatives could be explored, such as changing the person's responsibilities and/or providing him or her with training to reduce the accent.

Ethnic jokes and ridicule are a common type of humor that can have negative effects on minority ethnic workforce groups. There are as many ethnic jokes as there are ethnic groups; many jokes are the same, substituting different ethnic groups around the punch line. It is also common for employees to make fun of mannerisms and accents, clothing, and hair styles of coworkers who are from different ethnic groups. Ethnic jokes may be considered harmless in some company cultures and be overlooked or excused. However, just as racial and sexual humor are considered offensive and should not be tolerated in the workplace, so too should ethnic jokes; ridicule of members of an ethnic group should not be tolerated. Often, the most effective method to combat offensive humor is to stand up and speak out against it.

Finally, stereotypes are the most pervasive problem ethnic minorities confront in the workplace. Stereotypes are usually distortions about various characteristics of a specific group. Of course, people often assume that every person within a particular ethnic group possesses these characteristics. For example, tall males from any ethnicity or race are often stereotyped by others as being proficient in basketball. African American men and women are often stereotyped as being good singers and dancers. Additionally, many African American men and women report firsthand experience of colleagues expressing genuine surprise at their ability to excel in the workplace, academia conflicting with the stereotypes. The most difficult aspect of stereotypes is they're deeply ingrained in American culture. Stereotypes are so pervasive that they are generally accepted without question. One strategy to deal with ethnic stereotypes is to point it out and initiate a strategy for inquiry to determine its validity in the current case. It is important to consider claims of discrimination, prejudice, and racism on a case-by-case basis by resisting the urge to consider the claims of one group over another.

Employee Efforts Supporting the Inclusion of Ethnicity in the Workforce

As stated previously, ethnic jokes and humor can have negative effects on ethnic groups. According to Esty et al. (1995), in order to prevent ethnic stereotyping from occurring in the workplace, employees must be made aware that stereotypes fade away over time with daily contact with ethnic groups (p. 100). Employees must also be willing to:

- Speak up and out against ethnic insults and typecasting in the workplace when they occur and
- Ask international employees questions about their culture rather than make incorrect statements about it. International employees welcome the opportunity to share information about their culture with colleagues (p. 100).

Chapter Summary

Although related to the construct of race, ethnicity is separate and has a profound impact on interactions in the workforce. Ethnic groups are identified in relation to the dominant culture of the society in which they live, and their ethnic identity requires shared perceptions that there are within-group similarities and across-group differences. However, all persons within any particular group are not necessarily carbon copies of one another. In addition, ethnicity can only emerge in the context of relationships and interaction with others. Ethnicity, according to Nagel (1994), is created and re-created based upon situations and the volition of the individuals engaged in interaction with one another. In reference to workforce diversity, the characteristics of minority or subordinate groups in the United States are unequal treatment, distinguishing physical or cultural traits, involuntary membership, awareness of subordination, in-group marriage, and minority members' lacking the knowledge about ways of working, being, and knowing in American culture.

Definition of Key Terms

Accent—A mode of pronunciation, such as pitch or tone, emphasis pattern, or intonation and characteristic (Dictionary.com/accent).

Ascribed status—Social status (e.g., race or gender) that people have little or no choice about occupying (Kottak, 2006, p. 310).

Assimilationist model—The process of change a minority ethnic group may experience when moving to a country where another culture dominates (p. 303).

Culture—A distinctive human activity which refers to customary behavior and beliefs that are learned through interaction with society and include knowledge, beliefs, arts, morals, laws, customs, and any other capabilities and habits acquired by man as a member of society (p. 271).

Discrimination—"Refers to policies and practices that harm a group and its members" (p. 307).

Ethnic group—A group of people who share certain beliefs, values, habits, customs, and norms because of their common background (p. 290).

Ethnicity—Ethnicity "is revealed when people claim a certain identity for themselves and are defined by others as having that identity" (p. 290).

Hypodescent—A rule of descent that assigns social identity on the basis of ancestry, applied mainly in the United States, and used to divide American society into groups that have been unequal in their access to wealth, power, and prestige (p. 290).

Intrinsic racism—"The belief that a (perceived) racial difference is sufficient reason to value one person less than another" (p. 297).

Mixed race—A person who has parents of two different ethnic classifications.

Multiculturalism model—Opposite of the assimilationist model, it encourages the practice of cultural-ethnic traditions (p. 303).

Prejudice—"Devaluing a group because of its assumed behavior, values, capabilities, or attributes" (p. 306).

Race—A "socially constructed term derived from contrasts perceived and perpetuated in societies, rather than from scientific classifications based on common genes" (as cited by Kottak, 2006, p. 293).

Racial classification—A political issue involved in access to resources, including jobs, voting districts, and federal funding of programs aimed at minorities (p. 296).

Stereotypes—"Fixed ideas, often unfavorable, about what the members of a group are like" (p. 306).

Critical-Thinking Discussion Questions

1. How significant is your ethnicity to your individual identity?

2. In what ways do you believe that your ethnic identity has caused you to be the victim of prejudice or discrimination in the workforce?

3. What are some common issues and concerns surrounding ethnicity in the workforce, for example, language, accent, jokes/ridicule, and stereotypes, have you experienced? How were these situations resolved?

4. Has there ever been a time when you were mislabeled ethnically because of racial characteristics?

5. Have there been times when your individual ethnic identity has been in conflict with your collective ethnic identity? If so, how? How did you resolve the conflict?

6. Name two ways that race and ethnicity differ.

CaseStudy: Muslim Religious Attire in the Workplace

Ajanta Bashar is a South Asian woman from Bangladesh who has been living in the United States for 12 years. Ajanta speaks English very well and is familiar with American culture and customs. After seeing a position advertised at a dry cleaner, Ajanta called the dry cleaner and spoke to the manager, who interviewed her over the phone. The manager liked her so much, she offered her the job over the phone. When Ajanta arrived for her first day of work, the manager seemed startled by her appearance. Ajanta has dark skin and wears a hijab (Muslim religious and cultural head cover), but her clothing was consistent with American culture. The manager brusquely stated that she had found someone "better suited for the job" and sent her home with no other explanation.

Unwilling to give up, Ajanta called the next day to speak with the manager about why she was rejected for the position when she arrived at the dry cleaner after she had been hired over the phone. The manager responded that she felt the dry cleaner's customers may not be comfortable if serviced by someone who was a Muslim after 9/11. The manager told Ajanta that if she were willing to not wear her hijab on the job, she would reconsider hiring her. Ajanta told the manager that her head covering is a part of her ethnic identity and she would not remove the hijab. The manager told her there was nothing she could do. Ajanta hung up the phone feeling rejected. "What can I do now?" she thought to herself. Will other companies reject me for the same reason?

Discussion Questions

1. What should Ajanta do?
2. What would you do if you were the manager of the dry cleaner?
3. Do you think employees and customers should be more supportive of Ajanta's hijab? Explain you answer.
4. Do you think the employees of the dry cleaner need ethnicity training regarding how to work with people of different ethnicities?
5. What strategies in the chapter support the inclusion of ethnicity in the workplace as it applies to Ajanta's situation?

References

Ethnicity (2013). Oxford dictionaries. Retrieved from http://oxforddictionaries .com/us/definition/american_english/ethnicity

Esty, K., Griffin, R., & Hirsch, M. S. (1995). *Workplace diversity: A manager's guide to solving problems and turning diversity into a competitive advantage.* Holbrook, MA: Adams Media Corporation.

Gold, S. J. (2007). Race and ethnic consciousness. In G. Ritzer (Ed.), *Blackwell Encyclopedia of Sociology.* Blackwell Publishing. Blackwell Reference Online. Retrieved from www.sociologyencyclopedia.com

Jenkins, R. (2007). Ethnicity. In G. Ritzer (Ed.), *Blackwell Encyclopedia of Sociology.* Blackwell Publishing. Blackwell Reference Online. Retrieved March 9, 2010, from www.sociologyencyclopedia.com

Kottak, C. P. (2006). *Anthropology: The exploration of human diversity.* New York: McGraw-Hill.

Nagel, J. (1994). Constructing ethnicity: Creating and recreating ethnic identity and culture. *Social Problems, 41*(1), 152–176.

Schaefer, R. T. (2004). *Racial and ethnic groups.* (9th ed.). Upper Saddle River, NJ: Pearson Education.

Shore, L. M., Chung-Herrera, B. G., Dean, M. A., Ehrhart, K. H., Jung, D. I., Randel, A. E., et al. (2009). Diversity in organizations: Where are we now and where are we going? *Human Resource Management Review, 19,* 117–133.

U.S. Census Bureau. (2008). Retrieved from www.census.gov/2008

7

DEVELOPING HUMAN RESOURCE DEVELOPMENT COMPETENCIES TO MANAGE SEXUAL ORIENTATION AND TRANSGENDER DIVERSITY ISSUES IN THE WORKFORCE

Michael P. Chaney and Lisa Hawley

Chapter Overview

Increasingly, human resource development (HRD) is integrating issues of diversity into theory, research, and training. However, the inclusion of diversity typically centers on race and ethnicity. Often excluded from workplace diversity discussions are issues involving lesbian, gay, bisexual, and transgender (LGBT) individuals. Culturally competent HRD practitioners must understand the inherent complexities associated with the multiple identities of LGBT individuals. Therefore, this chapter begins by defining important terms and constructs related to sexual orientation, and gender identity and expression. To further enhance HRD workers' understanding and awareness of LGBT individuals, this chapter will explore models of sexual identity development. The chapter goes deeper to examine specific demographic trends associated with LGBT people, such as estimated population sizes and relationship, educational, and employment statuses. We go on to discuss how these demographic characteristics influence LGBT individuals especially in the workplace. We also present societal attitudes toward LGBT communities and how these attitudes often carry over into the workplace. Moreover, we examine manifestations of anti-LGBT attitudes in the workplace in the forms of discrimination, harassment, and heterosexist workplace policies. This chapter navigates some of the complex and often difficult challenges that many LGBT individuals experience in the workplace, such as disclosing sexual orientation to colleagues. The chapter proceeds to focus specifically on the unique needs of transgender individuals. Historically, transgender individuals have been grouped together with the LGB community, which has often resulted in invisibility and within-group oppression. In this chapter, specific workplace policies such as the Employment Non-Discrimination Act (ENDA) are discussed, as well as issues affecting some transgender workers such as transitioning in the workplace. To help HRD professionals effectively work with transgender employees, Competencies for Counseling Transgender Clients in the areas of career and lifestyle development are presented. The chapter concludes with strategies for HRD workers to create nonheterosexist and transpositive work environments.

Learning Objectives

After reading this chapter, along with completing the chapter summary questions and the case discussion questions, you will be able to:

- Know appropriate terms and definitions used to describe individuals who comprise the LGBT communities
- Be familiar with different models of sexual identity development
- Have an understanding of the relationships between heterosexual privilege, heterosexist and transphobic policies, and oppression, especially as they relate to LGBT employees in the workplace
- Be aware of workplace issues that are specific to LGBT employees
- Recognize transgender issues in the workplace and be familiar with transpositive strategies for working with transgender employees
- Identify strategies for creating nonheterosexist and transaffirming work environments
- Describe ethical practices when working with LGBT employees

Conceptualizing Identity

Defining identity requires integrating a complex set of variables layered in experience. Arredondo and Glauner (1992) developed a model that describes identity as a set of characteristics or dimensions where some are fluid and others remain static. The model focuses on factors of personal identity and consists of three dimensions. **Dimension A** consists of characteristics that one is born with such as ethnicity, nationality, disability, age, genetics, gender, and sexual orientation. **Dimension B** consists of characteristics that are changeable and often influenced by the individual, such as religious and spiritual identity, educational background, career choice, and relationship and marital status. Lastly, **Dimension C** consists of historical events such as the Great Depression, Stonewall Uprising, September 11th, natural disasters, and economic downturns. Each of these dimensions influences how one views oneself as well as others' perceptions of an individual. For example, a 24-year-old recent college graduate, working in retail and planning to disclose her sexual orientation to her family in the fall, is experiencing financial difficulty due to underemployment. In the context of Arredondo's model, there are characteristics such as age and the economic downturn, which are unchangeable. Yet, an individual also has choice about career and partnership decisions that influences one's identity. One of the roles of the HRD practitioner is to understand the complexity of identity within the dynamics of a workplace. Sexual orientation and gender, as identity characteristics, necessitates knowledge and awareness within the HRD community. Sexual minorities for the purpose of this chapter include members of the LGBT communities.

Defining Lesbian, Gay, and Bisexual Identities

Terms used to describe nonheterosexual orientations have changed through the centuries and have received a great deal of attention in the early 1900s when sexual behavior was increasingly being studied. One of the most influential of these researchers was Alfred Kinsey, who examined the sexual behavior of men and women. In his research, he attempted to operationalize sexual practices. Kinsey, Pomeroy, and Martin (1948b) developed the Kinsey Scale, a continuum of sexual behavior. On one end of the continuum is same-sex sexual behavior (homosexuality) and at the other end of the continuum is opposite-sex sexual behavior (heterosexuality). All humans fall somewhere along the continuum as it relates to their sexual and affectional behaviors, feelings, and thoughts. It is important to note that an individual may experience homosexual or heterosexual feelings and thoughts and not act on them. Nonetheless, one's identity incorporates a sexual orientation that fits their construction of self. In general, a **homosexual** is an individual who is innately inclined to have romantic and/or sexual relationships with a person of the same gender. **Heterosexual** individuals are innately inclined to have romantic and/or sexual relationships with people of the opposite gender. **Bisexuality** refers to individuals who experience affectual feelings and/or physical attractions to both men and women. It should be noted that the term *homosexual* has a historically negative connotation. Homosexuality was listed as a mental illness in the Diagnostic and Statistical Manual of Mental Disorders up until 1973. As a result, LGB individuals do not typically use the term "homosexual" to describe themselves. The terms *lesbian, gay men,* and *bisexual* are generally used. Competent HRD practitioners will always ask their clients how they wish to be referred to. Table 7.1 includes important terms with their definitions related to sexual orientation and gender identity and expression. Please note that *transgender* is defined later in the chapter. Transgender is related to gender identity and expression and is distinct from sexual orientation. Yarber, Sayad,

Table 7.1

Bisexual: Emotional and sexual attraction to both sexes.

Gender identity: A person's internal sense of being male or female.

Heterosexual: Emotional and sexual attraction between members of the other sex.

Gender role: The attitudes, behaviors, rights, and responsibilities that society associates with each sex.

Homosexuality: Emotional and sexual attraction between members of the same sex.

Sexual identity: One's self label or self-identification as a heterosexual, lesbian, gay, or bisexual.

Sexual orientation: The pattern of sexual and emotional attraction based on the gender of one's partner.

Transgender: Individuals whose appearance and behaviors do not conform to the gender roles ascribed to people of that sex.

and Strong (2010) suggested that gender, gender identity, and gender role are "conceptually independent" of sexual orientation.

Sexual Identity Development

Currently, there are several identity models that conceptualize marked stages that LGB individuals often go through (Cass, 1979; Troiden, 1989). The Cass Identity Development Model is a framework with six stages. The stages are fluid and not meant to be benchmarks an individual must complete. They are common indicators used to help HRD professionals lend voice to the experiences of one's lesbian or gay identity development. The first stage is **Identity Confusion**, which is when first awareness takes place that one might be lesbian or gay. Due to societal and social pressures, the individual may minimize her or his feelings or may view the same-sex experience as "experimenting" or "a one-time event." The overarching question of "who am I?" is often the focus of this stage. The second stage, **Identity Comparison,** is marked with a tension between one's past understanding of self to a current understanding of self as possibly lesbian or gay. One might self-isolate or deal with grief and loss issues associated with the cost of accepting the new identity. In the workplace, one might experience difficulties connecting with others or may limit one's participation, especially if the individual views the workplace as hostile toward lesbian and gays. In the third stage, **Identity Tolerance**, the individual is developing an appreciation of their new identity. They involve themselves more fully in lesbian or gay culture. An individual may develop a new set of friends that are supportive and/or knowledgeable about lesbian/gay culture. During this stage, one may begin disclosing ("come out") her or his sexual orientation identity to family, friends, and close coworkers identified as being safe and supportive. In the workplace, an individual will often observe both direct and indirect oppressive incidents and make decisions about disclosure. The fourth stage, **Identity Acceptance**, is characterized by the individual increasing contact with others in their sexual group community. The individual no longer simply tolerates their new identity, but begins to move toward acceptance. Being part of their new identity subculture becomes an important part of their life. However, there is still an element of tension experienced as the individual struggles to develop strategies for reducing incongruencies between public self and private self. The fifth stage is **Identity Pride**, which is associated with positive feelings and reactions to one's identity as a gay person, as well as a need to share their identity with others. The person also begins to engage and bring their "two worlds" together—the newly accepted gay identity and their previous sense of self. The **Identity Synthesis** stage is the final stage, in which the individual experiences a sense of wholeness. Their sexual identity is not their defining identity but an integral part of their identity (Cass, 1979).

Troiden's Homosexuality Identity Development Model (1989) focuses on the following stages: **Sensitization, Identity Confusion, Identity Assumption,** and **Commitment**. Similar to Cass (1979), this model begins with a sense of uncertainty and progresses to an increased sense of self-acceptance, motivation, and commitment to develop social connections.

To help understand the identity development process of bisexual individuals, recent models have been conceptualized. For example, Brown (2002) proposed a four stage model that resembles the afore-mentioned identity development models. In the first stage, **Confusion** about one's identity is experienced. **Finding and Applying the Label** of bisexuality is the second stage. In the third stage, a bisexual individual begins **Settling into the Identity**. During the fourth and final stage, **Identity Maintenance**, the bisexual person is integrated into the bisexual community and may serve as a source of support for individuals looking for others like themselves (Brown, 2002). It should be noted that the preceding stage models are not necessarily linear.

The identity development of sexual minorities is an important aspect for the HRD manager to consider. Employees may experience emotional and social turmoil and confusion depending on their own unique experiences. If working at an employee assistance program (EAP) or managing diversity education, using these stage theories as a framework will often normalize the individual's experience. Let us now examine the LGB communities a little more closely.

A Closer Look at Lesbian, Gay, and Bisexual Communities

Population Analysis

Although there is no way to know for sure how many LGB individuals reside in the United States because objective assessments of LGB population size at the national level do not exist, historical data and more recent research provide estimations. These estimations are disputatious because they likely do not include individuals who are not comfortable disclosing their sexual orientation, LGB children and adults who have not yet realized an LGB identity, and individuals who are heterosexually married who also identify as LGB. As mentioned earlier, one of the first studies to quantify the number of lesbian and gay people was conducted by Alfred Kinsey. Based on their research, Kinsey, Pomeroy, and Martin (1948a, 1948b) reported that approximately 10% of males and 2% to 6% of females were primarily gay and lesbian. Janus and Janus (1993) reported that 9% of men and 5% of women identified as gay and lesbian in their study. As stated above, it is extremely difficult determining the number of LGB individuals for two reasons. First, there is a lack of objective estimate protocol. For example, although the U.S. Census includes a category for same-sex "unmarried partners," that category does not take into consideration single lesbian and gay individuals, lesbian and gay couples who do not live together or do not label their relationship as "unmarried partners," or bisexual individuals. Second, bisexual individuals are often excluded from epidemiological studies. However, a 2011 study for the National Center for Health Statistics found that approximately 1% of men 18 to 44 years old identified as bisexual, 2% identified as gay, and 4% identified as something other than heterosexual or bisexual. In the same study among women 18 to 44 years old, 3.5% reported being bisexual and 1% lesbian Albeit the aforementioned statistics demonstrate discrepancies in the number of LGB individuals, the available data provides HRD practitioners with a general idea of how many Americans may identify as LGB. Overall, it is estimated that 9 million Americans (18 years or older) self-identify as LGB (Gates, 2011).

Relationships and Educational Status

Culturally competent HRD practitioners must have knowledge about LGB relationships and the educational trends of LGB workers because workplace and federal policies often affect these facets of LGB identity.

Contrary to popular belief, many LGB individuals are not single. In fact, Elizur and Mintzer (2003) reported that 40% to 60% of gay men and 45% to 80% of lesbians are partnered. More recent data reported similar results. Black, Sanders, and Taylor (2007) found that approximately 50% of gay men and 63% of lesbians are partnered. These results are important because they debunk a common stereotype that most lesbians and gay men are promiscuous. When same-sex relationships are examined more closely, it has been found that partnered lesbians and gay men tend to be older and are more likely to be White (Carpenter & Gates, 2008). The fact that partnered lesbians and gays tend to be older is likely a developmental issue. It is possible that with age comes comfort or acceptance with one's sexual identity, which allows an individual to be more open to the idea of a relationship. It is also possible that partnered lesbians and gay men are more likely to be White because as research has shown, other cultures (e.g., African Americans) tend to be more disapproving of LGB individuals than Whites (Lewis, 2003). This disapproval would make it less likely for individuals to openly express their sexual orientation, which likely would prevent these individuals from getting into same-sex relationships.

In regard to educational status, lesbians and gay men are generally highly educated. It has been reported that lesbians and gay men are more educated than their heterosexual counterparts (Black et al., 2007). This is consistent with past research that has estimated 45% of gay male couples have college degrees compared to 20% of the general heterosexual population (Black, Gates, Sanders, & Taylor, 2002). Interestingly, although many gay men have college degrees, gay men who attend college are less likely to pursue graduate education. Among lesbians, it is estimated that 25% have earned college degrees compared to 16% of heterosexual married women (Black et al., 2002). Knowing the percentage of lesbian and gay individuals with college degrees is extremely relevant because higher education has been found to be related to individuals being more likely to identify as LGB and/or more likely to live in a predominantly LGB neighborhood (Barrett & Pollack, 2005). In their pivotal study exploring the economic trends of lesbians and gay men, Black and colleagues (2007) reported that, in regard to academic studies, lesbians were more likely to major in areas that are not "stereotypical female." On the other hand, gay men were more likely to focus their studies in areas that were historically associated with females. These results illustrate the complexity of the intersection of gender roles and sexual orientation. Moreover, these results have implications for the employment and social economic status of LGB workers.

Employment and Social Economic Status

There is a general myth that LGB individuals are wealthy. As a result of this stereotype, LGB individuals are often provided the label **HINK** (high income, no kids) or **DINK** (dual income, no kids). This myth is often perpetuated by individuals who oppose civil rights initiatives for the LGB community because it is assumed that if LGB people are affluent and have expendable incomes, then they do not need civil protections. Not only does this generalization make it seem that LGB individuals do not need civil rights, but it also creates a myth that LGB people might not need other services such as social, economic, and health-related services (Lind, 2004).

The truth is that most LGB individuals do not have expendable incomes. When earnings are examined and compared to their heterosexual counterparts, a salient discrepancy is revealed. In one of the first studies to explore LGB earnings in comparison to heterosexual workers, Badgett (1995) found that gay and bisexual men earned on average 11% to 27% less than their heterosexual peers. The same study also revealed that lesbians and bisexual women earned approximately 12% to 30% less than their heterosexual counterparts. The latter results further demonstrate sexism in relation to salary discrepancies. More recent research has shown that openly gay and bisexual men earn approximately 30% to 32% less than heterosexually married men, and openly lesbian and bisexual women earn approximately 17% to 38% more than heterosexually married women (Blandford, 2003). Black et al. (2007) reported similar trends that partnered gay men generally have lower wages and income than men in heterosexual relationships, and lesbians generally have significantly higher wages and income than their heterosexual counterparts. Black and colleagues (2007) used the term **lesbian premium** to explain the reasoning behind their higher market earnings. According to this theory, upon realization of a lesbian identity and the possibility of a future that does not resemble a "traditional" household, some lesbians and bisexual women may invest more heavily in education and career-oriented activities. This in turn would likely lead to higher-paying jobs. Another explanation as to why lesbians and bisexual women on average earn more than corresponding heterosexuals could be due to lesbian and bisexual women being unusually successful at finding employment in male-dominated fields, whereas gay and bisexual men are overrepresented in jobs traditionally held by women relative to other male workers (Blandford, 2003). Men working in traditionally "female" occupations often earn lower pay. This phenomenon has been termed the **gay male penalty**. Employers tend to award compliance to masculinity and stereotypical male traits (assertiveness, power, strength, etc.) and chasten values of femininity. This illustrates the intersection of heterosexism and sexism.

Attitudes Toward LGB Individuals

Societal Attitudes

Although societal attitudes toward LGB individuals appear to be improving overall, many Americans continue to have negative attitudes toward and beliefs about the LGB communities. For example, in one study, although 76% of Americans reported being comfortable interacting with lesbians and gay men in social settings, 50% of Americans had negative views of gay men and 48% had negative attitudes toward lesbians (Pew Research Center for the People and the Press, 2003). In a recent Gallup Poll (2008), 48% of Americans responded that living a life as a lesbian or gay man was morally wrong. Sometimes, negative attitudes directed toward LGB people can lead to violence. According to the U.S. Department of Justice, Federal Bureau of Investigation 2008 Hate Crime Statistics, there were 1,297 hate crimes related to sexual orientation, the third highest category of all hate crimes. There were 921 antimale hate crimes and 156 antifemale hate crimes reported. These numbers are likely underrepresented because most anti-LGBT violations go unreported due to shame or fear of further repercussions.

As a result of the divided attitudes and beliefs among Americans, it makes it difficult for LGB individuals to know to whom it is safe to disclose sexual orientation and/or gender identity. Research has shown that there are certain factors that predict individuals' positive and negative attitudes toward LGB individuals. A strong predictor of positive attitudes toward LGB individuals is prior experience with these communities. That is, the more interaction we have with people who identify as LGB, anti-LGB attitudes are decreased (Brown & Henriquez, 2008; Herek & Glunt, 1993). Education has also been shown to affect positive attitudes toward LGB individuals. Specifically, Lambert, Ventura, Hall, and Cluse-Tolar (2006) found that high education had a positive effect on anti-LGB attitudes. Moreover, individuals with advanced education are more likely to be willing to extend rights to and interact with LGB individuals.

We briefly mentioned factors that influence an individual's positive attitudes toward the LGB communities. There are also elements that predict negative attitudes toward the LGB communities. For example, race, religiosity, and political conservatism have been found to contribute to anti-LGB attitudes (Brown & Henriquez, 2008). African Americans were more likely than European Americans to have negative attitudes about LGB people. Additionally, individuals who regularly attended religious services were more likely to have anti-LGB feelings. These results are not surprising given that many churches relay messages that LGB people are sinful and immoral. Interestingly, when race is controlled for, religiosity emerges as the primary predictor of anti-LGB attitudes (Schulte & Battle, 2004).

Attitudes in the Workplace

As described above, societal attitudes toward the LGB communities are divided. In some ways, Americans are becoming more tolerant and in other ways heterosexist beliefs are thriving. Within the workplace, the attitudes of coworkers of LGB employees tend to be more negative than that of the general population. This is exemplified by The Williams Institute on Sexual Orientation Law and Public Policy report that found up to 43% of LGB workers verbally or physically abused or had their workplace vandalized, and approximately 90% of transgender workers experience workplace harassment (as cited in Burns & Krehely, 2011). It seems that although heterosexual workers may view themselves as accepting and tolerant of LGB colleagues, the research shows that this is not in fact the case. Embrick, Walther, and Wickens (2007) found that among heterosexual workers who express liberal viewpoints, especially as they relate to LGB issues, these same individuals often demonstrate actions that are inconsistent with their words. For example, a heterosexual employee may express that she has "no problem working with gay men," but during her lunch hour with colleagues she tells anti-LGB jokes. One explanation given for this behavior is that it maintains **heterosexual privilege**.

There are three themes that have been identified related to the negative attitudes of heterosexuals toward their LGB coworkers (Embrick et al., 2007). The first theme is blatant detestation of LGB individuals. This could be due to a lack of exposure to LGB individuals, personal beliefs, negative past experiences with LGB individuals, or homophobia. The second theme is "don't ask; don't tell." This means that some heterosexual coworkers' negative attitudes are a result of LGB visibility in the workplace. These individuals would rather have their LGB coworkers not disclose their sexual orientation in the workplace. Disclosure in the workplace for LGB individuals is risky because being open about one's LGB identity has been linked to direct physical threats and sexual harassment (Williams, Giuffre, & Dellinger, 2009). The third theme associated with why some heterosexuals have negative attitudes toward their LGB coworkers is ostracism and fear. When a dominant cultural group experiences fear as a result of another cultural group, it is often because the dominant group feels its privileges are being threatened. Additionally, lack of awareness and knowledge of the nondominant group can lead to ostracism and fear. With all of this knowledge about what contributes to the negative attitudes toward LGB workers, HRD practitioners are in a good place to begin working with employers to create work environments that are safe, both psychologically and physically, for all employees.

Workplace Concerns

Discrimination

Common fears and issues experienced by LGBT employees include fear of dismissal, job discrimination, refused employment, harassment, unequal treatment in promotions, and other work-related insults.

Badgett, Lau, Sears, and Ho (2007) reported that the rate of discrimination complaints by sexual minorities was comparable to the rate of sex discrimination complaints by women. Reviews of studies between 1992 and 1999 found that 16% to 68% of LGB respondents experienced discrimination in the workplace. More recent studies report similar findings. Studies suggest discrimination is occurring in the workplace for LGBT workers. In a sampling of the New Jersey Supreme Courts, discrimination was experienced as denied employment (17%), denied promotion (28%), negative performance evaluation (21%), teased or harassed (29%), and received unequal pay (10%).

Chojnacki and Gelberg (1994) identified four levels of discrimination in work settings for lesbian and gay employees. Level 1, **Overt Discrimination**, and Level 2, **Covert Discrimination**, indicate discriminatory practices occurring. Level 3, **Tolerance**, and Level 4, **Affirmation**, indicate less discriminatory policies and practices. The degree of discrimination within each level influences different expectations of the leaders in HRD. Overt discrimination requires quick and transparent actions to eliminate the discrimination. Level 2 requires the HRD leaders to understand the subtle transgressions and address them. Level 3 requires both direct and indirect actions, as well as policies which are inclusive of sexual minorities. Level 4 requires continued maintenance of antidiscrimination practices and an inclusive positive work environment.

Institutional Discrimination

Institutional discrimination refers to any type unjust practice or discriminatory behavior toward a person or groups of people by the government, agencies, businesses, or public institutions. A salient example of institutional discrimination was the "Don't Ask, Don't Tell" (DADT) policy adopted by the U.S. Armed Services in 1994. The policy was based on the following premise: If the employer (armed services) does not ask about your sexual orientation and an individual chooses not to disclose an LGBT identity, then the individual was "safe" from dismissal unless a person was observed behaving in such acts. This policy was counter to what we know about sexual identity development, specifically, the more one becomes comfortable with her or his sexual identity there tends to be an increased need to come out to others. To date, approximately 13,500 service men and women have been dismissed since the implementation of DADT (Servicemembers Legal Defense Network, 2010). As of May 2010, the U.S. Legislature had developed a compromise bill that would repeal DADT (10 USC s. 654). In December 2010, the U.S. Senate voted 65–31 to end DADT, and President Barack Obama signed a landmark law repealing the ban on gay men and lesbians openly serving in the military. This action was due in part to LGBT groups advocating on their own behalf for the policy to be repealed.

Harassment

For many LGBT employees, the workplace is a setting in which many hours are spent and quality productivity is expected. For the manager, the goal is a safe work environment and a positive work culture. These are simple role expectations; yet, workplace culture is based on a complex set of human interactions, as well as planned work goals and company expectations. Avoiding discrimination, harassment, and violence in the work setting is an important priority for the HRD practitioner. One task for the HRD practitioner is to gauge the work environment for incidents of harassment and discrimination. **Harassment** in the workplace may include physical, emotional, and verbal activities to create a hostile environment for the LGBT worker. Volokh (1997) suggested any speech in the workplace that is severe or pervasive enough to create a hostile or abusive work environment based on race, religion, sex, national origin, or sexual orientation is considered harassment. Similarly, **sexual harassment** is offensive or unwelcomed sexual behavior in the workplace. Bullying and physical confrontation are other types of harassment influencing the work environment. Measuring harassment in the workplace is difficult due to fears of retribution and underreporting. HRD workers need to be at the forefront to respond to harassment and take measured steps to deal with reported incidents and the parties involved. Two legal cases dealing with workplace harassment are presented at the end of this chapter. To address harassment, the workplace institution must be committed to policies that identify and address workplace harassment as unacceptable and inclusive of multiple identities.

Family and Employee Benefits

Two of the most practical issues affecting some LGBT individuals are family issues and employment benefits. Approximately one-fifth of an employee's salary comes from benefit packages. Therefore, same-sex parents not eligible for benefits experience an economic loss compared to others. Recent legislative acts such as the Defense of Marriage Act (1996) have created confusion among states and companies whether interpretation includes benefits. For example, 22 states and the District of Columbia currently provide domestic partner benefits for their state workers, leaving 28 states lacking benefits for LGBT families (Human Rights Campaign Foundation, 2012). Fortune 500 companies outpace federal and state organizations for domestic partner policies. The higher a Fortune 500 company ranks, the more likely it is to include health benefits for LGBT employees and their partners. As recent as June 2010, the Obama Administration issued a memo extending domestic partner benefits to federal employees. This, along with the repeal of the DADT, suggests a government shift in more inclusive federal policies for LGBT workers.

The importance of these benefits to quality of work life has been well documented. HRD research has reported that employee benefits help families balance work and family, improves employee retention, and improves work performance (Hornsby & Munn, 2009). HRD professionals are also involved in policies to develop and activate benefits. Most commonly, organizations require documentation validating domestic partnerships. Policies differ from organization to organization, yet common documentation includes proof that one is over 18 years old, unmarried, unrelated, in an intimate caring and mutual relationship, and has no other legal marriage/partner relationship and documentation of legal and financial commitment including affidavits. Documentation may include shared bank accounts, health directives, and a shared mortgage. Second, the HRD representative often takes on the role of diversity advocate. If partner benefits increase the quality of work–life balance and provides a positive work environment, then advocating within the institution for fair and equitable benefits is another responsibility of the HRD professional. The fact that the most powerful and highly economically resourced companies provide family benefits demonstrates the value placed on such policies.

Career Development Issues

The career development of sexual minorities is an underdeveloped area of research. Gedro (2009) suggested the current dearth of career development research is indicative of the pervasive heterosexist-dominant perspective. Even less research has focused on career development among bisexuals and transgender individuals (Pope et al., 2004). In the following section, we briefly explore some of the developmental career concerns of LGB individuals because the culturally responsive HRD practitioner should advocate for and promote workplace policies that are inclusive of LGBT workers. Workplace environments that are not inclusive of LGBT workers influence the career development of these communities. Contrasting the career development of heterosexual workers, many LGBT individuals choose careers solely based on their sexual orientation. Sexual identity development and career development often occur during the same life-span stages of late adolescence to young adulthood (Gedro, 2009). The combination of the fear of disclosure and rejection likely limits time and effort spent on one's career achievement.

Inaccurate stereotypes often segment LGBT individuals into job classifications that are based on preconceived notions of what it means to be LGBT. Gedro (2009) suggested that many gay men experience stereotyped work roles (e.g., hairdresser, flight attendant) and traditional male gender role expectations that limit their employability. On the other hand, many lesbians tend to have more occupational choices and often do not fit into gender-oriented stereotypes. These occupational stereotypes contribute to some of the workplace limitations experienced by LGBT workers. The term **lavender ceiling** is often used to describe the limited advancement and inequitable wage earnings of many "out" LGBT workers.

Coming Out

Coming out is the process many LGBT individuals go through when they self-disclose their sexual orientation and/or gender identity to others. For some individuals, coming out in the workplace can be a positive experience. For other individuals, numerous repercussions might be experienced as a result of coming out at work.

In a national sample of LGB employees, Ragins, Singh, and Cornwell (2007) found individuals' fear of stigma was reduced when the work environment was perceived as supportive. The cost of disclosing is often based on fear of social isolation, job loss, and career development. The same study found employees fearful of disclosing their identity led to less positive career attitudes, fewer promotions, and more physical stress-related symptoms. Most important, coworker support was an influence in decreased fear associated with disclosure. Key to an individual's experience is the underlying need to experience a sense of belonging and social support. In a related study, Huffman, Watrousrodrigues, and King (2008) found supervisor support was significantly related to job satisfaction, and coworker support was related to outness at work. McDonald and Hite (2005) suggested that HRD needs to support supervisors to develop greater awareness of their role in affecting fairness and equality in the workplace, especially as it relates to LGBT employees.

Transgender Issues in the Workplace

Historically, when issues of sexual orientation are discussed, transgender individuals are grouped in with LGB individuals. We chose to explore workplace issues affecting the transgender community separately for a couple of reasons. First, transgender individuals are often underrepresented in the professional literature. Although they may be "grouped in" with other sexual minority communities, their unique issues are often neglected. Second, the workplace issues and needs of the transgender community are unique and specific and deserve attention. Davis (2009) referred to transgender issues as one of HRD's newest challenges and opportunities.

Transgender is an umbrella term used to describe individuals whose anatomy and/or appearance may not conform to traditional gender roles. Ellis and Eriksen (2002) conceptualized transgender as a category used to describe individuals who experience discrepancies between biological sex and gender identity. Transsexuals, cross-dressers, drag kings/queens, and intersex individuals all have different meanings and fit under the transgender umbrella. Defining each of these terms is beyond of the scope of this chapter, but to better understand the differences between each of these categories under the transgender spectrum, see Ellis and Eriksen's work. A current term, **gender queer**, is frequently being used among younger individuals because it is viewed as a more fluid construct than transgender. Someone who defies boundaries of gender identity and sexual orientation would be described as gender queer (e.g., may view self as both man and woman, neither man or woman, or as some other gender). We now want to explore the complex developmental process of transgender identity.

Transgender Identity Development

If you were going on a trip to a place you have never been to before, you most likely would bring a map or use a global positioning system (GPS) to help get you to your destination quickly and without obstacles. In a similar way, HRD professionals who have knowledge of transgender identity development processes have a "map" and understanding to more effectively work with transgender workers in a culturally responsive and transaffirming manner. Traditional models of human development are not necessarily applicable to transgender individuals because these models tend to construct gender and gender roles in traditional, binary, biologically based conceptions. Mallon (1999) was one of the first researchers to propose that transaffirming, nonstigmatizing models of transgender identity development were needed.

Based on a qualitative examination of transgender adults, Morgan and Stevens (2008) described an identity developmental process common among many transgender individuals. Based on themes reported by the participants, the researchers presented the process of transgender identity development in life stages. Starting in **childhood**, a feeling of mind–body dissonance is experienced (Morgan & Stevens, 2008).

In other words, although the child may have male genitalia, the child feels and thinks that he is a female. This causes a significant amount of distress and discomfort. During **puberty** is another time when the transgender individual often experiences mind–body dissonance. The bodily changes that occur during puberty are stressful and sometimes embarrassing for most adolescents; for transgender adolescents who often feel like their first and secondary sex characteristics do not match the gender that they perceive themselves to be, it can be traumatizing. For many transgender adolescents, discomfort and anxiety during puberty is so intense that it is not uncommon for some to engage in binding practices (binding of developing breasts and penises to make them appear flat or nonexistent) and self-mutilation to attempt to remove sex organs and breasts. According to Morgan and Stevens, in **adulthood**, many transgender individuals continue to manage the gender dissonance they experience. The researchers described this period as "biding time" until the individual transitions. The final stage in this process is **transition**. This is the process of adjusting their bodies to their preferred gender (Morgan & Stevens, 2008). Transition for many transgender individuals brings contentment and a sense of wholeness. A limitation of this model of identity development is that it assumes the only resolution of gender dissonance is transitioning. Moreover, the study on which this model resulted is based on the narratives of 11 female-to-male transgender adults and may not be generalizable to all transgender individuals.

The next model we are going to discuss is a more comprehensive, 14-stage Transsexual Identity Formation Model (Devor, 2004). Although transsexualism is just one point on the transgender continuum, most transgender individuals go through these same stages and report similar experiences during their developmental processes. Albeit this is a stage model, not everyone goes through the stages in the same way, at the same speed, in the same order, nor will everyone end up in the same place. Every individual's experience is unique.

The first stage of the Transsexual Identity Development Model is **Abiding Anxiety**. In this stage, the individual might experience a sense of anxiety about not feeling congruent in one's body and/ or social/gender roles. Many transgender individuals report feeling this anxiety as part of their earliest childhood memories. Typically, the anxiety is centered on gender issues and relations (Devor, 2004). Stage 2, **Identity Confusion About Originally Assigned Gender and Sex,** is characterized by questioning whether or not one is supposed to be the gender or sex into which they were born. In this stage, children may make statements to parents that they are the opposite gender or that they desire to be the opposite gender. During puberty, when many transgender adolescents' bodies do not develop into the ones they desired, depression, anxiety, and sometimes suicidal ideation result. It is also during this stage that individuals will attempt to resolve the identity confusion by diligently attempting to conform to social standards of appropriate gender expression. Stage 3, **Identity Comparison About Originally Assigned Gender and Sex,** is characterized by individuals attempting to balance living as their originally assigned gender, while at the same time finding ways to express their need to belong to the opposite gender. Individuals in this stage compare themselves to behaviors and identities that they have observed in others of their gender. Learning about the existence of transsexualism or transgenderism is the fourth stage of the model. **Discovery of Transsexualism or Transgenderism** for many is the moment that everything makes sense to the person. Depending on the individual, some people may accept their transgender identity quickly, while others may take years to get to a point of self-acceptance. For individuals who may not accept a transgender identity quickly, they might proceed through the next few stages more slowly. Stage 5, **Identity Confusion About Transsexualism or Transgenderism,** is marked by individuals wondering if they might be transgender. In order to resolve some of the confusion, they may seek out information via community resources or the Internet. In Stage 6, **Identity Comparisons About Transsexualism or Transgenderism,** the individual is engaged in a process of comparing the self to people of the originally assigned gender, other transgender individuals, and to individuals who belong to genders to which the individual may be transitioning (Devor, 2004). The goal of this process is for the transgender person to discover which comparison results in greatest mirroring of the transgender individual's subjective experience. Once individuals start to realize that they may be transgender, they begin to disconnect from their originally assigned gender or sexual identity. **Tolerance of Transsexual or Transgender Identity**, Stage 7, is illustrated by individuals beginning to apply the identity of transgender to themselves. They may make statements such as, "I am likely transsexual." They may also begin to tell others that they are transgender. The disconnection from the originally assigned gender or sex is even greater in this stage than in the previous stage as the individual moves closer to transitioning genders. Stage 8, **Delay Before Acceptance of Transsexual or Transgender Identity**, is a stage of information gathering for the individual. They delay making concrete decisions about their identity until they have enough information about transgenderism to make sure that whatever decision is made will bring them contentment. In this stage, they may seek out other transgender peers for support and validation of self. They may also participate in reality-testing experiences to see if they could fully accept their transgender identity. Stage 9, **Acceptance of Transsexual or Transgender Identity**, is demonstrated by statements from the individual such as, "I am transgender."

Although not all transgender individuals go through physical or social transitions, many do. For those who choose to transition, they may experience a **Delay Before Transitioning**, Stage 10. The delay is due to the individual taking care of practical and logistical tasks that must be accomplished before the transition process can begin (e.g., discussing the process with employers, planning finances, setting up a support system). **Transition** is the eleventh stage. This stage might involve alterations in physical presentation of the self, counseling, surgical procedures, hormone replacement therapy, and so on. Not all transgender individuals go through the transition process. Stage 12, **Acceptance of Post-Transition Gender or Sexual Identity**, is very similar to Stage 9. Over time, individuals feel empowered now that the social expression of their gender identity is congruent with how they view themselves. They begin to appreciate what it means to be a person of the gender into which they transitioned. Self-acceptance replaces dissonance. The thirteenth stage, **Integration**, takes place when the person who has transitioned becomes integrated into society. A person who has reached the final stage, **Pride**, has achieved a personal sense of pride in one's transgender identity. The individual is able to discuss their transidentity comfortably and openly. Individuals in this stage may also be involved in political and social change efforts, advocating for the rights of other transgender individuals. It should be noted that the pride stage might be experienced simultaneously with earlier stages (Devor, 2004)

Antidiscrimination Policies for Transgender Workers

Although businesses and organizations are increasingly including sexual orientation in workplace nondiscrimination policies, gender identity and expression frequently are left out. This is exemplified by recent statistics (Human Rights Campaign Foundation, 2010) that show 88% of Fortune 500 companies had some form of a nondiscrimination policy in place that included sexual orientation. Only 57% of Fortune 500 companies had nondiscrimination policies that included gender identity and expression. Another area that illustrates the devaluation of transgender individuals in the workplace is that it is currently legal to be fired from a job in 29 states based on sexual orientation, however, in 34 states an individual can be fired from by an employer for being transgender. The **Employment Non-Discrimination Act** (ENDA) is a proposed bill in Congress that would provide basic protections against discrimination related to sexual orientation and/or gender identity and expression in the workplace (Human Rights Campaign, 2010). The bill has been introduced in Congress since the mid-1990s, but it has not successfully passed. It was believed that the bill would pass if transgender issues were not included on the bill, and therefore transgender protections were removed. Recently, ENDA has been reintroduced to Congress with transgender protections included on the bill because of the urging of House Representative Barney Frank. It was crucial that the transgender community be included in the bill due to unique workplace issues that they often experience.

Transitioning

Transitioning is the process in which some transgender individuals engage to make gender identity and expression congruent. There are three primary steps by which some transgender persons may choose to begin the transition process including hormonal therapy, the real-life experience, or sex reassignment surgery. In the first phase, individuals may begin the transition process by taking hormones associated with the other sex (i.e., estrogen to men or testosterone to women). For most transgender individuals who begin hormonal treatment, they begin to experience alterations to their voice, as well as changes in physical appearance. The second phase in the transition process for some transgender people is **the real-life experience**. During this experience, the person is expected to live full time as the gender into which he or she is transitioning for an extended period of time, while meeting regularly with a counselor to process the experience. This includes maintaining full-time employment, functioning as a student, or volunteering, and legally obtaining a gender-appropriate first name (Coleman et al., 2011). It is during the real-life experience when many transgender individuals experience a tremendous amount of discrimination and harassment in the workplace because it is typically at this point when many disclose for the first time to employers their transgender identity. Often, the HRD practitioner is to whom the disclosure is first made. It is not uncommon for transgender persons to lose their jobs during the transition process due to discrimination. Many transwomen ("male-to-female") lose positions of power on the job because they are seen as no longer competent once they transition (Griggs, 1998). On the other hand, many transmen ("female-to-male") are viewed as more valuable than they were as women since transitioning (Schilt, 2006). This demonstrates that transgender individuals can experience both sides of sexism, as the privileged and oppressed. Many transgender individuals report being aware of the gender discrimination that takes place in the workplace (Connell, 2010).

The third phase of the transition process for some transgender individuals is **sex reassignment surgery (SRS)**, also called sex affirmation surgery. In order to qualify for phalloplasty or vaginoplasty, an individual must have been involved in successful hormone treatment for 12 months and a successful 12-month, real-life experience (Coleman et al., 2011). Sex affirmation surgery is an individual decision, and not all transgender people feel the need to have surgery to feel whole. For those individuals who choose to go through sex affirmation surgery, many experience discrimination and prejudice from coworkers post-transition. Schilt and Connell (2007) interviewed transmen and transwomen about their experiences transitioning in the workplace. Some participants reported that coworkers excluded them from social circles post-transition. Moreover, coworkers even questioned the authenticity of the gender into which participants transitioned (Schilt & Connell). For example, some coworkers would reference their transgender peers by their birth genders rather than by the genders into which the employees transitioned.

Job Training

Other workplace issues relevant to the transgender community include the need for job training. Many transgender individuals have difficulty finding employment due to discrimination. One study reported that 47% of transgender individuals believed their identity and/or their presentation contributed to their inability to find employment (Reback, Simon, Bemis, & Gatson, 2001). The same study reported that 28% of transgender participants had lost a job due to their transgender identity. As a result of the disproportionately high rates of unemployment and job discrimination among the transgender community, many transgender individuals get involved with sex work to financially support themselves. It is estimated that 24% to 75% of transgender individuals participate in sex work (Herbst et al., 2008). A recent study that examined the social service needs of transgender individuals found the greatest need was job training (Kenagy & Hsieh, 2005). HRD practitioners are in a great position to meet the job training needs of the transgender community. Because some of the needs of the transgender community are unique, it is recommended that HRD practitioners gain knowledge and skills to competently work with this population. The Association for Lesbian, Gay, Bisexual, and Transgender Issues in Counseling (ALGBTIC), a division of the American Counseling Association, has produced a set of **Competencies for Counseling Transgender Clients** (Burnes et al., 2010). A subsection of the competencies are related to Career and

Lifestyle Development. It is recommended that HRD practitioners implement the following competencies:

- Assist transgender clients with exploring career choices that best facilitate identity formation and job satisfaction.
- Recognize that existing career development theories, career assessment tools, employment applications, and career counseling interventions contain language, theory, and constructs that may be oppressive to transgender and gender-conforming individuals.
- Acknowledge the potential problems associated with career assessment instruments that have not been normed for the transgender community.
- Challenge the occupational stereotypes (e.g., sex work, entertainment careers) that restrict the career development and professional decision making of transgender clients, or respect decisions to remain in entertainment careers, while also being prepared to affirm that these are valid jobs for those who are satisfied working in these fields.
- Acknowledge and understand how the interplay of discrimination and oppression against transgender individuals adversely affect career performance and/or result in negative evaluation of their job performance, and thus may limit career options resulting in underemployment, less access to financial resources, and overrepresentation in certain careers.
- Demonstrate awareness of the high degree of discrimination that transgender individuals have historically experienced in the workplace and how this discrimination may affect other life areas (e.g., housing, self-esteem, family support).
- Demonstrate awareness of and skill in addressing employment issues and challenges for transgender individuals who have experienced transition, those who may choose to transition, and those who may not opt to transition while in the workplace and recognize the diversity of experiences for transgender individuals who choose to transition while in the workplace.
- Explore with clients the degree to which government (i.e., federal, state, and/or local) statutes, union contracts, and workplace

policies protect workers against employment discrimination based on gender identity and expression. In cases where there is not protection of transgender employment rights, provide information on advocacy and support efforts.

- Link clients with transgender mentors and resources that increase their awareness of viable career options.
- Provide employers with consultation and education on gender identity issues and ways to facilitate workplace changes, such as restrooms, locker rooms, staff education, and creating a respectful, inclusive environment.
- Assist with empowering transgender individuals to advocate on their own behalf as appropriate in their workplace context (i.e., micro-level or macro-level) and/or offer to engage in this advocacy with the client's consent if the client would benefit from a direct workplace psychoeducation/training on transgender issues and safety in the workplace.
- Advocate for gender identity and gender expression antidiscrimination policies in the workplace as they are applicable on both micro-level (e.g., in the workplace) and macro-levels (e.g., in the local and larger communities where we live and with policy makers and legislators) (Burnes et al., 2010).

Creating a Nonheterosexist Work Environment

Language and the Workplace

Returning to Arredondo's model of individual differences, how one thinks about their identity often influences how they define themselves. Language is a powerful tool to express inclusiveness and model a safe environment in a work group. The HRD representative is in a position to maximize this tool. To use language as a tool, one must be knowledgeable of current trends in diversity. For example, when referring to a "homosexual" person one should consider using *lesbian* or *gay*. As previously mentioned, the term *homosexual* is considered outdated and holds a derogatory connotation. In addition, the term *heterosexual* is often associated with power and privilege (Rocco, Landorf, & Delgado, 2009). As both academics and practitioners, we recommend adopting what we refer to as **situational language**, the adjusting of language based on the context of the interaction. For example, in a work environment, we may refer to someone's sexual orientation using her or his terminology appropriate for a workplace. If a person refers to himself as a gay man, an HRD professional may inquire, "Are there any issues you experience as a gay man as it relates to your work?" In a more relaxed setting with family or friends, language that is shared and deemed appropriate by the particular norms of the group is used.

The HRD representative needs to consider that some individuals who experience oppression will sometimes reclaim power by using language that is considered derogatory. Whereas this is not always appropriate for the workplace environment, one should note this phenomenon. For example, two self-identified lesbians may use the word "dyke" in a casual lunch conversation as they build a sense of camaraderie. If two heterosexual individuals use the same term in a casual lunch conversation, this would be considered offensive. Semantics and definitions are ever-changing and fluid. Educating oneself of appropriate terminology is a valuable exercise to increase one's cultural competence. More important, the HRD practitioner is to model culturally sensitive language, as well as enact interventions when offensive language occurs in the workplace.

Discourse

Robinson-Wood (2009) described cultural identities as dominant or nondominant discourses. A **dominant discourse** is a narrative associated with the dominant voices in society. These are the most common voices heard in the media, or the identities seen in people who hold positions of power in the workplace (e.g., White, male, heterosexual, able-bodied, Christian) and have attributes often viewed as necessary for success. **Nondominant discourse** represents voices less visible or voices that are often viewed negatively, which impacts their influence in the dominant culture. For example, individuals in the lower economic strata often experience stereotypes of being "lazy" or "lacking proper manners," perpetuating the practice of limiting their power as a group.

In conclusion, the current work environment is not value-free. Yet, in HRD it is our role to recognize values (our own and others) and how they may influence the work experiences and environments of LGBT employees. Second, if values evolve into discrimination, harassment, and an overall hostile environment, then redirecting the work culture to one that is committed to diversity and devoid of oppressive practices toward particular groups is key.

Chapter Summary

The issue of LGBT workers is complex. The career development and workplace experiences of these communities includes socioeconomic inequalities (Badgett, 1995), employment mobility (Gedro, 2009), and discrimination (Chojnacki & Gelberg, 1994). The lack of inclusion of LGBT policies within workplace diversity practices is well documented (Human Rights Campaign Foundation, 2012). Throughout this chapter, we described in detail the current issues, workplace practices, and approaches to increase HRD professionals' competence to work effectively with LGBT employees.

The HRD professional has a crucial role in understanding and implementing a workplace environment that is safe for all workers. Although research in this area is limited, studies suggest inclusive benefits and policies (Hornsby & Munn, 2009) and education about LGBT individuals are beneficial to the overall work environment. For the LGBT worker, this includes implementing inclusive policies, and preventing and disrupting discriminatory behaviors, including harassment. Therefore, exposure to LGBT communities and education about LGBT cultural issues is imperative for the culturally competent HRD professional.

Definition of Key Terms

Affirmation—The fourth level of discrimination in work settings for lesbian and gay employees that requires continued maintenance of antidiscrimination practices and an inclusive positive work environment.

Arredondo's Personal Identity Model—A model that describes identity as a set of characteristics or dimensions where some are fluid and others remain static. Dimension A consists of unchangeable characteristics that one is born with, such as ethnicity, nationality, disability, age, genetics, gender, and sexual orientation. Dimension B consists of characteristics that are changeable and often influenced by the individual, such as religious and spiritual identity, educational background, career choice, and relationship and marital status. Dimension C consists of historical events such as the Great Depression, the civil rights movement, September 11th, natural disasters, and economic downturns.

Bisexual—Refers to individuals who experience affectual feelings and/or physical attractions to both men and women.

Cass's Identity Development Model—A framework of six stages that LGB individuals often go through. Stage 1 is Identity Confusion, which is when first awareness takes place that one might be gay. Stage 2 is Identity Comparison, which is marked with a tension between one's past understanding of self to a current understanding of self as possibly lesbian or gay. Stage 3, Identity Tolerance, is where the individual is developing an appreciation of their new identity. Stage 4 is Identity Acceptance, when the individual begins to place positive associations on their gay/lesbian identity and begins to accept their identity. Stage 5 is Identity Pride, which is associated with positive feelings and reactions to one's identity as a gay person, as well as a need to share their identity with others. The final stage is Identity Synthesis, in which the individual experiences a sense of wholeness.

Covert discrimination—Level 2 of discrimination in work settings for lesbian and gay employees that indicates discriminatory practices are occurring, requiring HRD leaders to understand the subtle transgressions and address them.

DINK—A label assigned to LGB individuals as a result of a general myth that LGB individuals are wealthy, meaning, "dual income, no kids."

Dominant discourse—A narrative beholden to the dominant voices in society, most common identities viewed in the media, or the identities seen in people who hold positions of power in the workplace, for example, White, male, heterosexual, able-bodied, Christian, etc.

Employment Non-Discrimination Act—A proposed bill in Congress that would provide basic protections against discrimination related to sexual orientation and/or gender identity and expression in the workplace that was introduced in the mid-1990s; it has not successfully passed but has been reintroduced with transgender protections.

Gay male penalty—Phenomenon where men working in traditionally "female" occupations often earn lower pay due to employers' awarding compliance to masculinity and stereotypical male traits and chastening values of femininity.

Gender queer—Someone who defies boundaries of gender identity and sexual orientation who, for example, may view self as both man and woman, neither man or woman, or as some other gender.

Harassment—In the workplace it is the physical, emotional, and verbal activities that create a hostile environment for the LGBT worker.

Heterosexual—Individuals who are innately inclined to have romantic and/or sexual relationships with people of the opposite gender.

Heterosexual privilege—Privileges afforded heterosexual individuals as opposed to LGB individuals within the workplace.

HINK—A label assigned to LGB individuals as a result of a general myth that LGB individuals are wealthy, meaning, "high income, no kids."

Lavender ceiling—A term used often to describe the limited advancement and inequitable wage earnings of many "out" LGBT workers.

Lesbian premium—A theory that explains the reasoning behind the higher market earnings of lesbians, whose wages and income are generally significantly higher than their heterosexual counterparts. This may be due to lesbian and bisexual women investing more heavily in education and career-oriented activities, therefore leading to higher paying jobs.

Nondominant discourse—Represents voices less visible that are often viewed negatively, which impacts their influence in the dominant culture; for example, individuals in the lower economic strata often experience stereotypes of being "lazy" or "lacking proper manners," perpetuating the practice of limiting their power as a group.

Overt discrimination—Level 1 of discrimination in work settings for lesbian and gay employees that indicates discriminatory practices are occurring, requiring HRD leaders to take quick and transparent actions to eliminate the discrimination.

Sex reassignment surgery—Also called sex affirmation surgery, it is the third phase of the transitioning process, following successful hormone treatment for 12 months and a successful 12-month, real-life experience in which some transgender individuals engage to make gender identity and expression congruent.

Sexual harassment—Offensive or unwelcomed sexual behavior in the workplace.

Situational language—The adjusting of language based on the context of the interaction. In the work environment reference to someone's sexual orientation uses her or his terminology appropriate for a workplace. In a more relaxed setting with family or friends, language that is shared and deemed appropriate by the particular norms of the group is used.

Tolerance—Level 3 of discrimination in work settings for lesbian and gay employees that requires both direct and indirect actions, as well as policies which are inclusive of sexual minorities.

Transgender—An umbrella term used to describe individuals whose anatomy and/or appearance may not conform to traditional gender roles.

Transitioning—The three-step process in which some transgender individuals engage to make gender identity and expression congruent. The steps include hormonal therapy, the real-life experience, and/or sex reassignment surgery.

Troiden's Homosexuality Identity Development Model—A model that focuses on four stages: Sensitization, Identity Confusion, Identity Assumption, and Commitment. It begins with a sense of uncertainty and progresses to an increased sense of self-acceptance and motivation to develop social connections.

Critical-Thinking Discussion Questions

1. Using Arredondo's model, which individual differences related to your own identities are salient in relation to your professional life (e.g., gender, sexual identity, educational experiences)?

2. As a human resource professional, describe the nature in which nondiscrimination policies are written. Second, in your current work, is there a nondiscrimination policy, and does the policy include or exclude sexual orientation and/or gender identity?

3. Describe your use of situational language. Specifically, how do you change your language in reference to diversity issues depending on your environment? Or are you consistent in your use of language regardless of situation?

4. Discuss your understanding of the definitions for LGBT individuals, including the complexity and values attached to these definitions.

5. LGBT people are at risk of experiencing workplace discrimination. Discuss your role in prevention and intervention to confront discriminatory practices.

6. What are some of the stereotypes you have about LGBT individuals? Where did you learn these stereotypes? Are stereotypes positive or negative?

7. As an HRD professional, what are you able to do to promote positive attitudes in the workplace toward LGBT coworkers? How would you deal with homophobic employees?

8. What are some of the "privileges" you will bring to your work environment? How will these privileges influence employees from the nondominant culture?

9. How might you advocate for transgender employees?
10. As an HRD worker, who would be most challenging for you to work with: a lesbian, a gay man, a bisexual man, a bisexual woman, or a transgender person? Explain.

Critical Essay Questions

1. How might an individual's level of sexual identity development relate to their level of job satisfaction?
2. What is (are) the function(s) of heterosexual privilege? What are some examples of heterosexual privilege in an employment setting?
3. Is it important for a lesbian, gay, bisexual, or transgender employee to "come out" at work?
4. Homosexuality was removed from the Diagnostic and Statistical Manual of Mental Disorders (DSM) in 1973. Why do you think gender identity disorder remains listed as a mental illness in the DSM-IV-TR?
5. How does heterosexism and transphobia in the workplace negatively affect heterosexual workers?

Legal Perspectives

Workplace case law tends to fall into three main areas: (1) reports of workplace harassment; (2) discrimination for employment at hiring and/or promotion: and (3) accessing equal benefits. The following two court cases describe harassment in the workplace of sexual minorities.

Moreau vs. Qwest Communications Inc.

In 2006, Donald Moreau filed an employment discrimination lawsuit against Qwest Communications Inc. The basis of the lawsuit according to public records is severe antigay harassment by coworkers. The plaintiff described being referred to as "faggot" and antigay literature placed on his desk. He described coworkers' efforts to get him fired and feeling unwelcomed. During his employment, the plaintiff received strong performance reviews and reported concerns to management. Following fact-finding by the Denver Anti-Discrimination Office (DADO), the enforcement agency of the city's antidiscrimination policies found the workplace to be hostile and recommended training for workers. Qwest Communications Inc. did not comply with the DADO report, and Mr. Moreau left his place of employment and filed a lawsuit. The case was resolved out of court in April 2007 with a mutually agreed-upon settlement.

Dunbar vs. Footlocker Inc.

Similarly, in 2004 Kevin Dunbar experienced harassment as an employee of Footlocker Inc. The plaintiff reported being disparaged in front of costumers and reported receiving harassing comments from coworkers. Following a written complaint to management, the confidential complaint was read in front of coworkers. After transferring to another store, he was soon fired. A lawsuit followed based on the company not implementing its antidiscrimination policy. A settlement was reached, and the company implemented training to "vigorously" train its employees and managers about antigay harassment.

In both cases, settlements were reached. Examining these cases further, the HRD practitioner benefits from being involved at the first complaint filed by an employee. The formal complaint by the employee provides the mechanism for the HRD representative to intervene appropriately. The lack of intervention discussed in each case is evident. Attempts to enact an intervention are not evident. The responsibility of HRDs to implement antiharassment training and consequences for violating workplace policy at the time of the complaint is vital. In each case, a department transfer was the first course of action. Yet, both transfers resulted in continued harassment and/or discrimination. Therefore, changing situations is one response, especially, if the environment is intolerable, but this does not change the culture of the workplace environment. Culture changing within the company requires "buy in" from management and the empowerment of the Human Resources Department to develop policy as well as implement procedures when policy is violated. Therefore, if in both cases the supervisors and managers acted on the complaint by intervening with the particular employees to resolve the issues, then lawsuits could be mitigated. It is worth noting that in both cases, settlements were reached, indicating the companies were adverse to further pursuit of litigation. Most companies desiring to avoid negative publicity and lawsuits benefit from antiharassment policies with specific procedures and guidelines and provide training to identify harassment and techniques to resolve issues for all employees, especially supervisors.

Case Study: Michele

Miguel is a successful, 32-year-old senior project manager at a prestigious information technology firm. Miguel is the only Latino individual and the only person of color at the senior level within the firm. Miguel joined the firm seven years ago as a computer programmer. He is now a well-respected member of the firm. The firm currently has policies in place that protect employees against discrimination based on sexual orientation, but not gender identity.

Ever since Miguel was a young child he always felt different. As a child, he was rejected by other boys and, as a result, socialized with female peers. When asked what he wanted to be when he grew up he would say, "I want to be a girl when I grow up." When Miguel turned 12 years old, he started sneaking into his sister's closet to wear her clothes when no one else was in the house. The sense of relief and exhilaration that Miguel experienced while wearing his sister's clothes caused him also to feel isolated and anxious.

It was in college when Miguel began to accept a transgender identity, after working with a LGBT-affirmative counselor for a couple of years. Although Miguel began to accept a transgender identity, Miguel had not made a commitment yet to live full time as a woman. Miguel had disclosed to some family members and close friends about being transgender, and in general he has received support from these individuals. Still, Miguel did not feel entirely complete.

Now 32 years old and a star within the IT firm, Miguel has made the difficult decision to transition, including having gender affirming surgery. Miguel has been working with a therapist for the past year to help prepare for the psychological and physical aspects of the transition. Miguel, who now goes by the name Michele in nonprofessional aspects of her life, has not disclosed to any coworkers or human resources workers that she identifies as transgender and that she has decided to transition. Michele is about to begin her real-life experience. To prepare for the real-life experience and to gradually get her coworkers used to her transition, Michele started to grow her hair longer and gradually began to wear accessories typically associated with women (e.g., earrings, nail polish, neutral-colored make-up). Additionally, Michele began hormone therapy, which has caused feminization of her voice and body. Since Michele has started the transition process, she has found notes addressed to her on her desk and in the men's bathroom with messages such as "Faggot," and "Get out Freak!" Because of the escalating harassment, Michele decided to talk to the human resources manager. Michele disclosed to HR that she is, in fact, in the process of transitioning and that she would like the support of the firm because she has no intention of leaving. Two weeks later, Michele was called into the office of the vice president of the firm. Michele was told that although she was a good worker, she was a representative of the firm and the firm no longer wanted her to work directly with clients on projects. Additionally, the executives believed that Michele's transition has caused an overall disruption to the entire firm. Due to these factors, the vice president let Michele go.

Discussion Questions

1. Was letting Michele go the right thing to do?
2. As an HRD professional, how would you have handled Michele's case?
3. How do you feel about transgender individuals?
4. How might you advocate for future transgender employees at this firm?

References

Academy of Human Resource Development Standing Committee on Ethics and Integrity (1999). Academy of human resource development standards on ethics and integrity. Retrieved from www.ahrd.org/associations/10425/files/ethics_standards.pdf
Arredondo, P., & Glauner, T. (1992). *Professional dimensions of identity model.* Boston: Empowerment Workshops.
Badgett, M.V.L. (1995). The wage effects of sexual orientation discrimination. *Industrial and Labor Relations Review, 48*(4), 726–739.
Badgett, M., Lau, H., Sears, B., & Ho, D. (2007, June). Bias in the workplace: Consistent evidence of sexual orientation and gender identity discrimination. The Williams Institute.

Barrett, D.C., & Pollack, L.M. (2005). Whose gay community? Social class, sexual expression, and gay community involvement. *The Sociological Quarterly, 46,* 436–456.

Black, D., Gates, G., Sanders, S., & Taylor, L. (2002). Why do gay men live in San Francisco? *Journal of Urban Economics, 51*(1), 54–76.

Black, D.A., Sanders, S.G., & Taylor, L.J. (2007). The economics of lesbian and gay families. *Journal of Economic Perspectives, 21*(2), 53–70.

Blandford, J.M. (2003). The nexus of sexual orientation and gender in the determination of earnings. *Industrial and Labor Relations, 56*(4), 622–642.

Brown, M.J., & Henriquez, E. (2008). Socio-demographic predictors of attitudes towards gays and lesbians. *Individual Differences Research, 6*(3), 193–202.

Brown, T. (2002). A proposed model of bisexual identity development that elaborates on experiential differences of women and men. *Journal of Bisexuality, 2*(4), 67–91.

Burns, C., & Krehely, J. (2011). Gay and transgender people face high rates of workplace discrimination and harassment: Data demonstrate need for federal law. Retrieved from www.americanprogress.org/wp-content/uploads/issues/2011/06/pdf/workplace_discrimination.pdf

Burnes, T.R., Singh, A.A., Harper, A.J., Harper, B., Maxon-Kann, W., Pickering, D.L., Moundas, S., & Hosea, J. (2010). American Counseling Association competencies for counseling with transgender clients. *Journal of LGBT Issues in Counseling, 4,* 135–159.

Carpenter, C., & Gates, G.J. (2008). Gay and lesbian partnership: Evidence from California. *Demography, 45*(3), 573–590.

Cass, V.C. (1979). Homosexual identity formation: A theoretical model. *Journal of Homosexuality, 9,* 105–126.

Chojnacki, J.T., & Gelberg, S. (1994). Toward a conceptualization of career counseling with gay/lesbian/bisexual persons. *Journal of Career Development, 21,* 3–10.

Coleman, E., Bockting, W., Botzer, M., Coehn-Kettenis, P., DeCuypere, G., Feldman, J., Fraser, L., et al. (2011). Standards of care for the health of transsexual, transgender, and gender-nonconforming people, version 7. *International Journal of Transgenderism, 13,* 165–232.

Connell, C. (2010). Doing, undoing, or redoing gender? *Gender & Society, 24*(1), 31–55.

Davis, D. (2009). Transgender issues in the workplace: HRD's newest challenge/opportunity. *Advances in Developing Human Resources, 4,* 109–120.

Defense of Marriage Act, H.R. 3396 (1996).

Devor, A.H. (2004). Witnessing and mirroring: A fourteen stage model of transsexual identity formation. *Journal of Gay & Lesbian Psychotherapy, 8*(1), 41–67.

Elizur, Y., & Mintzer, A. (2003). Gay males' intimate relationship quality: The roles of attachment security, gay identity, social support, and income. *Personal Relationships, 10,* 411–435.

Ellis, K., & Eriksen, K. (2002). Transsexual and transgenderist experiences and treatment options. *The Family Journal, 10,* 289–299.

Embrick, D.G., Walther, C.S., & Wickens, C.M. (2007). Working class masculinity: Keeping gay men and lesbians out of the workplace. *Sex Roles, 56,* 757–766.

Gallup (2008, June). Americans evenly divided on morality of homosexuality. Retrieved from www.gallup.com/poll/108115/Americans-Evenly-Divided-Morality-Homosexuality.aspx

Gates, G.J. (2006, October). Same-sex couples and the gay, lesbian, bisexual population: New estimates from the American Community Survey. Retrieved from the Williams Institute, UCLA School of Law website: www.law.ucla.edu/williamsinstitute/publications/SameSexCouplesand GLBpopACS.pdf

Gates, G.J. (2011). How many people are lesbian, gay, bisexual, and transgender? Retrieved from http://williamsinstitute.law.ucla.edu/research/census-lgbt-demographics-studies/how-many-people-are-lesbian-gay-bisexual-and-transgender/

Gedro, J. (2009). LGBT career development. *Advances in Developing Human Resources, 11,* 54–66.

Griggs, C. (1998). *S/he: Changing sex and changing clothes.* New York: Berg.

Herbst, J.H., Jacobs, E.D., Finlayson, T.J., McKleroy, V.S., Neumann, M.S., & Crepaz, T.J. (2008). Estimating HIV prevalence and risk behaviors of transgendered person in the United States: A systematic review. *AIDS and Behavior, 12,* 1–17.

Herek, G.M., & Glunt, E.K. (1993). Interpersonal contact and heterosexuals' attitudes toward gay men: Results from a national survey. *Journal of Sex Research, 30*(3), 239–244.

Hornsby, E.E., & Munn, S.L. (2009). University work-life benefits and same-sex couples. *Advances in Developing Human Resources, 11,* 67–81.

Huffman, A.H., Watrousrodrigues, K.M., & King, E.B. (2008). Supporting a diverse workforce: What type of workforce is meaningful for lesbian and gay employees? *Human Resource Management, 47,* 237–253.

Human Rights Campaign (2010). Employment non-discrimination act. Retrieved from www.hrc.org/issues/workplace/enda.asp

Human Rights Campaign Foundation (2012). Corporate equality index 2013: Rating American workplaces on lesbian, gay, bisexual, and transgender equality. Retrieved from www.hrc.org/files/assets/resources/Corporate EqualityIndex_2013.pdf

Janus, S.S., & Janus, C.L. (1993). *The Janus report on sexual behavior.* New York: Wiley.

Kenagy, G.P., & Hsieh, C.M. (2005). Gender differences in social service needs of transgender people. *Journal of Social Service Research, 31*(3), 1–21.

Kinsey, A.C., Pomeroy, W.B., & Martin, C.E. (1948a). *Sexual behavior in the human female.* Philadelphia: W. B. Saunders.

Kinsey, A.C., Pomeroy, W.B., & Martin, C.E. (1948b). *Sexual behavior in the human male.* Philadelphia: W. B. Saunders.

Lambert, E.G., Ventura, L.A., Hall, D.E., & Cluse-Tolar, T. (2006). College students' views on gay and lesbian issues: Does education make a difference? *Journal of Homosexuality, 50*(4), 1–30.

Lewis, G.B. (2003). Black-white differences in attitudes toward homosexuality and gay rights. *Public Opinion Quarterly, 67,* 59–78.

Lind, A. (2004). Legislating the family: Heterosexist bias in social welfare policy frameworks. *Journal of Sociology and Social Welfare, 31,* 21–35.

Luther, S. (2009, September 21). How Fortune-ranked companies stack up on LGBT workplace policies. Retrieved from Human Rights Campaign, www.hrcbackstory.org/2009/09/how-fortune-ranked-companies-stack-up-on-lgbt-workplace-policies/

Mallon, G.P. (1999). Preface: An ecological perspective of social work practice with transgendered persons. In G.P. Mallon (Ed.), *Social services with transgendered youth.* Binghamton, NY: Harrington Park Press.

McDonald, K.S., & Hite, L.M. (2005). Reviving the relevance of career development in human resource development. *Human Resource Development Review, 4,* 418–439.

Morgan, S.W., & Stevens, P.E. (2008). Transgender identity development as represented by a group of female-to-male transgendered adults. *Issues in Mental Health Nursing, 29,* 585–599.

National Center for Health Statistics (2011). Sexual behavior, sexual attraction, and sexual identity in the United States: Data from the 2006–2009 national survey of family growth. Retrieved from www.cdc.gov/nchs/data/nhsr/nhsr036.pdf

Pew Research Center for the People and the Press (2003). Religious beliefs underpin opposition to homosexuality. Washington, D.C.: Author. Retrieved from http://peoplepress.org/reports/display.php3?ReportID=197

Pope, M., Barret, B., Syzmanski, D.M., Chung, Y.B., Singaravelu, H., McLean, R., & Sanabria, S. (2004). Culturally appropriate career counseling with gay and lesbian clients. *Career Development Quarterly, 53,* 158–177.

Ragins, B.R., Singh, R., & Cornwell, J.M. (2007). Making the invisible visible: Fear and disclosure of sexual orientation at work. *Journal of Applied Psychology, 92,* 1103–1118.

Reback, C.J., Simon, P.A., Bemis, C.C., & Gatson, B. (2001). *The Los Angeles transgender health study: Community report.* Los Angeles: Author.

Robinson-Wood, T.L. (2009). *The convergence of race, ethnicity, and gender: Multiple identities in counseling.* Columbus, OH: Merrill.

Rocco, T., Landorf, H., & Delgado, A. (2009). Framing the issue/framing the question: A proposed framework for organizational perspectives on sexual minorities. *Advances in Developing Human Resources, 11,* 7–24.

Schilt, K. (2006). Just one of the guys? How transmen make gender visible at work. *Gender & Society, 20*(4), 465–490.

Schilt, K., & Connell, C. (2007). Do gender transitions make gender trouble? *Gender, Work, & Organization, 14*(6), 596–618.

Schulte, L.J., & Battle, J. (2004). The relative importance of ethnicity and religion in predicting attitudes towards gays and lesbians. *Journal of Homosexuality, 47*(2), 127–142.

Servicemembers Legal Defense Network. (2010). About "don't ask, don't tell." Retrieved from www.sldn.org/pages/about-dadt

Troiden R.R. (1989). The formation of homosexual identities. *Journal of Homosexuality, 17*, 43–73.

U.S. Department of Justice, Federal Bureau of Investigations. (2009). Hate crime statistics, 2008. Washington, D.C.: Author. Retrieved from www2.fbi.gov/ucr/hc2008/index.html

Volokh, E. (1997). What speech does "hostile work environment" harassment law restrict? *Georgetown Law Journal, 85*, 627.

Williams, C.L., Giuffre, P.A., & Dellinger, K. (2009). The gay-friendly closet. *Sexuality Research & Social Policy, 6*(1), 29–45.

Yarber, W.L., Sayad, B.W., & Strong, B. (2010). *Human sexuality.* New York: McGraw-Hill.

8

SOCIAL CLASS AND DIVERSITY IN THE WORKFORCE

Marilyn Y. Byrd, Jose Martinez, and
Chaunda L. Scott

Chapter Overview

This chapter will examine ways that social class is manifested in the workforce. First, an explanation will be given of the social class economic structure in America, including a description of levels of social class within the economic structure. Next, a discussion on social class in the working environment and ways that social class can be manifested and perceived from a noneconomic perspective will be given. Examples will be provided of ways that social class can create bias as well as reinforce privilege in the workplace. The chapter will conclude with a discussion on emerging perspectives of social class in America.

Learning Objectives

After reading this chapter, along with completing the chapter summary questions and the case discussion questions, you will be able to:

- Identify and explain the American social class structure
- Define classism and levels of classism
- Discuss the noneconomic perspectives of social class
- Discuss emerging discourse on social class

The Social Class Structure in America

Social class refers to one's economic position in society. Historically, social class has represented a socioeconomic social stratification that is measured in terms of education, occupation, wealth, and income. Income refers to wages, while wealth refers to assets minus debts (Kimmel & Aronson, 2009). **Social stratification** is the process by which resources are distributed in society (Beeghley, 2005). In the United States, social stratification has created biases and prejudices between individuals and groups in workplace settings. Consequently, social class can also refer to the socially disadvantaged status of individuals who have been subjected to racial, ethnic, or cultural bias because of their identity as a member of a group without regard to their individual qualities (U.S. Small Business Administration, 2004).

Classism is a consequence of social class structures and refers to the differential treatment based on social class or perceived social class.

> Classism is the systematic assignment of worth based on social class; policies and practices set up to benefit more class-privileged people at the expense of the less class-privileged people, resulting in drastic income and wealth inequality and causing basic human needs to go unmet; the rationale and the culture which perpetuates these systems and this unequal valuing. . . . Classism is held in place by a system of beliefs and cultural attitudes that ranks people according to economic status, family lineage, job status, level of education, and other divisions (Class Action, 2013).

Classism can be manifested in the workforce through individual (behaviors and attitudes), institutional (policies and procedures), or cultural (norms) practices.

Gilbert (2008) proposes there are six social classes in the United States: the **privileged classes**, made up of a *capitalist* class (1%) and an *upper-middle class* (14%); a **majority class**, consisting of a *lower-middle class* (30%) and a *working class* (30%); and a **lower class** that includes the *working poor* (13%) and the *unemployed underclass* (12%).

Closer examination of the social classes is necessary for understanding and further discussion of ways that individuals are privileged or marginalized based on their social class.

Salient Features of the Privileged Classes

The privileged classes represent varying degrees of power in the United States. This group is often classified as having inherited wealth or "old money" (e.g., Rockefellers) or "new money" as represented in earned wealth (e.g., Bill Gates, Oprah Winfrey) (SparkNotes Editors, 2006). According to Thompson and Hickey (2008), the privileged classes dominate corporate America and significantly influence the nation's political, educational, religious, and other institutions. Moreover, this group exhibits a strong sense of group solidarity by attending the same prestigious private schools and holding membership in the same exclusive clubs.

Leondar-Wright and Yeskel (2007) offer further descriptions of this group and suggest that two distinct categories exist within this group: the ruling class and the owning class/rich.

> The ruling class is the stratum of people who hold positions of power in major institutions of the society. (Appendix 13C)
>
> The owning class/rich is the stratum of families who own income-producing assets sufficient to make paid employment unnecessary. (Appendix 13C)

While identifying with this group according to wealth (inherited or accumulated) is a fundamental criterion, individuals that become instantly wealthy (e.g., lottery winners who may have originally been working class or working poor class) do not automatically become an accepted member of the privileged classes. In this instance, status is a perception that accompanies social class. **Status** is a "subjective phenomenon, a sentiment in people's minds . . . members of a status group generally think of themselves as a social community, with a common lifestyle" (Gilbert, 2008, p. 8).

Salient Features of the Majority Classes

Beeghley (2005) points out that the majority of the population in the United States is middle class. In a *USA Today* commentary, Vice President Joe Biden said, "Quite simply, a strong middle class equals a strong America. We can't have one without the other" (Biden, 2009). However, there has been some debate on how this group is defined.

Purnell (2010) pointed out that the "middle class in America is extremely amorphous due to the sheer variety of definitions that most people in this country use to explain themselves in relation to other people" (p. 34). While income should be a straightforward indicator of the majority class, defining this group has become quite elastic (Haugen, Musser, & Kalambakal, 2010).

Survival and potential for prosperity are essential features of this group. Furthermore, the life chances of the middle class are good. **Life chances** are the better (or worse) chances in life a person has depending on the person's social class, lifestyle, life expectancy, health, education, marital happiness, and so on (Sernau, 2001). Historically this group consisted of entrepreneurs, small-business owners, and occupations that controlled their own production. The new middle class now includes professional and managerial occupations that control the labor of others (Gilbert, 2008).

Salient Features of the Lower Classes

The lower class experiences greater inequality and is characterized by struggle, insufficiency, and limited education. Leondar-Wright & Yeskel (2007) point out two groups within the lower class: (1) the working group of individuals whose income depends on hourly wages for labor or on other nonmanagerial work or very small business activity that does not require higher education, and (2) the poverty class, which is the stratum of families with incomes persistently insufficient to meet basic human needs.

Individuals within this group are either looking for opportunities to "push up" or have accepted their position in life and simply work to meet the daily needs of life. Belief in the American Dream is most salient within this group.

Noneconomic Perspectives Emerging from Social Class Identities

From a broad sociological perspective, discussions on social class in the United States generally focus on the capitalist and economic state of Americans. In this section, three noneconomic perspectives of social class will be examined and examples of individual, institutional (organizational), and cultural classism will be provided. First, stereotyping and the harmful effects on some targeted social groups will be discussed. Second, the intersection of social class with other forms of difference that can create multiple experiences of disadvantage will be examined. Third, the intersection of social class with forms of privilege that can reinforce the power of the power-holder will be explored.

The Psychological and Physiological Effects of Classism

Classism is a consequence of one's perceived social class. As such, classism is a form of **social oppression** (Hardiman, Jackson, & Griffin, 2007).

> Social oppression perpetuates the belief that some social groups are superior or normal and establishes systems of advantage and privilege for these groups while simultaneously defining other social groups as inferior and deserving of disenfranchisement, exploitation, and marginalization. The oppressors are members of dominant social groups privileged by birth or acquisition, who knowingly or unknowingly exploit and reap unfair advantage over members of oppressed groups. Members of oppressor groups are also trapped by the system of social oppression that benefits them, and are confined to roles and prescribed behavior for their group. (p. 37)

In addition to social oppression, classism can produce emotional and psychological consequences. For example, the media and popular culture portray social groups in negative ways and project negative images that create unintentional social bias. **Social groups** are groups of people that share physical, cultural, or social characteristics that typically target them for social oppression, and experiences of disadvantage, marginalization, and subordination (e.g., racial, ethnic, immigrant, gender, and even emerging categories such as disabilities) (Hardiman, Jackson, & Griffin, 2007). These images transfer to workplace environments in such ways that can be socially damaging and serve to reinforce cultural classism. The negative consequences of cultural classism can be affective to the psychological and physical well-being of individuals who are "looked down on" and disrespected in their workplaces because of their perceived social class. Culturally induced language such as *ghetto, trailer trash, low class,* and so on, that translates prejudice and bias against persons based on their perceived social class are other negative effects of classism. Another consequence is experiencing isolation and feelings of "not fitting in." For example, a workplace where conversations in the break room frequently bring up the latest designer fashions, the "best" places to order a shrimp dinner, or the best ski resort to spend winter vacation could be embarrassing to the newcomer who comes from a less privileged background and is looking for ways to connect to and become a part of their new environment.

Consequently, when cultural classism is internalized, the results could be anxiety, stress, low self-esteem, health problems, absenteeism, depression, and experiencing the **second-class citizen syndrome**. The second-class citizen syndrome refers to feelings of inferiority or experiencing feelings of inadequacy or "not living up" to the standards of others in the group. Individuals that experience this syndrome are often targets of institutional or organizational classism.

In work settings, social class separates the powerful from the powerless. Furthermore, "the ability to achieve goals is highly correlated with class, people with similar interests often act in concert and discriminate against others, even though they are not formally organized into groups" (Beeghley, 2005, p. 24). There are several practical implications that emerge from social stratification of social class: access (or lack of access) to resources, information, networks, opportunities, and other essentials that are critical for achieving success or fulfillment at work.

The Intersection of Social Class with Other Forms of Difference

Other systems may intersect with social class and thereby create bias toward marginalized social groups. For example, the **good ol' boy network** is a social networking system that allows racial prejudice to linger and endure and as a result creates a social stratification usually across racial lines. In addition, this system serves to keep a barrier in place that excludes women from social circles where opportunities may exist to advance. In this instance, social class creates a social stratification across gender lines. The following vignette is an example of institutional or organizational classism and highlights ways that bias is manifested through social networking:

> Jessica, an African American woman, held a mid-management corporate position. Based on her annual reviews over the past years, she was

progressing nicely toward executive management. But when an executive management position became available, Jessica applied but the position was given to Claudia, a White woman and a former employee of the organization. Claudia had resigned three years prior for personal reasons. Although she had left the organization, she had maintained contact with some of the top managers in the organization and was still in the social clique. She frequently went to lunch with "higher ups" in the organization and attended church with others. In fact, it was during one of these social encounters that Claudia learned about the forthcoming position. So when the position was advertised, she applied as an external applicant and got the position. Returning to an executive management position was simply a matter of Claudia expressing her desire to return to the organization. The fact that Jessica had the qualifications, experience, tenure with the organization, and all those things that are assumed to guarantee advancement appeared to be irrelevant. In Jessica's mind, she felt like a second-class citizen.

While Jessica's racial status may not have directly influenced the decision as to who would get the job, Claudia's association with executive management within her former organization was a clear advantage. In this example, race and social class intersected to create a disadvantage for Jessica. Despite the fact that laws have created more opportunities for protected groups of people based on race, sex, age, religion, and so on, and have sought to bring about greater equality for these groups, social settings such as churches and social groups such as local women's clubs, garden clubs, civic clubs, soccer mom's groups, and others, are still highly segregated. In social settings, people continue to prefer interaction with and maintain social relationships with those like themselves. These informal sites are sources for inside information to formal organizations and provide exposure to those seeking to gain entrance.

In addition, access and the freedom to exercise one's power and authority often lies in informal social networking systems (Gostnell, 1996). But in many instances women, particularly in predominantly male environments, are excluded from this network. The following is excerpt of one woman's account of the socialization aspect of her job as the Chief Information Officer (CIO) (Byrd, 2008):

My position is CIO in the Information Technology Department of my organization. I am the first woman to hold this position. Currently I am the only woman in an administrative management position. And although my title is CIO, I am not considered part of the executive management team—which is kind of funny in and of itself. And from a socialization perspective, I am not on their (other administrative and executive managers') social invitation list. For one thing, they all play golf and squash, and these are the type of social gatherings where information is freely shared. I don't play golf or play squash. I have often seen guys from my department leave the office to have lunch together in the congenial way that men have when they are together. I am quite sure they end up discussing events of the morning, discussing employees, those sorts of things, over lunch. These are the types of situations that many women are left out of. Many times I discover second-hand information that directly affects my responsibilities in the department.

In my first job fresh out of college, I learned quickly that after work happy hour is another setting where you can get a lot of information about what is going on in the organization. And sometimes when people have a couple of drinks, you find out so much! In my current position, it's a little bit different—it's more of social cliques and I am not in the social clique. So the challenge is trying to figure out how to enter the male world. Now there are other social contexts in which I *can* cross over. For instance, if I joined the local country club, I could place myself into their world. And if they see me they might, say, "Hey you want to join us?" But I should not have to go to that extent in order to get the information that I need. One thing I *have* done is to involve my children in soccer. Two of the department's executive managers have children who also play soccer. So that is a way I have learned to get to know some of these guys in an outside social setting.

The above excerpt is another example of institutional or organizational classism. Furthermore, it exemplifies how this CIO's gender may have played a role in her being intentionally or unintentionally locked out of the male social network. Moreover, this example highlights how this CIO's position was (intentionally or unintentionally) controlled by excluding her position from the formal executive management team.

Intersection of Social Class and Privilege

The good ol' boy social networking system supports class privilege, an advantage of power holders within an organization. **Privilege** "refers to the rights, benefits, and advantages automatically received by being a member of the dominant group regardless of intentions" (Sensoy & DiAngelo, 2009, p. 348). This system also functions to re-enforce the use of power (e.g., granting favors for friends outside the established rules and regulations that have been established for an organization). This aspect of the good ol' boy system supports Weber's (1968) definition of power. According to Weber, **power** is the ability of an individual in a social relationship to achieve his or her will regardless of resistance by others. The following vignette is an example of ways this system is manifested through the use of power.

> Kyle is a first-generation college graduate. Despite financial assistance in the form of partial scholarships and student loans, his family struggled to send him to college. His family income was slightly over the limit that would have qualified him for full government grants. He excelled at his grades and graduated with top honors. After graduating, he landed an entry-level management position with a large corporation. Kyle worked hard the first year and was commended during his annual review for his hard work. He was informed that he was on track for the next mid-management position that came open. As it turned out, when the next mid-management position became vacant, the job went to the son of the VP's good friend and college buddy. Kyle was disappointed, but he refused to let this show of favoritism affect his job performance. Kyle came from a family who believed that hard work pays off and eventually reward will come.

In this vignette, class privilege worked as an "unearned advantage through personal contacts" to the benefit of the VP's friend's son. Furthermore, class privilege in this instance is a manifestation of institutional (organizational) classism.

Moreover, Kyle showed belief in the American Dream, the ideology that education and hard work are the keys to success, and success is the door to wealth. Individuals from lower social classes see education as a way to "be anything you want to be." The hidden assumption behind the American Dream however, is that the playing field is even. While higher social classes also ascribe to the notion of the American Dream, education is taken for granted, and many times their success in corporate America, or other professions, is already decided (or can be decided) by the social networking system.

According to Orman (2011), a new American Dream is emerging, one that is more realistic and more attainable. The new American Dream is rooted less in achieving success that is measured in terms of wealth, but in being able to meet basic needs and being able to live comfortably, but responsibly.

The Significance of Discussions on Social Class in Higher Education

Higher education is a vibrant arena to identify and dismantle social class bias and prejudice (Class Action, 2013). As universities and colleges increase their efforts to diversify their campuses, consideration needs to be given to the assimilation process for lower-income class and first-generation students. The culture students will encounter in these settings is usually more representative and responsive to the middle- to upper-class students. Therefore, creating a model for inclusion at the institutional level is a beginning point for impacting social change at the organizational level.

Unfortunately, in the United States, there have been limited discussions on the topic of social class, including classroom discussions (Borrego, 2011). Discussions on social class in the classroom can provide a valuable learning opportunity for students to understand power and privilege as it relates to working and living productively with diverse colleagues and neighbors. This learning experience is also "important for both working-class students who often feel that they do not fit into the academic environment and for students of relative class privilege who often are unconscious of how certain advantages shape their lives" (p. 2). In order for students to fully understand the concept of social class, their relationship to social class, and the role of social class in the workplace and the greater global society, workforce diversity course discussions must be expanded to include a module on "social class diversity."

New Directions for Discourse of Social Class in the Workforce

The American social class structure is replicated in the workforce through social groups. But there has been limited discourse on social class and diversity of groups within social groups. For example, there are variations of Hispanics, such as those who are Cuban Americans versus Mexican Americans. For this reason, more discourse on the awareness and understanding of social group diversity within social class structures is needed because that awareness and understanding has not materialized in a substantial way.

In addition, unequal treatment given to individuals within the same economic social class needs to be considered. For example, middle-class African Americans who are not necessarily treated as middle class experience cultural classism. Although economic similarities exist, racial differences override economic similarities.

Another emerging and significant aspect of social class is the **working military class**, a work group that does not reflect the traditional civilian workforce. The members of the working military class are "warriors who come primarily from rural America and our country's inner cities" (Glantz, 2009, p. 70). The working military class reflects the poorer background of those who enlist and who are hoping for better opportunities in the military. A salient characteristic of this group is the overrepresentation of minorities and the practically non-existence of the upper class and bottom class (Halbfinger & Holmes, 2003). With the exception of those with a desire to pass on a family tradition of military service, the nation's educated and wealthy youth have shunned the military. On the other hand, those from the bottom lower class may be underrepresented because they do not meet the requirements for enlistment.

Recent high school graduates with little desire to go to college choose the military because it is alluring with its offer of benefits and potential for learning a trade. Others gravitate to the military to pursue a skill. Still others are looking for an opportunity and a "way out" of their existing conditions. Some workers that are already in the workforce gravitate toward the military because they are not moving ahead in their current occupation or employment. The military, as a working environment, is described as a "more egalitarian and racially harmonious society, one in which prejudice is trumped by meritocracy, discipline, and the need to survive" (Halbfinger & Holmes, 2003, p. 6). The workplace is a dynamic environment, and college graduates entering the workforce will need increased social knowledge that is foundational for equal treatment of all types of social groups in this setting.

Chapter Summary

This chapter presented the economic structure of social class in America and discussed some of the salient features of American social class structure. The chapter then discussed noneconomic perspectives of social class and ways individuals can experience disadvantage or privilege based on their perceived social class affiliation. The chapter concluded with emerging perspectives of social class and the workforce.

Definition of Key Terms

Classism—The institutional, cultural, and individual set of practices and beliefs that assign differential value to people according to their socioeconomic class; and an economic system that creates excessive inequality and causes basic human needs to go unmet (Leondar-Wright & Yeskel, 2007, Appendix 13).

Good ol' boy network—Social networking system that allows bias and prejudice to linger and endure and as a result creates a social stratification usually across forms of difference.

Life chances—The better (or worse) chances in life a person has depending on the person's social class, lifestyle, life expectancy, health, education, marital happiness, and so on (Sernau, 2001).

Lower classes—Consists of the working poor and the unemployed underclass.

Majority classes—Consist of a lower middle class and a working class.

Power—The ability for an individual in a social relationship to achieve his or her will regardless of resistance by others (Weber, 1968).

Privilege—The "rights, benefits, and advantages automatically received by being a member of the dominant group regardless of intentions" (Sensoy & DiAngelo, 2009, p. 348).

Privileged classes—The upper class, which consist of the rich and power-ful, and the upper-middle class, which consists of educated and wealthy professionals.

Second-class citizen syndrome—Refers to feelings of inferiority or experi-encing feelings of inadequacy or "not living up" to the standards of others in the group.

Social class—One's economic position in society. Historically, social class has represented a socioeconomic social stratification that is measured in terms of education, occupation, wealth, and income.

Social groups—Groups of people that share physical, cultural, or social char-acteristics that typically target them for social oppression, and experiences of disadvantage, marginalization, and subordination (e.g., racial, ethnic, immi-grant, gender, and even emerging categories such as disabilities) (Hardiman, Jackson, & Griffin, 2007).

Social oppression—Perpetuates the belief that some social groups are supe-rior or normal and establishes systems of advantage and privilege for these groups while simultaneously defining other social groups as inferior and deserving of disenfranchisement, exploitation, and marginalization (Hardi-man, Jackson, & Griffin, 2007, p. 37).

Social stratification—The process by which resources are distributed in society (Beeghley, 2005).

Status—A "subjective phenomenon, a sentiment in people's minds . . . mem-bers of a status group generally think of themselves as a social community, with a common lifestyle" (Gilbert, 2008, p. 8).

Working military class—The poorer background of many veterans hoping for better opportunity in the military; warriors who come primarily from rural America and our country's inner cities (Glantz, 2009, p. 70).

Critical-Thinking Discussion Questions

1. Compare and contrast social class from an economic and non-economic perspective.

2. How does the concept of life chances apply in a concrete way to social class?

3. What do you think accounts for the difficulties in defining the middle class?

4. Discuss the impact of social class and ageism.

5. What steps should organizations take to address issues of social class bias in the workplace?

Case 1: Classism at Lake Shore Bank

Jade was very excited about her new job as new accounts administrator at Lake Shore Bank. The job not only paid well, but the position itself was everything Jade ever dreamed. She had worked her way through college, and many of the jobs she had worked were menial, manual-labor types of jobs. She vowed that once she got her degree, she would never look back on those days. Now that she had her degree and had landed a "prestigious" job, Jade felt very pleased with herself. After a few days at the bank, Jade began to pay attention to some of the conversations that took place in the break room or just conversations in general among the staff. For instance, during lunch one day, she was sitting with a group of ladies that commented about the "trailer trash" that came into the bank to cash their welfare checks. Couldn't they just go to the local supermarket and cash their checks? Then there was the time she overheard two women conversing about the tacky clothes that the new teller wears. One of the ladies laughingly suggested they take the teller shopping since she obviously does not know how to choose classy, stylish clothing. Jade was uncomfortable each time she overheard these comments, but she remained silent. She was actually not surprised about these two women in particular looking down on someone's clothing. In the short while she had been with the bank, Jade noticed these two women were always talking (in a boastful sort of way) about their expensive lifestyles. They were obviously quite taken with themselves.

The incident that really struck a chord with Jade was the day she witnessed a VP demeaning one of the janitorial staff for not watering the plants in her office. The woman screamed at the janitor, "You people should be glad you have a job. But obviously you don't appreciate your job very much if you are too lazy to tend to the plants!" Jade was embarrassed for the janitor because she remembered a time when she worked manual-labor jobs. People seemed to think that the type of work you do determines the type of respect you receive. Jade pondered what she should do.

Discussion Questions

1. What type of classism is being shown in this incident? Support your response.
2. Why do you think Jade remained silent the first few times she witnessed classism?
3. Do you think Jade should approach the VP about what she witnessed? Why or why not?
4. Do you think individuals in work settings have the responsibility to speak out against biased attitudes such as classism?

Case 2: Degradation of Hispanic Lower Social Class

The Chi Omega sorority chapter of Penn State University was being investigated after a photograph surfaced of a party laden with Mexican stereotypes in the fall of 2012 (Murray, 2012). The members were dressed in ponchos and sombreros and wore fake mustaches. One displayed a sign saying, "Will mow lawn for weed + beer," while another showed a sign that said, "I don't cut grass. I smoke it." The president of the sorority issued an apology, while the university's public relations director said that the university was appalled that this level of insensitivity would be displayed. The sorority's communications director also responded that the behavior was a degradation of a group of people.

This incident brings to light concerns in relation to social class and diversity. The outfits were obviously stereotypical of the Mexican culture, when in truth, the vast majority of people in Mexico do not wear ponchos or sombreros. Apparently, the point was to classify and convey the assumption that people of Mexican descent or Mexican-origin are yard workers, smoke grass, drink beer, and sport moustaches. This misconception raises a concern that people of Mexican descent are being depicted in the lowest socioeconomic class, which serves as a denigration of their culture and reinforces the stereotypes of Mexican culture.

In general, U.S. society has tended to treat people in lower socioeconomic classes in a derogatory manner, regardless of their skin color. The perception that the lower class are less worthy even subjects this group to lesser pay, which further perpetuates their economic status. The sorority's depiction of the Mexican culture is a microcosm of what many in society have come to perceive, given the socialization by the media and others about class positions. Source: Murray, R. (2012, December 5). Penn State sorority girls busted for offensive photos at Mexican-themed party. *New York Daily News.*

Discussion Questions

1. If you had been a member of the Penn State sorority, would you have gone along with your fellow sisters' degradation of the Mexican culture or would you have spoken up about the degrading nature of depicting people of Mexican descent in such a manner?
2. Does this incident have implications about the social class of this group or the sorority as a whole?
3. Is it likely that the sorority does not interact with people of Mexican descent, or even have members that are of Mexican descent?
4. What do you think should have been the consequences of their actions?

References

Beeghley, L. (2005). *The structure of social stratification in the United States.* Boston: Pearson.

Biden, J. (2009, January 30). Time to put middle class front and center [Editorial]. *USA Today.* Retrieved March 11, 2011, from www.usatoday.com

Borrego, S. E. (2011). Class on campus: Breaking the silence surrounding socioeconomics. *Diversity Digest, 11*(3), 1–4. Retrieved March 19, 2011, from Diversity web: An interactive resource hub for higher education, www.diversityweb.org/DiversityDemocracy/vol11no3/index.cfm

Byrd, M. (2008). To enter and lead: Renegotiating meanings of leadership and examining leadership theory of social power from the perspectives of African American women leaders in predominantly white organizations (Doctoral dissertation, Texas A&M University). Retrieved from http://repository.tamu.edu/bitstream/handle/1969.1/ETD-TAMU-2711/BYRD-DISSERTATION.pdf?sequence=1

Class Action. (2013). What is classism. Retrieved March 10, 2013, from www.classism.org/about-class/class-definitions

Gilbert, D. (2008). *The American class structure in an age of growing inequality.* Los Angeles: Pine Forge Press.

Glantz, A. (2009). *The war comes home.* Berkeley: University of California Press.

Gostnell, G. M. (1996). The leadership of African American women: Constructing realities, shifting paradigms (Portland State University, ProQuest Digital Dissertations). (UMI No. 9701103).

Halbfinger, D. M., & Holmes, S. A. (2003, March 30). Military mirrors working-class America. *New York Times.* Retrieved March 11, 2011, from www.nytimes.com

Hardiman, R., & Jackson, B. (2007). Conceptual foundations for social justice education. In M. Adams, L. A. Bell, & P. Griffin (Eds.), *Teaching for diversity and social justice* (2nd ed., pp. 35–66). New York: Routledge.

Haugen, D., Musser, S., & Kalambakal, K. (Eds.). (2010). *The middle class: Opposing viewpoints.* Farmington Hills, MI: Greenhaven Press.

Kimmel, M., & Aronson, A. (2009). *Sociology now.* Boston: Pearson, Allyn & Bacon.

Leondar-Wright, B., & Yeskel, F. (2007). Classism curriculum design. In M. Adams, L. A. Bell, & P. Griffin (Eds.), *Teaching for diversity and social justice* (2nd ed., pp. 309–334). New York: Routledge.

Murray, R. (2012, December 5). Penn State sorority girls busted for offensive photos at Mexican-themed party. *New York Daily News.*

Orman, S. (2011). *The money class: Learn to create your new American Dream.* New York: Spiegel & Grau.

Purnell, B. (2010). The middle class is in debt. In D. Haugen, S. Musser, & K. Kalambakal (Eds.), *The middle class: Opposing viewpoints.* Farmington Hills, MI: Greenhaven Press.

Sensoy, O., & DiAngelo, R. (2009). Developing social justice literacy: An open letter to our faculty colleagues. *Phi Delta Kappan, 90*(5), 345–352.

Sernau, S. (2001). *Worlds apart.* Thousand Oaks, CA: Pine Forge Press.

SparkNotes Editors. (2006). SparkNote on social stratification and inequality. Retrieved June 30, 2013, from www.sparknotes.com/sociology/social-stratification-and-inequality/

Thompson, V. E., & Hickey, J. V. (2008). *Society in focus: An introduction to sociology.* (6th ed.). Boston: Pearson.

U.S. Small Business Administration. (2004). Small Business Act (15 USC 637). Retrieved August 25, 2010, from www.sba.gov/regulations/sbaact/sbaact.html

Weber, M. (1968). *Economy and society.* Totowa, NJ: Bedminster Press. (Original work published 1920).

PART III
DIVERSITY IN THE WORKFORCE: EMERGING TRENDS

9

SPIRITUALITY AND DIVERSITY IN THE WORKFORCE

Marilyn Y. Byrd

Chapter Overview

This chapter discusses the concept of spirituality as an emergent workforce diversity topic. Although it is not a new idea, forms of spirituality are now emerging in more contemporary forms in the workplace. Spirituality will be further examined as a process that can lead to social justice outcomes.

Learning Objectives

After reading this chapter, along with completing the chapter summary questions and the case discussion questions, you will be able to:

- Conceptualize varying definitions of spirituality
- Recognize the need for studying workplace spirituality
- Discuss the business perspective of spirituality in the workplace
- Discuss social justice as an emerging perspective of spirituality in the workplace

Defining Spirituality—Varying Perspectives

A growing topic in workplace diversity is spirituality. Moore (2008) points out that spirituality is a relatively unexplored area of workplace diversity. Moreover, identifying individual differences in expressing spirituality provides a rationale for addressing spirituality as a workplace diversity topic. "In practice, spirituality in the workplace is an umbrella term for a plethora of loosely related policies and practices that focus on the recognition of 'soul' at a personal and at an organizational level" (Gockel, 2004, p. 158).

Spirituality in the workplace is an idea of revolutionary potential that requires more clarity and theoretical understanding (Butts, 1999). Because the focus of spirituality is on the whole person, the idea of spirituality should include the various and diverse ways that people express their spiritual values (Hicks, 2002). Spiritual diversity is the concern for and acceptance of the multiple ways that individuals express their spirituality in the workplace. Therefore, a universal definition of spirituality does not allow space to negotiate spiritual diversity.

Spirituality is the interconnectedness with self and others (Mitroff & Denton, 1999). It is a timeless and universal concept that gives purpose and meaning, encouragement and hope. Smith (2001a) defines workplace spirituality as the various ways we express our spirituality at work, both for personal support and in making ethical, just decisions.

Spirituality conveys a feeling of empowerment that enables one to transcend the ordinary and envision that which is sacred in everyday life (Gockel, 2004). It is a source of deep faith and willpower and grants one with a sense of calmness and peace. It is that which comes from within, beyond the survival instincts of the mind. Each of us has a spiritual center, which is our connection to this source of inner knowing (Guillory, 1997). Spirituality in the workplace centers on a wide range of individual experiences both within and outside of formal religion (Tisdell, 2003).

Having considered these varying perspectives, we might ask: "What is the role of spirituality in bringing about more culturally inclusive workplace settings?" According to Tisdell and Tolliver (2000), it means "bringing one's heritage and full authentic self in facilitating the process. It means being connected to something greater and grander than self and connecting that awareness with culturally and spiritually grounded approaches to [working] . . ." (p. 244). Spirituality can take on numerous forms of human experience. In this respect, spirituality in itself is diverse. The dynamics between work and life have generated a need for individuals to "achieve personal stability . . . and realize that our inner wisdom is the only source that will sustain our adaptation and stability in the long run" (Guillory, 1997, p. 214).

The Need to Study Workplace Spirituality

Miller and Miller (2005) believe that the growing interest in workplace spirituality is due to the evolution in consciousness we are experiencing as human beings. Furthermore, "spirituality allows people of all religions to work together in harmony, even in the secular world of business" (p. 12). We often face situations or obstacles in our work that are challenging or frustrating. Connecting to our spiritual selves allows us to withdraw and gather strength. When we emerge, we are energized, prepared to face the challenges, and ready to complete the task.

Connecting to a spiritual nature provides the stimulus for motivation. In addition, spirituality has motivational qualities, and motivation stimulates creativity and productivity. Miller (1999) says that motivation to be creative can be clearly understood within the context of spirituality. Therefore, motivation is a driving force for developing new products, improving customer service, and creating other business or organizational values. Likewise, motivation is a driving force that helps to overcome challenges to achieving these values. According to Miller, creativity often requires tapping into an inner character (our spirituality) to face and overcome uncertainties and fears. As a result, spirituality can be empowering in confronting challenges that can affect work productivity and consequently impact business performance.

Guillory (1997) points out that connecting to a spiritual source benefits individuals in work environments in several ways. First, spirituality creates inner meaning and motivation about work. Second, it creates inner peace in one's self. Third, it is a natural desire to help others grow, learn, and succeed. Finally, spirituality respects and values individual and group dignity.

Covey (1990), celebrated author and professor, makes an important connection to workforce diversity and spirituality. According to Covey, a spiritual dimension of one's life helps grant a source of meaning and purpose and helps one to achieve balance between work and life. Engaging in spiritual activities helps one to discover and understand the meaning and purpose of work and reinforces commitment and values. While individuals may share a common need to engage in spirituality, the path to making a spiritual connection may not be the same.

Current Perspective of Workplace Spirituality—A Business Perspective

In the past decade, some organizations have adopted a business model that promotes a spiritual workplace (Stanczak & Miller, 2002). Rather than identifying with religious ideals, this model subscribes to optimizing human resource development by valuing trust, faith, justice, respect, and love. The intended outcome is to affect productivity and profitably. Another element of the spiritual workplace is creating a space where workers can connect to a personal source of spirituality and minimize the everyday stress and potential burnout created in the workplace. Furthermore, research suggests that spirituality has a therapeutic effect that is useful when experiencing change in workplace settings.

Conflict, pressures of the job, the changing nature of work environments, loss of a job, increased job responsibilities, lack of individual purpose, and the like are challenges that produce a spiritual process in search of a resolution (Guillory, 1997). Groen (2004) says that workplaces do not necessarily set out to create soulful spaces. Rather, activities and workshops such as leadership development training, workshops, and seminars allow spaces for individuals to go "beneath the surface" for greater meaning-making experiences.

Organizations that are spiritually centered might provide activities that support the mental and physical well-being of employees. **Spiritual-centered organizations** are organizations that recognize the need to provide a means for employees to maintain a healthy balance of work and life. Some organizations are offering onsite pastoral care or access to ministers to provide spiritual and religious services to employees who are in need of immediate or ongoing spiritual care due to work or family crises. Wellness programs, grief counseling, ethics training, fitness centers, yoga, flexible work time, onsite child care, and meditation and relaxation rooms are other examples of ways that employees can revitalize the soul (Uhrich, 2001). Furthermore, spiritually centered organizations are more likely to incorporate ethics, character, and values into training programs (Gockel, 2004). In service-based organizations, a spiritual-centered focus might be expressed by encouraging employees to be more empathic and caring of customers, while managers would be expected to develop more personal relationships with staff (Burack, 1999; Gockel, 2004).

According to Wagner-Marsh and Conley (1999), organizations can create a spiritually based organizational culture by practicing six key concepts: honesty with self, articulation of the corporation's spiritually based philosophy, mutual trust and honesty with others, commitment to quality and service, commitment to employees, and selection of personnel to match the corporation's spiritually based philosophy. Wagner-Marsh and Conley promote a fourth wave of the spiritual workplace that argues for the spiritual transformation of organizations.

Organizations should be proactive rather than reactive in using a spiritually based philosophy. Gockel (2004) points out:

> Starting a business meeting with the Lord's Prayer or questioning the social message behind a new advertising campaign might have gotten a manager laughed out of the board room in the 1980s, but spirituality in all its forms is experiencing a renaissance in the workplace. . . . Change of any kind requires a certain amount of faith that allows individuals to let go of what they know and to try something new. The continuous change projected in the modern economy demands the confidence to make decisions in the face of best guesstimates and to retool quickly when an individual's leaps do not land him or her in a desired place. Helping clients manage stress and cultivate strength through meditation, prayer, and other spiritual practices can provide an anchor to promote resilience in times of great uncertainty. (p. 165)

In light of recent scandals and unethical conduct that has occurred in the business world, spirituality is emerging as a movement that is centered on morality and ethics in the workplace (Smith, 2001a). For this reason, spiritual-centered organizations are placing emphasis on leadership that is accountable, proactive, and socially responsible.

Furthermore, individuals are beginning to insist that their spirituality be valued in the same way as their knowledge and skills (Smith, 2001b). In the same manner that knowledge and skills cannot be separated from the self, so is one's spirituality a part of self. Spirituality is formed from life experiences beginning from childhood and can be formed with or without religious instruction. As a result, life experiences direct and shape an individual's spirituality. While spiritual experiences are common in formation, spiritual disciplines or the practices of spirituality in a specific direction can vary.

Models for Applying Spirituality in Work Environments

Until recently, spirituality has been generally associated with religious literature, which did not lend itself to research methodologies (MacDonald, 2000). However, there is a lack of research and theory that explains spirituality in relation to diversity. Spirituality is now appearing in professional literature in relation to physical and psychological well-being in organizational and institutional settings.

Spirituality spans a range of disciplines such as anthropology, sociology, theology, and education. Because of this, varying concepts of the phenomenon exist, which has created a lack of knowledge that addresses the theoretical principles of spirituality. However, the field of education has contributed considerable literature toward spirituality in a learning environment. Because of the similarities between the educational and professional work environment, research from the field of education is useful for exploring the nature of spirituality in a diverse workforce.

Elizabeth Tisdell, a leading scholar in the field of education who has conducted extensive research on the cultural relevance of spirituality and learning, says religion is an "organized community of faith that has written codes of regulatory behavior, whereas spirituality is more about one's personal belief and experience of a higher power or higher purpose" (Tisdell, 2001, p. 1). Tisdell (2003) offers the following principles of spirituality:

- Spirituality and religions are not the same, but for many people they are interrelated.
- Spirituality is an awareness and honoring of wholeness and the interconnectedness of all things through the mystery of what

many people refer to as the Lifeforce, God, higher-power, cosmic energy, Buddha nature, or Great Spirit.

- Spirituality is fundamentally about making meaning.
- Spirituality is always present (though often unacknowledged) in the learning environment.
- Spiritual development constitutes moving toward authenticity.
- Spirituality is about constructing knowledge through unconscious and symbolic processes.
- Spiritual experiences can occur unexpectedly and lead to transformation of self.

Garcia-Zamor (2003) asserts there is a spiritual awakening in the U.S. workplace. This trend is prevalent because more employers have taken a humanistic approach for creating a more fulfilling work environment. The assumption being that employees who are fulfilled through expressing their spirituality are happy, creative, and productive. On the other hand, when employees are discouraged from expressing their spirituality, a dispirited environment is created and results in low morale, absenteeism, and greater turnover.

Cash, Gray, and Rood (2000) believe that to treat religion and spirituality as mutually exclusive is problematic. The use of "a common term such as support, ethics, morals, beliefs, mission, values, spiritual contemplation, and community involvement makes the distinction between the two practices difficult to explain" (p. 127). Furthermore, legal mandates that require companies to adhere to religious accommodations may, in fact, promote spiritual practices such as prayer rooms and activities that support a spiritual aspect of one's religion. Moreover, further problematic is the interpretation as to when one employee's spiritual expression infringes upon another person's right. Whereas religion is a protected class under the Civil Rights Act of 1964, an individual's spiritual expression may not necessarily constitute a religious practice, although another individual may perceive it as such. Therefore, Cash et al. (2000) recommend "an open, non-categorized interpretation of the concept of belief, both religious and secularly spiritual" and "re-interpret religious belief to include religious, spiritual, strongly held values of whatever origin" (p. 127).

According to Jurkiewicz and Giacalone's (2004) values framework, the degree of workplace spirituality evident in a culture is thus indicated by the positive expression of these 10 values: benevolence (showing acts of kindness), generativity (leaving something behind for those who follow), humanism (bringing about the greater good of humanity), integrity (having high values), justice (having expectations of being treated fairly), mutuality (fostering a feeling of community), receptivity (encouraging supportive and open relationships with coworkers), respect (demonstrating consideration and concern), responsibility (empowering people), and trust (creating an environment that encourages loyalty and security). Organizational cultures that foster these values are believed to have a positive effect on motivation, commitment, and adaptability.

A study by Mitroff and Denton (1999) created five organizational models that describe how an organization can be religious or spiritual. The *religious*-based organization can express positive values toward religion and spirituality or positive values toward religion and negative values toward spirituality. The *evolutionary* organization expresses strong affiliation with a particular religion and later adopts values that are more ecumenical. The *recovering* organization is guided by principles used by programs such as Alcoholics Anonymous to foster spirituality. The *socially responsible* organization is guided by the spiritual values of the founders or heads (e.g., Greyston Bakery). In a *values-based* organization, the owners or heads are not guided by any particularly religion or spirituality. Mitroff and Denton (1999) suggest that each model has a fundamental, underlying principle of hope. The principle of hope expresses the organization's basic principle of trust. If an organization places trust in its values and ethical principles, performance, productivity, and profits should follow.

Emerging Forms of Spirituality in the Workplace

Spirituality is emerging as a topic that empowers individuals in the workplace to challenge and change systems of oppression by embracing the soul and spirit. In this respect, spirituality addresses both individual and organizational levels of the work environment.

Garcia-Zamor (2003) says that spirituality can be manifested in two levels: individual and organizational. At the individual level, spiritual values of the individual are expressed even before employment.

These individuals would make known their concerns about whether or not the culture of the organization was accepting of their spiritual values. These spiritual values do not necessarily relate to a specific religion. The issue of concern to management should be focused on how productivity is affected if an individual is not permitted to express his or her spirituality. At the organizational level, management understands that spiritual values are connected to the individual and that people connect their spirituality to their work ethics. Therefore, organizational performance can be impacted by an individual's spiritual values.

At the individual level, spirituality is one's personal belief and experiences of a Lifeforce—a higher power or higher purpose (Tisdell, 2001). However individuals seeking to freely express their spiritual convictions in the work environment may encounter some of the same biases that are experienced by other diverse groups.

Individuals will seek to associate themselves with organizations that are perceived as spiritual workplaces. "When the inner self connects to one's work, work and the inner self seem to know no limits" (Burack, 1999, p. 284). In a spiritual workplace, individuals feel motivated to reach their fullest potential through creativity, emotions, and intelligence. Ultimately, organizations will be more profitable. Therefore, organizations must learn to capture the spiritual energy of their employees.

Spirituality engages one's passion. This type of passion is not of an erotic nature but rather an intense feeling that fuels our convictions and beliefs. For instance, spirituality played a large role in the engagement of people's passion in the Civil Rights Movement (Tisdell, 2001). Individuals that come from diverse and marginalized groups often draw upon some personal element of spirituality that forces them to give voice to their oppressions and their experiences in workplace settings. From this awareness, they are capable of constructing knowledge, which empowers them to take action for a more equitable and just workplace. Therefore, spirituality is one of the ways people make meaning of their experiences.

Dialogue and storytelling are spiritual activities that are emerging to address sociocultural issues in the workplace (Groen, 2004). **Sociocultural** refers to the dynamics and power that can be used to oppress based on one's gender, race, or social class (Merriam &

Caffarella, 1999). Moreover, spirituality has been embraced as a source of strength for members of socially disadvantaged groups. **Socially disadvantaged** refers to being subjected to racial or ethnic prejudice or cultural bias because of one's identity as a member of a group without regard to individual qualities (U.S. Small Business Administration, 2004). For example, belief in God has been a source of strength for African American women who seek strength to endure triple social oppressions stemming from race, gender, and social class oppression. In this respect, spirituality has been utilized as a coping strategy that in many instances has led to an **enlightened revelation** (Byrd, 2013).

With roots in Kant's categorical imperative philosophy of universal individual rights, an enlightened revelation is a process of engaging one's inner peace to endure the everyday experiences of one's socially disadvantaged status. Experiencing a negative event can lead to critical reflection, which can lead to meaning-making as a person tries to make sense of the experience. By taking action, an anticipated and expected outcome is social change and social justice. Social change and social justice have the capacity to bring about liberation and emancipation. Figure 9.1 illustrates the enlightened revelation framework.

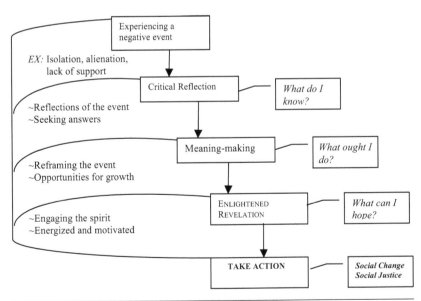

FIGURE 9.1   Enlightened Revelation: Spiritually Relevant Framework
© Byrd, 2013

Emancipatory spirituality seeks to affirm an individual's compassion for a just society by challenging systems of oppression (Lerner, 2000). Spirituality is not simply a system of religious beliefs. "Rather, spirituality comprises articles of faith that provide a conceptual framework for living everyday" (Hill-Collins, 1998, p. 245).

The participants in a study conducted by Byrd (2008) expressed spirituality as a powerful force when confronting negative experiences in the workplace. The narratives of the participants in this study indicated that socially disadvantaged groups often engage in an emancipatory spiritual process when facing social oppression. The following is an excerpt from an interview with one of the participants from this study. The participant, an African American woman and a former leader at a state agency, described how her deep and abiding faith in God was not only the source of her strength for coping, enduring, and surviving social oppression in her work environment—it was the source of her empowerment for challenging unjust systems that allow social oppression to thrive. This example further illustrates how dialogue is an emerging form of spirituality that brings about spiritual release.

> The first thing is to trust God to level the playing field. Because if you do not, you will spend a lot of your energy trying to make things right that really you do not have the ability to make right. The second thing is to learn to pack your own emotional chute and take care of yourself. Make sure that you are whole within yourself. Because you cannot control how other people feel about you nor can you control how they react to you. But you can control your inner peace. And that is another part of your spirituality you have to know. For me, it is knowing who God is and knowing He is going to take care of me. In the beginning my boss used little strategies to cut ground from under me. I was already an established manager when she arrived. And because she was also racist, when she came she tried to turn everybody against me (including the employees who reported directly to me). I had gotten everybody to know me and we were all . . . together. But then she started creating little groups again. She would pull people in for little special meetings, without including me or informing me. She always operated in a crisis mode and every time she came into my office—it was a problem. It was never

anything that I had done right. And so the first thing I knew, my blood pressure was racing. I am wondering to myself, What have I got to deal with now? Then the Lord just gave me a strategy . . . and this was just for me . . . it was stop, drop, and roll. The stop was to be still and know that God was ultimately in control. Be still and know that I'm God. Stop all this other that's going on. You need to come to peace. When this adrenalin is going on, that's not the way God meant for you to live. So the first thing was be still. . . . I stopped and I was still. And then drop. Your personal investment is you don't want to look dumb, you don't want to look incompetent. You don't want this person to take advantage of you. But you've got to trust God that the other person's motives are not your concern. Your motives are your concern. Have you acted out of a lack of integrity? Or have you done anything . . . if you have not, then stop, drop—drop your personal investment in the outcome because God has promised to take care of you. And so no matter what is going to come of this, I don't have to worry about it. And the other was roll—instead of me trying to struggle with whatever this is that comes out of her mouth, and trying to make it right and give her an answer—what I can do is cast my cares on God. That is, trust God to take care of me and then just deal with the situation and leave the results to Him. Because at first my heart is racing, I'm trying to figure out what's wrong so I can fix it. And then I got so calm when I saw her coming that immediately I went into a biofeedback response. My heart rate would slow down deliberately to keep her from triggering that adrenalin rush in me and getting me all fired up. And once I learned that strategy it was so good for me, and I carried it over into other areas of my life. Stop. Be still and know that I am God. Drop. Drop your personal investment and outcomes because God is going to take care of you. Roll. Cast your cares on God because He cares for you. Not only does He care for you He's going to do something about it. He has the capability of doing something about it. But that was the strategy that I stumbled onto maybe and it helped me finish out my career with great peace. God is responsible for outcomes and I'm responsible to walk it out. That is . . . I know that it's going to have a good ending no matter what it is because God has promised to take care of me. But some things you just need to walk through . . . it doesn't look very good in the middle. I heard T. D. Jakes say on the TV the other day—he said you know the beginning and the end. But you don't know the middle. So I've learned to walk it out in the middle. And the middle is that the just should live by faith. (Original interview data, Byrd, 2008; reprinted: Byrd, 2009)

Emancipatory spirituality brings about a spiritual consciousness that has the power to evoke social change. **Social change** refers to acts of advocacy for the cause of changing society in a positive way (Horton & Freire, 1990). Social change actions can evolve suddenly or over a period of time, affecting either a wide or limited scope of people. Social change is the result of efforts taken to ensure social justice for all members regardless of race, gender, sexual orientation, religion, nation, and so on. **Social justice** refers to "the process of remedying oppression due to race, ethnicity, interracial conflict, class conflict, gender distinction, religious differences including exploitation, marginalization, and powerlessness. Questions that implicate issues of a power imbalance within society are considered social justice issues" (Edwards & Vance, 2001, p. 63).

Expressing one's spirituality does not mean enforcing spiritual values. Instead it means connecting to the spirit within when confronted with disempowering experiences. It means drawing on spiritual values to advocate for equitable and socially just work environments. Spirituality gives rise to a new paradigm where individuals are drawing upon their spiritual values as a tool for social change.

Chapter Summary

In this chapter, spirituality was presented from a business perspective and from a social justice perspective. Organizations and businesses are incorporating spirituality as a means of individual well-being from the stressors associated with life at work. Individuals are also embracing spirituality as a means of coping with oppression that stems from being identified as socially disadvantaged. The enlightened revelation spiritually relevant framework was discussed as a coping strategy for oppression. As an emerging perspective, the latter has potential for bringing about individual emancipation and organizational social change.

Definition of Key Terms

Emancipatory spirituality—Seeks to affirm an individual's compassion for a just society by challenging systems of oppression.

Enlightened revelation—Process of engaging one's inner peace to endure the everyday experiences of one's socially disadvantaged status.

Social change—Acts of advocacy for the cause of changing society in a positive way.

Social justice—Remedying oppression due to race, ethnicity, interracial conflict, class conflict, gender distinction, and religious differences including exploitation, marginalization, and powerlessness.

Socially disadvantaged—Being subjected to racial or ethnic prejudice or cultural bias because of identity as a member of a group without regard to the individual qualities.

Sociocultural—The dynamics and power that can be used to oppress based on one's gender, race, or social class.

Spiritual-centered organizations—Organizations that recognize the need to provide a means for employees to maintain a healthy balance of work and life.

Spiritual workplace—Environment whereby individuals feel motivated to reach their fullest potential through creativity, emotions, and intelligence.

Spirituality—That which comes from within, beyond the survival instincts of the mind; possessing a spiritual center, which is the connection to this source of inner knowing.

Critical-Thinking Discussion Questions

1. Visit the website for Greyston Foundation (http://greyston.org/index.php?who_we_are). How does this business illustrate principles of spirituality and social justice?
2. Do you believe that organizations should incorporate spirituality into training programs? Why or why not?
3. Discuss how workplace spirituality supports the principle of ethics.

Case Study

Vickie, an administrative assistant who has her own office, likes to listen to contemporary gospel music. Occasionally Vickie will tune in to her favorite contemporary gospel radio station and listen to gospel music play softly while she works. Melinda, a worker from another office who often comes to Vickie's office on business-related matters, has complained to

Vickie's boss saying that she "cannot tolerate" that kind of music and feels that Vickie should not be allowed to listen to that particular station while at work. Vickie's boss later approaches her saying that it is OK to play music softly, but she should listen to a more neutral station.

Discussion Questions

1. Research and explain the EEOC's statement on religious discrimination and religious expression.
2. Based on your interpretation, are Vickie's rights being violated? Why or why not?
3. How does the EEOC make a distinction between the practice of one's religion and the expression of one's spiritual beliefs?

Legal Perspective

The Equal Employment Opportunity Commission (EEOC) brought a religious discrimination suit against ConocoPhillips on behalf of a long-term pipe fitter at the Bayway Refinery in Linden, New Jersey. Clarence Taylor, a deacon and lay leader of his church, was required to work Sundays for two months in 2006. Taylor requested religious accommodation but was denied and was required to work a schedule causing him to miss Sunday services for two months.

The U.S. District Court in Newark found that Taylor's rights were violated according to Title VII of the 1964 Civil Rights Act. This legislation mandates that employers make reasonable accommodations for employees' sincerely held religious beliefs. According to the EEOC, employers are expected to explore other alternatives, such as flexible work time, shift swapping, etc. as needed in order to conform to an employee's request for reasonable accommodations. Taylor was also granted monetary award in the civil action and provided with 40 hours of additional vacation leave.

ConocoPhillips was further ordered to provide training to all Bayway management/supervisory employees in federal laws prohibiting religious discrimination at an onsite location. Training for all other current employees would be conducted as computer-based training. (*Source:* www.eeoc.gov/eeoc/newsroom/release/5–28–09a.cfm)

References

Burack, E. H. (1999). Spirituality in the workplace. *Journal of Organizational Change Management, 12*(4), 280–291.

Butts, D. (1999). Spirituality at work: An overview. *Journal of Organizational Change Management, 12*(4), 328–331.

Byrd, M. (2008). To enter and lead: Renegotiating meanings of leadership and examining leadership theory of social power from the perspectives of African American women leaders in predominantly white organizations (Doctoral dissertation, Texas A&M University). Retrieved from http://re-pository.tamu.edu/bitstream/handle/1969.1/ETD-TAMU-2711/BYRD-DISSERTATION.pdf?sequence=1

Byrd, M. (2013). Emancipatory spirituality: A philosophical & social justice perspective. *Proceedings of the Academy for Human Resource Development,* Arlington, VA: AHRD.

Byrd, M. Y. (2009). Telling our stories of leadership: If we don't tell them they won't be told. In M. Byrd & C. Stanley (Eds.), Giving voice: The socio-cultural realities of African American women's leadership experiences. *Advances in Developing Human Resources* (pp. 582–605). doi:10.1177/1523422309351514

Cash, K. C., Gray, G. R., & Rood, S. A. (2000). A framework for accommo-dating religion and spirituality in the workplace. *Academy of Management Executive, 14*(3), 124–134.

Covey, S. R. (1990). *The seven habits of highly effective people.* Melbourne: The Business Library.

Edwards, P., & Vance, S. (2001). Teaching social justice through legal writing. *The Journal of the Legal Writing Institute, 7,* 63–86.

Garcia-Zamor, J. (2003). Workplace spirituality and organizational perfor-mance. *Public Administration Review, 63*(3), 355–363.

Gockel, A. (2004). The trend toward spirituality in the workplace: Overview and implications for career counseling. *Journal of Employment Counseling, 42,* 156–167.

Groen, J. (2004). The creation of soulful spaces and the organizational context. *Organizational Development Journal, 22*(4), 19–30.

Guillory, W. (1997). The living organization: Spirituality in the workplace. Retrieved from www.innovint.com/downloads/default.asp

Hicks, D. A. (2002). Spiritual and religious diversity in the workplace. Implica-tions for leadership. *The Leadership Quarterly, 13,* 379–396.

Hill-Collins, P. (1998). *Fighting words: Black women and the search for justice.* Minneapolis: University of Minnesota Press.

Horton, M., & Freire, P. (1990). *We make the road by walking: Conversations on education and social change.* Philadelphia: Temple University Press.

Jurkiewicz, C. L., & Giacalone, R. A. (2004). A values framework for mea-suring the impact of workplace spirituality on organizational performance. *Journal of Business Ethics, 49*(2), 129–142.

Lerner, M. (2000). *Spirit matters.* Charlottesville, VA: Hampton Roads Publishing.

MacDonald, D. A. (2000). Spirituality: Description, measurement, and relation to the five factor model of personality. *Journal of Personality, 68*(1), 153–197.

Merriam, S. B., & Caffarella, R. S. (1999). *Learning in adulthood.* San Fran-cisco: Jossey-Bass.

Miller, D. R., & Miller, W. C. (2005, September). Interview on spirituality in the workplace. *Effective Executive.* ICFAI University Press, India. Retrieved from www.globaldharma.org/Files%20-%20Adobe%20Acrobat/Publications/SBL%20ICFAI%20Interview%20on%20Spirituality.pdf

Miller, W. C. (1999, October/November). Spirituality, creativity and business. *The Inner Edge, 2*(5), 20–22. Retrieved from www.workplacespirituality.info/SpiritualityCreativityBusiness.html

Mitroff, I. I., & Denton, E. A. (1999). A study of spirituality in the workplace. *Sloan Management Review, 40*(4), 83–92.

Moore, T. W. (2008). Individual differences and workplace spirituality: The homogenization of the corporate culture. *Journal of Management and Marketing Research,* 79–93. Retrieved from www.aabri.com/manuscripts/08060.pdf

Smith, N. (2001a). Does spirituality belong in the workplace? Retrieved July 4, 2010, from www.workplacespirituality.info/article1002.html

Smith, N. (2001b). What is workplace spirituality? Retrieved July 4, 2010, from www.workplacespirituality.info/article1001.html

Stanczak, G. C., & Miller, D. E. (2002). *Engaged spirituality: Spirituality and social transformation in mainstream American religious traditions, report supplement.* Center for Religion and Civic Culture, University of Southern California. Retrieved July 3, 2010, from http://crcc.usc.edu/docs/Engaged SpiritualityAppendix.pdf

Tisdell, E. J. (2001). *Spirituality in adult and higher education.* ERIC Clearinghouse on Adult Career and Vocational Education, Columbus, OH. Retrieved from www.ericdigests.org/2002-3/adult.htm

Tisdell, E. J. (2003). *Exploring spirituality and culture.* San Francisco: Jossey-Bass.

Tisdell, E. J., & Tolliver, D. E. (2000). *The role of culture and spirituality in teaching for social change in adult higher education classes.* Paper presented at the Midwest Research to Practice Conference in Adult, Continuing, and Community Education, University of Wisconsin, Madison.

Uhrich, D. (2001). Spirituality in the workplace: A review of the literature. Retrieved from www.wiktel.net/monarch/resource/spirit.pdf

U.S. Small Business Administration (2004). Small Business Act (15 USC 637). Retrieved August 25, 2010, from www.sba.gov/regulations/sbaact/sbaact.html

Wagner-Marsh, F., & Conley, J. (1999). The fourth wave: The spiritually-based firm. *Journal of Organizational Change Management, 12*(4), 292–301.

10

INTERGENERATIONAL TENSIONS IN THE WORKFORCE

Brenda Lloyd-Jones and Jody A. Worley

Chapter Overview

The purpose of this chapter is to focus on intergenerational tensions in the workforce. It accomplishes this aim by defining some basic terms and concepts essential to the study of generations in the workforce and exploring four theoretical perspectives associated with generations and ageing in the workforce. In addition, this section examines the concept of work values and generational profiles and discusses its critical relation to the development of tensions in the workplace among and between generations. Finally, the chapter provides empirical data on generations in the workplace, presents a diversity model that focuses on generational differences in the workforce, and concludes with strategies for managing intergenerational conflict.

Learning Objectives

After reading this chapter, along with completing the chapter summary questions and the case discussion questions, you will be able to:

- Define the basic terminology used in the literature on generational differences
- Discuss the characteristics associated with each of the four generational cohorts in the workforce
- Identify ways in which theoretical perspectives are used to predict and explain intergenerational tensions in the workforce

- Develop an awareness of generational differences and how they can lead to intergenerational conflict at work
- Understand why organizations are concerned about intergenerational problems and the strategies they use to address intergenerational conflict in the workplace
- Explain communication practices that help to create a successful intergenerational workforce
- Discuss current approaches for understanding and managing generational diversity in the workplace

Four distinct generations of American workers currently compose the contemporary workforce (Lancaster & Stillman, 2002; Reynolds, 2005; Zemke, Raines, & Filipczak, 2000). The age demographic of the workforce has shifted considerably within a few decades (Pitt-Catsouphes & Smyer, 2007), and employees are working with coworkers who are as old as their parents and as young as their children (Zemke et al., 2000). The multigenerational workforce has garnered widespread attention that primarily focuses on comparisons between the generational groupings and the distinctive generational differences that often create tensions among the cohorts (Zemke et al., 2000).

According to Glass (2007), the generations share more similarities than differences; however, the subtle differences in their perspectives of work can impact how they view the workplace and potentially generate tensions between generational cohorts in the workplace. Research literature suggests that the presence of generational cohort groupings in organizations can have important consequences in employee attitudes, behaviors, and expectations (Dencker, Joshi, & Martocchio, 2007).

The purpose of this chapter is to focus on intergenerational tensions in the workforce. It accomplishes this aim by defining some basic terms and concepts essential to the study of generations in the workforce and exploring four theoretical perspectives associated with generations and ageing in the workforce. In addition, this section examines the concept of work values and generational profiles and discusses its critical relation to the development of tensions in the workplace among and between generations. Finally, the chapter provides empirical data on generations in the workplace, presents a diversity model that focuses on generational differences in the workforce, and concludes with strategies for managing intergenerational conflict.

Basic Terminology and Distinctions

Generational differences are widely discussed in both the popular press and business-oriented books, and the investigation of generations in the workforce has led to a proliferation of terms used to describe various aspects of the phenomenon. According to Reeves and Oh (2007), "The nomenclature used to label the generations is not standardized because the various people writing about generational differences have come up with a variety of different names to label the various generations" (p. 295). Researchers, theorists, and practitioners tend to use terms in very different ways. Therefore, it is useful to define some of the terms.

Generation is a recurrent term in the literature on generational differences in the workplace and refers to people born in the same general time span who are approximately the same age and have in common key historical or societal experiences (Kupperschmidt, 2000; Smola & Sutton, 2002). Accordingly, distinct life-defining events (see Figure 10.1) during a generation's formative years influence and define the generation's (Zemke et al., 2000) common value systems that distinguish them from people who came of age at different times (Twenge, Campbell, Hoffman, & Lance, 2010).

The authors suggest that the life-defining events or broad "forces are strongest during an individual's childhood and adolescence; for example, work values remain relatively stable from early adolescence to young adulthood" (Twenge et al., 2010, p. 1120). Sociologists indicate that the time-span of each generation is approximately two decades, after which it diminishes into the background as the next generation comes of age (Schaeffer, 2000; Shepard, 2004). A **generational cohort** is defined as a group of people who have grown up (e.g., adolescence or young adult) during the same time while sharing similar external events (e.g., media, critical economic and social events, and popular culture) that create cohesiveness in values, attitudes, and preferences, which remains relatively constant throughout the cohort's lifetime and results in a social personality distinct to each generational group

1930s:	Great Depression
	Election of FDR
1940s:	Pearl Harbor
	D-Day
	Death of FDR
	VE Day and VJ Day
	Hiroshima and Nagasaki
1950s:	Korean War
	TV in every home
	McCarthy HCUAA hearings
	Rock 'n' Roll
	Salk polio vaccine introduced
1960s:	Vietnam
	Kennedy elected
	Civil Rights Movement
	Kennedy/King assassinations
	Moon landing
	Woodstock
1970s:	Oil Embargo
	Nixon resigns
	First PCs
	Women's Rights Movement
1980s:	*Challenger* explosion
	Fall of Berlin Wall
	John Lennon shot
	Reagan elected
1990s:	Desert Storm
	Oklahoma City bombing
	Death of Princess Diana
	Clinton scandals
2000s:	September 11
	Human Genome Project
	War on Terrorism
	(Iraq, Afghanistan)
	War in Darfur
	Energy crisis
	Digital technology
	(Google, YouTube, smartphones)
	Climate change
	Dot-com and housing bubbles
	Obama elected
2010s:	Earthquakes (Haiti, China, Chile)
	British Petroleum (BP) Gulf of Mexico oil spill

Figure 10.1 Defining Events
Adapted from Zemke, Raines, & Filipczak, 2000.

(Howe, Straus, & Matson, 2000; Twenge et al., 2010). According to these authors, the effect of the September 11th terrorist attacks will probably vary between people who were 11 or 31 years old at that particular time.

An alternate perspective of generations in the workforce presumes that despite workers' ages, life experiences, and career goals, ultimately employees may be "generic" (Jurkiewicz & Brown, 1998, p. 29) in their job expectations and classifying employees by generations may be misguided (Jorgensen, 2003; Yang & Guy, 2006). According to Gordon and Steele (2005), "It is always dangerous to describe or stereotype different generations' characteristics since individuals within that generation do not always fit the qualities ascribed to them" (p. 2). Twenge et al. (2010) add that "there are much greater differences in job performances within age groups than between age groups, and the same is true of the generations (p. 1137). There are average differences; however, ample variation exists within each generation. Further, in a review of the literature on generational differences in the workforce, Reeves and Oh (2007) found that authors disagree about which span of years should encompass any one generation, which underscores the large variance among the distinguishing characteristics within any given generation. Depending on the source, the birth ranges of the four generational groups can vary and overlap by as much as seven or eight years (Zemke et al., 2000). Our society has given each generation a specific label to separate the cohorts from each other, "although most research suggests that cohort effects are linear rather than categorical, with steady change over time rather than sudden shifts at birth year cutoffs" (Twenge et al., 2010, p. 1120).

Whereas researchers and social scientists who study different age groups acknowledge that the ascribed generational categories are inconsistent and do not align with every individual, there is some agreement that particular qualities and preferences generally apply to each of the generations. Raines (2003) is a primary writer in this area and has developed widely accepted classifications or generational profiles of the generational cohorts. The following section uses Raines's categories of generational cohorts (see Table 10.1) to briefly describe the four diverse generations in the current workforce (the Veterans, Baby Boomers, Generation X, and Millennials).

Table 10.1   Four Generations Comprise the Workforce

GENERATIONAL COHORT	TIME SPAN
Veteran generation	Born between 1921 and 1940
Baby Boomer generation	Born between 1941 and 1960
Generation X	Born between 1961 and 1980
Millennial generation	Born between 1981 and 2000

Veteran Generation (born 1921–1940)

Veterans are the oldest generation in the workforce and identified by the label of the "Silent generation" as a result of a perceived quiet, industrious demeanor. This generation includes individuals born before 1940 and is also known as Traditionals and Matures. The Veteran generation was influenced by historical defining events such as the Great Depression, the Pearl Harbor Attack, and World War II. The Veterans range in age from 70 to 89 years old and have been characteristically described as conservative with resources (Jenkins, 2007), as having a sense of obligation, and as observing fiscal restraint (Niemiec, 2000). While 95% of the Veteran generation are retiring from the workforce, they currently represent about 8% of the workforce (Murphy, 2007). In the workplace, members of the Veteran generation value loyalty, respect for authority, and hard work. Contrary to popular belief, members of this generation tend to search out technological advancement and are interested in learning new ways of doing work (Zemke et al., 2000).

Baby Boomer Generation (born 1941–1960)

The **Baby Boomer** generation is currently the largest cohort in the workforce, comprising 44% of the U.S. workforce (Murphy, 2007) and capturing individuals born between 1941 and 1960. Occupying many leadership and management positions, the Boomers' current age range is from 50 to 69 years old, and they are referred to as the baby boom due to the 17 million babies born during that period (O'Bannon, 2001). Defining historical events such as the Civil Rights Movement, the Vietnam War, and the Kennedy and King assassinations influenced the Boomer generation (Zemke et al.,

2000). Characterized as optimistic, idealistic, and believing that hard work and sacrifice are the price to pay for success, Boomers are credited with starting the "workaholic" trend (Glass, 2007). They define themselves by their professional achievements, positions, perks, and prestige (Kane, 2009). Work values characteristic of the Boomer generation include teamwork, collaboration, and group decision making (Zemke et al., 2000).

Generation X (born 1961–1980)

Generation X is a significantly smaller cohort compared with the Baby Boomer generation in the workforce and accounts for 33% of the U.S. labor force (Murphy, 2007). Born between 1961 and 1980, members of Generation X range in age from 30 to 49 years old. They were influenced by defining events such as the global energy crisis, Tandy and Apple PCs, massive corporate layoffs, MTV, AIDS, and technology (Murphy, 2007). Also called Gen Xers, the "X" symbolizes the namelessness of the cohort. Although the members of this generational cohort grouping were aware of their own existence, they were overshadowed by the enormous number of individuals in the Boomer generation (Beutell & Wittig-Berman, 2008). The offspring of the Boomer generation, individuals of Generation X grew up in households in which their parents worked long hours. Subsequently, Gen Xers learned to fend for themselves (Macky, Gardner, & Forsyth, 2008), securing the label "latch-key kids." They observed their parents contend with a period of a stagnant job market, limited wage mobility, and corporate downsizing. According to Twenge et al. (2010), Gen Xers had a "substantially higher probability of witnessing their parents' divorce or job loss due to downsizing than had any prior generation" (p. 1120). Consequently, members of Generation X are disillusioned with corporate America (Zemke et al., 2000). In the workplace, Generation Xers values work–life balance (Glass, 2007), feedback, continuous learning (Clochesy, 2008), and leadership based on competency (Zemke et al., 2000). Gen Xers have strong technical skills (Zemke et al., 2000), are results oriented (Crampton & Hodge, 2006), and embrace diversity (Twenge et al., 2000).

Millennial Generation (born 1981–2000)

Members of the **Millennial** generation include individuals born between 1981 and 2000, and they are currently 10 to 29 years old. The offspring of a supportive home and recipients of parental excesses (Niemiec, 2000), Millennials are described as confident and ambitious (Kersten, 2002). Millennials are also called Generation Y, Nexters, and Generation Me (GenMe). With numbers estimated as high as 70 million, Millennials represent the fastest-growing cohort of the U.S. workforce. They currently comprise 15% of the workforce, with 22 million workers (Murphy, 2007). They have been influenced by defining events such as the bombing of the Federal Building in Oklahoma City, Columbine High School shootings, the September 11th terrorist attacks, corporate scandals in WorldCom and Enron, the beginning of the Iraq War, and Hurricane Katrina (Murphy, 2007). Additionally, this generation grew up with technology, including the personal computer, PDAs, laptops, Blackberries, and social networking (e.g., Facebook, Myspace, Twitter), which makes them accustomed to getting access to information quickly (Twenge et al., 2010). At work they are described as "tech savvy"; they like informality, learn quickly (Twenge et al., 2010), and value team work, collective action, and diversity (Zemke et al., 2000). Further, "millennials are more individualistic and self-focused, inspiring the label Generation Me" (Twenge et al., 2010, p. 1118).

In sum, four generations are working together in the contemporary workplace. Similar to the discourse on race, gender, and class, scholars often conceptualize generational differences as another form of diversity and tend to underscore the intersections among the categories that result in misunderstanding and resentment between the generational cohorts at work (Raines, 2003).

According to the research literature, race, ethnicity, and culture are individual differences that most qualified researchers and self-professed authorities represented in the generational literature ignore (Reeves & Oh, 2007). The primary exception to this finding is Twenge (2006), who gives considerable attention to race. With regard to race, her analysis concludes that GenMe (equivalent to the Millennials) "will continue the shift toward equality across race" [and] "that race will become less important as a defining characteristic" (p. 214).

Theoretical Perspectives

Theoretical frameworks associated with generations and generational diversity in the workforce provides a lens by which to examine the ways in which each generation views the world. The significance of theory in this context is its ability to explain and predict intergenerational tensions in the workforce.

Generation Theory

The generational perspective, which is commonly ascribed to Mannheim (1952), emphasizes the importance of social factors in human development. Accordingly, generational models view development as an interaction between the individual and the social events that happen and influence the cohort. Scott (2000) elaborates on the generational approach in describing its effects:

> . . . those born at the same time may share similar formative experiences that coalesce into a "natural" view of the world. This natural view stays with the individual throughout their lives and is the anchor against which later experiences are interpreted. People are thus fixed in qualitatively different subjective areas. (p. 356)

Scott's explanation supports the notion of ascribed generational categories, which are used to delineate generational cohort groupings in the workplace. These common life experiences, including historical and social events, create cohesiveness in values, attitudes, and beliefs that result in a social character or personality distinct to each generational cohort. These generational personalities are formed through socialization and remain relatively stable throughout the cohort's lifetime.

Disengagement Theory

Central to the discussion of generations in the workplace is the intersection of age and work. Social gerontologists, who study the ageing process and its affect on individuals and society, draw from a number of theoretical perspectives. Among the most popular is **disengagement theory** (Cumming & Henry, 1961), which submits that there is a mutual process of withdrawal that happens between ageing individuals and society. Ageing individuals willingly withdraw from society as they experience a decrease in their capacities. Similarly, society withdraws from ageing individuals to permit younger people to occupy the former statutes of older individuals. In this way, the stability of the society is maintained and social roles are passed, without contest, from one generation to the next (Perry & Perry, 2009). Disengagement theory is useful in predicting the impact of the shift in age demographics on the workforce as it relates to succession planning in organizations, as well as recruitment within organizations whereby employees who reach retirement age (i.e., older generations) exit the workforce and younger people (i.e., younger generations) enter the workforce or transition into vacant positions, which may foster potential for intergenerational tensions and conflict in the workforce. Additionally, many organizations are especially concerned about the retirement of the Boomers, who according to Kane (2009) are retiring at a rate of 8,000 per day. Apprehension within organizations centers on an unprecedented loss in skilled labor that is predicted to dramatically impact the workforce. Subsequently, many organizations are developing and implementing phased retirement programs to address skills shortages.

Modernization Theory

Another theory that some social scientists use to explain the changing social status of ageing adults is **modernization theory**. This theory posits that as the society becomes more modern, the status of older people diminishes. In an industrial and postindustrial society like the United States, emphasis is placed on youth and the importance of highly skilled occupations for which the elderly are not prepared. Subsequently, the elderly relinquish status (Aboderin, 2004). This theory can be extended to contemporary organizations that value and seek workers with technological proficiency, therefore providing opportunities for training and development. Furthermore, as Generations X and Y workers bring to the workforce work-related skills that Veterans and Boomers may not have, the younger generations either advance to managerial roles in which they supervise older workers or transition into positions of former older workers who are now retirees. This scenario, as well, presents the opportunity for intergenerational conflict at work.

Activity Theory

Activity theory, the polar opposite of disengagement theory, assumes that older people who remain active, substituting outdated roles with current ones that also require interaction with others are best adjusted (Dowd, 1975). Activity theory can help to explain the importance placed on training, development, and continuing education in many organizations, providing opportunities for older workers to update existing or acquire new technological skills, which benefits the workers and the organization. Occupational analysts, researchers, and practitioners use elements of these four theories to diagnose and explicate the social dynamics of American generations in the workforce.

Generational Differences in the Workplace

Although several generational groupings have simultaneously occupied the same workplace in the past, the distinct generations were usually separated from each other as a result of occupational segregation in the workplace (Kogan, 2007). Traditionally, workplaces were stratified by job positions, and generations such that older employees held upper-management positions, middle-aged employees tended to occupy middle-management positions, and younger workers, usually lacking work experience, were commonly placed in entry-level positions (Kogan, 2007). Unlike earlier organizations, members of various generations work more closely together in the modern workplaces that Zemke et al. (2000) refers to as **generational mixing** (p. 10). In addition to working together, the distinctive generations compete for advanced opportunities in the workplace. The organizational management literature increasingly underscores a shift in the validity and use of the traditional model that conceptualizes power, resources, and job position flowing from older employees to younger employees in the contemporary workplace (Kreitner & Kinicki, 2007). Accordingly, advancement in the organization is linked less to seniority and more to merit. For example, a Generation X employee could manage a Traditional or Baby Boomer employee.

Further, the generational personality or identity is also likely to influence individual's work behavior and the expectations of work responsibility of others (Gursoy, Maier, & Chi, 2008). Due to generational differences, these expectations vary from generation to generation. Therefore, people from different generations may have difficulty understanding others' perspectives on work, which can be "stressful, confusing, and frustrating in a workplace" (Zemke, et al., 2000, p. 11) and possibly lead to intergenerational conflict. For instance, Veteran employees were influenced by the social experience of the Great Depression and tended to be savers and less likely to take risks because they experienced significant hardships at an informative age (Meredith, Schewe, & Karlovich, 2002). Accordingly, they bring their own unique values and perspectives to the workplace, which influence their loyalty to the organization and characterizes them as hardworking, respectful, and silent employees. Influenced by the Vietnam War and the Civil Rights Movement, the Baby Boomer generation learned that diligent work over time produces desired outcomes. Subsequently, Boomer employees are credited with inventing the "60-hour workweek" (Meredith et al., 2002), and they work long hours to achieve organizational goals, receive recognition of their job performance, and live a lifestyle that reflects their work ethic. Baby Boomer workers tend to be competitive in the workplace as a result of the large size of the Boomer generation. Influenced by their parents' long work hours taking them away from home and their "workaholic" tendencies, Generation X employees tend to avoid extended work hours in an effort to achieve work–life balance, prioritizing their personal lives over their work lives. These employees are described as independent workers who are self-reliant, resourceful, and outspoken, which are skills that likely reflect Gen Xers' social experience as latch-key children. Similar to the other three generational cohorts in the workplace, Millennials manifest a distinct personality profile as well. The Millennials were influenced by key social events such as the Internet, the September 11th terrorist attacks, and the recession and at work tend to search out opportunities for professional growth and development, adapting quickly in the face of change and uncertainty. Moreover, in a study on generational differences in the workplace, Twenge et al. (2010) found that GenMe and Gen Xers place a higher value on leisure time than the Boomer generation. They explain,

> GenX and especially GenMe grew up witnessing these social and labor trends and enter the workforce with the expectation of increasing work hours, the need for a dual-income household, and limited vacation time, it makes sense that the value of additional leisure time is particularly strong among theses cohorts. . . . However, given that GenMe values extrinsic reward more than Boomers did, the combination of not wanting to work hard but still wanting more money and status verifies the sense of entitlement many have identified among GenMe. (p. 1134)

According to Zemke et al. (2000), Millennials most closely resemble the Veteran employees in their perspectives. However, Twenge et al. (2010) challenges this proposition by highlighting a disconnect between GenMe's value of leisure time (e.g., not wanting to work overtime) and expectation of more status and compensation. These researchers attribute this inconsistency to GenMe's sense of overconfidence—not just confidence—that is typical of GenMe, also called the Millennials. Additionally, the study findings suggested that "the importance of intrinsic values has declined slightly over the generations, suggesting the younger generations are not necessarily searching for meaning at work. However, intrinsic values are still among the job characteristics rated most highly by GenMe" (Twenge et al., p. 1134).

Intergenerational Tensions in the Workforce

The interaction between members of different generations is known as **intergenerationality** (Raines, 2003), and intergenerational tensions often result from misunderstandings of and the lack of respect for generational groups. Intergenerational problems are of concern to organizations because they have been shown to affect job satisfaction, retention, and turnover (Zemke et al., 2000). Additionally, theorists predict organizations that employ a broad spectrum of generations will experience challenges in resolving the conflict that results from the varied needs of each generational cohort. Perry and Perry (2009) refer to **conflict** as a clash between incompatible people, ideas, or interests and describe it as diametrically opposed to cooperation. In the workforce, conflict between and among generations manifests as intergroup conflict. As an illustration, an older generation and a younger generation arguing over work and life expectations are engaged in intergroup conflict. For example, Boomers may disapprove of Gen Xers because they conclude their workday promptly at 5 p.m., which for Boomers reflects an unwillingness to work hard and "go the extra mile."

By contrast, the Gen Xers frown on the Boomers for remaining late at work, which suggests to Xers a lack of work–life balance and existence outside of work. According to a Twenge and colleagues' study (2010), Gen Xers valued extrinsic values higher than GenMe and the Boomers generation. These scholars suggested that "economic forces" could explain this effect.

> . . .for example, GenX and GenMe have seen a consistent increase in the demand for and cost of higher education and the necessity of dual-income households, while simultaneously being required to work more hours. Thus, the increased desire for extrinsic rewards and more leisure time could be in part a reflection of the increased financial demands and the decrease in leisure time characterizing the U.S. workplace. (p. 1134)

Intergenerational engagement can create tensions in the workplace due to generational differences in values, perspectives, work styles, communication styles, and attire preferences. Unfortunately, the outcome of differences among generational cohorts in the workplace often generate **intergenerational conflict**, which Zemke et al. (2000) defines as "differences in values and views, and ways of working, talking and thinking that set people in opposition to one another and challenge organizational best interests" (p. 11). A few specific differences between generations include communication styles, work values (i.e., views about loyalty and acceptance of change), and habits and comfort with technology.

Work Values

Generational theory suggests that fundamental value differences exist between those of different generations. Generational differences in

work values can affect the perceived fit of employees with the organization (Twenge et al., 2010, p. 1137). Kreitner and Kinicki (2007) define
values as an "enduring belief in a mode of conduct" or desired outcome
(p. 78). Whereas **espoused values** refer to the stated values and norms
that are preferred by an organization, and **enacted values** refer to the
values and norms that are actually displayed by employees (Kreitner &
Kinicki, 2007). Organizational climates often reflect the values and
goals of founding members of organizational leaders; at the time, these
leaders are largely Boomers. GenMe employees who are newcomers to
an organization may experience a person–organization misfit caused
by generational differences and differing work values from founding
members or organizational leaders (Twenge et al., 2010). The blend-
ing of people of different generations in the workplace suggests that
employees can bring their own unique values, which sometimes leads
to conflict among the generations.

Empirical findings identify intergenerational differences in values
(Smola & Sutton, 2002), in world views, in perspectives on work (Gursoy et al., 2008), communication styles, and attire preferences (Raines,
2003). These differences between generations can be a source of considerable conflict in the workplace (e.g., Jurkiewicz, 2000; O'Bannon,
2001; Society for Human Resource Management, 2004).

According to Gursoy et al. (2008), these generational differences are
likely to generate additional conflicts in the workforce. Glass (2007)
identifies work ethic as a major work value that often results in conflict
among generational cohorts in the workplace.

Work Ethic

Each generational group has a unique pattern of behavior based on
their shared experiences (Kupperschmidt, 2000; Smola & Sutton,
2002; Westerman & Yamamura, 2007). For instance, Veterans value
hard work and believe in paying their dues. They become aggravated
when they perceive that younger generations do not work as hard nor
as many hours as they do, which is often due to Generation X and the
Millennials' use of technological options such as telecommuting or
having a virtual office, which Veterans and Boomers may view as dis-
tracting from a unified, productive work environment (Glass, 2007).

Veterans often feel that their career, for the most part, defines them (Murphy, 2007). Similar to their Veteran parents, Baby Boomers value hard work. However, the difference between Veterans and Boomers is that Boomers work diligently because they perceive it necessary for upward mobility, whereas Veterans work hard because they believe it is the right thing to do.

While Generation X works hard, their focus is on results and the completion of the assignment on or before the due date. Whereas Boomers are working hard to climb the corporate ladder, Gen Xers are working hard to create more time to balance work and personal obligations. The Millennials' perspective differs from the older generations in that Millennials value technology as a tool for multitasking, outcome as priority rather than how or where the work was done, and they value positive feedback more so than the other generations (Glass, 2007).

Smola and Sutton (2002) explored differences among generations with regard to work values and beliefs. Through a comparison of a survey completed in 1974 among workers and a simplified version of the same survey in 1999, three questions are answered:

a. Are there generational differences in work values among today's employees?
b. Are the values of today's workers different from those of 1974?
c. Do work values remain constant or change as workers grow older?

Smola and Sutton (2002) concluded that as the times change, so do work values across generations, and the need for companies to accommodate these changes is paramount.

Westerman and Yamamura's (2007) research into the generational preferences of work environment fit found goal orientation to have greater influence on satisfaction and intent to remain with the organization for Generation X, whereas relationship fit had greater influence for Baby Boomers' satisfaction and intention to remain. Neither study (Smola & Sutton, 2002; Westerman & Yamamura, 2007) measured generational differences for the newest group to enter the workforce, Generation Y (Millennials; born between 1980 and 1994). Gen Y or

Millennials are seen to be influenced by technology advances and have observed parents being affected by corporate downsizing similar to the experience of Gen Xers. Thus, Smola and Sutton (2002) purport that Gen Y will want even higher salaries, flexible work arrangements, and more financial leverage than Gen X.

Vendramin (2009) makes a distinction between generational tensions related to work and those related to employment by suggesting that areas of tension between generations are not related to work, but rather employment. The discourse of one generation regarding another is more contentious when employment is at stake and that perhaps those who feel more threatened by competition in work are most divisive. By contrast, Hess and Jepsen (2009) report only small but significant differences between generational cohort groupings with regard to perceptions of work.

Communication

Communication is another work value, and the differing modalities of communication often produce tension among generational cohorts. Understanding the communication styles and preferences of each generational cohort may help in reducing intergenerational tensions at work. As a group, Veterans are private and typically do not share their feelings and thoughts immediately, hence the label the "silent generation." In the workplace, Veterans prefer face-to-face or written communication and value verbal and public acknowledgment of their experience. Similarly, Baby Boomers value highly face-to-face and voice-to-voice communication. While most have acquired computer skills, Boomers use technology less often than younger generations. They prefer an open, direct, and relational style of communication, which allows opportunities for questions (Glass, 2007). Since their technology skills are acquired, Boomers may be less apt to incorporate these skills into their daily work regime (Gordon & Steele, 2005). While Generation X employees have a preference for e-mail as a primary communication tool, they tend to use whatever communication method is most efficient. They appreciate an informal communication style and favor short sound bites rather than lengthy lectures. Most Millennial employees prefer instant messaging, text messaging (or Twitter or Yammer), and e-mails and often post to various social networking sites much more frequently than older generations. They favor an informal, humorous mode of communication and dislike condescending, patronizing language (Zemke et al., 2000). The older generations regard the Millennial's overreliance on e-mail, particularly in situations where tensions are brewing, as a lack of interpersonal competency. Conversely, the younger generations view the older generations' preference for face-to-face communication as resistance to change, as it relates to digital forms of communications.

In an international survey conducted by Kelly Services (2010) examining communication style, Kelly Services obtained responses of approximately 100,000 people in 34 countries covering North America, Europe, and Asia Pacific. Survey participants included the three main workplace generations—Gen Y (aged 18 to 29), Gen X (aged 30 to 47), and Boomers (aged 48 to 65). Findings suggest that Gen Y is increasingly using instant messaging, however all generational cohorts overwhelmingly prefer face-to-face communication. Research findings suggest that by addressing issues such as internal communications, it is possible to manage the generational divide in the workplace, increase performance, and address interpersonal tensions. The research findings on communication with generations in the workplace indicate that employees of all generations want to be heard and feel respected.

Ando and Kobayashi (2008) study seniority systems in organizations that have at least three generations employed. Overall, the authors use an economic model of overlapping generations to demonstrate that seniority solves much of these generational conflicts in the sense that action directed toward future planning is sustainable in equilibrium.

Strategies for Managing Intergenerational Conflict in the Workplace

Much of the literature on generational difference in the workforce emphasizes the importance of engaging the best talent of all four generations. The overarching goal is to match generational preferences with strategies that assist employees in increasing performance and productivity and reducing the intergenerational tensions. Sago (2000) offers the following suggestions for dealing with generational issues that are often found in the workplace.

- **Minimize personal generational framework.** It is only natural for people to look at the world through their own set of values and experiences. In terms of intergenerational interactions, people judge others by their own framework that has been heavily influenced by their generation's formative events, traits, and characteristics. In dealing with members of other generations, it is important to minimize the use of lenses that tint how people and circumstances are judged.
- **Build knowledge and skills.** Increasing the knowledge and skills of the workforce can not only improve productivity, but it can also be a valuable tool for retaining staff. Having seen the parents of their generation suffer through the layoffs of the 1970s and 1980s, younger workers especially value training and education, and attainment of more skills makes employees more marketable in the job market. However, worker improvement programs actually encourage younger employees to stay with an organization longer.
- **Deal with changing work–life expectations.** One variable that has undergone a massive transformation is the changed perception of the desire to balance work and life. For the Veterans and Boomers, the prevailing attitude was "live to work." People tended to build or strengthen their self-identity from their professions. Conversely, Gen Xers and Gen Yers are more likely to "work to live." Jobs afford the means to experience and enjoy other facets of life.

While generational differences are inevitable, organizations can manage intergenerational tensions by focusing on the strengths, experiences, and potential of each generational cohort.

Creating a Successful Intergenerational Workforce

Zemke et al. (2000) suggest "aggressive communication" and "difference deployment" as two keys to creating a successful intergenerational workforce (p. 153). In aggressive conversations, generational conflicts and potential conflicts are realized. Underlying assumptions and unrecognized criteria or stereotypes are at the foundation of many generational differences. In aggressive, forward communication, the negative interactions and behaviors in the workplace can be redirected to positive activities where different perspectives and alternative points of view contribute to rather than detract from collaborative efforts. Therefore, effective and efficient communication practices often characterize companies in which an intergenerational workforce works best. These organizations have created a structure such that small group discussion, generationally integrated staff meetings, and conversations about different views and perspectives are common. Intergenerational conflict is often characterized by passive-aggressive behaviors and verbal attacks. Generational diversity is perhaps best managed when an organizational structure allows time for employees to talk about what members from different generational cohorts find interesting and rewarding about work and what type of work environment is most productive. For example, views on alternative work schedules, work load, and workplace policies on initiatives like flexibility scheduling and telecommuting may vary across generations. A structure that allows time to communicate alternative views reflective of diverse sets of values and approaches to work contributes to a workplace that attracts and retains people with differing needs and expectations of work and employment.

Difference deployment is what Zemke et al. (2000) refers to as the strategic use of employees with different backgrounds, experiences, skills, and viewpoints to strengthen interpersonal relations in a variety of workplace contexts. In organizations that practice difference deployment, there is intentional effort to integrate diverse perspectives and incorporate differences into work practices. "Generationally savvy organizations value the differences between people and look at differences as strengths" (Zemke et al., 2000, p. 154). This notion of difference deployment is consistent with the "learning and effectiveness" paradigm introduced by Thomas and Ely (2001) as a framework for effectively managing diversity in the workplace.

Managing Generational Diversity

There are, of course, a variety of approaches for understanding and attempting to manage diversity in the workplace. Each perspective or framework for understanding the issues focuses on slightly different aspects that result in different levels of effectiveness given the context in which it is implemented. Among the various ways for understanding and managing diversity in the workplace are approaches that emphasize assimilation, accommodation, celebration of differences, or education and learning. Key aspects of each of these perspectives are presented in Figure 10.2.

Approaches to diversity management that aim to *assimilate* are characterized by intentional efforts to reconcile an imbalanced demography in the workforce. This approach is based on the notion that minority characteristics will assimilate and become more like the mainstream. Organizations that follow this approach may actively recruit and hire individuals from each generational cohort, but maintain an underlying

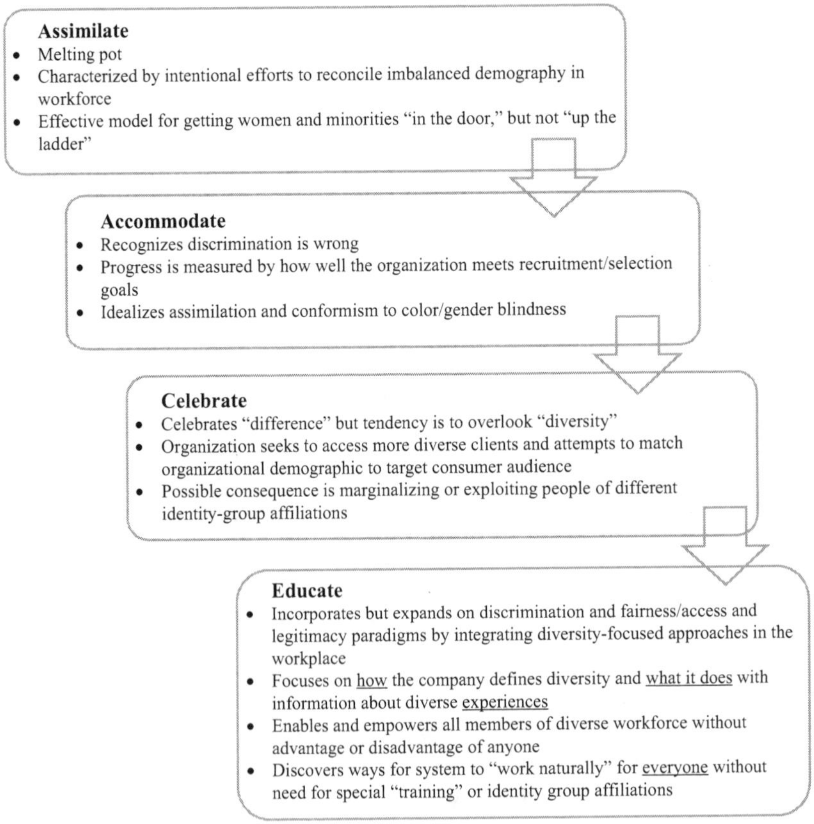

Assimilate
- Melting pot
- Characterized by intentional efforts to reconcile imbalanced demography in workforce
- Effective model for getting women and minorities "in the door," but not "up the ladder"

Accommodate
- Recognizes discrimination is wrong
- Progress is measured by how well the organization meets recruitment/selection goals
- Idealizes assimilation and conformism to color/gender blindness

Celebrate
- Celebrates "difference" but tendency is to overlook "diversity"
- Organization seeks to access more diverse clients and attempts to match organizational demographic to target consumer audience
- Possible consequence is marginalizing or exploiting people of different identity-group affiliations

Educate
- Incorporates but expands on discrimination and fairness/access and legitimacy paradigms by integrating diversity-focused approaches in the workplace
- Focuses on how the company defines diversity and what it does with information about diverse experiences
- Enables and empowers all members of diverse workforce without advantage or disadvantage of anyone
- Discovers ways for system to "work naturally" for everyone without need for special "training" or identity group affiliations

Figure 10.2   Model for Managing Diversity

assumption that work values and the prioritization of work relative to nonwork will be as alike and easily predictable as possible. In the pursuit of sameness, these approaches often do not take full advantage of the human resources available from individuals who happen to be outside of the mainstream identity group. Although assimilation approaches are effective for getting diverse populations "in the door," they have had less success helping individuals from non-majority identity groups "up the ladder" to supervisory management or leadership positions.

Likewise, approaches that aim to *accommodate* recognize the injustice inherent in negative discrimination. Thomas and Ely (2001) suggest that this "discrimination and fairness paradigm" idealizes assimilation and conformism to color and gender blindness. Zemke et al. (2000) argue that "generationally blind organizations" also operate as if to homogenize employees and fit them to a single template of the "good employee" (p. 154). A generationally friendly work environment is one in which there is open communication and differences are valued and discussed as sources of individual and organizational effectiveness.

A more common model for practice in organizations is one that seeks to access more diverse clients and attempts to match the organizational demographic to target consumer audiences. These approaches *celebrate* "differences" but overlook "diversity" in pursuit of differentiation. Managing diversity by celebrating differences comes with a possible consequence of marginalizing or exploiting people of different identity-group affiliations.

The generational diversity in the current available workforce offers access for organizations to deploy differences in skills, perspectives, and values across the lifespan. Strategic and effective deployment of skills that takes full advantage of the strengths of a diverse workforce requires a willingness to *educate* and learn about the generational differences.

A legitimacy and learning paradigm incorporates but expands on the discrimination and fairness paradigm and the access and legitimacy paradigm by integrating diversity-focused approaches to learning from everyone in the workplace. This approach promotes equal opportunity in ways that work naturally for everyone without imposing special training sessions or workshops designed to orient individuals who are not already viewed as part of the mainstream. The aim is to enable and empower all members of a diverse workforce without advantage or disadvantage to anyone. As such, organizations internalize differences among the workforce so that it learns and grows because of the diversity resources, not despite them. The focus, then, is on how the company defines diversity and what it does with information about diverse experiences among the workforce.

Chapter Summary

Four generations are currently working side by side in the U.S. workforce. The distinct generations are referred to as Veterans (1921–1940); Baby Boomers (1941–1960); Generation X (1961–1980); and Millennials (1981–2000). Older, middle-age, and younger employees share common work responsibilities. However, unique work values, communication preferences, and expectations of these distinct generations may differ seriously. These differences between generations tend to make conflict in the workplace inevitable. Consequently, organizations are becoming increasingly interested in understanding the needs and preferences of each generation in the workplace and in managing generational tensions, particularly since this kind of conflict has been linked to overall job dissatisfaction, ineffective performance, and employee attrition.

Key to understanding generations in the workforce is awareness of the generational perspective, which posits that individuals born during the same general time span experience significant life events that happened during their formative years and subsequently influenced their world view. It is this inherent view that characterizes and identifies each generation, and in addition to generating a generational personality, it serves as a relatively stable template for successive experiences. To illustrate this concept, consider the Boomers generation that came of age during the civil and women's rights era. Many individuals of this generation are revered in today's society as advocates and activists for human rights and social justice issues.

Generational differences often emerge in the workforce due to the expectations, desires, and views that tend to vary from generation to generation. Employees from one generation, for instance, may have difficulty understanding another generation's ways of doing work, which can produce feelings of stress, aggravation, and tension. Intergenerational tensions in the workforce are often the result of interaction between generations at work, increasing the potential for conflict over contradictory work values, expectations, and preferences among generations in the workplace.

Managing intergenerational conflict involves a variety of methods, including practical applications such as minimizing personal generational framework, building knowledge and skills, and dealing with work–life preferences. Researchers identify "aggressive communication" and "difference deployment" as two important tactics to creating a successful intergenerational workforce. The focus is on effective interpersonal and open communication skills. Assimilation, accommodation, celebration of differences, or education and learning are approaches for understanding and attempting to manage generational diversity in the workplace. The literature on generational difference in the workforce emphasizes the importance of engaging the best talent of all four generations. Although generational differences have received less attention as a dimension of diversity when compared with gender, race, and ethnicity, differences among generations are increasingly impacting the workforce and garnering attention from practitioners, theorists, and researchers.

Definition of Key Terms

Activity theory—The polar opposite of disengagement theory, it assumes that older people who remain active, substituting outdated roles with current ones that also require interaction with others, are best adjusted.

Aggressive communication—Proposes that the negative interactions and behaviors in the workplace can be redirected to positive activities.

Baby Boomer generation—Born between 1941 and 1960, this is currently the largest cohort in the workforce, comprising 44% of the U.S. workforce. The Boomers are referred to as the baby boom due to the 17 million babies born during that period.

Conflict—A clash between incompatible people, ideas, or interests and described as diametrically opposed to cooperation.

Difference deployment—Refers to the strategic use of employees with different backgrounds, experience, skills, and viewpoints to strengthen interpersonal relations in a variety of workplace contexts.

Disengagement theory—Submits that there is a mutual process of withdrawal that happens between ageing individuals and society. Ageing individuals willingly withdraw from society as they experience a decrease in their capacities. Similarly, society withdraws from ageing individuals to permit younger people to occupy the former statutes of older individuals. In this way, the stability of the society is maintained and social roles are passed, without contest, from one generation to the next.

Enacted values—Refers to the values and norms that are actually displayed by employees.

Espoused values—Refers to the stated values and norms that are preferred by an organization.

Generation—People born in the same general time span who are approximately the same age and have in common key historical or societal experiences.

Generation theory—Emphasizes the importance of the social factor in human development. Accordingly, generational models view development as an interaction between the individual and the social events that happen and influence the cohort.

Generation X—Born between1961 and 1980, this is a significantly smaller cohort in the workforce compared with the Baby Boomer generation and accounts for 33% of the U.S. labor force. They are also called Gen Xers.

Generational cohort—Defined as a group of people who have come of age (e.g., adolescence or young adult) about the same time while sharing similar external events that create cohesiveness in values, attitudes, and preferences, which remains relatively constant throughout the cohort's lifetime and results in a social personality distinct to each generational group.

Generational mixing—Refers to the practice of various generations working closely together in the modern workplaces.

Intergenerational conflict—Refers to the differences in values, views, ways of working, talking, and thinking that set people in opposition to one another that challenge organizational best interests.

Intergenerationality—The interaction between members of different generations.

Millennial generation—Born between 1981 and 2000, Millennials are also called Generation Y, Nexters, and GenMe. They currently comprise 15% of the workforce, with 22 million workers.

Modernization theory—Posits that as the society becomes more modern, the status of older people diminishes. In an industrial and postindustrial society like the United States, emphasis is placed on youth and the importance of highly skilled occupations for which the elderly are not prepared. Subsequently, the elderly relinquish status.

Values—Enduring belief in a mode of conduct or desired outcome.

Veteran generation—Born between 1921 and 1940, this is the oldest generation in the workforce and is identified by the label of the "silent generation" as a result of a perceived quiet, industrious demeanor. This generation includes individuals born before 1940 and is also known as Traditionals and Matures.

Critical-Thinking Discussion Questions

1. List and describe the four generations in the workforce.
2. Describe the concept of generational personality.
3. Discuss an alternative view of generations.
4. Compare disengagement theory and activity theory.
5. Provide an example of intergroup conflict in the workplace.
6. How might the workplace culture be cultivated to foster positive intergenerational relations?
7. What are three strategies for managing intergenerational conflict in the workplace? What is the overarching goal in the process of managing this type of conflict?
8. Compare strategies for managing generational diversity that aims to assimilate with a strategy that celebrates differences.
9. What are specific components of the education and learning approach to managing generational diversity in the workplace?
10. What is the interplay between differences in work values and intergenerational tension in the workplace?

Case Study 1: Generational Communication Differences

Sam Gladstone, vice president for customer relations in a medium-sized electronics company, is concerned about the efficiency and effectiveness of customer service delivery for a few of the company's most popular products. Sam organized a highly functioning work team consisting of members from several different generations to recommend solutions for addressing customer complaints. After several weeks of collecting information from unsatisfied customers and from individuals within the company responsible for direct customer service delivery, the team discovers a pattern of complaints from younger workers about the curt tone from managers and supervisors. Specifically, younger workers report feeling disrespected when they receive commands rather than requests from supervisors and managers. The customers reported that customer service representatives were disrespectful and often seemed short with them. When the team reported these findings to Sam he suspected that the tension between younger workers and older managers and supervisors is spilling over to interactions between customer service representatives and the customers.

Discussion Questions

1. What are some strategic approaches that Sam Gladstone might consider in working toward resolving the communication differences and generational tensions between younger workers and older managers/supervisors?
2. What generational differences in communication style may be contributing to the tensions experienced in the workplace?
3. While there are a variety of approaches for understanding and attempting to manage diversity in the workplace, which approach (perhaps unintended) may currently be in operation?

Case Study 2: Intergenerational Tensions—Differing Communication Styles

Stacy Altman, general manager of a small debt-consolidation company, is concerned about the interpersonal tensions she has observed building among employees from different generations. All of the staff members are committed to achieving organizational goals, and the company consistently receives strong positive feedback for providing high-quality customer service. However, Stacy has observed several exchanges during staff meetings that have her concerned about how well some of the staff will be able to continue to work together as a team. Some of her older employees complain that the younger workers are "self-centered, difficult to interact with, and overly service-focused." Younger employees respond that the older workers are "stodgy, slow, and resistant to change when it comes to the use of technology." When Stacy listens to the younger and older employees interact, she notices that they use very different language depending on whether they are communicating with coworkers from their own generation or from an older or younger generation. For example, she notices that when Millennials talk with each other, they use words like *sweet, mega, dawg, NOT, whatever, LOL, don't even,* or *chill.* However, as a Boomer, she remembers using words like *groovy, bummer, bummed out,* and *gnarly.* It is becoming increasingly clear to Stacy why the employees from the older generation perceive younger people as using too much slang, having poor communication skills, and being difficult, entitled, and service-focused, yet she wonders if they are really that much different. When these now older people were the age of Millennials today, previous generations characterized them in similar ways.

Discussion Questions

1. What strategy would you recommend for Stacy to consider in her attempt to resolve this intergenerational tension?
2. As a general manager, how might Stacy create a successful intergenerational workforce team and manage the generational diversity in her organization?
3. What generational differences in communication style may be contributing to the tensions experienced in the workplace?

References

Aboderin, I. (2004). Modernisation and ageing theory revisited: Current explanations of recent developing world and historical Western shifts in material family support for older people. *Ageing and Society, 24,* 29–50. doi:10.1017/S0144686X03001521

Ando, M., & Kobayashi, H. (2008). Intergenerational conflicts of interest and seniority systems in organizations. *Journal of Economic Behavior & Organization, 65,* 757–767. doi:10.1016/j.jeb0.2006.01.005

Beutell, N.J., & Wittig-Berman, U. (2008). Work–family conflict and work–family synergy for generation X, baby boomers, and matures: Generational differences, predictors, and satisfaction outcomes. *Journal of Managerial Psychology, 23,* 507–523.

Clochesy, J.M. (2008). A generational shift in the diversity landscape. *Diversity Factor, 16,* 22–29.

Crampton, S.M., & Hodge, J.W. (2006). The supervisor and generational differences. *Proceedings of the Academy of Organizational Culture, Communications and Conflict, 11,* 19–22.

Cumming, E., & Henry, W. (1961). *Growing old.* New York: Basic Books.

Dencker, J., Joshi, A., & Martocchio, J.J. (2007). Employee benefits as context for intergenerational conflict. *Human Resource Management Review, 17,* 208–220. doi:10.1016/j.hrmr.2007.04.002

Dowd, J.J. (1975). Aging as exchange: A preface to theory. *Journal of Gerontology, 30,* 584–594.

Glass, A. (2007). Understanding generational differences for competitive success. *Industrial and Commercial Training, 39,* 98–103.

Gordon, V.N., & Steele, M.J. (2005). The advising workplace: Generational differences and challenges. *NACADA Journal, 25,* 26–30.

Gursoy, D., Maier, T.A., & Chi, C.G. (2007). Generational differences: An examination of work values and generational gaps in the hospitality workforce. *International Journal of Hospitality Management, 27,* 448–458. doi:10.1016/j.ijhm.2007.11.002

Hess, N., & Jepsen, D.M. (2009). Career stage and generational differences in psychological contracts. *Career Development International, 14,* 261–283. doi:10.1108/13620430910966433

Howe, N., Strauss, W., & Matson, R.J. (2000). *Millennials rising: The next great generation.* New York: Vintage.

Jenkins, J. (2007). Leading the four generations at work. Retrieved February 21, 2010, from www.amanet.org/movingahead/editorial.cfm?Ed=452

Jorgenson, B. (2003). Baby boomers, generation X and generation Y. Policy implications for defense forces in the modern era. *Foresight, 5,* 41–49.

Jurkiewicz, C.E. (2000). Generation X and the public employee. *Public Personnel Management, 29,* 55–74.

Jurkiewicz, C.L., & Brown, R.G. (1998). GenXers vs. Boomers vs. Matures. *Review of Public Personnel Administration, 18*(4), 18.

Kane, S. (2009). Multi-generational workforce. Retrieved February 22, 2010, from http://legalcareers.about.com/od/practicetips/a/multigeneration.htm

Kelly Services. (2010). Kelly global workforce index. Retrieved February 25, 2011, from http://easypr.marketwire.com/easyir/msc2.do?easyirid=95BBA2C450798961

Kersten, D. (2002, November 15). Today's generations face new communication gaps. *USA Today.* Retrieved March 1, 2010, from www.usatoday.com/money/jobcenter/workplace/communication/2002-11-15-communication-gap_x.htm

Kogan, M. (2007). Human resources management: Bridging the gap. Retrieved March 3, 2010, from www.govexec.com/features/0901/0901s1.htm

Kreitner, R., & Kinicki, A. (2007). *Organizational behavior.* New York: McGraw-Hill Irwin.

Kupperschmidt, B.R. (2000). Multigeneration employees: Strategies for effective management. *Health Care Manager, 19,* 65–76.

Lancaster, L.C., & Stillman, D. (2002). *When generations collide: Who they are. Why they clash. How to solve the generational puzzle at work.* New York: Harper Collins.

Macky, K., Gardner, D., & Forsyth, S. (2008). Generational differences at work: Introduction and overview. *Journal of Managerial Psychology, 23,* 857–861. doi:10.1108/0268394081004358

Mannheim, K. (1952). *The problems of generations. Essays on the sociology of knowledge.* London: Routledge and Kegan Paul.

Meredith, G.E., Schewe, C.D., & Karlovich, J. (2002). *Defining markets, defining moments: America's 7 generational cohorts, their shared experiences, and why businesses should care.* New York: Hungry Minds.

Murphy, S.A. (2007). Leading a multigenerational workforce. Retrieved January 24, 2010, from http://assets.aarp.org/www.aarp.org_/articles/money/employers/leading_multigenerational_workforce.pdf

Niemiec, S. (2000). Finding common ground for all ages. SDM, Management. Retrieved February 12, 2010, from www.emeraldinsight.com/journals.htm?articleid=1463342&show=pdf

O'Bannon, G. (2001). Managing our future: The Generation X factor. *Public Personnel Management, 30,* 95–109.

Perry, J.A., & Perry, E.K. (2009). *Contemporary society: An introduction to social science.* Boston: Pearson.

Pitt-Catsouphes, M., & Smyer, M.A. (2007, June). The 21st century multi-generational workplace (Issue Brief 09). Chestnut Hill, MA: Center on Aging and Work. Retrieved March 15, 2010, from http://agingandwork .bc.edu/documents/IB09_MultiGenWorkplace_000.pdf

Raines, C. (2003). *Connecting generations: The sourcebook for a new workplace.* Menlo Park, CA: Crisp Publications.

Reeves, T.C., & Oh, E.J. (2007). Generation differences and educational technology research. In J.M. Spector, M.D. Merrill, J.J.G. van Merrienboer, & M. Driscoll (Eds.), *Handbook of research on educational communications and technology* (pp. 295–303). Mahwah, NJ: Lawrence Erlbaum Associates.

Reynolds, L.A. (2005). Communicating total rewards to the generations. *Benefits Quarterly, 21*(2), 13–17.

Sago, B. (2000). Uncommon threads: Mending the generation gap at work. Retrieved February 22, 2010, from www.asaecenter.org/PublicationsResources/ articledetail.cfm?ItemNumber=13100

Schaeffer, J. (2000). Kemper Reports (Winter-Spring). Kemper Distributors, Inc., Chicago, IL.

Scott, J. (2000). Is it a different world to when you were growing up? *The British Journal of Sociology, 51,* 355–76.

Shepard, S. (2004). Managing the Millennial. *Consultative Education in Global Telecommunications.* Shepard Communications Group, LCC.

Society for Human Resource Management. (2004). *Generational differences survey report.* Alexandria, VA: Author.

Smola, K.W., & Sutton C.D. (2002). Generational differences: Revisiting generational work values for the new millennium. *Journal of Organizational Behavior, 23,* 363–382. doi:10.1002/job.147

Thomas, D.A., & Ely, R.J. (2001). Making differences matter: A new paradigm for managing diversity. In *Harvard Business Review on managing diversity.* Boston: Harvard Business School Press.

Twenge, J.M. (2006). *Generation me: Why today's young Americans are more confident, assertive, entitled—and more miserable than ever before.* New York: Free Press.

Twenge, J.M., Campbell, S.M., Hoffman, B.J., & Lance, C.E. (2010). Generational differences in work values: Leisure and extrinsic values increasing, social and intrinsic values decreasing. *Journal of Management, 36*(5), 1117–1142. doi:10.1177/0149206309352246

Vendramin, P. (2009, March). *Age diversity and intergenerational relationships at the workplace.* Paper Presented at the 4th Conference of Young People & Societies around the Mediterranean, Forli. Retrieved March 15, 2010, from www.ftu-namur.org/fichiers/Forli-Vendramin.pdf

Westerman, J.W., & Yamamura, J.H. (2007). Generational preferences for work environment fit: Effects on employee outcomes. *Career Development International, 12,* 150.

Yang, S.M., & Guy, M.E. (2006). GenXers versus boomers: Work motivators and management implications. *Public Performance & Management Review, 29,* 267.

Zemke, R., Raines, C., & Filipczak, B. (2000). *Generations at work: Managing the clash of Veterans, Boomers, Xers, and Nexters in your workplace.* New York: American Management Association.

11

LINGUISTIC PROFILING IN THE WORKFORCE

Claretha Hughes and Ketevan Mamiseishvili

Chapter Overview

This chapter seeks to provide an understanding of how linguistic profiling has become an issue in today's workforce. Linguistic profiling is not a new phenomenon. It has existed for centuries; however, as the workplace has become more diverse, the occurrences of this type of profiling have become more prevalent. The chapter provides examples of linguistic profiling in the workplace and presents ways to recognize it and resolve problems that may arise as a result.

Learning Objectives

After reading this chapter, along with completing the chapter summary questions and the case discussion questions, you will be able to:

- Recognize examples of linguistic profiling in the workplace
- Analyze linguistic profiling case studies
- Identify potential legal and ethical issues related to linguistic profiling in the workplace
- Understand cultural, economic, and technological implications of linguistic profiling

Linguistic Profiling in the Workforce

Native Americans have the only valid claim on the American dialect in the United States. Besides Native Americans, everyone in

America is an immigrant or descendant thereof. The discussions and debates surrounding linguistic profiling would be null and void if the previous statements were accepted and respected in the American workplace; however, we know this to be untrue, thus the need for this chapter.

What is linguistic profiling? Baugh (2000) stated, "Linguistic profiling is based upon auditory cues that may be used to identify an individual or individuals as belonging to a linguistic subgroup within a given speech community, including a racial subgroup" (p. 363). Smalls (2004) defined linguistic profiling as the "term used to describe inferences that are often made about a person's speech. Inferences may include where a speaker is from, whether he/she is male or female, or whether he/she is native born to the United States" (p. 1). Incidents of linguistic profiling have reached the highest office in the United States, the President of the United States of America, since the election of President Barack Hussein Obama as the first African American president. It was noted by Heilemann and Halperin (2010) that some citizens believed that had then-candidate Obama chosen to use or had a noticeable "Negro" dialect during the 2008 presidential campaign, he probably would never have been elected. The history of linguistic profiling goes well beyond the American shorelines, but for this text we are going to limit our discourse to linguistic profiling in the American workforce.

Linguistic profiling research officially began after the *King v. Ann Arbor* Black English case of 1979 (Smitherman & Baugh, 2002). Within the *King v. Ann Arbor* case, the judge ruled that school-aged children must be taught regardless of their speech "deficiencies" as identified by their school district. Linguistic profiling may be one of the most subtle forms of discrimination in the U.S. workplace (Anderson, 2007; Rahman, 2008; Smalls, 2004; Squires & Chadwick, 2006). Baugh (2000) noted that "Linguistic profiling has been accepted as legal in some instances and illegally discriminatory in others" (p. 363). Often, linguistic profiling is accomplished during the interview process, especially with the introduction of telephone interviews (e.g., Atkins, 1993; Giles, Wilson, & Conway, 1981; Purkiss, Perrewe, Gillespie, Mayes, & Ferris, 2006). Many potential job candidates may have been screened out during the telephone interview, but it is hard to discern whether or not they did not effectively respond to the inter-view questions or whether they were discerned to have a dialect or tone of voice that the interviewer did not like or understand. It is a subtle form of bias. According to Rahman (2008), the perceptions of listeners are impacted by the interaction and overlap of meaning. Indi-viduals may have preconceived positive or negative attitudes regarding specific dialects that can impact their decisions.

Three key workplace implications of linguistic profiling that will be discussed are (1) cultural, (2) workplace and global economic, and (3) technological.

Cultural Implications

Within all organizations there are cultural implications that pertain to how they function. People within an organization often represent a diversity of cultures. They may be local, regional, national, and/or international. Yet, they are all asked to work together and communi-cate effectively to help the organization succeed. Communication is the thread that links people together within and across organizations, and without effective communication, success may be limited.

Lippi-Green (1997) explains that at the start of the communication process, people make immediate social evaluations based on the per-son's language or accent, which is directly linked to that person's race, ethnicity, or homeland. Rahman (2008) found that racial identity was identified by listeners in 28 seconds; Anderson (2007) showed that the same could be determined in only 16 seconds. Purnell, Idsardi, and Baugh (1999) found that 70% of their race or ethnicity subjects were identified correctly just after listeners heard them say the word "hello." The impact of the speed of identification is felt when judg-ments that impact an individual's potential for employment, ability to purchase or rent a home, and the ability to purchase home insurance are made almost instantaneously (Fischer & Massey, 2004; Massey & Lundy, 2001; Purnell et al., 1999; Rahman, 2008; Squires & Chad-wick, 2006).

The short time element suggests that there is an inane discrimina-tory culture of linguistic profiling within the American workforce. The ability to routinely reject and negatively impact a person's ability to prosper based on an auditory judgment may not be right, but it may not be illegal either. Baugh (2000) comments that:

> The challenge is to have the wisdom and patience to tolerate others whose linguistic backgrounds differ substantially from our own—to accentuate the benefits of preferential linguistic profiling while discarding the tradition of discriminatory linguistic profiling that fans the embers of racial discord, to the detriment of fairness. (pp. 363–364)

This begs us to consider the question of whether linguistic profiling is an ethical or legal issue. Rahman (2008) found that

> Speech that displays the exclusive use of features without regional or African American ethnic association leads to high judgments of standardness with concomitant perceptions of education, higher social class, and appropriateness for use in mainstream business environment. (p. 167)

Individuals use variations in language to construct themselves as social beings (Lippi-Green, 1997). Based on the analysis of 30 years of empirical work in sociolinguistics, Lippi-Green concludes that linguistic variations and social identity are naturally linked. Asking individuals to give up their accents means asking them to give up their social allegiances and "suppress or deny the most effective way they have of situating themselves socially in the world" (Lippi-Green, 1997, p. 63). It is illegal to ask people to change their religion, gender, race, or ethnicity. Then why is it okay to ask individuals to reject their language if the language is what defines the individual as a social being? As we ponder these issues, there may be legal consequences that have not yet been tested. How is it that we separate language from race and ethnicity without violating current law?

Individuals are often judged on the basis of how they speak and what language forms they use rather than the language content (Lippi-Green, 1997). Certain accents or dialects activate biased perceptions and judgments about a person's social status, personality traits, educational attainment, or intelligence (Atkins, 1993; Giles et al., 1981; Lippi-Green, 1997; Nesdale & Rooney, 1990; Purkiss et al., 2006). There is even a perceived link between intelligence and Standard English (e.g., Lippi-Green, 1997; Rahman, 2008); however, there is no statistical proof of this. One has to effectively define intelligence to validate this perception. If the standard is unattainable for those not exposed, that does not equate lack of intelligence. It may only require more time to acquire that particular knowledge and/or skill. Or, even better, a more accurate assessment of intelligence. Slaves did not speak Standard English; yet, they were intelligent enough to engineer many institutions and physical structures in America including the White House, the city of Washington, D.C., and the United States Capitol Building.

Linguistic profiling in its present state suggests and often requires those who do not speak "appropriate" Standard English to give up their culture. Why should this be acceptable, especially when the meaning of what is being said and communicated is clearly understood? There is no known economic depreciation that occurs as a result of someone's dialect or tone; yet, many are discriminated against in the workplace for having this natural difference. Issues of linguistic profiling need to be further researched and rectified to improve the workplace and community environment. Segregation in housing and discrimination in the cost of insurance and real estate has had a negative impact on the socioeconomic status or racial and ethnic communities in the United States (Smalls, 2004).

There is also a dilemma faced by many African Americans in the U.S. workforce. They are often forced to determine how to talk in the workplace by choosing between their community of birth and the "perceived" standard of excellence, in this case, what White America perceives to be best in order to obtain and/or retain a position for which they are otherwise qualified (Rahman, 2008). The issue of concern is not skill or performance qualification, but fear that linguistic profiling will be used to legally discriminate against them in the workplace. Smitherman and Baugh (2002) found that "racially distinct communities had resulted in linguistically distinct communities" (p. 8). Thus, many African Americans and nonnative speakers may become insecure once they realize that they are being judged based upon their origination from a distinct community of which they had no control.

Nonnative speakers of English are also often subjected to discrimination and prejudice in the workplace based on their foreign accents.

A foreign accent, even when it is perfectly well understood and clearly not a barrier to communication, may invoke very negative reactions and emotions from listeners (Lippi-Green, 1997; Munro, Derwing, & Sato, 2006). Stereotyping and discrimination on the basis of foreign accent occurs in a wide range of workplace settings, even at academic institutions, where we would expect that high level of education would bring some protection to foreign-born individuals from accent discrimination and bias (Lippi-Green, 1997; Munro et al., 2006). According to Lippi-Green (1997), "there is a strong resistance in the U.S. to teachers with foreign accents, and nowhere is that resistance so loudly voiced as in the university setting" (p. 124). Foreign-born instructors are often exposed to the same prejudice and stereotypes as other nonnative speakers of English in the United States, because "a Ph.D. cannot render anyone accentless" (Lippi-Green, 1997, p. 126).

Previous research has indicated that perceptions of foreign-born instructors' accents may influence judgments and evaluations of their teaching effectiveness (e.g., Manrique & Manrique, 1999; Rubin & Smith, 1990; Skachkova, 2007; Thomas, 1999). Skachkova's (2007) study that examined the academic life of 34 immigrant women professors in the United States suggested that accent was "the most problematic aspect of immigrant professors' teaching" (p. 707). Foreign-born women in Skachkova's study reported that their accents negatively affected students' course evaluations of their teaching quality and performance. Similar sentiments are expressed by Rong (2002) who notes that "a foreign appearance accompanied by an accent may immediately discount an instructor's credibility" (p. 136). Similar to African Americans, foreign-born faculty members may turn out to be excellent communicators and effective teachers, but they are often immediately discredited and challenged because of their foreign accents (Lippi-Green, 1997).

Of course, there are instances when the lack of language proficiency results in the communication failure in the classroom between a faculty member and a student. However, evidence suggests that the problem is generally not the language and communicative competence of the foreign-born instructors, but the perceptions about the accentedness of their speech (Lippi-Green, 1997; Rong, 2002; Rubin, 1992; Rubin & Smith, 1990; Skachkova, 2007). Evidence suggests that the accent that identifies the instructor as foreign "triggers expectations of poor teaching ability" (Rubin & Smith, 1990, p. 350). For example, Rubin and Smith's (1990) study is a good illustration of how listeners' language attitudes influence their perceptions of foreign instructors' teaching effectiveness. Based on the matched guise technique, 92 undergraduate students in Rubin and Smith's study were asked to listen to highly and moderately accented versions of 4-minute classroom lectures that were recorded in advance: one on a natural science and one on a humanities topic. Each participant listened to only one lecture topic given with either high or low levels of accent, while simultaneously looking at a photograph of either an Asian or a European looking instructor. Neither high nor low accented speech affected comprehension in this study, but "the higher the level of *perceived* accentedness, the lower the teaching ratings" were (Rubin & Smith, 1990, p. 349). In other words, "the degree to which subjects *believed* the speech samples were accented (as opposed to the level of actual accent)" influenced their ratings of foreign-born teaching assistants' teaching credibility (Rubin & Smith, 1990, p. 349).

Interestingly, not all foreign accents evoke the same reactions and stereotypes from listeners, because often discrimination on the basis of accent or dialect is not about the language itself, but about "the social circumstances and identities attached to that language" (Lippi-Green, 1992, p. 242). Nonnative speakers of Asian, African, and South American languages are subjected to even greater prejudice because these accents are linked to non-White race and signal "a third-world homeland" (Lippi-Green, 1997, p. 238). When the accent is linked to a specific race or a national origin, listeners' preconceived stereotypes about that ethnic or racial group are immediately activated and they cannot hear objectively. The results from Hosoda and Stone-Romero's (2010) study support Lippi-Green's (1997) observations. The study found that the job applicants with French accents were viewed more positively than applicants with Japanese accents for positions that required high levels of communication skills, even when for some study participants it was more difficult to comprehend the French than the Japanese accent. Hosoda and Stone-Romero suggest that the stereotypes associated with Asians may have influenced the study participants when making employment decisions and evaluating the applicants' fit for the job.

Why should African Americans or any racially or ethnically different individuals spend their productive work hours worrying about how they sound when their White peers know what they mean when they speak? There are many studies that measure productivity in the workplace. A wonderful future study could investigate how much productive time is lost due to linguistic profiling fears. Consider, for example, the time spent by thousands of students filling out faculty evaluations and determining whether or not they could understand their professor's "spoken language"—at the end of the semester, no less. Then consider the employees who analyze these data based on rating results and the time spent by faculty trying to understand what is actually being evaluated as opposed to focusing on course content, research, or service.

Workplace and Global Economic Implications

Throughout the world workplaces are continuously evolving to meet the global economic needs of diverse communities. Success within these workplaces is elevating the economic prosperity of people from all walks of life. Yet, there are still barriers that must be overcome for continuous improvement to occur. One of these barriers is linguistic profiling. There are many workplace and global economic implications that may occur as a result of linguistic profiling. Some implications to consider include:

- Cultural isolationism
- Diminished productivity
- Legal discrimination in hiring
- Reduced team/group effectiveness
- Reduced global economic activity
- Individual insecurity regarding job security

Cultural Isolationism

The culture of an organization is often considered to be its major strength. Every day, struggles of being discounted because of an accent or having to change the way one communicates may put a huge strain on employee morale and create an unnecessary stress (Thompson,

2006). Reduced employee morale adversely affects their job performance. When employees are culturally isolated because of their use of language or accent, their performance is potentially reduced.

Diminished Productivity

Linguistic profiling can lead to diminished productivity when the employee's ability to communicate is ridiculed and discounted simply due to a dialect or accent. Not only is the individual's ability to produce diminished but also the capability of those who are linguistically profiling their peers is being affected. Their time is spent judging dialect and/or accent and not focusing on the organization's business processes and procedures.

Legal Discrimination in Hiring

Legal discrimination in hiring occurs because of linguistic profiling. It is a subtle form of bias that is very difficult to detect and prove. While overt forms of discrimination have declined over time, "subtle—often unconscious and unintentional—forms continue to exist" (Dovidio, 2001, p. 845). These implicit forms of contemporary prejudice that are often triggered by such subtle cues as accent pose "unique challenges to the legal system" and "to the equitable treatment of members of disadvantaged groups" (Dovidio, 2001, p. 845). This type of discrimination sometimes leads to the inability to recruit and/or retain the most qualified job candidates (e.g., Atkins, 1993; Dovidio & Gaertner, 2000; Hosoda & Stone-Romero, 2010; Purkiss et al., 2006). Organizations must be aware of the potential loss of revenues and the extra time spent on recruiting efforts after bypassing candidates due to tone, dialect, and/or accent and must engage in "renewed efforts to develop new, effective techniques to combat contemporary racial bias" (Dovidio, 2001, p. 846).

There is a "relationship between Black education and American economic policy" (Smitherman, 1981; Smitherman & Baugh, 2002, p. 11). This relationship is actualized through the denial of jobs because of a lack of education and linguistic profiling with an education. The *King v. Ann Arbor* case may have opened the door for education despite linguistic profiling, but many economic doors may have been closed to and are still being closed to Blacks because of linguistic profiling.

Reduced Team/Group Effectiveness

Many organizations use teams and/or group work to attempt to boost workplace performance and productivity. Yet, teams and groups may be undermined when diversity within these teams and groups are diminished due to discrimination against members because of dialect or accent. Even unconscious and unintentional biases that could be triggered by such subtle cues as ethnic accents can adversely affect group processes (Dovidio, 2001). Interracial groups whose members display implicit or explicit bias against other team members are not only less cohesive and friendly, but they are also less efficient and productive (Dovidio, 2001). Dovidio also found that teams who were free from prejudice solved the problems more quickly and displayed a high level of satisfaction with teamwork and the outcomes. Biased judgments and stereotypes triggered by accents may also affect the selection of the team members. Accents often evoke the stereotypes that listeners hold about a particular ethnic or racial group that can unconsciously affect their decisions of who they prefer to work with within the group (Atkins, 1993; Lippi-Green, 1997). For example, Asian Americans are often considered highly competent, but at the same time they are stereotyped as quiet, reserved, and lacking interpersonal and leadership skills (Hosoda & Stone-Romero, 2010; Lin, Kwan, Cheung, & Fiske, 2005; Wu, 1997). These preconceived judgments, when activated by such subtle cues as accents, can affect the team member selection process or even a specific task assignment.

Reduced Global Economic Activity

Global economic activity has been shown to be the future of revenue growth as the world becomes "flatter" (Friedman, 2005). Yet many organizations will lose out on this potential growth because of linguistic profiling. The best-qualified candidate may not sound the way we prefer; thus, the decision must be made to determine what is most important: the way an individual sounds or what the individual can do to enhance the growth of our organizations.

The global economy is intertwined to the extent that there is 24-hour communication amongst people of different cultures and languages. Language tolerance and inclusion facilitates the expansion of global economic activity. If this communication is hindered, the accelerated growth that has been fruitful for many nations may slow down. Most economic growth is occurring in countries where Standard English is not the norm; thus, countries may become afraid to invest in places where there is a lack of tolerance of language differences. Linguistic profiling need not be the reason for reduced global economic activity among nations.

Individual Insecurity Regarding Job Security

Individuals collectively come together to form organizations. Each individual must feel valued to provide peak performance within the organization. When an individual is insecure regarding their job security because of their dialect or accent, the organization loses. It loses productivity, employee loyalty, and cultural cohesiveness. How can an individual be expected to perform when there is a lack of trust that they will retain their job? How can they provide the best service to customers when they are consistently being judged because of their accents or dialects? Dell computers experienced some of these issues with their call centers in India. Many Americans stopped purchasing Dell computers because they did not want to talk to technical support or customer services representatives who had distinctively Indian accents regardless of their expertise.

Organizations are going to be tasked to address all of these issues if they hope to remain competitive within the global economy. Human resource development professionals will be called upon to develop training systems and organizational development processes that will enhance the employees' ability to understand and avoid these potential pitfalls to organizational success.

Technological Implications

There are many ways that technology is being used by organizations and individuals to address linguistic profiling concerns. In the academic environment, minority and foreign faculty are choosing to teach online. Often in this environment, there is no long-term verbal communication with students; yet, these faculty members are still subject to evaluations that ask students to evaluate their spoken English even if it is not occurring.

Many organizations are using websites to allow customers to self-service or receive 24-hour chats with customer service representatives as opposed to telephone conversations. These techniques may not be directly stated to have become standard as a result of linguistic profiling, but they are effective techniques that can be incorporated to assist organizations and individuals as they attempt to deal with speech discrimination.

Binary language is the number one form of communication in the world. Throughout the world, it is becoming the language of choice, even if unknown to its users. Many individuals who use computers do not know that they are using binary language, but it is the best way to avoid linguistic profiling. Its success is experienced most in social media settings such as Facebook, Myspace, and Twitter. There is constant communication without extensive linguistic profiling. Participants do not care how other participants sound; they just receive the information supplied and use it to meet their needs.

As organizations expand the use of technology within the workplace, they have the potential to reduce linguistic profiling. Binary language can be used by organizations as a way to determine content value. For example, individuals can look for common ground through focusing upon content and not the means of how they receive the content. Is the content less valuable because the person who provided it spoke with a different dialect, tone, or accent? What is the organization's priority: producing or providing a first-quality product or discerning employee dialect, tone, or accent?

Chapter Summary

Linguistic profiling is an evolving issue in the global economy. Many organizations are competing globally for diverse talent. Yet, some may be self-sabotaging their success by instinctively discriminating against potential employees based upon their accent, tone, or dialect. They may not be aware of the extent to which this may be negatively impacting their potential for success. As the world continues to become flatter (Friedman, 2005), employers must be aware of the cultural, economic, and technological solutions that can provide them with the most competent employees. Without understanding the impact that linguistic profiling may have on their workplaces, they are open to more legal or ethical dilemmas that may reduce their competitiveness in the global marketplace.

Squires and Chadwick (2006) suggested that by not including linguistic profiling in racial discrimination research, the extent to which discrimination persists will be understated and be "less effective in protecting basic civil rights" (p. 413). They also noted that "the fundamental way people communicate by simply talking to each other, is often the basis today for determining who gets what and why" (p. 413). This statement is powerful, yet it may be perceived as too simplistic. Many workers may think they are simply talking to their coworkers and superiors in the workplace when, in fact, they are being discriminated against because of their dialect, accent, and/or natural tone. "To speak freely in the mother tongue without intimidation, without standing in the shadow of other languages and peoples" is a basic human right that every person deserves (Lippi-Green, 1997, p. 243).

Definition of Key Term

Linguistic profiling—Smalls (2004) defined linguistic profiling as the "term used to describe inferences that are often made about a person's speech. Inferences may include where a speaker is from, whether he/she is male or female, or whether he/she is native born to the United States" (p. 1). According to Baugh (2000), "linguistic profiling is based upon auditory cues that may be used to identify an individual or individuals as belonging to a linguistic subgroup within a given speech community, including a racial subgroup" (p. 363).

Critical-Thinking Discussion Questions

1. In what types of career fields is linguistic profiling most likely to occur?
2. Describe a situation in which you or someone you know has been linguistically profiled.
3. Can you think of a situation where you may have linguistically profiled someone?
4. To what extent does linguistic profiling affect economic prosperity of individuals?
5. Is linguistic profiling during the interview process a legal or an ethical issue?

6. Develop a training program to teach interviewers how to not linguistically profile potential employees during the interview process.
7. Describe the key competencies that the interviewer must possess to avoid linguistic profiling.
8. In what ways can technology be used to limit linguistic profiling in the workplace?
9. What can organizations do to develop a culture of linguistic tolerance?
10. Since there are civil rights laws that protect against racial, national origin, and ethnic bias in the workplace, should the dialect, tone, and accent of these workers also be protected?

Case Study 1

On April 30, 2010, the *Wall Street Journal* reported that the Arizona Department of Education was grading teachers based upon their fluency of the English language. They were judging whether teachers were heavily accented or ungrammatical in their speech. The Department sent evaluators into schools to assess teachers. Many of these teachers were Hispanics.

The EEOC notes that employment decisions that are made based on foreign accent do not violate Title VII of the Civil Rights Act of 1964 if the job requires effective oral communication in English. The employer has to provide a job description based on an accurate job analysis that explicitly states that effective oral communication in English is a requirement for the job.

The No Child Left Behind Act allows states to determine the meaning of fluency, but the Act requires that students be taught by teachers who are fluent in English to receive federal funds.

Discussion Questions

1. Provide pros and cons regarding Arizona's decision to hire teachers based on their accent.
2. Should there be standards to fire teachers based upon pronunciation and/or accent?
3. Should states be allowed to determine the meaning of fluency, especially regarding this case where many of the children are foreign speakers and teachers are trying to meet the school proficiency standards of the NCLB Act? Why or why not?

Case Study 2

Often, linguistic profiling occurs during the interview process, especially with the introduction of telephone interviews. Many potential job candidates may have been screened out during the telephone interview. It is hard for managers and supervisors to discern whether or not candidates are being linguistically profiled. Managers, supervisors, and job candidates do not know if candidates effectively respond to the interviewer questions or whether they were discerned to have a dialect or tone of voice that the interviewer did not like or understand.

Discussion Questions

1. Describe what would cause someone to linguistically profile a job candidate during a telephone interview.
2. Provide evidence of how applicant's accent, tone, or dialect can trigger adverse selection decisions by interviewers.

References

Anderson, K. T. (2007). Constructing "otherness": Ideologies and differentiating speech style. *International Journal of Applied Linguistics, 7*(2), 178–197.

Atkins, C. P. (1993). Do employment recruiters discriminate on the basis of nonstandard dialect? *Journal of Employment Counseling, 30,* 108–118.

Baugh, J. (2000). Racial identification by speech. *American Speech, 75,* 362–364.

Dovidio, J. F. (2001). On the nature of contemporary prejudice: The third wave. *Journal of Social Issues, 57*(4), 829–849.

Dovidio, J. F., & Gaertner, S. L. (2000). Aversive racism and selection decisions: 1989–1999. *Psychological Science, 11*(4), 315–319.

Fischer, M. J., & Massey, D. S. (2004). The ecology of racial discrimination. *City & Community, 3*(3), 221–241.

Friedman, T. L. (2005). *The world is flat: A brief history of the 21st century.* New York: Farrar, Straus, & Giroux.

Giles, H., Wilson, P., & Conway, A. (1981). Accent and lexical diversity as determinants of impression formation and perceived employment suitability. *Language Sciences, 3*(1), 91–103.

Heilemann, J., & Halperin, M. (2010). *Game change.* New York: HarperCollins.

Hosoda, M., & Stone-Romero, E. (2010). The effects of foreign accents on employment-related decisions. *Journal of Managerial Psychology, 25*(2), 113–132.

Lin, M. H., Kwan, V.S.Y., Cheung, A., & Fiske, S. T. (2005). Stereotype content model explains prejudice for an envied outgroups: Scale of anti–Asian American stereotypes. *Personality and Social Psychology Bulletin, 31*(1), 34–47.

Lippi-Green, R. (1999). *English with an accent: Language, ideology, and discrimination in the United States.* New York: Routledge.

Manrique, C. G., & Manrique, G. G. (1999). *The multicultural or immigrant faculty in American society.* Lewiston, NY: The Edwin Mellen Press.

Massey, D. S., & Lundy, G. (2001). Use of Black English and racial discrimination in urban housing markets: New methods and findings. *Urban Affairs Review, 36*(4), 452–469.

Munro, M. J., Derwing, T. M., & Sato, K. (2006). Salient accents, covert attitudes: Consciousness-raising for pre-service second language teachers. *Prospect, 21*(1), 67–79.

Nesdale, A. R., & Rooney, R. (1990). Effect of children's ethnic accents on adults' evaluations and stereotyping. *Australian Journal of Psychology, 42*(3), 309–319.

Purkiss, S.L.S., Perrewe, P. L., Gillespie, T. L., Mayes, B. T., & Ferris, G. R. (2006). Implicit sources of bias in employment interview judgments and decisions. *Organizational Behavior and Human Decision Processes, 101,* 152–167.

Purnell, T., Idsardi, W., & Baugh, J. (1999). Perceptual and phonetic experiments on American English dialect identification. *Journal of Language and Social Psychology, 18*(1), 10–30.

Rahman, J. (2008). Middle-class African Americans: Reactions and attitudes toward African American English. *American Speech, 83*(2), 141–176. doi:10.1215/00031283–2008–009

Rong, X. L. (2002). Teaching with differences and for differences: Reflections of a Chinese American teacher educator. In L. Vargas (Ed.), *Women Faculty of Color in the White Classroom* (pp. 125–145). New York: Peter Lang Publishing.

Rubin, D. L. (1992). Non-language factors affecting undergraduates' judgments of non-native English-speaking teaching assistants. *Research in Higher Education, 33*(4), 511–531.

Rubin, D. L., & Smith, K. A. (1990). Effects of accent, ethnicity, and lecture topic on undergraduates' perceptions of nonnative English-speaking teaching assistants. *International Journal of Intercultural Relations, 14,* 337–353.

Skachkova, P. (2007). Academic careers of immigrant women professors in the U.S. *Higher Education, 53,* 697–738.

Smalls, D. L. (2004). Linguistic profiling and the law. *Stanford Law & Policy Review* (15 Stan. L. & Pol'y Rev 579), 1–22.

Smitherman, G. (Ed.). (1981). Black English and the education of Black children and youth. *Proceedings of the National Invitational Symposium on the King Decision.* Detroit: Wayne State University Center for Black Studies.

Smitherman, G., & Baugh, J. (2002). The shot heard from Ann Arbor: Language research and public policy in African America. *The Howard Journal of Communications, 13,* 5–24.

Squires, G. D., & Chadwick, J. (2006). Linguistic profiling: A continuing tradition of discrimination in the home insurance industry. *Urban Affairs Review, 41*(3), 400–415.

Thomas, J. (1999). Voices from the periphery: Non-native teachers and issues of credibility. In G. Braine (Ed.), *Non-native educators in English language teaching* (pp. 5–15). Mahwah, NJ: Lawrence Erlbaum Associates.

Thompson, C. (2006). Using a language that's not your own: Experience of multicultural employees. *Diversity Factor, 14*(2), 30–36.

Wu, D.T.L. (1997). *Asian Pacific Americans in the workplace.* Lanham, MD: AltaMira Press.

12

PERSONAL/PHYSICAL APPEARANCE STIGMATIZING IN THE WORKFORCE

Cynthia Sims

Chapter Overview

Are employers allowed to prohibit religious garb? Can certain hairstyles be banned in the workplace? These questions will be answered in this chapter as personal and physical appearance stigmatizing is described. Stigmatizing based on one's outer appearance can result from a lack of understanding and sensitivity to individual expression and diversity, which can lead to discriminatory policies and practices within organizations. As personal and physical appearance discrimination cases increase, human resource development (HRD) and human resource management (HRM) professionals must deliberately explore and address this emerging workforce diversity issue, not only in the United States but globally.

This chapter begins with a discussion of the significance of appearance. Next, various aspects of appearance stigmatizing are explained, and relevant legislation is presented. The chapter ends with a summary that includes recommendations for preventing and/or eliminating the negative outcomes of personal and physical appearance stigmatizing. A list of key terms and applicable legislation is also provided.

Learning Objectives

After reading this chapter, along with completing the chapter summary questions and the case discussion questions, you will be able to:

- Explain the significance of appearance as self-expression
- Discuss how appearance conveys one's dimensions of diversity
- Summarize what personal/physical appearance stigmatization encompasses
- Identify laws that address personal/physical appearance discrimination
- Cite a case that addresses personal/physical appearance discrimination

Why Is Our Appearance So Important to Us?

Both literature and clothing capture the spirit of the time in which they are created. Both are art forms. One is language art and the other one is both an artifact and a mentifact. Literature and clothing both can be nonverbal but a powerful means of communication. (Skinner & Chowdhary, 1998, p. 175)

One of the most obvious ways we express our identities is through our personal and physical appearance. Although we may desire to look like someone else at different stages in our lives, for example, we want to have the physique of a model or athlete when we are teenagers, we are still unique, and our appearance represents our individuality.

In diversity terms, Loden Associates, Inc. (2010) stated that physical abilities and characteristics are primary dimensions of diversity, along with others, including race, ethnicity, age, gender, sexual orientation, class, income, and spiritual beliefs. These characteristics are primary because they shape our identity, values, and self-image. When people do not like the way we look, for example, we may view ourselves as unattractive or lacking. Conversely, when we are told that we are beautiful, our self-image is more positive.

Loden Associates (2010) further explain that primary dimensions of diversity are immutable—that is, it is highly unlikely that they will be changed. For example, you cannot change your ethnicity or race. Yet, if certain primary dimensions change, our identity may change as well. For example, if you become paralyzed, your lifestyle and self-identity are likely to change. Furthermore, if we are asked to change, hide, or renounce our primary dimensions of diversity, or if others do not accept us due to our primary dimensions of diversity, we can feel insulted and disrespected. If your employer disallows certain hairstyles, for example, you may feel that your physical characteristics are devalued.

Some of these dimensions can be seen by others, but a few cannot. However, through our appearance, we can communicate to others our primary dimensions of diversity. For example, one's religious garb can express his or her religion.

Secondary dimensions, on the other hand, can change at various points in one's life, for example, work experience, organization role/level, geographic location, family status, military experience, work style, communication style, education, and most recently added, first language and political beliefs (Loden Associates, 2010). These dimensions are not always as apparent, yet again, they can be presumed by our appearance. For example, one's military experience can be determined by the amount of ribbons displayed on his or her uniform.

Why Do We Stigmatize?

Stigma is socially constructed and based on person–environment interactions.
(Hurley-Hanson & Giannantonio, 2006, p. 455)

In every culture, there are preferred behaviors and appearances. Each culture determines what behaviors and appearances are acceptable and valued or improper and undesirable. When people violate the norms of a culture, they are seen as socially unacceptable, and stigmas are attached.

Many times we are stigmatized based on how others perceive our appearance and the assumed associated dimension(s) of diversity. In the workplace, personal and physical stigmatizing can lead to unlawful practices and policies. Let's explore examples of personal and physical appearance stigmatizing in the workplace, particularly when appearance is seen as a communication of primary and secondary dimensions of diversity. Let's also examine what the laws state about appearance in the workplace and why attempts to change, conceal, devalue, and/or ignore dimensions of diversity in the workplace are considered illegal.

Personal Appearance Stigmatization

We dress to establish an identity and to fit in with some subculture while rejecting others. (Green hair or brown? Dreads or straighteners? Make-up or none? Brooks Brothers suits or T-shirts and jeans? Miniskirt and stilettos or jeans and Birkenstocks?) (Fisk, 2006, p. 1111).

Personal appearance includes the following: clothing, tattoos, piercings, makeup, and hairstyles. These are considered mutable characteristics because they can be changed or voluntarily worn.

Our clothing says a great deal about "how we see and feel about ourselves and how we construct ourselves for the rest of the world to see. Most people give careful thought to how they dress as a part of defining who they are" (Fisk, 2006, p. 1111). When we choose our clothes and adornment, we choose how we represent ourselves. We may intentionally inform others of our spiritual beliefs, ethnicity, and income, to name a few, by our choice in attire and adornment. However, we do not choose how others will perceive us because of our appearance.

Many organizations have formal dress code policies and/or appearance policies, and others have unwritten policies that stem from the culture of the organization. Prospective and current employees are usually informed directly of the organizational dress code or appearance requirements, which may include the use of uniforms, business attire, and grooming stipulations during the hiring process, employee orientation, and/or via written company policy. A sense of an organization's preferred attire and adornment can also be determined by one's peers, duties, work role/level/status, or general organizational traditions. Some organizations, however, do not consider employees' primary dimensions of diversity or their need for self-expression through clothing, body art, piercings, and makeup when creating these formal or informal policies. Many times, stigmas are attached to certain forms of expression, so limitations are set. When employers create dress code/appearance policies that stifle the voluntary or involuntary expression of employees' dimensions of diversity, it is likely that the policy is unlawful.

Personal appearance stigmatizing can result in policies that consciously or unconsciously discriminate against a person's dimension(s) of diversity. Examples include, but are not limited to the following:

- If an employer believes women are more attractive and desirable with revealing clothing and makeup and less so without it, women may be required to wear sexually explicit attire and/or makeup. (gender issue)
- If employers view Muslims as terrorists, they may prohibit religious garb, such as hijabs and other adornment, in the workplace. (religion/spiritual beliefs issue)
- If an employer feels that earrings on males look feminine and, therefore, inappropriate, men may be discouraged from wearing earrings in the workplace. (gender issue)
- If an employer believes sagging pants and large gold chains are too urban or thuggish, a workplace policy forbidding loose-fitting jeans, limiting jewelry size, and requiring belts on males may be created. (gender, class, race, and ethnic issues)

What the Law States About Personal Appearance–Based Hiring and Dress Codes

More employees are becoming aware of their rights to express themselves through their personal appearance. Hence, cases involving employment-related discrimination based on appearance are increasing. Cases involving personal appearance can be linked to language in laws (regarding race, color, religion, national origin, or sex) that prohibit workplace discrimination.

Race/Color/National Origin

Title VII of the Civil Rights Act of 1964 is clear about what constitutes discriminatory practices in the workplace regarding race, color, and national origin, and considers these as protected classes. Disallowing certain forms of expression can be considered discrimination because there may be a "disparate impact on [a] . . . particular protected class" (Fowler, 2001, p. 33). Since race is protected under Title VII, for example, limiting certain hairstyles that are worn by those within a specific race can be racial discrimination, especially when the policy is subjective and not evenly enforced.

Religion/Spiritual Beliefs

When employees wear clothing or adorn themselves, they may be communicating their religion. An employer is limited by the law when setting dress codes. The U.S. Equal Employment Opportunity Commission (n.d. e) states:

> Unless it would be an undue hardship on the employer's operation of its business, an employer must reasonably accommodate an employee's religious beliefs or practices. This applies not only to schedule changes or leave for religious observances, but also to such things as dress or grooming practices that an employee has for religious reasons. These might include, for example, wearing particular head coverings or other religious dress (such as a Jewish yarmulke or a Muslim headscarf), or wearing certain hairstyles or facial hair (such as Rastafarian dreadlocks or Sikh uncut hair and beard). It also includes an employee's observance of a religious prohibition against wearing certain garments (such as pants or miniskirts). (para. 1)

Sex/Gender

Although employers can require makeup, they cannot perpetuate gender stereotypes by requiring women to use makeup or clothing that objectifies them. Employers must have evenly enforced policies that have similar grooming standards for males and females to ensure equality, for example, having a hair length requirement and/or well-kept nails for males when there is a similar policy for women.

Physical Appearance Stigmatization

Physical Appearance

Physical appearance includes the following characteristics: attractiveness, skin tone, facial features, hair texture, weight, height, physical disabilities, age, and pregnancy. These characteristics are considered immutable because you normally cannot change them. (Your age, weight, height, and pregnancy status will eventually change, but not immediately.) In some instances, however, people have sought to change their physical appearance to assimilate, feel accepted, gain power and privilege, or avoid discrimination.

Much of our physical appearance is biologically based, inherited from our parents. We may like or dislike our physical features, seek to enhance them, or aspire to change them if possible. Some of our physical abilities and disabilities may change at certain periods in our lives, yet others will remain. When our employers and coworkers deem our physical appearance unacceptable, the workplace can be an uncomfortable environment in which to work.

Immutable Physical Characteristics

Cultures associate stigmas to certain immutable features, attaching positive and negative values to them. For example, in the African American culture, a light skin tone is a marker of beauty, and dark skin is viewed negatively. Also, "As in . . . Asian countries such as Japan, . . . lighter skin pigment also represents membership of the elite, or the middle class" (Aizura, 2009, p. 311). Other racial and ethnic groups harbor these beliefs, causing problems in the workplace within and external to their racial and ethnic groups. For example, "based on the color of their skin, dark-skinned Blacks historically have experienced more [workplace] discrimination—both from Whites and members of their own race—than lighter-skinned Blacks, according to the EEOC" (Mirza, 2003, p. 62). For these reasons and others, some darker-skinned people invest in skin bleaching creams to try to lighten their skin and become accepted.

Height is another immutable physical characteristic that one does not change (after growth has ended). There are stigmas associated with height, and above-average height is usually valued more than a shorter stature. "Tallness is considered powerful . . . because of its link to masculinity, in that the male body claims more space. On the flip side, the shorter body takes up less space, and is perceived as feminine, which invokes passivity and powerlessness" (Butera, 2008, p. 14). This heightism is a serious workplace issue in the United States and other countries, as height is associated with power and dominance. In some Asian countries, for example, a certain height is a requirement for many jobs (Coonan, 2006) and even college entrance. Height also grants status and power. For these reasons, some Asians pursue surgery that includes breaking their lower legs and inserting lengthening instruments in order to increase their height.

Physical appearance stigmatizing can result in policies that consciously or unconsciously discriminate against a person's dimension(s) of diversity. Examples include, but are not limited to, the following:

- If an employer believes that darker-skinned people are less intelligent, he or she may hire a light-skinned person over a dark-skinned person. (skin tone, race, and ethnicity issue)
- If employers deem thin employees as more capable than overweight employees, they may promote a thin employee with fewer skills over an overweight employee. (weight issue)
- If an employer feels a pregnant prospective employee will be less available to work after the child is born, he or she may not hire a pregnant woman.
- If employers believe a 53-year-old employee will have difficulty learning their companies' latest technology, they may not include the employee in training.

What the Law States About Immutable Physical Characteristics

Immutable appearance cases are becoming more common and growing. However, there is "sparse current law on the topic of immutable appearance discrimination" (James, 2008, p. 669). When immutable appearance characteristics are linked to language in federal laws (race, color, religion, national origin, sex, disability, and pregnancy), cases for discrimination can be filed.

Race/Color

"Equal Employment Opportunity Commission statistics show an increasing number of skin tone discrimination charges, which increased by 125% since the mid-1990s" (Sims, 2006, p. 1200). For this reason,

Title VII has been updated to include language that broadens the definition of color. Expanding the clause under race/color discrimination to include "personal characteristics associated with race (such as hair texture, skin color, or certain facial features)" (U.S. Equal Employment Opportunities Commission, n.d. d, para. 1) makes the law more inclusive of the types of discrimination that occur. And,

> Although Title VII does not define 'color,' the courts and the Commission read 'color' to have its commonly understood meaning—pigmentation, complexion, or skin shade or tone. Thus, color discrimination occurs when a person is discriminated against based on the lightness, darkness, or other color characteristic of the person. (U.S. Equal Employment Opportunities Commission, n.d. a, para. 1)

Title VII has broadened its language under color; however, Greene (2008) challenges courts' lack of use of the law. She states:

> Many Title VII cases have arisen when an applicant's or employee's non-conformity with an employer's policy barring certain hairstyles or clothing has resulted in an adverse employment action, such as a denial or termination of employment. Generally, courts have not deemed an adverse employment action resulting from an applicant's or employee's non-conformity with an employment policy banning the display of mutable characteristics commonly associated with a particular racial or ethnic group, a violation of Title VII's proscription against racial, color, or national origin discrimination. These cases have largely been unsuccessful because of courts' narrow interpretations of Title VII's prohibitions against race, color, and national origin discrimination. Courts have viewed these protected categories as encompassing only "immutable characteristics" such as skin color and, in some instances, hair texture. Courts have also been less inclined to expressly hold that employment decisions based on racial, color, or ethnic stereotypes violate Title VII. Therefore, courts have hindered the efficacy of Title VII to achieve its mandate to ensure that individuals are not denied equal employment opportunities on the basis of race, national origin, and color. (p. 1355)

Race and color may also be impacted by less obvious characteristics, including facial hair. For example, "a 'no-beard' employment policy that applies to all workers without regard to race may still be unlawful if it is not job-related and has predisposition to a skin condition that causes severe shaving bumps" (U.S. Equal Employment Opportunities Commission, n.d. b, para. 2). This type of case can also be considered a disability according to the Rehabilitation Act because pseudolfolliculitis barbae (shaving bumps) is a common condition that afflicts African American men (Fowler-Hermes, 2001).

Height/Weight/Disability/Medical Condition/Pregnancy

Some employers impose height and weight requirements on their employees. However, "height and weight requirements tend to disproportionately limit the employment opportunities of some protected groups and unless the employer can demonstrate how the need is related to the job, it may be viewed as illegal under federal law" (U.S. Equal Employment Opportunities Commission, n.d. c, para. 1)

Stigmatization based on weight is a commonly ignored issue in the workplace. Latner, O'Brien, Durso, Brinkman, and MacDonald (2008) stated in their study:

> Because it is not widely recognized as a form of prejudice, there is no taboo on weight-biased beliefs. Members of the out-group (in this case, non-overweight individuals) do not question their biased beliefs, and members of the in-group agree that these beliefs are fair, justified and internalize them as truths. If weight bias were recognized as a legitimate and important form of prejudice, then the out-group might be less likely to maintain the stereotype, as people do not wish to be identified as being prejudiced. Furthermore, as is historically the case when social injustices are recognized, the in-group might initiate a mainstream movement toward equality and begin to develop self-pride. (p. 1151)

Since federal laws do not specifically address weight, it is difficult to win cases of weight discrimination or unfair treatment in the workplace. Only San Francisco and Washington, D.C., have laws that address weight discrimination, so more legislation is needed regarding this dimension of diversity.

The appearance of pregnancy communicates to others one's family status, which is a second dimension of diversity. Workplace policies that unfairly target a woman who is pregnant can exist. The Pregnancy Discrimination Act dictates what actions are deemed unlawful. Federal law reads:

> Under Federal law, if an employee is temporarily unable to perform her job due to pregnancy or childbirth, the employer must treat her the same as any other temporarily disabled employee. For example, if the employer allows temporarily disabled employees to modify tasks, perform alternative assignments or take disability leave or leave without pay, the employer also must allow an employee who is temporarily disabled due to pregnancy to do the same. (U.S. Equal Employment Opportunities Commission, n.d. c, para. 1)

Employees with general disabilities are a protected class. When an employer imposes certain restrictions on employees with physical disabilities, they violate the Americans with Disabilities Act and possibly the Rehabilitation Act (for federal employees).

Chapter Summary

Our appearance is very meaningful to us, and we want others to respect and value the ways in which we communicate our identities. Even if others do not agree with our forms of self-expression, body type, and/ or other physical features, we want our employers to become more aware of how personal and physical stigmatizing can perpetuate policies and practices that devalue and ignore our dimensions of diversity, which can eventually negatively impact how employees interact and work. It is very important, therefore, that employers and employees understand the micro and macro implications of personal and physical appearance stigmatizing in the workplace.

Employers and their personnel must be aware of legislation that addresses unlawful workplace policies and practices that stem from personal and physical stigmatizing. Laws change as appearance discrimination cases increase, so it is also imperative that employers and employees stay informed of evolving diversity language and applicable cases. Consistent diversity training should be utilized to provide opportunities to learn and discuss these diversity issues and their implications.

Employers must also develop a workplace environment that recognizes and values the diversity of its employees and provides opportunities for them to benefit from their differences. Research has shown that as a result, not only is the bottom line positively impacted, but employees are happier, morale increases, and turnover decreases.

Definition of Key Terms and Legislation

Americans with Disabilities Act of 1990—Makes it illegal in the private sector and in state and local governments to discriminate against a qualified person with a disability. It requires that employers reasonably accommodate the known physical or mental limitations of an otherwise qualified individual with a disability who is an applicant or employee, unless doing so would impose an undue hardship on the operation of the employer's business.

Heightism—Prejudice against people, male and female, of below-average stature.

Pregnancy Discrimination Act—Amended Title VII to make it illegal to discriminate against a woman because of pregnancy, childbirth, or a medical condition related to pregnancy or childbirth.

Section 501 of the Rehabilitation Act of 1973—Prohibits employment discrimination in the federal sector against individuals with disabilities.

Stigmatize—To label unacceptable based on cultural norms, stereotyping, or prejudice.

Title VII of the Civil Rights Act of 1964—Makes it illegal to discriminate against someone on the basis of race, color, religion, national origin, or sex.

U.S. Equal Employment Opportunity Commission—The federal body responsible for enforcing laws regarding workplace discrimination.

Critical-Thinking Discussion Questions

1. What does our appearance convey about us?
2. Why is physical appearance considered a primary dimension of diversity?
3. Name five secondary dimensions of diversity that can be communicated through our appearance.

4. Explain how physical appearance can be linked to the language of federal laws.

5. Discuss why it is difficult to prove discrimination that results from perceived personal/physical appearance stigmatizing.

6. Name two laws that prohibit discrimination based on the dimension(s) discussed above.

7. Give two personal examples of both mutable and immutable characteristics. Discuss a time when someone treated you unfairly because of the examples you just identified.

8. Is physical appearance stigmatizing mostly a female or male issue? Explain why.

9. Can employers refuse a request to wear religious garb because it might be offensive to others?

10. Name three ways employers can prevent or address unlawful policies and practices that are a result of personal stigmatizing.

Case Study 1—Pregnant Employee at the Front Reception Desk: Is This a Case of Physical Appearance Stigmatizing?

Lucille is an excellent receptionist at Sarah C. Howard School for Girls. She has outstanding oral communication and customer service skills, which she has enhanced in the five years that she has been employed there. The teachers, parents, and students have all commended her on how personable she is, and she has even served as a mentor for many of the students.

One day, Lucille announced to her supervisor, Assistant Principal Ann Smith, that she was four-months pregnant. Lucille explained that she and her boyfriend were very happy about the pregnancy, but she wanted to wait until she was past her first trimester before she shared the news with her colleagues. Ann thanked Lucille for confiding in her.

One month later, Lucille received a letter from Ann in her mailbox. The letter explained that Lucille would be briefly transferred to the back workroom to assist with secretarial duties. Lucille was stunned because she loved the reception area and the duties she performed. She made an appointment to speak with Ann. During her meeting with Ann, the following conversation took place:

Lucille: Thank you for agreeing to meet with me so soon. I am just anxious to know why I am being removed from the front desk. I really enjoy my current position and even excel at it.

Ann: Yes, Lucille. I know that. I am concerned, however, that your condition, especially now that your pregnancy is apparent, may send the wrong message to our students. I am also trying to avoid having to move you later to accommodate some of your anticipated needs.

Lucille: I don't understand. I have close relationships with many of the students. They know me well. What message would I send? And why would you have to move me later?

Ann: I actually have another meeting in two minutes. We can discuss this issue another time. I spoke with the two part-time workroom staff, Ashley and Tyler, last week. They have both agreed to share your hours when you switch jobs. The move will be tomorrow. By the way, I noticed last week that you haven't been wearing your engagement ring anymore.

Exercise

Circle the words in the case above that communicate Lucille's dimensions of diversity. On the bottom of this page, write down the protected class (the legislation discussed in this chapter), if any, to which the dimensions can be linked.

Discussion Questions

1. What dimensions and protected class(es) did you select? Why?
2. Do you believe this is a case of physical appearance stigmatizing? Why or why not?
3. What advice would you give Lucille and Ann?

Homework

Research pregnancy discrimination cases. In a 200-word essay, explain if your opinion was supported or challenged by the information you found.

Case Study 2—The National Basketball Association Player Dress Code: Is This a Case of Personal Appearance Stigmatizing?

In 2005, the National Basketball Association (NBA) implemented a new dress code for its players. Commissioner David Stern established this policy to ensure players represent the NBA League in a professional manner, particularly when they are participating in team or league business. The following is a list of items (which has been taken directly from the NBA website, www.nba.com/news/player_dress_code_051017 .html) that players are not allowed to wear:

- Sleeveless shirts
- Shorts
- T-shirts, jerseys, or sports apparel (unless appropriate for the event [e.g., a basketball clinic], team-identified, and approved by the team)
- Headgear of any kind while a player is sitting on the bench or in the stands at a game, during media interviews, or during a team or league event or appearance (unless appropriate for the event or appearance, team-identified, and approved by the team)
- Chains, pendants, or medallions worn over the player's clothes
- Sunglasses while indoors
- Headphones (other than on the team bus or plane, or in the team locker room)

The following is a list of the required "Business Casual" attire:

- A long- or short-sleeved dress shirt (collared or turtleneck), and/or a sweater
- Dress slacks, khaki pants, or dress jeans
- Appropriate shoes and socks, including dress shoes, dress boots, or other presentable shoes, but not including sneakers, sandals, flip-flops, or work boots

Exercise

Circle clothing and adornment which you feel may communicate the players' dimension(s) of diversity. On a sheet of paper, write down the item(s). Next to each item, write the dimension that it could communicate. Next to the dimension, write the protected class (taken from any of the legislation discussed in this chapter), if any, to which it can be linked.

Discussion Questions

1. Why did you identify the item(s), the dimension(s), and the protected class(es)?
2. Do you believe this is a case of physical appearance stigmatizing? Why or why not?
3. Do you feel Commissioner Stern's policy is discriminatory? Why or why not?
4. What changes, if any, would you make to the policy?

Assignment

Research the NBA dress code policy and others' opinions about it. Compare your opinion to what you found. In a 200-word essay, explain if your opinion was supported or challenged by either more information about the policy or the opinions you found.

References

Aizura, A. Z. (2009). Where health and beauty meet: Femininity and racialisation in Thai cosmetic surgery clinics. *Asian Studies Review, 33,* 303–317.

Butera, L. E. (2008). Height, power, and gender: Politicizing the measured body (Unpublished master's thesis, Bowling Green State University, Bowling Green, OH).

Coonan, C. (2006, November 6). Long legs to remain fantasy for petite Chinese. *The Independent.* Retrieved from www.independent.co.uk/news/world/asia/long-legs to-remain-fantasy-for-petitechinese-423134.html.

Fisk, C. L. (2006). Privacy, power, and humiliation at work: Re-examining appearance regulation as an invasion of privacy. *Louisiana Law Review, 66*(4), 1111–1146.

Fowler-Hermes, J. (2001). The beauty and the beast in the workplace: Appearance-based discrimination claims under EEO laws. *Florida Bar Journal, 75*(4), 32–38.

Greene, W. D. (2008). Title VII: What's hair (and other race-based characteristics) got to do with it? *University of Colorado Law Review, 79*(4), 1355–1394.

Hurley-Hanson, A. E., & Giannantonio, C. M. (2006). Recruiters' perceptions of appearance: The stigma of image norms. *Equal Opportunities International, 25*(6), 450–463.

James, H. R. (2008). If you are attractive and you know it, please apply: Appearance based discrimination and employers' discretion. *Valparaiso University Law Review, 42*(2), 629–73.

Latner, J. D., O'Brien, K. S., Durso, L. E., Brinkman, L. A., & MacDonald, T. (2008). Weighing obesity stigma: The relative strength of different forms of bias. *International Journal of Obesity, 32*(7), 1145–1152.

Loden Associates, Inc. (2010). Primary and secondary dimensions of diversity. Retrieved from www.loden.com/Site/Dimensions.html

Mirza, P. (2003, December). A bias that's skin deep. *HR Magazine,* 62–67.

Sims, C. (2006). Broadening the scope of diversity: Implications for the recruitment and retention of minority faculty. *Proceedings of the Annual Academy of Human Resource Development International Research Conference, 1* (pp. 1199–1205). Columbus, OH.

Skinner, S. L., & Chowdhary, U. (1998). Testing the myths of aging stereotyping: Reflection through clothing and appearance related information in a compendium. *Educational Gerontology, 24*(2), 175–181.

U.S. Equal Employment Opportunity Commission (EEOC). (n.d. a). Facts about race/color discrimination. Color discrimination. Retrieved from www.eeoc.gov/eeoc/publications/fs-race.cfm

U.S. Equal Employment Opportunity Commission (EEOC). (n.d. b). Pre-employment inquiries and height and weight. Retrieved from www.eeoc.gov/laws/practices/inquiries_height_weight.cfm

U.S. Equal Employment Opportunity Commission (EEOC). (n.d. c). Pregnancy, maternity & parental leave. Retrieved from www.eeoc.gov/laws/types/pregnancy.cfm

U.S. Equal Employment Opportunity Commission (EEOC). (n.d. d) Race/color discrimination. Race/color discrimination & employment policies/practices. Retrieved from www.eeoc.gov/laws/types/race_color.cfm

U.S. Equal Employment Opportunity Commission (EEOC). (n.d. e). Religious discrimination. Religious accommodation/dress and grooming policies. Retrieved from www.eeoc.gov/laws/types/religion.cfm

13

VISIBLE AND INVISIBLE DISABILITIES IN THE WORKFORCE: EXCLUSION AND DISCRIMINATION

Chaunda L. Scott and Marilyn Y. Byrd

Chapter Overview

This chapter begins with an introduction, followed by a summary of the historical models that inform an understanding of disabilities. Next, the Civil Rights movement and its relationship to disability rights will be highlighted, followed by a discussion on disability and unemployment. The next section will discuss technology and its role in improving the quality of life for people with disabilities to participate in the workforce. The last section will discuss disability activism and empowerment as a source to overcome the stigma of having a disability. The chapter concludes with a chapter summary, definition of key terms, critical-thinking discussion questions, and two case studies.

Learning Objectives

After reading this chapter, along with completing the critical-thinking discussion questions and the case discussion questions, you will be able to:

- Describe how the historical models of disability inform understanding today
- Describe how the Civil Rights Movement helped the disability rights movement

- Describe what barriers individuals with disabilities face in unemployment
- Describe how technology assists people with disabilities to participate in the workforce
- Describe people with disabilities who have overcome barriers and the next steps regarding advancing disability rights

Introduction

The laws can force services for individuals with disabilities, but only time and effort can change public attitudes. (Gollnick & Chinn, 2002, p. 188)

The World Health Organization (2001) defines disability as a set of conditions, many of which are created by society, that can deny, prevent, or restrict full participation by people with a perceived or self-disclosed infirmity. In the workplace, people with disabilities have a "reduced ability to perform tasks one would normally do at a given stage in life" (Schaefer, 2010, p. 408).

As of 2010, there were roughly 56.7 million individuals in the United States that have a disability, of which 38.3 million are considered severely disabled (Brault, 2012). The U.S. Department of Labor's (2012) current population survey reported that the risks for an individual becoming disabled in his or her lifetime are greater than might be expected. Twenty-five percent of today's 20-year-olds will become disabled before they reach retirement (Council for Disability Awareness, 2012).

The more visible and commonly encountered states of disability are: blindness, deafness, inability to walk, mental incapacity, and other obvious forms of mental or physical impairment that alter a person's ability to function as a whole person. However, there are some disabilities that are less visible such as chronic medical conditions, depression, disorders, injuries, and learning impairments that cause a person to be unable to function at "normal" capacity (Davis, 2005). Nonetheless, people with disabilities face a daily struggle to overcome prejudices and biases that are associated with their disability. Schaefer (2010) explains that people with disabilities will experience prejudice in their communities because: (1) society views these individuals based on what they cannot do rather than what they can do; (2) access to buildings and transportation services is limited and thus greatly hinders their chances to find and secure a job; and (3) society in general restricts them "in ways that are unnecessary and unrelated to any physical infirmity" (p. 408).

Stigmatizing people with disabilities can be traced back to Biblical and ancient Greek history (Pelka, 2012). In the scriptures, people with deformities or noticeable defects were considered "unclean" or "unfit" and in some way deserving of the fate they had been dealt. Uncleanliness was also equated with ungodliness which translated into meaning that a person was not fit to approach God. Rose (2003) says that perceptions of the ancient Greeks, with their images and depictions of the perfect body and other notions such as the infanticide of deformed infants, has carried over into our common consciousness, thus maintaining the perception that people with disabilities are inherently flawed.

Furthermore, the struggle against disability discrimination has been largely ignored in education curriculum (Office of Disability Employment Policy, n.d.). Advocates for disability rights have sought to encourage the integration of disability history into educational programs not only to increase an awareness of disability discrimination but to enhance the development of people and recognize the contributions that some individuals with disabilities can make to the workplace.

Perceptions and biases against people with disabilities is a historical problem that continues to pervade today's workforce. Given the long history of exclusion and discrimination of people with disabilities, educators, practitioners, and students should be familiar with historical models of disability that inform an understanding of how disability is perceived: the moral model, the medical model, the rehabilitation model, and the disability model.

Historical Models of Disability

A central aim of disability research along with disability civil rights efforts is to raise awareness of what it means to be disabled in the United Stated (Kaplan, 2000). Kaplan points out four **models of disability** that have been used to illustrate how individuals experience various visible and invisible disabilities.

First, the moral model, the oldest of the models, is grounded in the idea that having a disability is a sin and is a source of embarrassment for the person with the disability. This model not only fosters exclusion but promotes a sense of self-disapproval and lack of self-worth. Second, the medical model, emerging during the 19th century, supports the view that a disability is something that needs to be treated medically. Third, as the medical model gained acceptance and support in American society, the rehabilitation model evolved. This model posits that individuals with disabilities should pursue various types of medical "training, therapy, or counseling" to address their disabilities (Kaplan, 2000). Fourth, the most modern of the four models, the disability model, regards a disability as a common state of being—as opposed to an uncommon state of being. The disability model also identifies societal inequity as a serious social ill "experienced by persons with disabilities and as the cause of many of the problems that are regarded as intrinsic to the disability under the other models" (p. 355). This model is most useful in explaining "the role that social circumstances play in creating disabling conditions" (Stein & Stein, 2007, p. 1221). Hence, in the workplace, by understanding disability as a common state of being, people with disabilities can be ensured a more inclusive and participatory workplace environment.

The Civil Rights Movement and Disability

The enactment of key pieces of legislation, such as the **Rehabilitation Act of 1973** and the **Americans with Disabilities Act** (ADA) of 1990, as well as the role that disability activists have played in the disability rights movement are central to establishing equal rights and opportunities for people with disabilities (Fleischer & Zames, 2011). As was mentioned previously, disability activists have played an influential role in taking political action in support of disability rights. Therefore, the 1960s Civil Rights Movement provided the perfect backdrop for disability activists to join the quest for equal opportunities for people with disabilities. The most dramatic action taken by this group was the 1977 "San Francisco 504 sit-in." Activists and supporters staged a sit-in at a San Francisco federal building demanding enforcement of Section 504 of the Rehabilitation Act of 1973. The San Francisco sit- in sparked similar movements across the country. Section 504 of the Act protects people with disabilities from being excluded from receiving federal funding and being denied benefits from programs receiving federal funding based on their disability status.

The ADA was passed by Congress in 1990 for the purpose of prohibiting discrimination against people with disabilities in "private sector employment, public services, public accommodations, transportation and telecommunications" (Gollnick & Chinn, 2002, p. 171). For example, in the workplace, organizations were mandated to provide reasonable accommodations for people with disabilities by readjusting, redesigning, reconfiguring, or reconstructing workplaces so that this group would have the same rights, privileges, and quality of work life as people without disabilities. Public transportation vehicles such as buses and trains along with transportation stations were also required to become user friendly to assist the disabled population with their transportation needs (Gollnick & Chinn, 2002) by adding such additions as wheelchair lifts, wheelchair reserved seating areas and wheelchair safety seat belts. However, despite the progress that has been made by legislation and the advocacy of disability activists and supporters, the struggle for disability equality continues.

Disability and Unemployment

As previously highlighted in this chapter, individuals with disabilities, despite their protected class status, represent "about two-thirds of working age people . . . in the United States [that] are unemployed" (Schaefer, 2010, p. 409). This problem may be related to the fact that individuals with disabilities were regularly turned down from being admitted into mainstream educational institutions, unless they were planning to take "special education" courses (Ryan, 2011). Ryan additionally notes that it has only been 41 years since the passage of such legislation as the Rehabilitation Act of 1973 and the American with Disabilities Act (ADA) of 1990. Both of these Acts were influential in making mainstream educational institutions more accommodating for individuals with disabilities. Because of these laws, educational opportunities have assisted individuals with disabilities in attaining employment (Ryan, 2011). To illustrate this point, in 2010, 41.1% of individuals between the ages of 21 and 64 that had a disability gained employment, along with "27.5% of adults with severe disabilities" (Brault, 2012, p. 10).

Results of ongoing research by the Job Accommodation Network (JAN) in partnership with the University of Iowa's Law, Health Policy, and Disability Center (LHPDC) report that employers can make workplace accommodations for employees with disabilities at a low cost and high impact. Significant findings of the JAN ongoing research are:

1. Employers contact JAN for information and solutions for the purpose of retaining valued and qualified employees.
2. The majority of employers report no or little cost in making accommodations for employees with disabilities.
3. Employers report that the accommodations they implement are effective.
4. Employers report direct and indirect benefits after making accommodations for employees with disabilities.

This research study concluded that retaining valued employees and increasing the employee's productivity are the top two benefits for making workplace accommodations for people with disabilities (JAN, 2013). Indirect benefits include improved interactions with other employees, overall company morale, and overall company productivity.

Technology and Quality of Work for People With Disabilities

For many individuals with physical and mental impairments, technology has significantly improved the quality of work, thus helping people with disabilities participate more actively in the workplace. However, the results of a recent study conducted by Harris, Owen, and De Ruiter (2012) disclosed that for many individuals with disabilities, access to technology posed several problems for the study participants. For example, the researchers found that the study participants did not have the right technological skills to access and navigate various technologies they encountered. Second, the researchers found that the study participants noted they did not have the financial resources to purchase technological equipment that would accommodate their disability. Third, the researchers found that it was often difficult for the study participants to keep their skills current due to constantly changing technologies. Finally, the researchers found that the study participants had unfavorable feedback toward online links to beneficial resources, primarily because online links are not always updated and consequently do not provide needed information.

The findings made by Harris et al. (2012) provide insight on the limitations of technology and other resources that could enhance the quality of work and life for people with disabilities, concluding that, "parity of participation in civic engagement enables marginalized groups to be agents of social change" (p. 81). Identifying ways that people with disabilities can be empowered at work is the first step to social change. The next step is a more participatory approach to research and greater collaboration among advocacy groups, researchers, scholars, and practitioners to learn of other ways that technology can be improved to better meet the needs of individuals with disabilities in the workforce (Harris et al., 2012).

Disability Rights—Overcoming Barriers

To date, advocacy for disability rights has remained in the forefront through the actions of activists and other champions for the cause. For example, the entertainment industry is noted for publicly portraying the careers of celebrities who have self-disclosed their disabilities. Celebrities such as Cher, Tom Cruise, Michael J. Fox, and Danny Glover, to name a few, have chosen to foreground their respective disabilities. Identifying with one's disability is a source of empowerment and helps to shift the focus toward being successful and overcoming the stigma (Johnstone, 2004). Therefore, celebrity self-disclosure has served to promote not only disability rights but a sense of identity. However, greater efforts are needed to eradicate the discrimination and biases that individuals with disabilities encounter in the workplace.

Tororei (2009) poignantly states, "persons with disabilities must be able to access the workplace and the work" (p. 12). To achieve this, employers have not only a legal but a moral obligation to offer a workplace environment that creates a feeling of independence, self-worth, job satisfaction, and dignity, and provides opportunities to interact and connect with others and consequently enjoy the same rights and privileges that are available to individuals in that environment.

Another crucial element of advancing the rights of people with disabilities in the workplace is cultivating and developing talent (Stein & Stein, 2007). Traditionally, the mindset of disability in the workplace has been one of "invisibility" and absence from the everyday routine (Tororei, 2009). However, invisibility "undermines the dignity and self-worth" that enables people with disabilities "to live and express their humanity" (p. 12). Therefore, overcoming barriers requires opportunities for training and development that contributes to more meaningful work.

Chapter Summary

Discrimination and exclusion of people with disabilities has existed throughout the history of Western civilization. Examples from the past have served as models that inform an understanding of disability even today. It is apparent that there are many ways to understand disability, but it is important to judge who is disabled on an individual basis. Advocates on behalf of people with disabilities have worked to ensure a more inclusive work environment and as a result have helped to produce laws to ensure equity and fairness for this group. However, barriers such as biased perceptions and inadequate accommodations, to name a few, still prevent full participation in the workplace for people with disabilities. In addition, the state of unemployment for individuals with disabilities is a growing concern. Technology has significantly enhanced opportunities for individuals with disabilities to participate in the workforce, but greater advocacy for equity and fairness is needed.

Definition of Key Terms

Americans with Disabilities Act 1990—This act "prohibits discrimination against people with disabilities in employment, transportation, public accommodation, communications, and governmental activities. The ADA also establishes requirements for telecommunications relay services" (Americans with Disabilities Act 1990).

Disability—A disability is defined as a set of conditions, many of which are created by society, that can deny, prevent, or restrict full participation by people with a perceived or self-disclosed infirmity (World Health Organization,

2001); a "reduced ability to perform tasks one would normally do at a given stage in life" (Schaefer, 2010, p. 408).

Models of disability—Four models that are used to ground one's understanding of how disability is perceived: the moral model, the medical model, the rehabilitation model, and the disability model.

Rehabilitation Act of 1973—Protects disabled individuals from discrimination by employers and organizations that receive federal financial assistance (Rehabilitation Act of 1973).

Critical-Thinking Discussion Questions

1. Discuss the purpose and impact of the key legislation impacting people with disabilities as presented in this chapter.

2. Conduct an Internet search and locate other legislation that has resulted from the advancement of disability rights, including disability rights in the area of education. Discuss how this legislation has been useful in advancing disability rights.

3. What purpose do disability models serve?

4. Discuss how the medical model of disability has impacted the treatment of people with disabilities.

5. What recommendation(s) do you have for improving the quality of life for people with disabilities?

6. What technologies, other than those named in the chapter, could help people with disabilities perform more effectively in the workplace?

Case Study 1: Mike's Story

Until two years ago, Mike Doe was a fireman in Texas. Mike served the last two years in Iraq with the United States Army before he was injured in a Jeep that turned over while he was in combat. Mike's injury was severe, and he lost his left arm. Now that Mike is back home in Texas, he needs help finding out how the Americans with Disabilities Act (ADA) can best serve him. Because you work for ADA as Mike's counselor, you want to use the ADA laws to provide him with a resource plan regarding what ADA assistance is offered to injured war veterans. Refer to the U.S. Department of Veteran Services website at www.va.gov to develop your three-page resource plan to be presented in a class discussion.

Case Study 2: Accommodations for a New Hire

Diana Jayson has been in a wheelchair since a car accident in 2003 left her paralyzed from the waist down. Looking at this as a minor setback, Diana continued to pursue her education and earned her Bachelor of Science degree in Information Technology online from a public university in South Carolina in 2005. Anxious to work in her field, Diana applied for a network manager position at a communications company that provides telecommunication services to the Northwest district of South Carolina. When the human resources manager, Ellen McDonald, saw Diana's resume, she knew Diana was a good candidate for the position and called her. After talking for a few minutes about the job requirements and Diana's qualifications, Ellen requested Diana come in for an interview.

When Diana arrived for the interview, Ellen was surprised to see Diana in a wheelchair. Ellen decided to hold the interview in a conference room that could accommodate Diana's wheelchair comfortably. Ellen took Diana's coat and hung it in the coat room. Then she sat down across from Diana and began the interview. "I was very impressed by your resume, Diana," Ellen said. "Tell me a little about your experience in IT." Diana told Ellen about her classroom experience developing programs for course assignments and how she couldn't wait to put her new skills into practice. While Diana was enthusiastically describing the class assignments, Ellen was considering how she could make accommodations for Diana in the office. She thought, "The hallways are pretty narrow in our office building, but we do have handicap-accessible parking with a ramp and an electronic door. However, I'm not quite sure how I can accommodate the wheelchair in the break room, copy room, and service area."

After the interview, Ellen thanked Diana for coming to the interview. "Did you have any difficulty finding our building and getting inside?" Ellen asked. Diana replied, "No, actually, your building was very easy to access and your office was easy to find. I had no problems whatsoever." Once alone in her office, Ellen thought about the interview. "Well, she has the skills, but not the experience. And, I'm not real sure about the cost required to make the entire office wheelchair accessible. Maybe, I'll talk to Rick in IT and see what he thinks about getting a wheelchair in the service area. I'll also have to talk to Steve in HR to see what our policies are for people with disabilities." Ellen began looking through the other applicants' resumes. "Boy, I wish I had known she was in a wheelchair before I got my hopes up."

Discussion Questions

1. What are some of the no-cost solutions Ellen can make to accommodate Diana's wheelchair?

2. What environmental obstacles can you imagine exist in the break room, copy room, and service area?
3. What are some of the benefits to hiring Diana?
4. How should Ellen handle the decision to not hire Diana?

References

Americans with Disabilities Act of 1990 (ADA), 42 U.S.C. §§ 12101-12213 (2000).

Brault, M. W. (2012). Americans with disabilities: 2010. Household economic studies. Current population reports. U.S. Department of Commerce Economic and Statistics Administration. Washington, D. C: U. S. Census Bureau. Retrieved April 8, 2013, from www.census.gov

Council for Disability Awareness (2012). *Chances of disability: Me disabled.* Retrieved April 8, 2013, from www.disabilitycanhappen.org/chances_disability/

Davis, N. A. (2005). Invisible disability. *Ethics, 116*(1), 153–213.

Fleischer, D., & Zames, F. (2011). *The disability rights movement: From charity to confrontation.* Philadelphia; PA: Temple University Press.

Gollnick, D. M., & Chinn, P. C. (2002). *Multicultural education in a pluralistic society* (6th ed.) Upper Saddle River, NJ: Merrill Prentice Hall.

Harris, S. P., Owen, R., & De Ruiter, C. (2012). Civic engagement and people with disabilities: The role of advocacy and technology. *Journal of Community Engagement and Scholarship, 5*(1). Retrieved April 8, 2013, from: http://jces.ua.edu/civic-engagement-and-people-with-disabilities-the-role-of-advocacy-and-technology/

Job Accommodation Network (Original 2005, Updated 2007, Updated 2009, Updated 2010, Updated 2011, Updated 2012, Updated 2013). *Workplace accommodations: Low cost, high impact.* Retrieved October 30, 2013, from http://AskJAN.org/media/lowcosthighimpact.html

Johnstone, C. J. (2004). Disability and identity: Personal constructions and formalized supports. *Disabilities Studies Quarterly, 24*(4). Retrieved October 29, 2013, from: http://dsq-sds.org/article/view/880/1055

Kaplan, D. (2000). The definition of disability—Perspective of the disability community. *Journal of Health Care Law and Policy, 3*(2), 352–364.

Office of Disability Employment Policy (n.d.). *Disability history: An important part of America's heritage.* U. S. Department of Labor. Washington, D.C.

Pelka, F. (2012). *What we have done: An oral history of the disability movement.* Amherst: University of Massachusetts Press.

Rehabilitation Act of 1973, Pub. L. No. 93-112, 87 Stat. 355 (codified as amended in scattered sections of 15 U.S.C., 20 U.S.C., 29 U.S.C., 36 U.S.C., 41 U.S.C., and 42 U.S.C.).

Rose, M. L. (2003). *The staff of Oedipus: Transforming disability in ancient Greece.* Ann Arbor: University of Michigan Press.

Ryan, D. J. (2011). *Job search handbook for people with disabilities.* Indianapolis, IN: JIST Works Publishing.

Schaefer, R. (2010). *Racial and ethnic groups* (12th ed.). Upper Saddle River, NJ: Pearson.

Stein, M. A., & Stein, P. J. S. (2007). Beyond disability civil rights. *Hastings Law Journal, 58,* 1203–1240.

Tororei, S. K. (2009). The right to work: A strategy for addressing the invisibility of persons with disability. *Disability Studies Quarterly, 29*(4), 12.

U.S. Department of Labor, Bureau of Labor Statistics. (2012). Labor force statistics from the current population Survey. Retrieved October 27, 2013, from www.bls.gov/cps/cpsdisability_faq.htm#Identified

World Health Organization. (2001). *International classification of functioning, disability and health: Short version.* Geneva, Switzerland: World Health Organization.

14

Re-Emergence of Racial Harassment and Racial Hate Symbols in the Workforce

Marilyn Y. Byrd and Chaunda L. Scott

Chapter Overview

In Chapter 2, race was discussed as a protected class under Title VII. In this chapter, the impact of racism and the re-emerging ways that racism exists is discussed. Racial hate symbols will be examined, and the historical significance associated with these symbols will be explained. The emotional effect of racism will also be explored. This chapter concludes with a discussion of diversity education as a necessary action for addressing racial harassment.

Learning Objectives

After reading this chapter, along with completing the critical-thinking discussion questions and the case discussion questions, you will be able to:

- Distinguish between racial discrimination and racial harassment
- Identify the historical significance of racial hate symbols
- Discuss the emotional impact of racial harassment
- Discuss racial harassment in the work environment
- Examine diversity training as adequate for addressing racial harassment

A perception exists in our society that racism has been eradicated by legislation (Byrd & Scott, 2010b). However, actions that constitute racism continue to be a problem in the U.S. workplace. In its very essence, racism involves not only negative attitudes and beliefs but also the social power that enables these behaviors to translate into disparate outcomes that disadvantage other races or offer unique advantages to one's own race at the expense of others (Feagin & Vera, 1995). "Racism is more than a matter of individual prejudice and scattered episodes of discrimination" (p. ix) . . . Rather, it can be further conceptualized as "the socially organized set of ideas, attitudes, and practices that deny African Americans and other people of color the dignity, opportunities, freedoms, and rewards that this nation offers white Americans" (p. 7).

Racism has three fundamental components (Jones, 1997). First, **racism** is rooted in beliefs about group differences (stereotypes) that are assumed to reflect fundamental biological differences. Second, racism involves an individual making well-differentiated negative evaluations and feelings about another racial group (prejudice). Whether or not the other group is described explicitly as inferior, the individual believes his/her group to be superior. Third, racism reflects the disparate treatment of groups (discrimination) by individuals and institutions in ways that perpetuate negative beliefs, attitudes, and outcomes. Racism may be demonstrated in the form of racial harassment or racial discrimination.

Encounters or experiences of **racial harassment** involve "thoughts, behaviors, actions, feelings, or policies and procedures that have strong hostile elements intended to create distance among racial group members after a person of color has gained entry into an environment from which he or she was once excluded" (Carter, 2007a, p. 79). Racial discrimination is a selectively unjustified negative behavior toward members of a target group that involves denying "individuals or groups of people equality of treatment which they may wish" (Allport, 1954, p. 51). Although both are forms of racism, there is a distinction between racial harassment and racial discrimination.

Racial discrimination is socialized racist actions captured in attitudes, behaviors, policies, and strategies for the purpose of maintaining racial group separatism (Carter, Forsyth, Williams, & Mazzula, 2007).

In addition, racial discrimination refers to episodes of avoidance whereas harassment pertains more to experiences of hostility. While racial discrimination is primarily applicable to unfair practices such as hiring, firing, promotion, and so on, racial harassment applies to conduct that creates a hostile, offensive, or intimidating work environment that has the potential to negatively impact an individual's ability to perform his or her job. Targets of racial harassment are subjected to racist actions that are "intended to communicate or make salient the target's subordinate or inferior status because of his or her membership in a non-dominant racial-group" (Carter & Helms, 2002, p. 5). Examples of racial harassment include ethnic slurs, derogatory statements or insults, and verbal or physical abuse.

Racial profiling is also a good example of contemporary racial harassment in professional work settings and professional fields due to the fact it also targets individuals based on their race, ethnicity, religious beliefs, or national origin who *appear* as if they may be *dangerous* according to the personnel in charge (American Civil Liberties Union, 2005). Instances of contemporary racial profiling highlighted by the American Civil Liberties Union (2005) include:

- Law enforcement officers without just cause regularly questioning, detaining, and ticketing African Americans and other dark-skinned minorities while driving for no just cause. These incidents are most commonly known as "driving while Black and Brown."
- Airline security guards as a result of September 11th have been detaining and denying Arabs, Muslims, and South Asians entry into the airport because they look similar to past terrorists.
- Airline pilots also as a result of September 11th have instructed travelers on aircrafts to deplane because one or more traveler's ethnic background and appearance has provoked fear and concerns among other travelers and the flight crew.

Socialized racist actions can become integrated with everyday practices in such a way that these actions become actualized and reinforced through routine situations as highlighted above (Essed, 1991). Essed developed a theoretical explanation for interpreting a situation as stemming from racism. First, the individual experiencing the event should have some general knowledge about the cultural and historical background of racism in order to distinguish an acceptable practice from an unacceptable one. Second, there needs to be a method of making a comparison with some other situation or context in which to fit this particular act. Third, a systemic analysis of the situation should be made that considers the context (place and actors involved), the complication (what was not acceptable), the explanation (what is the indicator[s] that racism was the intent), the argumentation (why the action was racially charged), and the reaction (how the subject responded). The impact of everyday racism in its various forms is **racial oppression.** Racial oppression is produced by using power and privilege to relegate a racial group to a subordinate status.

Historical Significance of Racial Hate Symbols

The system of slavery in the United States is a period when African natives were captured, transported, and sold as property. During this period, which lasted from the mid-1600s until about 1865, Whites exercised dominance, control, and intimidation over Africans (and subsequently American-born African people). The era of slavery established a racial divide that is ultimately the source of racism in this country.

Racial harassment is a lingering form of historical racism. One way that racial harassment is practiced is through the use of **racial hate symbols**. These symbols reflect hostile, violent, degrading, intimidating, or offensive racist acts against African Americans, some of which trigger images of death. Nooses are an example of a racial hate symbol. Nooses date back to the slavery era when Africans and African Americans were lynched as a form punishment for rebelling against their owners or for reasons that demonstrated the perceived authority and superiority of Whites over African Americans. In the post-Civil War era, nooses were linked to mob-like lynchings carried out by the Ku Klux Klan, a White supremacist group formed initially as a social fraternity organization. During that time, the Klan's mission was to maintain social order and preserve White supremacy. The organization later evolved as a terrorist group. To African Americans, nooses symbolize this period in history when they were targets for racial violence merely because of their skin color. In addition, nooses depict a period of segregation and subjugation, which were the essence of racism and discrimination in the United States (Hudson, 2008).

Since the Jena Six episode, the re-appearance of nooses has become a re-awakening of this symbol of hatred toward African American people. The Jena Six were a group of African American teens who were arrested in December 2006 after a fight in which a White student was beaten and suffered multiple bruises. The fight was the result of racial tensions at the Jena, Louisiana, high school where nooses (in school colors) were discovered hanging from a tree on school property. Immediately following Jena Six, there was an outbreak of noose-related incidents involving institutions of learning. A noose was found hanging on the office door of a Black professor at Teachers College, Columbia University in October 2007. In July 2010, a noose was found hanging in a campus building at the University of California, San Diego. During Black History Month, a KKK-style hood was found draped over a campus statute at that same university. According to DiversityInc (2010), 78 nooses have been reported in government buildings, schools, and workplaces.

Cross burning is another form of racial harassment that has historical roots and is commonly associated with the ideology of the Ku Klux Klan. The burning of crosses was often part of Klan rallies and, in some instances, served as a ritual at the site of a lynching.

> Klansmen burned churches and schools, lynching teachers and educated blacks. Black landowners were driven off their property and murdered if they refused to leave. Blacks were whipped for refusing to work for whites, for having intimate relations with whites, for arguing with whites, for having jobs whites wanted, for reading a newspaper or having a book in their homes. Or simply for being black. (Wormser, 2003, p. 25)

During the early period of desegregation, crosses were burned on the lawns of Black families to communicate the message that these families were not welcome in White neighborhoods. According to Bell (2004), state courts have negotiated First Amendment challenges to cross burning statutes. Rather than being treated as a hate crime, that should be prosecuted, cross burning has been deemed as constitutionally protected hate speech. In addition to nooses and cross burning, racist graffiti, posters, cartoons, drawings, pictures, confederate or swastika signs, and other similar visual displays of a racial nature against African Americans are invading the U.S. workplace (Thomas, 2010).

Another way that racial harassment is conveyed is through the use of technology. The media and the Internet are sources that provide an avenue for hate sentiment to be sustained. Blogs and websites that invite and encourage racist sentiments used to demean, degrade, insult, and offend Blacks and other ethnic groups are common. These media sources allow access to individuals who advocate racist sentiment. However, because the First Amendment "gives voice" to this type of sentiment, racial harassment lingers.

The subjection of racial harassment and the appearance of racial hate symbols are re-enactments of a mandated segregated era in this country referred to as the days of Jim Crow. Jim Crow was "synonymous with a complex system of racial laws and customs in the South that ensured White social, legal, and political dominance of Blacks. Blacks were segregated, deprived of their right to vote and subjected to verbal abuse, discrimination and violence without redress in the courts or support by the White community" (Wormser, 2003, p. xi).

In light of the allegations of racial harassment in work and public places, with the exception of segregation, the 21st century bears a strong resemblance to the Jim Crow era.

In *The Souls of Black Folks*, W.E.B. Du Bois (1903) made the now famous statement, "for the problem of the 20th century is the problem of the color-line." It is not without notice that the problem of the 20th century has spilled over into the 21st.

Emotional Impact of Racial Harassment

The emotional impact of racism, in general, on an individual's well-being is a topic that has received little attention in discussion of workforce diversity. Given the chronic and pervasive nature of racism that stems from the history of this country, it seems reasonable to argue that racism can cause people to become physically and emotionally vulnerable (Carter, 2007a). Furthermore, because racial harassment is hostile, aggressive, and takes the form of physical as well as verbal assaults, this conduct can be dangerous and criminal.

Encounters with racial harassment can produce nonpathological, race-based traumatic stress injury, a condition that involves emotional or physical pain or the threat of physical and emotional pain (Carter, 2007a). Research indicates that racial harassment has the potential for producing stress and stress-related psychological and physiological conditions. Race-based traumatic stress is a condition that results from racial harassment. This condition occurs suddenly, is beyond the target's control, and is emotionally painful (Carter, 2007a). The reactions to the event can be manifested through mental, physical, or emotional means.

Racial harassment can also be associated to demeaning situations where individuals are made to feel inferior. Racism should be labeled according to the actions taken (avoidance or hostility) so that specific psychological and emotional reactions can be addressed (Carter, 2006). An example of racism associated with avoidance would apply to situations where minorities were told there were no job openings. On the other hand, racism that is hostile in nature and illustrates demeaning and degrading conduct is enacted as racial harassment. This type of conduct involves situations and encounters where the target is humiliated and subjected to racial epithets, jokes, slurs, or taunts. Generally speaking, these are situations where the intent is that the individual (target) is made to feel inferior because of the color of their skin.

In the workplace, racial harassment is intended to communicate or make salient an inferior status because of membership in a nondominant racial group (Carter & Helms, 2002). In addition to physical and verbal assaults, racial harassment could take the form of assigning stereotypes such as being lazy or unintelligent (Carter, 2007b). Reactions to racial harassment evoke emotions such as anger, rage, shame, guilt, reduced self-esteem, and self-doubt.

Victims or targets of racial harassment have the option of filing a lawsuit or complaint through their organization, seeking the services of a mental health professional, or simply trying to cope with the situation and any lingering effects (Carter, 2007b). Linking the type of racial encounter to the individual's emotional and psychological reactions is a critical factor in assessing treatment as well as documenting emotional and psychological harm for pursuing litigation.

Racial harassment and racial discrimination should be treated as distinct events (Carter, 2007b). Should a complaint be filed, the target of the act must provide evidence that the intent to discriminate or harass is specifically ascribed to race. Organizations commonly respond to complaints of racism (discrimination or harassment) by trying to justify that factors other than race were responsible for the action. This strategy makes the person making the allegation appear to look foolish or overly sensitive. These types of tactics can produce additional stress for the individual having the experience because their perception of a racial event is challenged.

Racial Harassment in U.S. Work Environments

Since the presidential election of Barack Obama, a plethora of hate crimes have been noted in a variety of settings, including religious and governmental venues, nonprofit agencies, universities, and retail stores (Jacobs & Scott, 2010). In March 2010, customers at a Walmart Supercenter in New Jersey were angered, offended, and embarrassed when an unidentified voice came over the public address system ordering all Blacks to leave the store. The victims of this racial harassment were not only customers who were shopping at the store, but the Black employees of the supercenter. The alleged perpetrator, a 16-year-old male, is further indication that racism is not dying out but is being passed on through generations. Moreover, this incident suggests that racism is assuming new forms of harassment.

Ironically, a significant portion of workplace diversity research centers on the business case for diversity enhancing the bottom line (Bell, Connerley, & Cocchiara, 2009). In the example of Walmart, the context of a retail store impacts both customers and employees. In this example, the business case for promoting diversity in the workplace is challenged. Derogatory racial comments in this context can result in a loss of customers as well as result in lowered commitment and perhaps even turnover of employees. Given that reports of racial harassments in the form of hate symbols and hate speech has pervaded workplaces where multiple stakeholders are offended, it is obvious that the business case for diversity has failed to make a difference.

Racial harassment is "unconsciously" being taught in public schools. In May 2010, a Lumpkin County, Georgia, teacher allowed students to dress in KKK outfits, depicting the White supremacist hate group that had large chapters in Georgia, as part of a history class project. A Black student was approached and asked to assist in the re-enactment of a lynching.

Bonilla-Silva (2006) suggests that many White Americans view racism as a thing of the past, insisting that they view people as human beings rather than assigning them to a specific race, ethnicity, or other diverse group. If that is so, does this simply mean that the word "racism" is no longer being used, but racist practices are still being played out? Chapter 4 presented a discussion on race as a protected status under Title VII of the Civil Rights Act of 1964. This same legislation mandated the establishment of the Equal Employment Opportunity Commission (EEOC). The purpose of the EEOC is to investigate complaints of discrimination on behalf of members of a protected status. The EEOC has the power to file suit against employers found to be in violation of Title VII. In 2007, the EEOC reported almost 7,000 cases of race-based harassment (Bello, 2008).

Table 15.1 shows violations of Title VII settled by the EEOC from 2005 to 2010. The context of the complaints is provided to give an overview of the types of environments as well as the types of complaints.

Table 14.1   Violations of Title VII Settled by the EEOC from 2005 to 2012

YEAR	EMPLOYER INDUSTRY	COMPLAINT
2012	Transportation	Permitting multiple incidents of hangman's nooses and racist graffiti, comments, and cartoons
2011	Wholesale	Permitting physical and offensive verbal harassment based on race and national origin (Ex: N-words and using the term "African bastard").
2010	Custom Home Manufacturer	Permitting display of racial symbols (namely, nooses), racially offensive pictures, and use of the "N" word
2009	Car dealership/New York	Permitting derogatory comments and using racial epithets and racial slurs including the "N" word against a 16-year-old Black student apprentice; permitting the display of racist symbols
2008	Military Contractor	Threats of death by lynching
2008	Furniture Manufacturer	Permitting use of N word, racial slurs, nooses
2007	Aviation/Alabama	Permitting KKK videos and display of nooses
2006	Car Retailer	Continuous subjection to racially derogatory remarks
2005	News Publisher	Daily subjection to racial epithets

Is Training a Solution for Addressing Racial Harassment?

Despite diversity training and race-relations programs conducted by corporations, racial bias and hatred is increasing in the U.S. workplace (Tahmincioglu, 2008). As discussed in this chapter, acts such as the appearance of nooses, burning crosses, and graffiti—along with the use of racial epithets and insults—are signals that racial harassment is flourishing.

Diversity training is now inclusive of a number of workplace diversity issues. The problem with diversity training programs is that many are canned and do not capture the specific issues that are occurring within a work environment.

> It isn't surprising that many people cannot make the distinction between racism to be reviled versus diversity to be embraced. On one hand, we must appreciate our differences to be diverse, but on the other hand, we must all be alike to avoid racism. While diversity is not something to be avoided, it cannot be forced, as with affirmative action programs, or it leads to division, resentment and yes, racism. (Larson, 2006)

The multidirectional focus of diversity initiatives in organizations has shifted from the original objective of sensitivity training programs that focused on sensitivity training (Byrd, 2007). However, training may not be an effective remedial solution for organizations that are experiencing problems with racial harassment. Searching for causal and contributing elements may yield greater results. Organizations that offer diversity training in an attempt to correct racial issues may be unsuccessful in their attempt. HR professionals might explore interventions such as distributing surveys to assess instances of reported mistreatment and conducting organization-wide workshops that focus on behavior modifications to induce modern racists to reconstruct discriminatory attitudes (Deitch et al., 2003).

The Black/White binary forms the primary paradigm for race relations in the United States and represents the major source of racial friction in the U.S. workplace. The racial harassment directed toward Blacks maintains a racial division and will continue to break down and destroy race relations. Improving race relations in organizations will require more than a training effort (Byrd, 2007). It will require creative and innovative efforts such as the one introduced at Motorola, management that is willing to recognize that racial behaviors do exist, and leaders who are willing to engage in organization-wide efforts to address the persistence of racial harassment. Indeed, diversity training is one of the top training interventions in organizations today, because it is intended to expose differences in people in hopes of creating greater harmony among the workforce. Differences in people are obvious. The problem is that the concept of diversity now encompasses a growing list of ways that people differ, which has tended to diffuse oppressive issues such as racism that can stem from racial differences. The late Elsie Cross, a pioneer in the field of diversity, explained, "While other differences may be important, these differences haven't led to the most egregious forms of discrimination in this country" as discrimination based on race (as cited in Caudron & Hayes, 1997, p. 122). Without real discourse about racism, diversity training will hold little value other than being another training effort.

Organizations' approach to diversity training generally speaks from a discrimination and fairness paradigm or access and legitimacy paradigm in terms of practices and processes of employment (Thomas & Ely, 2000). However, few diversity training programs in organizations approach diversity training from a social justice and emancipatory paradigm (Byrd & Scott, 2010a). Social justice is a moral obligation and reflects the highest standard by which individuals within organizations are treated (Mill & Bentham, 1987). For this reason, diversity training programs should reflect the realism and existence of social justice issues, such as racism, that derive from diversity in the workplace. Because the word *racism* evokes fear and implies blatant and deplorable forms of hatred, diversity training programs tend to skirt the topic.

Leadership and management in workplace settings should be willing to take action against all types of racial oppression (Byrd, 2007). In light of the persistence of racial oppression such as racial harassment, the following questions should be considered.

- Are diversity training programs inclusive of antiracist content?
- Do diversity training programs, videos, orientation programs, and the like discuss racial harassment in terms of racist undertones?

- Are organizations willing to implement social justice content into diversity training?
- Do leadership and management training programs include content for leaders on addressing and problem-solving racial harassment?
- Are diversity training programs designed to build race relations?

Alderfer, Alderfer, Bell, and Jones (1992) conceptualized a Race Relations Workshop as the educational component of a management education program to improve race relations. The catalyst for this undertaking was the premise of education as a tool for change. Forming the framework for this project was a manager's race relations competence. Race relations competence is "an element of overall managerial competence. A manager who is competent in race relations possesses certain kinds of knowledge about key issues in race relations and acts in specific ways with respect to racial issues" (p. 1263). Companies such as Motorola are also implementing diversity initiatives in an effort to improve race relations. The Cross-Country Diversity Network, consisting of human resource professionals from different organizations, was born from Motorola's efforts to respond to the needs and frustrations of a diverse workforce (Mai-Dalton, 1993).

The reality is that deplorable forms of hatred are actually being experienced in the workplace. As a result, the avoidance of discussions of racism allows individuals to hide their true racial viewpoints, which allows acts of racial harassment to thrive (Bonilla-Silva, 2006). In an effort to eradicate acts of racial discrimination and harassment in workplace settings presently and in the future, the following strategies are offered.

1. If you are a victim of racial discrimination and harassment in a workplace setting, report these acts **immediately** to upper management or your human resources department. If your workplace does not have a formal policy to address these demeaning and offensive acts, contact the Equal Employment Opportunity Commission (EEOC) (www.eeoc360.com/).
2. As an employee—don't ignore racial slurs (racial insults and smears) in work settings directed at colleagues from diverse back-

grounds. Speak out against their offensiveness by reporting these acts to upper management and your human resources department, who are responsible for responding to this issue.

3. As an employee—don't ignore visual signs of racial discrimination and racial harassment (e.g., nooses) in work settings directed at colleagues from diverse backgrounds. Speak out against their impropriety by reporting these demeaning visual signs of racial injustice to upper management and your human resource department, who are accountable for responding to these acts.

To address racial harassment, organizations will need to move from diversity training to diversity education targeting all levels of the organization (Byrd & Scott, 2010a). Shifting the focus to diversity education means moving beyond awareness that inappropriate racial conduct exists toward transforming the culture into one that is more open and receptive to the multiple forms of diversity that are emerging in the workplace. Providing diversity education in academic preparation and professional development training is necessary. Executives and managers are responsible for conveying the message and *operationalizing the practice of a hostile-free, stress-free climate where all individuals* have the opportunity to thrive and perform at an optimum level.

Chapter Summary

Racial harassment is a form of racism that is practiced through hostile and aggressive physical and verbal conduct and hate symbols. The growing number of complaints handled by the EEOC is indication that racial harassment continues to be a problem in U.S. society. Because the workplace simulates the broader society, racism is a pervasive and destructive force in the workplace.

There is no simple solution to social problems such as racism. However, organizations should begin examining the problem as a need for more inclusive and direct diversity education initiatives that directly target and address issues such as racial harassment.

Definition of Key Terms

Racial discrimination—Unjustified negative behavior toward members of a target group that involves denying individuals or groups of people equality of treatment which they may wish.

Racial harassment—Conduct that creates a hostile, offensive, or intimidating work environment that has the potential to negatively impact an individual's ability to perform his or her job.

Racial hate symbols—Symbols such as nooses, drawings, cross burning, and confederate or swastika signs that are associated with hostile, violent, degrading, intimidating, or offensive racist acts against African Americans. Some of these symbols have historical roots that trigger images of death.

Racial oppression—The outcome of racism by using power and privilege to relegate a racial group to a subordinate status.

Racial profiling—A form of racial harassment that targets individuals based on their race, ethnicity, religious beliefs, or national origin who appear as if they may be dangerous according to the personnel in charge (American Civil Liberties Union, 2005).

Racism—Accepted racist ideology and the use of power to deny other racial groups the basic dignity and freedoms awarded to one's own group.

Critical-Thinking Discussion Questions

1. How have companies such as Home Depot, Lockheed Martin, and others that have settled racial harassment lawsuits worked to improve their organization's image?
2. Do you think organizations should have policies that explicitly address racial hate symbols? Why or why not?
3. Is racial harassment addressed by the EEOC? Explain.
4. What are some of the remedies available for victims of racial harassment?

Visit: www.workplacefairness.org/raceharassment?agree=yes#2

Case Study: The Recurring Problem of Nooses in the Workplace

The emergence of nooses in the workplace as a symbol of racial harassment began in the 1990s (U.S. Equal Employment Opportunities Commission, 2000). The presence of nooses in the workplace represents not only a resistance to diversity but is a hostile example of racial harassment at the individual level (Thomas, 2010). When management does not address these types of incidents, resistance to diversity is now reflected at the organizational level. For example, Reginald Smith, an assembly plant worker, entered his work area one morning and was appalled to see a noose hanging from his equipment locker. Smith, the only African American worker in the plant's assembly area, immediately confronted his immediate supervisor, who downplayed the incident. Weeks later a second noose appeared on Smith's locker. This time Smith filed a complaint with the Equal Employment Opportunity Commission.

1. Identify the workforce diversity problem.
2. Describe the feelings Reginald may be experiencing given that he is the only African American worker and he is well aware of symbolic meanings associated with nooses.
3. Discuss the actions of Reginald's supervisor.
4. How could this problem be corrected? What framework presented in Chapter 2 would be useful in addressing this problem? Explain your response.

Legal Perspective

Equal Employment Opportunity Commission vs. Lockheed Martin

In August 2005, the Equal Employment Opportunity Commission (EEOC) filed a race discrimination lawsuit against Lockheed Martin on behalf of Charles Daniels. Lockheed Martin, the largest military contractor in the world, was alleged to have subjected Daniels to a racially hostile work environment and severe racial harassment where he was threatened with lynching. In addition to physical and death threats, Daniels was subjected to physical threats of violence and verbal abuse by coworkers and supervisors who used racial slurs and other offensive references to Blacks. Despite officials being aware of the harassment, the perpetrators were not disciplined. The EEOC settled a $2.5 million lawsuit with Lockheed Martin in January 2008 for racial harassment. (*Source:* U.S. Equal Employment Opportunity Commission, www.eeoc .gov/eeoc/newsroom/release/1–2-08.cfm)

References

Alderfer, C. P., Alderfer, C. J., Bell, E. L., & Jones, J. (1992). The race rela-tions competence workshop: Theory and results. *Human Relations, 45*(12), 1259–1273.

Allport. G. W. (1954*). The nature of prejudice.* Reading, MA: Addison-Wesley.

American Civil Liberties Union. (2005). Racial justice racial profiling—Racial profiling: Definition. Retrieved October 22, 2010, from www.aclu.org/racial-justice/racial-profiling-definition

Bell, J. (2004). O say, can you see: Free expression by the light of fiery crosses. *Harvard Civil Rights, Civil Liberties, 39,* 335–3. Retrieved October 16, 2010, from www.law.harvard.edu/students/orgs/crcl/vol39_2/bell.pdf

Bell, M., Connerley, M. L., & Cocchiara, F. K. (2009). The case for mandatory diversity education. *Academy of Management, Learning & Education, 8*(4), 597–610.

Bello, M. (2008). Racial harassment cases rise sharply. *USA Today.* Re-trieved July 24, 2010, from www.usatoday.com/news/nation/2008–02–05-nooses_N.htm

Bonilla-Silva, E. (2006). *Racism without racists: Color-blind racism and the per-sistence of racial inequality in the United States.* Lanham, MD: Rowman & Littlefield.

Byrd, M. (2007). Educating and developing leaders of racially diverse organiza-tions. *Human Resource Development Quarterly, 18*(2), 275–279.

Byrd, M., & Scott, C. L. (2010a). *Changing the culture: Diversity education for executives and managers of a multi-diverse workforce.* Session presented at the 4th annual meeting of the George Mason University Workforce Diversity Research and Practice Conference, Arlington, VA.

Byrd, M., & Scott, C. L. (2010b). Integrating dialogue on forms of racism within human resource development workplace diversity courses and workplace settings: Implications for HRD. In C. Graham (Ed.), *Proceed-ings of the 2010 Academy of Human Resource Development Conference of the Americas* (pp. 1315–1336). Knoxville, TN: Academy of Human Resource Development.

Carter, R. T. (2006). Race-based traumatic stress. *Psychiatric Times, 23*(14), 37–38.

Carter, R. T. (2007a). Racism and psychological and emotional injury: Recog-nizing and assessing *race*-based traumatic stress. *Counseling Psychologist, 35,* 13–105. doi:10.1177/0011000006292033

Carter, R. T. (2007b). Clarification and purpose of the race-based traumatic stress injury model. *The Counseling Psychologist, 35*(1), 144–154.

Carter, R. T., Forsyth, J., Williams, B., & Mazzula, S. (2007). Racism as a pre-dictor of psychological injury: Implications for psychology and the law. *Law Enforcement Executive Forum, 7,* 131–156.

Carter, R. T., & Helms, J. E. (2002, September). *Racial discrimination and ha-rassment: A race based traumatic stress disorder.* Paper presented at the Ameri-can College of Forensic Examiners Conference, Orlando, FL.

Caudron, S., & Hayes, C. (1997). Are diversity programs benefiting African Americans? *Black Enterprise, 27*(7), 121–128.

Deitch, E. A., Barsky, A., Butz, R. M., Chan, S., Brief, A. P., & Bradley, J. C. (2003). Subtle yet significant: The existence and impact of everyday racial discrimination in the workplace. *Human Relations, 56*(11), 1299–1324.

DiversityInc (2010). DiversityInc, Noose Watch. Retrieved October 21, 2010, from http://diversityinc.com/content/1757/article/2588/

Du Bois, W.E.B. (1903). *The souls of Black folk.* New York: New American Library.

Essed, P. (1991). *Understanding everyday racism: An interdisciplinary theory.* Newbury Park, CA: Sage.

Feagin, J. R., & Vera, H. (1995). *White racism.* New York: Routledge.

Hudson D., Jr. (2008, Winter). Banning the noose. *Intelligence Report, 132,* Southern Poverty Law Center.

Jacobs, J., & Scott, C. (2010, February). *Workplace violence—The persistence of hate crimes: Implications for HRD.* Presentation and Proceedings for the 2009 AHRD International Research Conference of the Americas. Washington, D.C.

Jones, J. M. (1997). *Prejudice and racism* (2nd ed.). New York: McGraw-Hill.

Larson, J. (2006, April 10). Diversity and racism. *American Chronicle.* Retrieved July 23, 2010, from: www.americanchronicle.com/articles/view/7846

Mai-Dalton, R. R. (1993). Managing cultural diversity on the individual, group, and organizational levels. In M. M. Chemers & R. Ayman (Eds.), *Leadership theory and research: Perspectives and directions* (pp. 189–215). San Diego, CA: Academic Press.

Mill, J. S., & Bentham, J. (1987). *Utilitarianism and other essays.* Edited by A. Ryan. New York: Penguin Group.

Tahmincioglu, E. (2008, January 13). Racial harassment still infecting the workplace. MSNBC. Retrieved July 23, 2010, from www.msnbc.msn.com/id/22575581/

Thomas, D. A., & Ely, R. J. (2000). Making differences matter: A new paradigm for managing diversity. *Harvard Business Review, 74*(5), 79–90.

Thomas, Y. (2010). Racial discrimination in the workplace. Retrieved July 24 2010, from www.you-can-learn-basic-employee-rights.com/racial-discrimination.html

U.S. Equal Employment Opportunity Commission (EEOC) (2000). *EEOC chairperson responds to surge of workplace noose incidents at NAACP Annual Convention.* Retrieved October 4, 2010, from www.eeoc.gov/eeoc/newsroom/release/7–13–00-b.cfm

U.S. Equal Employment Opportunity Commission (EEOC) (2008). Lockheed Martin to pay $2.5 million to settle racial harassment lawsuit. Retrieved July 24, 2010, from www.eeoc.gov/eeoc/newsroom/release/1-2-08.cfm

Wormser, R. (2003). *Rise and fall of Jim Crow.* New York: St. Martin's Press.

15

CROSS-CULTURAL TEAM OPPORTUNITIES AND CHALLENGES IN THE WORKFORCE WITH GLOBAL IMPLICATIONS

Trammell Bristol and Chaunda L. Scott

Chapter Overview

This chapter will address the challenges associated with cross-cultural teams from a global perspective. These types of teams are impacted by many issues, and in order to provide a comprehensive understanding of this topic, a discussion must begin with globalization and multinational corporations. Globalization has become more significant in recent years because of advances in technology, transportation, and communication. As a result, corporations have forged markets to sell their products and services in foreign countries.

In addition, since multinational corporations operate on an international level, they have to interact more with diverse cultures, including employing a diverse workforce. As a result, managing diversity has become a means by which multinational corporations have grown to understand the needs of its customers to become more competitive. While there can be success when culturally diverse members of the workforce function as a cross-cultural team, there can also be challenges. Therefore, it is imperative that corporations be willing to manage diversity in the workplace in an effective manner. This chapter will explore the challenges as well as the impact that cross-cultural teams can have when multinational corporations manage diversity.

Learning Objectives

After reading this chapter, along with completing the critical-thinking discussion questions and the case discussion questions, you will be able to:

- Explore the role of globalization and its impact on business in the modern world
- Discover how cultural diversity has impacted the business environment
- Develop an understanding of the significance of managing diversity in order to facilitate cross-cultural teams in the modern business environment
- Identify the characteristics that are needed for cross-cultural teams to be effective

Historical Perspective on Globalization

In the history of mankind, there has always been the exporting of products to other nations. The research of Moore and Lewis (2009) illustrates that trading has been part of our history since the first ships set sail. For example, the Romans set up companies that operated throughout the world and functioned much like private corporations. They elected CEOs and hired employees in other countries to represent their interest. The Romans established businesses that operated trade routes along the Red Sea and sailed to Ethiopia. Roman ships "could carry as much as 300 tons of wine, silver and other goods to India . . . [and] these same ships could carry back bulk shipments of Indian spices and Chinese silk" (Moore & Lewis, 2009, p. 4). Eventually, their ability to expand was limited because of travel. However, the Romans were instrumental in establishing international trade, albeit on a smaller scale, within in our society.

In modern times, advances in travel have enabled corporations to reach many countries. Advances in technology and media have also facilitated the growth of business internationally. According to Marquardt and Reynolds (1994), there are now more companies that operate outside of their country of origin, such as Honda and Motorola. For example, Honda originated in 1948 in Japan manufacturing motor bikes; now Honda has grown to manufacture not only motorcycles but also automobiles. Currently, North America accounts for more than 50% of the total sales of the company. Not only does Honda sell its products aboard, but it also manufactures them in countries abroad, such as Brazil and the United States (Honda Motor Company, 2009).

Another example of a company that has grown to operate in international markets is Motorola, founded in Chicago, Illinois, in the 1920s. Initially, Motorola's products included automobile car radios, televisions, and various telecommunication products. In the 1960s, the company expanded and marketed its products in eight countries, including Japan. Currently, the company manufactures communication and electronics products and employs people in 37 countries (Wiechmann, Ryan, & Hemingway, 2003).

Globalization Defined

The success of the aforementioned companies highlights the prevalence of businesses operating on an international level. Organizations that operate on an international level are multinational corporations. Now more than ever, companies are seeking opportunities to produce and distribute their products and services to more markets. This phenomenon has been termed *globalization,* and the corporation's focus is to conduct business internationally in order to maximize its profits. While globalization expands a company's earning potential, oftentimes there are benefits for the average citizen. First, a major benefit of globalization has been the expansion of goods and services in developing markets; this expansion has allowed consumers to obtain varied and less expensive products in their country (Kohut & Wike, 2008).

Second, globalization has facilitated the creation of job growth (Johnson, Lenartowicz, & Apud, 2006). Workers in developing economies are able to relocate to pursue new and better opportunities in countries with stronger economies. In addition, companies can build plants in cost-effective locations to manufacture and assemble their products.

Third, multinational companies are committed to making positive impacts abroad (Ali, 2001). For example, in 2006 General Electric Co. (GE)'s Developing Health Globally Program partnered with 11 ill-equipped hospitals in Ghana to make improvements to patient care.

Patients from the rural regions of the country walk to these hospitals for care. It was imperative for these hospitals to be able to enhance their technology; as a result of GE's involvement, these hospitals received newer equipment, including X-ray machines, ultrasound machines, patient monitors, infant warmers, water filters, and generators. The advances in technology at this hospital have facilitated marked improvements in the level of care for the patients.

Due to the technological advances in communication and transportation over the past 50 years, globalization has progressed (Rangan & Lawrence, 1999). This progress has lessened the distance between nations and, more significantly, facilitated changes in governmental policies to permit or increase trade. In fact, since 1989 "globalization has increased significantly . . . with the collapse of the Soviet bloc, the creation of a single Europe, the implementation of the North American Free Trade Agreement (NAFTA) and the establishment of the World Trade Organization (WTO)" (Johnson, Lenartowicz, & Apud, 2006, p. 525). The Soviet bloc inhibited foreign trade and investment within its borders; since its collapse, international companies have taken advantage of new business opportunities.

Since the creation of the WTO, European Union (EU), and NAFTA, three zones of economic activity have been cultivated to facilitate the free flow of goods, services, and capital within these nations. The WTO serves as a global governing body for trade policies between foreign companies. The second entity, the European Union, or EU, consists of 27 countries in Europe that in 1999 adopted the European currency system. The goal of the EU is for "goods, services, capital, and human resources to flow across national borders in Europe in a manner similar to the way they cross state lines in the United States" (Sherman, Bohlander, & Snell, 1998, p.631). The third entity, the North American Free Trade Agreement (NAFTA), was created to facilitate opportunities for trade and investment between Mexico, Canada, and the United States.

Challenges to Globalization

As with any business venture, globalization has its challenges. While some companies have been successful in operating on an international level, it has not gone without its challenges. In fact, there are several barriers to globalization. According to Rangan and Lawrence (1999), these barriers include: (a) policies that restrict trade and decrease competition from international players, (b) the costs of transportation and communication, (c) the use of collusive strategies of local corporations that ultimately inhibit or exclude competition from outsiders, and (d) a lack of knowledge of the culture and its preferences. Of the aforementioned barriers, it appears that culture is more difficult to address (Uday-Riley, 2006). According to Lillis and Tian (2009), multinational corporations can be ill-prepared to interact in global environments because they are not sensitive to the role of culture. One example of this is Hong Kong Disneyland. Disney knew that it wanted to bring its four themed lands, entertainment, and amusement park to China but this region was unfamiliar with the Disney characters. Initially, Disney Hong Kong was not received well and drew criticism from the government. According to Matusitz (2011), the barriers that Disney experienced were the result of making the Hong Kong Disneyland westernized and failing to capture the significance of the local culture. In order for Hong Kong Disneyland to survive, Disney had to adapt to local customs including labor practices so that the business venture would thrive. The above example illustrates that cultural differences can negatively impact a corporation's ability to thrive. The next section of the chapter will explore the concept of culture and how culture can be a challenge to globalization.

Culture and Its Significance for Globalization

In 1980, Geert Hofstede, an influential Dutch social psychologist and anthropologist, defined culture as "the collective programming of the mind which distinguishes the members of one group or society from those of another" (Berger, 1996, p. 3). The transmission of culture can come by means of parents and/or teachers relaying acceptable behavior and/or defining what is good or bad. These labels then program a person to prescribe positive or negative labels to other cultural groups. However, culture provides a context for understanding a person (e.g., what may be similar or different between cultures). Culture manifests itself as either implicit or explicit (Berger, 1996). For instance, implicit culture defines the meaning of life and our basic assumptions, such as making meaning of the things around us. Conversely, explicit culture defines our norms and values which become visible in music, architecture, food, language, dress, and so on. For multinational corporations, understanding this information provides a preliminary understanding of what may or may not appeal to a specific culture. In addition, culture provides a framework for understanding relationships, especially in the workplace, and the nature of how work is to be carried out.

Moreover, Hofstede understood that as more companies operate in different cultures, there needed to be an effective manner in which they could work. Hofstede's research in 1983 (Berger, 1996) created a framework for understanding cultural differences, and it has implications for teams in multinational corporations. There are four fundamental dimensions of culture: (1) power distance, (2) uncertainty avoidance, (3) individualism, and (4) masculinity.

1. Power distance—This concept assesses the extent to which members of a society accept that power is unequally distributed. A large power distance denotes that employee involvement is difficult to implement because of the autocratic management style. In this type of management style, employees look to management for approval. On the other hand, with a small power distance, employees are more independent and leadership is shared. In fact, employees collaborate and consult with leadership.

2. Uncertainty avoidance—This concept measures the degree to which people feel threatened by ambiguous situations; it can impact the creation of beliefs and institutions to avoid uncertainty. In cultures with high uncertainty avoidance, rules are important and they invent rituals, rules, and regulations to counteract risks. Risks are only taken within secure parameters. Conversely, in low uncertainty avoidance cultures, formality and paperwork are viewed as disruptive and unnecessarily bureaucratic. This low-scoring culture values risk-taking as part of the norm.

3. Individualism—This concept explores the extent to which people believe that their primary concern in life is the well-being of individuals and their immediate family, or the well-being of a wider grouping with a more extended network of support and loyalty. In highly individualistic cultures, meetings are seen as a

waste of time. While the individual may be part of a group, they see themselves as part of a team but may look for individual recognition. Additionally, this type of society values a competitive approach which is more individualistic because there is more of a focus on the individual. It demands that individuals produce in order for them to be rewarded. Most Western societies fall into this category. In contrast, collective cultures value consultation and collaboration; they operate as a team. The structure of the workplace encourages people to be productive and management listens to its employees. The team also shares in goal setting and is rewarded accordingly.

4. Masculinity—This concept measures the extent to which masculine values, such as success, money, and possessions, are given priority over "caring" values (or less masculine values), such as nurturing and sharing.

The purpose for using Hofstede's framework is to develop an understanding for not only your culture but also other cultures. When a person is able to analyze differences between cultures, it furthers the understanding of how cultural differences may impact the workplace and how to work most effectively within those differences.

Communication Across Cultures

According to Johnson et al. (2006), in most multinational corporations, part of an aspiring manager's career development is an assignment in one of its locations in a foreign country. While, "over 100,000 U.S. expatriates are sent overseas each year . . . the expatriate failure rate [is] estimated at between 40 and 55%" (Johnson et al., 2006, p. 526). Living in a foreign country can be a challenge because of adjusting to a different culture. What has been troubling is that at times these managers request to return home early and abandon their assignment. For corporations, this can be costly and "estimates range from $250,000 to $1 million" (Johnson et al., 2006, p. 526). These costs do not include expenses related to low productivity and damaged relationships for the corporation. Therefore, according to Matveev and Milter (2004), companies need to prepare managers to work in a different culture. Matveev and Milter argue that this can be accomplished by developing intercultural competence (IC). This type of training enhances the employee's knowledge about a foreign culture and language, but it also facilitates the understanding of how to interact with other cultures. Some of the skills include emotional and behavioral skills to accompany effective implementation, such as empathy, and the ability to manage anxiety and uncertainty.

Operating on a global level results in a need to be knowledgeable of the various cultures and the verbal and nonverbal forms of communication. What is often unrealized is that nonverbal communication accounts for the most important aspect of the message when communicating with someone from a different culture (Tirmizi, 2008). Misunderstanding a foreign culture can have grave consequences. For example, Ricks (1999) recounts the story of an American employee working in a Korean knitting mills plant in South Carolina. The American employee, trying to catch the attention of his Korean boss, crooked his finger to signal for him to move closer. This nonverbal gesture is considered vulgar in Korea. Hence, the boss was insulted and this misunderstanding almost cost this employee his job. This story illustrates that while communication is a joint activity, a clear understanding of the message depends upon the person receiving the information correctly. However, "even if a message is accurately transmitted and the meaning of the words are understood, the addressee may not 'understand' the message or comply with the speaker's intentions" (Orasanu, Fischer, & Davison, 1997, p.143). Therefore, the process of effective communication needs to ensure that the message has been understood (by clarifying the message) and that the message was transmitted as intended.

An important aspect of managing diversity encompasses understanding communication across various cultures. There are different facets of communication, which can include verbal and nonverbal forms. Clearly, the research highlights the significance of corporations being willing to invest in training their employees to understand all aspects of a specific culture. Communication training is one structure that an organization can implement to manage diversity effectively.

Diversity and Teams

According to Maznevski and Peterson (1997), a team encompasses a set of people who are working together to contribute to a project for the good of the organization. The team functions to make sense of and respond to a task that was assigned by the leadership of the organization. The team analyzes information and responds in accordance with the understanding of what the implications may have for their internal group process as well as the functioning of the organization. For example, a team can be given the assignment to plan and implement a reorganization of a business unit; the team begins by exploring the past history of the unit. The team then explores a broad array of sources (e.g., team members' own experiences, external sources, supervisors, etc.) to develop an understanding of the unit, with the goal of directing the organization in making a thorough and meaningful response for the future of the unit. Organizations have utilized teams as a means of conducting meaningful work and making informed decisions in organizations. As the nature of the business environment has changed, organizations have begun to form specialized teams to address contemporary issues.

Culturally diverse (e.g., race and gender) teams have been important in the modern business environment as companies seek to understand and make inroads into various niche markets (Ely & Thomas, 2001). The significance of culturally diverse teams has been discussed in the American management literature. Cox (2001) has argued that members of similar cultural identity groups have a similar understanding of the world. Therefore, the team that lacks diversity lacks the ability to operate as effectively in an environment that is culturally diverse. In order for groups to be effective, there needs to be representation in the numbers of those who are marginalized within the organization. "When group members share common goals and values, cultural diversity leads to more beneficial outcomes" (Ely & Thomas, 2001, p. 234). However, there are challenges for cross-cultural teams; these challenges result from the fact that cultural identity has been constructed by those in power. "Cultural identity [is] associated in the larger society with certain power positions such that some cultural identity groups have greater power, prestige and status than others"

(Ely & Thomas, 2001, p. 231). For example, in Western societies there are certain groups that have higher status and positions of power. Those with power are typically made up of White men, and in general, they hold more positions of power in organizations. As a result, in order for cross-cultural teams to be effective, a structure that mitigates these power issues needs to be implemented.

Ely and Thomas (2001) explored cultural diversity (i.e., racial diversity) to uncover how different companies utilized diversity to expand. They found that cultural diversity was most effective when one particular company utilized it as a resource "not only to gain entrée into previously inaccessible niche markets, but at its core, to rethink and reconfigure its primary tasks" (p. 265). This perspective, integration and learning, was effective because it prompted the team to see cultural diversity as a resource for learning and teaching. Therefore, knowledge that resulted from the culturally diverse teams enhanced the competitiveness of this company. In addition, the team viewed conflict as a means to facilitate constructive exploration of diverse views. The company that used the integration and learning perspective was able to increase its business opportunities in culturally diverse markets due to the aforementioned perspective.

In contrast, the other perspectives did not value the knowledge of those who were culturally diverse. These perspectives advocated for assimilation of minorities into the dominant culture. Therefore, knowledge from the culturally diverse was not valued, and these organizations failed to make strides in new and diverse markets. Ely and Thomas's (2001) research is significant because it highlights the importance of ensuring that the company adopts a framework that values managing diversity at its core business practices. Cox (2001) defines managing diversity as implementing systems and practices into the organization that values people's differences. This perspective enhances the advantages of diversity while minimizing the potential disadvantages. Hence, it is significant to ensure that organizations adopt a perspective that manages diversity in the workplace that is also in line with Ely and Thomas's integration and learning perspective.

While the above research focused on corporations in the United States, it highlights that managing diversity must be implemented so that potential challenges to cross-cultural teams can be minimized. As a result, corporations need to establish a culture of managing diversity in the workplace. Similarly, when multinational corporations operate in different cultures they must develop a way that will value the knowledge of its employees from those different cultures. "It is important for companies to realize that markets today are worldwide and cross-cultural. Being aware of and sensitive to cultural differences is a major factor in the world marketplace" (Lillis & Tian, 2009, p. 429). Therefore, the research on culturally diverse teams highlights the importance of managing diversity (e.g., valuing of and exposing employees to cultural diversity).

Cross-Cultural Teams

The material in this section will explore structures and support that organizations can utilize to manage diversity in the workplace, more specifically within cross-cultural teams. The literature highlights how cross-cultural teams can be utilized and facilitated most effectively.

A cross-cultural team can be defined as a team that potentially offers "innovative and higher-quality solutions to global business problems than do monocultural teams. They bring together people having information about different pieces of a multinational corporation's world. They also provide different frames of reference for projecting potential future scenarios for a multinational corporation" (Maznevski & Peterson, 1997, p. 61). What makes an effective cross-cultural team is the integration and building of knowledge from varied cultural perspectives. Cross-cultural teams also help multinational corporations "achieve autonomy and flexibility needed to serve a variety of customers in different regions while obtaining the efficiencies afforded by an integrated organization" (Snell, Snow, Davidson, & Hambrick, 1998, p. 147). Therefore, organizations need to implement a structure that will enhance the skills of its employees; not preparing employees can be detrimental.

What remains true is that in cross-cultural teams, there will be representation from different cultures. As a result, varied responses will be elicited and this may create conflict in the team. Specifically, when analyzing the collective and individualistic approach from Hofstede's framework, there are differences in how team members will interact. For example, individualistic cultures interact in the team to ensure that their own self-interests are preserved in the group. They will present their argument or idea and oppose those which directly contradict their own. In contrast, collectivist cultures will listen carefully to other group members and consider their arguments or ideas. Collectivists will not seek to contradict the contribution of others and will engage other team members to gain their input.

Teams, however, can be proactive in countering the challenges that cultural differences can bring. Maznevski and Peterson (1997) argue that teams need to incorporate processes which build respect, such as decentering and recentering, to address this problem. "Decentering is taking the perspective of others and explaining problems with respect to the differences in perspective rather than blaming them on other group members. Recentering calls for identifying or building a common view of the situation and a common set of norms" (p. 85). While conflicts may arise in cross-cultural teams, teams need to establish a respectful and engaging atmosphere in order to be effective.

Snell et al. (1998) conducted an international research project exploring cross-cultural teams and utilized 31 multinational corporations. Over a two-year period, they examined these teams and found that they generally analyzed three global concerns. The concerns included: a) local responsiveness, b) global efficiency, and c) organizational learning. Prior to implementing cross-cultural teams, two of the corporations, Ford and Glaxo Wellcome, conducted cross-cultural team-building programs. These programs surpassed the typical cultural awareness training and included discussing differences across cultures, as well as developing an awareness of cultural norms. In addition, the team-building programs focused on "developing coherent work processes that take advantage of differences on the team by establishing ground rules and protocols that integrate members (Snell et al., 1998, p. 152).

In another study, Evans (2006) explored the impact of cultural differences in a merger between French and British companies. As a result of the merger, the French and British managers were assigned to various cross-cultural teams. Initially, language was a barrier, so the company provided foreign-language classes for its managers. Over time, the teams were able to communicate effectively and team members made efforts to learn one another's language. The findings stress that, initially, teams may have difficulty working together. However, teams need to establish how they will communicate when there are different languages within the team. Evans's research illustrates that cultural differences do not have to be a barrier to the team's performance. Teams are able to surmount the challenges associated with cultural diversity and still be productive.

Matveev and Milter (2004) reviewed the literature on cross-cultural teams and found that in order for teams to be effective, the cross-cultural skills of the team members need to be developed. Failure of the team related to team members' being ill-prepared to work with other cultures. In the past, companies developed training programs to provide relevant knowledge to their employees about foreign cultures. These educational programs were created to provide the employee with intercultural competence (IC).

According to Matveev and Milter (2004) effective cross-cultural teams can be developed by using the IC model. The IC model has three components and incorporates: a) cultural knowledge, b) skills that are culturally relevant for the foreign culture, and c) personality orientation. First, cultural knowledge refers to information about cultural practices, such as the exploration of the differences in communication and interaction styles of the different cultures. In addition, team members have a level of comfort when communicating with different cultures and demonstrate flexibility in resolving conflicts. Second, members demonstrate skills that are perceived by different cultures as engaging. This would include using decentering and recentering as a means to be inclusive and obtain a diverse set of perspectives. Team members also possess valued skills such as the ability to understand and communicate team goals and roles. Third, team members possess a personality that exhibits empathy to foreign nationals and conveys an understanding of their perspective of the world.

Matveev and Milter used the IC model with a cross-cultural team of Russian and American managers who were employed by a multinational company. There were cultural differences between the managers, such as the American managers valued individualism, while the Russian managers' valued a more collectivistic approach. However, even with the cultural differences, the cross-cultural team was able to work together effectively. In addition, the managers highlighted that there were several components that would facilitate effective cross-cultural teams. Effective cross-cultural teams need to manage diversity; this is accomplished by incorporating structures and processes which facilitate open communication.

Understanding how teams function is another aspect of managing diversity in the workplace; organizations need to provide an understanding of the research that has been conducted on effective cross-cultural teams. For instance, employees need to be given skills that promote intercultural competence; possessing knowledge, respect, and understanding of different cultures is imperative. This type of learning opportunity requires specialized training from an expert in the field. In fact, the training needs to be more broadly understood throughout the organization so that it is valued in the workplace.

Conclusions

In order for multinational corporations to be able to capitalize on the effectiveness of cross-cultural teams, they must be willing to adopt a framework that values managing diversity. When it comes to implementing a cross-cultural team, there are certain components that multinational corporations need. First, the leadership from the multinational corporation needs to establish a framework that values managing diversity in every facet of its business practices. This framework must ensure that people's differences are acknowledged and the knowledge base that the employee brings to the workplace is valued. This will enhance the organization's ability to problem-solve and serve their markets better. Ely and Thomas's (2001) research is significant because they found that when companies adopt a framework that values managing diversity at its core business practice, they are successful in growing their business in markets previously unavailable to them (i.e., culturally diverse markets). In cross-cultural teams, they recommend that cultural diversity be used as a resource for learning and integrate that learning into developing effective and creative business practices.

Second, team members must engage in communication that is sensitive to cultural differences. Communication (both verbal and nonverbal) needs to ensure that the members of the team are in agreement. Using the framework of Matveev and Milter (2004) to develop intercultural competence (IC) is integral to cross-cultural teams. The three components of the model include the following: a) develop knowledge of the culture, b) develop skills that are culturally relevant for the foreign culture, and c) cultivate a personality orientation that embraces foreign cultures. The following bullets outline pertinent points when working with cross-cultural teams.

- Senior leadership needs to manage diversity by planning and implementing structures and practices that maximize the advantages of diversity while minimizing its barriers.
- Organizations need to bring in outside experts who can provide some direction and guidance on how to manage diversity in the workplace and utilize cross-cultural teams effectively.
- The team will establish the steps to share information across the team, and when the information needs to be distributed, they will outline the process that will be utilized.
- The team will establish rules for how the team will come to agreement and the best methods or processes for sharing and discussing information.
- The team will encourage and maintain open communication throughout the project. From the onset, the team will decide what will be the most effective means of communication for them and how progress will be documented during the project.
- The team needs to have open communication at all times; when there is much diversity on the team, there can be misunderstandings. The team must encourage people to discuss their feelings and show empathy toward one another. Team members will utilize decentering and recentering as a strategy to make progress with the team.
- When language can be a barrier for communication in the team, team members must look for opportunities to illustrate how they will effectively communicate. Perhaps the team will agree upon a language that the team will use for communicating in meetings and via written response.

- The team needs to promote an atmosphere of respect so that team members will feel comfortable talking in a different language. If interpreters are being used, the team needs to provide time for information to be processed and team members to dialogue if there are questions and to clarify information as needed.
- The team needs to create a team environment where cultural diversity is embraced and the knowledge from those who are diverse is utilized and valued.
- Team members will assess their own cultural identity, as well as their teammates', and understand how the various cultural differences may impact the team. The use of Hofstede's (in Berger, 1996) four fundamental dimensions of culture—power distance, uncertainty avoidance, individualism, and masculinity—can be utilized to understand how cultural differences may impact the functioning of the team and how work is carried out.
- The team will develop a proactive approach to uncover the challenges that cultural diversity may bring to the team.
- When other cultures are involved, the team must ensure that there is a climate of respect for the holidays and traditions of other cultures. Team members need to encourage openness and communication so that they are able to create a climate of respect for cultural diversity.
- When the team works together, they must develop an understanding of why cultural diversity is significant for their particular project. If there is, for example, a lack of cultural diversity on the team, they need to recruit team members who will be able to add to the knowledge base.

Chapter Summary

In conclusion, cross-cultural teams have become more prevalent with the expansion of globalization. The failure of cross-cultural teams has serious ramifications; "these projects often operate at higher costs, with higher risks and potentially a higher benefit" (Uday-Riley, 2006, p. 28). A review of the literature on cross-cultural teams highlights that there are benefits for multinational corporations, such as enhancing its profitability (Evans, 2006; Johnson et al., 2006; Krishna, Sahay, & Walsham, 2004; Matveev & Milter, 2004; Tirmizi, 2008; Uday-Riley, 2006). However, in order to capture these benefits, corporations must establish a structure that values cultural diversity. This structure begins with enhancing the skills of the team members, which include the ability to analyze integral dimensions of culture, facilitate knowledge of the culture, develop effective communication skills, and exhibit culturally sensitive skills (e.g., engagement, empathy, etc.).

Definition of Key Terms

Cross-cultural team—A cross-cultural team encompasses a culturally diverse set of employees who work together to offer innovative and higher-quality solutions to global business problems. Cross-cultural teams are utilized in multinational corporations because they bring together people who integrate and build knowledge from varied cultural perspectives to inform an international business economy.

Culture—Culture encompasses the collective basic norms and values and the ways that particular groups understand life, or make meaning of daily occurrences. Manifestations of culture can be uncovered in the group's music, language, dress, and so on.

Globalization—Globalization is the expansion of corporations to conduct business in foreign countries. The expansion enables a corporation to produce and distribute its products and services on an international level. This business endeavor enables the corporation to maximize its profits but also creates opportunities for people in less-developed economies, which include career opportunities and improving the quality of life for marginalized citizens.

Managing diversity—Planning and implementing systems and practices in the workplace that acknowledge and value cultural differences. This facilitates a workplace that integrates the knowledge of diverse members as a learning opportunity and allows the organization to be responsive to its different markets.

Multinational corporation—A multinational corporation is a business organization that operates on an international level to seek opportunities to produce and distribute its products and services worldwide. The organization's focus is to conduct business internationally, with the intent to maximize its profits.

Critical-Thinking Discussion Questions

1. What has led to the increase in globalization in our recent past? What have been some of the benefits of globalization for corporations and the individual person?

2. What have been some of the challenges related to the spread of globalization for corporations?

3. Suppose you are going to take an assignment to further your career development in a foreign country. What would you do prior to your departure to prepare yourself for this assignment?

4. When seeking to conduct business in a different culture, what should the company do to explore this different culture?

5. How does the average person come to develop an understanding of different cultures? Why is it important for businesses to understand different cultures?

6. For corporations, what are some of the benefits of implementing culturally diverse teams?

7. Why have there been challenges with implementing cross-cultural teams on national and international levels?

8. What are some of the aspects of communication that you would attend to when working with those who are culturally different? Discuss how you would address the concerns.

9. When exploring Hofstede's framework for understanding cultural diversity, what are the differences between the individualist and collectivistic cultures? What are some of the challenges that team members from these cultures may have?

10. Suppose that you were asked to assemble a global cross-cultural team for Acme Manufacturing (which is headquartered in Philadelphia, Pennsylvania). This corporation will be expanding its plant in Mexico and needs to explore how this will work best. The members of this team have not worked together previously; what would you do to create intercultural competence among the team members?

Case Study

The Acme Company recently merged with one of its foreign competitors in France. This merger was done because it would enable them to expand their product offerings and reach niche markets. Neither partner held overall control because there was an agreement on equal shareholding. The company maintains its divisions on both continents, but there is a plan to decentralize the company and much of the decision making. Human resources (HR) had to work diligently because there was a need to maintain the company's competitive edge by collaborating with the French and U.S. managers. In fact, the company had plans to expand their customer base and compete for business in other European countries. Therefore, they created a cross-cultural team that would include managers from both the United States and France. These managers were charged with developing a plan to enter the market in the southern region of France.

The company wanted to prepare the managers who would be part of the cross-cultural team. As a result, HR created a three-month training program that would enhance the cultural knowledge of the managers, which included several components. This training was conducted with the managers who would participate in the cross-cultural team. The foreign-language classes took place in their country of origin, but the other trainings were taken together by the managers over the course of several seminars. The objectives of the training included the following:

- Develop some level of proficiency in your nonprimary language (either French or English)
- Develop an understanding of culture and how culture can impact the functioning of the team and how work is carried out
- Develop skills to facilitate communication within the cross-cultural team
- Develop skills that exhibit cultural sensitivity when working with different cultures (e.g., empathy, decentering, recentering, etc.)

The first component of the training was intense foreign-language learning courses. The learning would focus on acquiring the skills of listening, speaking, writing, and reading the language. The primary goal of the foreign-language learning was stressing the importance of listening skills. HR reasoned that in the context of business, with time constraints, developing effective communication is essential to understanding culturally diverse team members. Next, the learning focused on expressing one's ideas in a simplistic style; they felt that this was paramount to ensuring that team members could communicate most effectively during discussions. Lastly, HR felt that in international business, written skills in a foreign language may be less significant.

Overall, the managers found that the training was helpful. Some of the managers complained that the motivation to learn a different language varied. The language learning component of the training was contingent upon the learners practicing the material outside of the classroom. When team members felt that others were not motivated to learn the language, problems in the team resulted.

Initially, this cross-cultural team had difficulty communicating because language was a barrier. The team found that they had to take the time to communicate when there were differences in the level of language proficiency. Over time, the team members found that clarification in written and verbal communication was needed. This required the team to take the time to do this and ensure that culturally responsive communication was done. Team members also demonstrated the use of decentering and were able to express the concerns of other team members in a respectful manner. However, when team members chose to communicate via e-mail, this wasn't necessarily the case. As a result, e-mails between managers of different languages were at times confusing.

In addition, the corporation made a mistake in their level of involvement. The corporation failed to communicate how cultural diversity would be utilized within the company and/or outline the significance of it for gaining entrée into different markets. Therefore, there was a breakdown in the level of commitment for this endeavor.

The final error was that team members did not develop a set of culturally relevant skills. The second component of the training focused on understanding the role that culture would play in the team. The team members were given information about how to understand and analyze one's culture as well as the culture of others. Each member then identified some potential challenges that may impact the team as a result of their differences and then engaged in problem-solving to diminish those problems. Third, the training focused on developing skills that would illustrate sensitivity to cultural diversity. The managers learned how to understand the world from the point of view of another culture and anticipated how to convey respect for other cultures.

Discussion Questions

1. HR developed several objectives for the training. Do you think that the objectives were sufficient to help the managers participate in the cross-cultural team?
2. Since the managers spoke different languages, what are some of the aspects that could have been implemented to facilitate written and verbal communication?
3. How could the corporation have improved this endeavor and created a more effective cross-cultural team experience?

References

Ali, A. (2001). Globalization: The great transformation. *Advances in Competitiveness Research, 9*(1), 1–9.

Berger, M. (1996). Introduction to cross-cultural team building. In M. Berger (Ed.), *Cross-cultural team building: Guidelines for more effective communication and negotiation* (pp. 1–10). New York: McGraw-Hill.

Cox, T., Jr. (2001). *Creating the multicultural organization: A strategy for capturing the power of diversity.* San Francisco: Jossey-Bass.

Ely, R., & Thomas, D. (2001). Cultural diversity at work: The effects of diversity perspectives on work group processes and outcomes. *Administration Science Quarterly, 46*(2), 229–273.

Evans, D. (2006). Creating value from cross-cultural teams: An example of Franco-British collaborative ventures. *Cross Cultural Management, 13*(4), 316–329.

Honda Motor Company: 2009 company profile (3rd ed.). In *Just Auto,* 22–23. Bromsgrove, UK.

Johnson, J., Lenartowicz, T., & Apud, S. (2006). Cross-cultural competence in international business: Toward a definition and model. *Journal of International Business Studies, 37,* 525–543.

Kohut, A., & Wike, R. (2008). Pew Presents . . . Assessing globalization: Benefits and drawbacks of trade and integration. *Harvard International Review,* 70–74.

Krishna, S., Sahay, S., & Walsham, G. (2004). Managing cross-cultural issues in global software outsourcing. *Communication of the ACM, 47*(4), 62–66.

Lillis, M., & Tian, R. (2009). Cross-cultural communication and emotional intelligence: Inferences from case studies of gender diverse groups. *Marketing Intelligence & Planning, 27*(3), 428–438.

Marquardt, M., & Reynolds, A. (1994). *The global learning organization.* New York: Irwin Publishing.

Matusitz, J. (2011). Disney's successful adaptation in Hong Kong: A globalization perspective. *Asia Pacific Journal of Management, 28,* 667–681.

Matveev, A., & Milter, R. (2004). The value of intercultural competence for performance of multicultural teams. *Team Performance Management, 10*(4/5), 104–111.

Maznevski, M., & Peterson, M. (1997). Societal values, social interpretation, and multinational teams. In C. Granrose & S. Oskamp (Eds.), *Cross-cultural work groups* (pp. 61–89). Thousand Oaks, CA: Sage.

Moore, K., & Lewis, D. (2009). *The origins of globalization.* New York: Routledge.

Orasanu, J., Fischer, U., & Davison, J. (1997). Cross-cultural barriers to effective communication in aviation. In C. Granrose & S. Oskamp (Eds.), *Cross-cultural work groups* (pp. 134–160). Thousand Oaks, CA: Sage.

Rangan, S., & Lawrence, R. (1999). *A prism on globalization: Corporate responses to the dollar.* Washington, D.C.: Brookings Institution Press.

Ricks, D. (1999). *Blunders in int'l business* (3rd ed.). Malden, MA: Blackwell Publishers.

Sherman, A., Bohlander, G., & Snell, S. (1998). *Managing human resources.* Cincinnati, OH: South-Western College Publishing.

Snell, S., Snow, C., Davidson, S., & Hambrick, D. (1998). Designing and supporting transnational teams: The human resource agenda. *Human Resource Management Journal, 37,* 147–158.

Tirmizi, A. (2008). Towards understanding multicultural teams. In C. Halverson & A. Tirmizi (Eds.), *Effective multicultural teams: Theory and practice.* New York: Springer.

Uday-Riley, M. (2006). Eight critical steps to improve workplace performance with cross-cultural teams. *Performance Improvement, 45*(6), 28–32.

Wiechmann, D., Ryan, A., & Hemingway, M. (2003). Designing and implementing global staffing systems: Part I—Leaders in global staffing. *Human Resource Management, 42*(1), 71–83.

16

RE-CONCEPTUALIZING AND RE-VISIONING DIVERSITY IN THE WORKFORCE: TOWARD A SOCIAL JUSTICE PARADIGM

Marilyn Y. Byrd

Chapter Overview

This chapter will re-conceptualize and re-vision the purpose, need, and goal for diversity in organizational and institutional workforce settings. A social justice paradigm will be introduced as a platform for organizations and institutions to enact organizational social justice.

Learning Objectives

After reading this chapter, along with completing the critical-thinking discussion questions and the case discussion questions, you will be able to:

* Re-conceptualize the meaning and focus of diversity
* Re-vision a paradigm shift for diversity from inclusion to social justice
* Describe a practical application of organizational social justice

Re-Conceptualizing the Meaning of Diversity

The commonly understood meaning of diversity is *the state of being different*. The term diversity became popularized in response to legislation that was enacted to bring about more equal representation for the socially disadvantaged. **Socially disadvantaged** refers to individuals protected by Title VII of the 1964 Civil Rights Act who are subjected to racial or ethnic prejudice or cultural bias because of identity as a member of a group without regard to their individual qualities (U.S. Small Business Administration, 2004). Research by Crocker and Major (1989) indicated that people who are perceived as deformed, mentally ill, retarded, obese, or unattractive are **socially stigmatized** and often subjected to cruel or unjust treatment because of their social disadvantage in society. Examples of other ways that people are socially disadvantaged or stigmatized are perceptions of their sexual orientation, religious affiliation, physical ability, or age (others may also apply).

Initially, the term diversity was applied to acknowledge the presence of a diverse workforce and the legislation that protected the rights of selected groups. Over the last 20 years, phrases such as *valuing diversity, appreciating diversity, promoting diversity, embracing diversity*, etc. became commonly encountered buzz phrases as organizations and the business world in general sought to convey a message of compliance to their constituents. Gradually, the term "diversity" has broadened and now encompasses an array of diverse perspectives as businesses and organizations have realized the competitive advantage that diversity brings to the bottom line. In this respect, the focus on diversity has shifted from the individual level to the organizational level as businesses and organizations have discovered how the diversity of the people benefits the interests of the organization. The new focus on diversity is being captured in terminology such as diversity of perspectives, diversity of thought, diversity of experience, diversity of education, etc. While achieving a competitive advantage through diversity has become the new focus, in the process, the lived experience of "being different" is rendered silent. **Lived experience** refers to the ways that people experience life based on their socially disadvantaged or socially stigmatized everyday reality.

Because topics such as racism, sexism, classism, intergenerational differences, racial harassment, etc., are not being appropriately captured under the more contemporary discussions of diversity as a competitive business advantage, the need to return the focus of diversity on the lived experiences of diverse groups has been the aim and goal of this textbook. Discussing the way diversity is experienced (by social groups), rather than how it is used (by the organization), creates space for diversity to be envisioned from a historical and contextual perspective. Therefore, it seems appropriate and necessary to re-affirm the original focus and need to have conversations about the lived experiences of diversity—not to relive past transgressions, but rather to *confront* past and emerging transgressions and social oppression that continue to deny full and equal participation, respect, and dignity for socially disadvantaged and socially stigmatized groups.

The preceding chapters have laid the foundation for a social justice paradigm that is dedicated to addressing social oppression. Social oppression was described in Chapter 8 as "the belief that some social groups are superior or normal and establishes systems of advantage and privilege for these groups while simultaneously defining other social groups as inferior and deserving of disenfranchisement, exploitation, and marginalization" (Hardiman, Jackson, & Griffin, 2007, p. 37). We expand that definition to include the "fusion of institutional and systemic discrimination, personal bias, bigotry, and social prejudice in a complex web of relationships and structures that shade most aspects of life" (Bell, 2007, p. 3). The outcome of social oppression is social injustice. **Social injustice** is the repression of an individual's right to full participation or capacity to realize their full potential in an organizational or institutional setting, regardless of their perceived social identity, lifestyle, cultural expression, or any other perceived category of difference. Because the discussions of diversity in the workforce have moved towards a competitive advantage, it is necessary to shift discussions of diversity to a social justice paradigm to capture the lived experiences of socially disadvantaged and socially stigmatized groups. In that way, we will have a clearer vision of how to respond and act with action-oriented practices that offer a remedy for social oppression.

A Social Justice Paradigm for Action-Oriented Organizations

Injustice anywhere is a threat to justice everywhere.

Dr. Martin Luther King, Jr.

According to Kuhn (1996), a paradigm provides a worldview of shared beliefs for a community of people to identify problems and create solutions. Thomas and Ely (1996) identified three diversity paradigms: discrimination/fairness, access/legitimacy, and learning/integration. The discrimination/fairness and access/legitimacy paradigms support legislation designed to enforce equal representation. The learning/integration paradigm focuses on learning from differences and recognizing multiple perspectives and culturally relevant information that certain groups bring to achieving competitive advantage. In recent years, organizations have begun adopting the term "inclusion," which focuses on developing an environment that enables all people to feel a part of the organization, to have equal access to opportunities that enables development and growth, and to contribute fully to the organization's success (Society for Human Resource Management, 2013; Thomas, 1992). The inclusion paradigm brings about "a sense of belonging: feeling respected, valued for who you are; feeling a level of supportive energy and commitment from others so than you can do your best work" (Miller & Katz, 2002, p. 147).

While the foregoing paradigms have served to represent perspectives of diversity in the workforce, none of these give voice to social justice. As Kuhn (1996) suggests, when current worldviews do not respond to current and emerging problems and dilemmas, a paradigm shift is needed. Social justice is a democratic, participatory, inclusive process for affirming human agency and working collaboratively to create change (Bell, 2007). It is a vision of a society where "all members are physically and psychologically safe and secure . . . able to develop their full capacities . . . and capable of interacting democratically with others" (p. 1). The purpose of a social justice paradigm is to create a platform to have conversations about "organisational undiscussables such as sexism, racism, patriarchy, and violence" (Bierema & Cseh, 2003, p. 24) that cause social oppression. Therefore, to fulfill the promise of *valuing diversity, celebrating diversity, appreciating diversity, promoting diversity, and embracing diversity*, we need to hear, understand, and appreciate the voice of social justice (Miller, 1994).

For example, a social justice paradigm would be an appropriate worldview to study the effects of microaggression. **Microaggression** refers to prejudicial behaviors that are demeaning, humiliating, unethical, disrespectful, and unjust and target socially disadvantaged and socially stigmatized groups. According to Sue et al. (2007), three categories, or levels, of microaggression occur that can inflict psychological and possible physical harm to the target: microinsult (demeaning remarks or comments); microassault (violent verbal or nonverbal attacks); and microinvalidation (attempts to devalue, discredit, minimize, negate, and/or nullify the background, culture, education, or expertise of the target). Microinvalidation sends that message: *I have the power to validate who you are.*

The term microaggression was coined in the 1970s by Chester Pierce, a psychiatrist who initially referred to racial microaggressions, particularly in referring to the African American race. **Racial microaggressions** are "commonplace verbal or behavioral indignities, whether intentional or unintentional, which communicate hostile, derogatory, or negative racial slights and insults" (Sue et al., 2007, p. 280). Researchers are now applying the term in a broader sense to include indignities, insults, and assaults directed toward other socially disadvantaged and socially stigmatized groups.

Despite legislation that has placed more mandates against discriminatory workplace processes and practices, microaggression transcends to a degree that inflicts harm—physical or mental, consciousness or unconscious, intentional or unintentional—which is an injustice to human dignity and worth. Furthermore, microaggression can occur in varying degrees of severity, which can contribute to an unpleasant and hostile working environment. Ford (2009) says that a hostile working environment is a facts-driven phenomenon that is based on the judgment of the decision-maker and his or her "understanding of morality, social justice, history, and the legislative purpose of Title VII" (p. 7). Consistent with Sue et al. (2007) is Ford's (2009) description of how the law broadly defines prejudicial behaviors that contribute to a hostile work environment:

- antilocution—feelings are freely expressed and shared with other like-minded individuals,
- avoidance—members of a disliked group are avoided altogether,
- discrimination—actions openly express dislike for certain groups,

- physical attack—extreme expression of dislike and hatred, and
- extermination—drawing parallels to historical examples by displaying symbols of annihilation (nooses, swastikas, racist graffiti) (p. 8).

Law and legislation does not clearly define prejudicial behaviors; nonetheless, employers are held accountable and liable for preventing a hostile workplace environment. Ford (2009) points out that the central purpose of enforcing the law in respect to a hostile work environment is to "inject morality and social justice into the workplace" (p. 5).

Another point that should be addressed is the context of work. For example, utility workers, delivery drivers, door-to-door salesmen, etc. are at work in a virtual environment but are still subjected to microaggression in the conduct of their work. In addition, healthcare providers (doctors, nurses, nursing assistants, etc.) are subjected to microaggression in their duty to care for patients who refuse (or someone refuses on their behalf) services because of the service worker's social categorization.

A social justice paradigm also creates a platform for discussions that exposes social power. Social power is a force that "results in some social groups having privilege, status, and access, whereas other groups are stigmatized, oppressed, and denied access" (Hardiman, Jackson, & Griffin, 2007, p. 58). Discussions of social power and its dominance in sustaining social oppression unveils the historical and contextual state of diversity. In doing so, *valuing diversity, celebrating diversity, appreciating diversity, promoting diversity, and embracing diversity* appear to be dichotomous statements in respect to the lived experience of diversity. For that reason, this textbook has promoted a paradigm that shifts discussions of diversity to one that emphasizes organizational social justice and establishing an organizational culture that extends beyond inclusion towards one that upholds human worth, respect, and dignity.

Action-Oriented Ways Organizations Can Practice Social Justice

In Chapter 3, **organizational social justice** was introduced as a state that organizations should seek to achieve so that everyone feels included, accepted, and respected, and whereby human dignity as well as equality are practiced and upheld. Organizational social justice represents a shift from viewing diversity in terms of representation and inclusion towards a new horizon that invokes a sense of agency and inspires individuals to reflect and take action against everyday micro-aggressions that deny them respect and dignity.

Organizations with social justice goals are concerned with eliminating oppression and are committed to "participatory democracy as the means of this action" (Murrell, 2006, p. 81). Furthermore, organizations with social justice goals proactively seek to ensure a diversity social climate that is supportive of socially disadvantaged and socially stigmatized groups. A **diversity social climate** is a pattern of attitudes and behaviors that represents the overall culture of an organization. A major influence of a diversity social climate is management's proactive stance against social oppression and social injustice. Some action strategies that demonstrate a concern for organizational social justice are: utilizing employee resource groups, practicing corporate social responsibility at the individual (employee) level, and creating a workforce social justice council.

Employee Resource Groups

Employee resource groups (ERGs) are gaining recognition as an opportunity that encourages employees to give voice or speak out about issues in the workplace. Research conducted by Roberson and Stevens (2006) suggests that allowing people from socially disadvantaged and socially stigmatized groups to describe incidents that pertain to ways that "discrimination, representation, management treatment, work relationships, levels of respect, and the diversity climate are salient" (p. 389) influences how individuals within these groups make meaning of their experiences. A progressive way that ERGs can be used in supporting social justice is holding periodic forums that are designed for sharing lived experiences. Sharing lived experiences is a way that an individual learns from having encountered or endured an oppressive event in an effort to make sense of that experience by reliving it with another person that is similarly located in society.

Corporate Social Responsibility

Corporate social responsibility (CSR) is an ethical practice that businesses and organizations undertake to illustrate responsibilities to stakeholders. Typically, organizations demonstrate CSR to stakeholders through external strategies such as charitable donations, environmental initiatives, and various community outreach initiatives. However, addressing CSR at the wider level minimizes the "social" aspect of internal issues at the individual and/or group level that could create a hostile environment for the socially disadvantaged and the socially stigmatized. Action strategies that demonstrate CSR at the individual level, for instance implementing policies that illustrate responsibility to employee social justice, are needed.

A progressive strategy that allows organizations to demonstrate CSR at the individual level is to issue a statement of conduct or revise current statements of conduct to reflect a moral obligation to respond to and take action against acts of social injustice in the workplace (including the virtual workplace). Another action strategy that demonstrates CSR at the individual level is incorporating specific language into mission and vision statements that demonstrate a proactive approach to social justice.

Workforce Social Justice Council

Organizations that commit to being socially responsible to its workforce support a social justice paradigm by creating a **workforce social justice council** (WSJC). The WSJC works in conjunction with human resources to ensure organizational social justice is practiced and upheld. The WSJC is responsible for making recommendations for proactive social justice policies and procedures and designing and implementing training and awareness workshops that are built around real problems and situations at all levels of the organization. The WSJC periodically solicits feedback from the entire workforce on the state of the organization's diversity social climate and empowers victims of social injustice to report occurrences to a higher authority.

Chapter Summary

This chapter explained the need to return the focus and need for having conversations on diversity to the lived experiences of social oppression. A shift to a social justice paradigm was explained as an emerging worldview that captures this experience. Organizational social justice was described as a goal for a paradigm shift. Practical ways that organizations can practice organizational social justice were provided.

Definition of Key Terms

Diversity social climate—A pattern of attitudes and behaviors that represents the overall culture of an organization.

Employee resource groups—Encourages employees to give voice or speak out about issues in the workplace; useful for providing upper management with insight on issues that could improve the organization's culture; also a useful source for mentoring and focusing on issues that relate to a particular community.

Inclusion—A sense of belonging: feeling respected, valued for who you are; feeling a level of supportive energy and commitment from others so that you can do your best work (Miller & Katz, 2002, p. 147; http://en.wikipedia .org/wiki/Inclusion_(value_and_practice)—cite_note-1).

Lived experience—Refers to the ways that people experience life based on their socially disadvantaged or socially stigmatized everyday reality.

Microaggression—Refers to prejudicial behaviors that are demeaning, humiliating, unethical, disrespectful, and unjust and that target socially disadvantaged and socially stigmatized groups.

Organizational social justice—The ideology that organizations operating through a representing agent seek to achieve a state whereby all individuals feel included, accepted, and respected and whereby human dignity as well as equality is practiced and upheld (Byrd, 2012).

Racial microaggression—Commonplace verbal or behavioral indignities, whether intentional or unintentional, that communicate hostile, derogatory, or negative racial slights and insults (Sue et al., 2007, p. 280).

Social injustice—Repression of an individual's right to full participation or capacity to realize their full potential in an organizational or institutional setting, regardless of their perceived social identity, lifestyle, cultural expression, or any other perceived category of difference.

Social justice—A "vision of society in which the distribution of resources is equitable and all members are physically and psychologically safe and secure" (Bell, 2007, p. 1).

Social oppression—The belief that some social groups are superior or normal and establishes systems of advantage and privilege for these groups while simultaneously defining other social groups as inferior and deserving of disenfranchisement, exploitation, and marginalization (Hardiman, Jackson, & Griffin, 2007 , p. 37).

Socially disadvantaged—Refers to individuals protected by Title VII of the 1964 Civil Rights Act who are subjected to racial or ethnic prejudice or cultural bias because of identity as a member of a group without regard to their individual qualities (U.S. Small Business Administration, 2004).

Socially stigmatized—Refers to individuals or groups who are perceived as deformed, mentally ill or retarded, obese, or unattractive and are often subjected to cruel or unjust treatment because of their social disadvantage in society.

Critical-Thinking Discussion Questions

1. Discuss how a social justice paradigm differs from the inclusion paradigm.
2. Conduct an Internet search of companies on DiversityInc's Top 50 list. Report on three companies that are practicing social justice advocacy and describe the type of social justice initiative being practiced. (www.diversityinc.com/the-diversityinc-top-50-companies-for-diversity-2013/)
3. Visit the EEOC website and search for two incidents whereby customer/patient preference has created a hostile working environment. How would the social justice paradigm provide a platform for addressing this type of discrimination? (www.eeoc.gov/eeoc/initiatives/e-race/caselist.cfm#customer)

Legal Perspective 1

In December 2012, an Atlanta-based manufacturing company was ordered to pay $500,000 in a race discrimination suit to 14 Black employees who worked at the company's South Dallas, TX, mill. The company reached a settlement with the EEOC on behalf of the plaintiffs who complained of being subjected to a hostile work environment and being exposed to violent, racist graffiti ("die, n——r, die"), racial slurs, the display of racist insignia such as swastikas, Confederate flags, "white power" and "KKK" logos, including the display of nooses at an employee workstation. Supervisors were aware of the incidents, but allowed the behavior to continue according to the complaints. The company is required to enact a graffiti abatement policy and undergo annual reviews of its compliance for two years. (*Source:* www.eeoc.gov/eeoc/initiatives/e-race/caselist.cfm#systemic)

Legal Perspective 2

In September 2012, Delano Regional Medical Center in Delano, California, was ordered to pay $975,000 to approximately 70 Filipino-American hospital workers in a landmark EEOC language discrimination lawsuit. The workers complained of a hostile working environment that subjected them to being berated, harassed, ridiculed, and reprimanded for speaking with an accent or using Filipino language. The lawsuit originated in 2006 when a "Filipino-American only" staff meeting was called. During this meeting, the workers were threatened and issued consequences for noncompliance with Delano's English only language policy. The workers were also subjected to being monitored by surveillance equipment, although other non-Filipino speaking workers who spoke other languages such as Spanish were not subjected to such treatment. Some Filipino workers reported being humiliated and threatened with arrest if they did not speak English. One Filipino employee's food was sprayed with air freshener when someone complained of hating Filipino food. Although over 100 Filipino workers signed a petition to report the harassment, management failed to investigate or take action. In addition to the monetary relief, Delano Regional Hospital was ordered to adopt a Title VII compliant language policy and to hire an EEO monitor to assist with compliant terms of the settlement. The hospital was also required to conduct antiharassment and antidiscrimination training at all levels. (*Source:* www.eeoc .gov/eeoc/newsroom/release/9–17–12a.cfm)

Case Study 1

This case is based on an actual incident.

In June 2013, a postal service worker, an African American male, was the victim of a prank that was alleged to have been initiated by a college fraternity. The postal worker delivered a large number of boxes addressed to "Reggin Toggaf" at the fraternity house. After delivering the boxes, he was told it was a prank and to read the name of the addressee in reverse order. The two words transposed revealed a racial slur and a slur directed towards gays. The postal worker admitted to being humiliated and insulted. The fraternity denied involvement, but the postal worker believed he was owed an apology.

Discussion Questions

1. Do you believe the university or the postal system is responsible for investigating this situation? Support your answer.
2. What type of microaggression does this resemble? Support your answer.
3. Discuss the incident in terms of the virtual workplace.

Case Study 2

Shameka, an African American woman, was in charge of a city tree trimming crew that was working to remove dead tree limbs near a neighborhood power line. One of the property owners, a white man in his early 60s, approached the workers complaining they were getting too close to his property and were going to damage his fence. The workers (all men) tried to ignore the property owner who was becoming more irate and agitated by the minute. Shameka, who was standing close by, noticed the encounter and had taken out her phone to record the encounter. She then approached the property owner with the intention of trying to assure him that her crew was abiding by city ordinance and was staying the proper distance from his property. The resident suddenly became belligerent and hostile, yelling a derogatory racial slur and sexually demeaning insult at Shameka. Catching her off guard, the resident spat in her face, then pushed her. Shameka immediately phoned her supervisor and reported the incident.

Discussion Questions

1. Do you think Shameka acted appropriately? Why or why not?
2. If you were Shameka's supervisor, how would you respond?
3. What type of microaggression does this incident describe? Support your answer.
4. Does the hostile work environment apply here? Why or why not?

References

Bell, L. A. (2007). Theoretical foundations for social justice education. In M. Adams, L. A. Bell, & P. Griffin (Eds.), *Teaching for diversity and social justice* (2nd ed., pp. 1–14). New York: Routledge.

Bierema, L. L., & Cseh, M. (2003). Evaluating AHRD research using a feminist research framework. *Human Resource Development Quarterly, 14*(1), 5–26.

Byrd, M. (2012). Theorizing leadership of demographically diverse leaders. In M. Paludi (Ed.), *Managing diversity in today's workplace: Strategies for employees and employers (Women and careers in management)* (pp. 103–124). Santa Barbara, CA: Praeger (ABC-CLIO).

Cox, T., Jr. (1992). *Creating the multicultural organization: A strategy for capturing the power of diversity.* San Francisco: Jossey-Bass.

Crocker, J., & Major, B. (1989). Social stigma and self-esteem: The self-protective properties of stigma. *Psychological Review, 96,* 608–630

Ford, R. O. (2009). A speech on hostile work environment. *Human Resources/Labor Relations Law Review, 1*(1), 5–16.

Hardiman, R., Jackson, B., & Griffin, P. (2007). Conceptual foundations for social justice education: Conceptual overview. In M. Adams, L. A. Bell, & P. Griffin (Eds.), *Teaching for diversity and social justice* (pp. 35–43). New York: Routledge.

Kuhn, T. S. (1996). *The structure of scientific revolutions* (3rd ed.). Chicago: University of Chicago Press.

Miller, F. A. (1994). Why we choose to address oppression. In E. Y. Cross, J. H. Katz, F. A. Miller, & E. W. Seashore (Eds.), *The promise of diversity: Over 40 voices discuss strategies for eliminating discrimination in organizations,* (pp. xxv–xxix). New York: Irwin.

Miller, F. A., & Katz, J. H. (2002). *The inclusion breakthrough: Unleashing the real power of diversity.* San Francisco, CA: Berrett-Koehler Publishers.

Murrell, P., Jr. (2006). Toward social justice in urban education: A model of collaborative cultural inquiry in urban schools. *Equity & Excellence in Education, 39,* 81–90.

Roberson, Q. M., & Stevens, C. K. (2006). Making sense of diversity in the workplace: Organizational justice and language abstraction in employees' accounts of diversity-related incidents. *Journal of Applied Psychology, 91*(2), 379–391. doi:10.1037/0021–9010.91.2.379

Society of Human Resource Management (2013). SHRM's diversity and inclusion initiative. Retrieved June 10, 2013, from www.shrm.org

Sue, D.W., Capodilupo, C. M., Torino, G. C., Bucceri, J. M., Holder, A.M.B., Nadal, K. L., & Equin, M. (2007). Racial microaggressions in everyday life: Implications for clinical practice. *The American Psychologist, 62*(4), 271–286.

Thomas, D. A., & Ely, R. J. (1996). Making differences matter: A new paradigm for managing diversity. *Harvard Business Review,* 79–90.

Thomas, R. (1992). *Beyond race and gender: Unleashing the power of your total work force by managing diversity.* New York: AMACOM.

U.S. Small Business Administration. (2004). Small Business Act (15 USC 637). Retrieved May 25, 2013, from www.sba.gov/regulations/sbaact/sbaact.html

Index

Please note: page numbers in *italics* followed by *f* indicate figures, by *p* indicate photographs, and by *t* indicate tables

integration diversity paradigm 337; legislative mandates 338, 339; lived experience 335, 336, 342; microaggression 337–8, 342; microassault 338; microinsult 338; microinvalidation 338; organizational social justice 339–40, 442; overview 334; paradigm defined 337; participatory democracy 340; physical attack 339; prejudice 335, 338–9; racial microaggression 338, 342; re-conceptualizing the meaning of diversity 334–6; social injustice defined 336, 342; social justice defined 342; a social justice paradigm for action-oriented organizations 336–9; socially disadvantaged 335, 343; socially stigmatized 335, 343; social oppression 336, 342; social power 339; Title VII of the Civil Rights Acts (1964) 335, 338–9; workforce social justice council (WSJC) 341

re-emergence of racial harassment and racial hate symbols 295–311; affirmative action 304; airline pilots 297; airline security guards 297; American Civil Liberties Union 297; confederate or swastika signs 300; cross burning 299; Cross-Country Diversity Network 306; diversity education 307; emotional impact of racial harassment 300–302; Equal Employment Opportunity Commission (EEOC) 303, 306; First Amendment 299, 300; Jen Six episode 299; Jim Crow laws 300; Ku Klux Klan 298, 299; law enforcement officers 297; law suits 301, 303; media and Internet 300; Motorola 305, 306; nooses and lynching 298–9; overview 295; prejudice 296; public schools

302–3; race-based traumatic stress 301; Race Relations Workshop 306; racial discrimination defined 296–7, 308; racial harassment defined 296, 308; racial harassment in work environments 302–3; racial hate symbols 298–300, 308; racial oppression 298, 308; racial profiling 297, 308; racism defined 296, 308; racist graffiti 300; sensitivity training 304; September 11 attacks 297; social justice and emancipatory paradigm 305; *The Souls of Black Folks* (Du Bois) 300; stereotypes 296, 301; Title VII violations 303, *303t*; training as a solution 304–7; visual displays of a racial nature 300

Rehabilitation Act of 1973: Section 501 275, 276, 277; visible and invisible disabilities 286, 287, 291
rehabilitation model of disability 286
relationships and educational status, sexual orientation 148–50
religion/spiritual beliefs, personal/physical appearance stigmatizing 271
religious garb, personal/physical appearance stigmatizing 266, 268, 271
reverse discrimination 38
Rockefellers 183
Roosevelt, Thomas R., Jr. 54
Roots (Haley) 39
Rosie the Riveter, gender 96, *99p*, *100p*
ruling class 183

Scott, Chaunda L. 3–33, 34–58, 125–41, 181–97, 283–94, 295–311, 312–33; *see also* cross-cultural team opportunities and challenges; ethnicity; historical perspectives; re-emergence of racial harassment and racial hate

pedagogy (CRP) 38; Critical Racism Pedagogy Model 35–41, *40f*; critical reflection (CR) 43; critical theory 37; critical theory school of thought 35, 37–9; cultural conscious (CC) 43; cultural racism 39; descriptive thinking (DT) 43; dialogic thinking (DIT) 43; diverse groups 53–4; Diverse Voices Conference Model 45–50, *48–9t*; Embedded Intergroup Relations Theory (EIRT) 53–4; framework defined 34, 55; higher education conference 45–50; individual racism 39; institutional racism 39; model defined 34, 55; Model for Creating Diversity (MCD) 50–2; Multicultural Organization Theoretical Framework 52–3; Oakland University 45; Organizational Development and Change Model (Lewin) 50–1; organizational justice 39; overview 34–5; Polyrhythmic Realities Framework 44–5; praxis (PX) 43; reverse discrimination 38; social justice 39, 40; Social Justice Critical Reflection Model (SJCRM) 42–3, *42f*; theoretical and practice-based paradigms 35; theory defined 34, 55; Trends in Mandating, Managing, and Leveraging Diversity in the Workforce Framework 1954–2014 (Scott) 14, 19, *20–6t*, 54; unfreezing/moving/refreezing/competitive advantage 51–2

theory, defined 34, 55; *see also* theories, models, and frameworks

Tisdale, Elizabeth 47, 206–7

Title VII, Civil Rights Act of 1964 (Amended in 1972 and 1991) 9, 11; gender 101, 117; and organizational culture 66; personal/physical appearance

stigmatizing 270–1, 274, 277; race 75; re-conceptualizing and re-visioning diversity 335, 338–9; religion 207; violations of (2005–2012) 303, *303t*

tokenism, gender 107

tolerance, sexual orientation 154, 171

trade, governmental policies on 315

Traditional generation ("silent generation") 223, 242

transgender issues 143, 158–67; antidiscrimination policies 163; Association for Lesbian, Gay, Bisexual, and Transgender Issues in Counseling (ALGBTIC) 165; Competencies for Counseling Transgender Clients 143, 165–7; competencies for human resource development practitioners 165–7; Employment Non-Discrimination Act (ENDA) 143, 163; gender discrimination 164; gender queer 159, 171; hormonal therapy in transitioning 163–4; identity development in life stages 159–60; job training 165; real-life experience in transitioning 164; sexism 164; sex reassignment surgery in transitioning 164, 171; sex work 165; transgender defined 145–6, *145t*, 158–9, 171; transitioning 143, 160, 162, 163–5, 172; transmen 164; Transsexual Identity Formation Model 160–3; transwomen 164; workplace harassment 152; *see also* sexual orientation

transitioning, transgender issues 143, 160, 162, 163–5, 171

Transsexual Identity Formation Model 160–3

Trends in Mandating, Managing, and Leveraging Diversity in the Workforce Framework 1954–2014 (Scott) 14, 19, *20–6t*, 54

About the Editors/Authors

Dr. Marilyn Y. Byrd is an assistant professor of Management and Marketing, University of Mary Hardin-Baylor, Belton, Texas. Dr. Byrd earned a BBA and an MBA from Sam Houston State University in Huntsville, Texas, and a Ph.D. in Human Resource Development from Texas A&M University, College Station, Texas. She teaches undergraduate and graduate courses in human resource management, organizational behavior, managerial communication, and business ethics at the University of Mary Hardin-Baylor in Belton, Texas. Dr. Byrd is a member of the Academy of Management and the Academy of Human Resource Development, where she serves as chairperson of the Workforce Diversity & Inclusion Steering Committee. In 2012, Dr. Byrd was recognized by the Academy of Human Resource Development for exemplary leadership. She currently serves as an Associate Editor for *Advances in Developing Human Resources* (ADHR), one of four journals affiliated with the Academy of Human Resource Development.

Dr. Byrd co-edited and authored the ADHR issue, *Giving Voice: The Sociocultural Realities of African American Women's Leadership Experiences*, with Dr. Christine A. Stanley, Texas A&M University. This issue was the first ADHR issue devoted exclusively to African American women's experiences. Most recently she co-edited and authored *Handbook of Research on Workforce Diversity in a Global Society*. She was appointed to participate in the Society of Human Resource Management Diversity & Inclusion Standards Task Force that was responsible for establishing standards for diversity professionals in the HR community. Dr. Byrd is interested in contributing to research and literature in the area of organizational social justice. Her other scholarly interests include leadership theorizing and issues emerging from racial diversity in the workplace.

Dr. Chaunda L. Scott is an associate professor and the graduate coordinator of the Master of Training and Development Program in the Department of Human Resource Development (HRD) housed in the School of Education and Human Services at Oakland University in Rochester, Michigan. She also serves as the diversity and inclusion specialist for the office of the dean in the School of Education and Human Services at Oakland University. Dr. Scott comes to Oakland University by way of The White House, The Harvard Graduate School of Education, and Teachers College Columbia University. At Oakland University, Dr. Scott teaches a variety of HRD courses in the Undergraduate HRD Program and Masters of Training and Development Program. She has also taught several courses in the Honors College. Her scholarly research interests lie in eradicating racism in society, workforce diversity education and training, human resource development, diversity integration in organizations, organizational justice, and tracking the status of Black South African women in the workplace post-apartheid.

Dr. Scott has also published her research in a number of respected national and international journals and is a recipient of a 2009 cutting-edge research award from the Academy of Human Resource Development. She has presented her research in such locations as Cape Town, South Africa; Oxford, England; Beijing, China; Limerick, Ireland; Montreal, Canada; Washington, D.C.; Chicago, Illinois; and Minneapolis, Minnesota. In addition to the above, Dr. Scott is the founder and president of the Diverse Voices Initiative. Created in 1999, Diverse Voices is a Michigan statewide higher education initiative that provides a supportive forum for Michigan higher education students, renowned scholars, business professionals, and community members to speak out in support of valuing all aspects of human diversity. Dr. Scott's professional service included serving as the first chairperson of the Academy of Human Resource Development's (AHRD) Cultural Diversity Committee/Special Interest Group. Currently, Dr. Scott serves as a member of the Academy of Human Resource Development, the Midwest Business Administration and Association International, and an appointed member of the Society of Human Resource Management (SHRM) Diversity & Inclusion Standards Task Force. Most recently in 2012, Dr. Scott served as a co-editor of the *Handbook on Workforce Diversity in a Global Society—Technologies and Concepts* published by IGI publishers in 2012. Most notable in 2013, Dr. Scott was named as one of the Top 25 Education Professors in Michigan by Online Schools Michigan.

About the Contributing Authors

Dr. Lisa Bass is an assistant professor of Educational Leadership and Policy at the North Carolina State University. She has a joint doctorate in Educational Leadership and Policy and Comparative and International Education. She has two master's degrees: the first in Business Administration and the second in Teaching. Her bachelor's degree is in Economics. Dr. Bass enjoys comparing educational systems from around the world and has traveled to Mexico, Ghana, Brazil, Hong Kong, and South Africa. Her primary research interest, however, is urban school reform through alternative approaches to schooling. Her goal is to positively impact urban education and the perceptions of urban youth. She often situates her analysis through the lens of ethical frameworks.

Dr. Trammell Bristol is a quality assurance coordinator employed by the Department of Children & Families in New Jersey, where she coordinates various adult education initiatives. In 2004, Dr. Bristol received her Ed.D. in Adult Education from Penn State University–Harrisburg. Her scholarly research interests include diversity management and equity issues. Dr. Bristol has published several articles and has presented her research at several international conference venues, including the Academy of Human Resource Development and the Adult Education Research Conference.

Dr. Michael P. Chaney is an associate professor in the Department of Counseling at Oakland University in Rochester, Michigan. He received his Ph.D. in Counseling from Georgia State University. As a licensed professional counselor and National Certified Counselor, he has provided mental health services to lesbian, gay, bisexual, transgender, queer, questioning, and intersex individuals and people living with HIV/AIDS. He is past-president of the Association of LGBT Issues in Counseling, a division of the American Counseling Association, and he is a regional trainer for the American Psychological Association's HIV Office for Psychology Education (HOPE) Program. Dr. Chaney has numerous publications in prestigious journals in the areas of addictions, sexual compulsivity and the Internet, sexual orientation, gender-identity and expression, social justice, and advocacy in counseling.

Dr. Lisa Hawley is an associate professor and the department chair in the Department of Counseling at Oakland University in Rochester, Michigan. She received her Ph.D. in Counselor Education at the University of South Carolina. Dr. Hawley's research interests include group and techniques training, socioeconomic issues and mental health, qualitative research methods, and professional identity and advocacy. At Oakland University, Dr. Hawley teaches the following courses: An Introduction to Counseling, Multicultural Counseling, Techniques in Counseling, Group Counseling, Advanced Group Counseling, Practicum, Internship, Program Evaluation, Human Sexuality, Dissertation Preparation, Program Evaluation, and Advanced Consultation. Dr. Hawley has also published her research in the following respected journals: *The Professional Identity of Counselor Educators, The Clinical Supervisor, The Journal for Specialists in Group Work, The Journal of Humanistic Education and Development, and The Family Journal: Counseling and Therapy for Couples and Families.*

Dr. Claretha Hughes is an associate professor in the Department of Rehabilitation, Human Resources, and Communication Disorders at the University of Arkansas and Director of the College of Education and Health Professions' Honors Program. She received her Ph.D. from Virginia Tech, and her research focuses on value creation through the use of human resource development and technology development. She is interested in the impact of values (a) on teaching and learning processes and motivation; (b) on organizational culture, change strategies, and leadership; and (c) on technology in the workplace environment and employee behavior. In 2012 Dr. Hughes received the R. Wayne Pace Book of the Year Award from the Academy of Human Resource Development for her book *Valuing People and Technology in the Workplace* and has been nominated for the American Academy of Management 2013 George R. Terry Book Award. In 2009, Dr. Hughes was acknowledged by the University Council of Workforce and Human Resource Education as an "Outstanding Assistant Professor."

Dr. Gaetane Jean-Marie is professor of educational leadership and department chair of Leadership, Foundations & Human Resource Education at the University of Louisville. For the past seven years, she held a joint appointment in African and African American Studies while an associate professor of educational leadership at the University of Oklahoma. Her research focuses on leadership development and preparation, effective leadership for educational equity in K–12 schools, women and leadership in K–12 and higher education context, and urban school reform. To date, she has over 60 publications which include books, book chapters, and academic articles in numerous peer-reviewed journals. She is the co-editor of *Women of Color in Higher Education: Turbulent Past, Promising Future* (2011) and *Women of Color in Higher Education: Contemporary Perspectives and New Directions* (2011) with Dr. Brenda Lloyd-Jones. Also, she is the editor of the *Journal of School Leadership*, book review editor of the *Journal of Educational Administration*, past chair/president of the Leadership for Social Justice AERA/SIG, and co-founder of Advancing Women of Color in the Academy (AWOCA).

Dr. Brenda Lloyd-Jones is an associate professor and associate chair of the Department of Human Relations at the University of Oklahoma. She received her Ph.D. in Education, Administration, and Research with an emphasis in Leadership at the University of Tulsa. Her research examines the intersections between gender, race, and generations in organizations. Co-editor (with Dr. Gaetane Jean-Marie) of a two-volume book: (1) *Women of Color in Higher Education: Turbulent Past, Promising Future* and (2) *Women of Color in Higher Education: Changing Directions and New Perspectives* (2011, Emerald Group Publishing Limited), she has also published in several peer-reviewed journals, including *Advances in Developing Human Resources* (ADHR). Her teaching centers on organizational studies in general and focuses on leadership access in the contexts of organizational justice. Recognized for her instructional strategies and teaching practices, she is also a professional speaker, experienced group facilitator, and certified mediator. An ardent community volunteer, she was honored with the Mayor's Commission on the Status of Women Award for Public Service. Accordingly, she is also interested in the parameters of volunteering and engages in research on the topics of community volunteers and leadership.

Dr. Ketevan Mamiseishvili is an associate professor of higher education at the University of Arkansas. She completed her doctorate at the University of Missouri in Educational Leadership and Policy Analysis. Prior to her current position, Dr. Mamiseishvili worked as a research assistant and evaluation coordinator in the Department of Student Life at the University of Missouri. She also taught English as a foreign language overseas in her home country of Georgia. She is actively involved in national professional associations, including American Educational Research Association, Association for the Study of Higher Education, and Association for Institutional Research. Her research focuses on foreign-born faculty work life, productivity, and job satisfaction in U.S. higher education.

Dr. Jose Martinez is a full professor of Sociology at the University of Mary Hardin-Baylor in Belton, Texas. He earned his Ph.D. in Sociology from the University of Texas. Dr. Martinez's research interests include race relations, social theory, and social class. He is a member of the American Sociological Association (Texas); the Association of Chicanos in Higher Education, Southwestern Council on Latin American Studies, and LULAC.

Mr. Terrance R. McClain is a doctoral candidate in Counseling at Oakland University. He is also a National Certified Counselor (NCC) and holds memberships in the American Counseling Association; American School Counselor Association; Association for Counselor Education and Supervision; Association for Spiritual, Ethical and Religious Values in Counseling; Association for Specialists in Group Work; Michigan Counseling Association; Michigan Association for Counselor Education and Supervision; Michigan Association for Specialists in Group Work; and the Association of Michigan School Counselors.

Dr. Cynthia Sims is an associate professor in the Department of Workforce Education and Development at Southern Illinois University Carbondale. She holds a Doctor of Education in adult and higher education, a Master of Arts in social work, a Master of Science in public service management, and a Bachelor of Science in business administration. Her research interests include workplace power, privilege, and diversity; the impact of colorism on women's career development; and the recruitment and retention of minorities in higher education. Dr. Sims is a member of the Association for Career and Technical Education and the Academy of Human Resource Development.

Dr. Jody A. Worley, an assistant professor in the Department of Human Relations at the University of Oklahoma, received his Ph.D. in educational psychology with emphasis in research methods, measurement, and statistics. His primary research interests include research methodology (e.g., survey design issues), organizational behavior/work-related issues (e.g., burnout, work–family conflict, workplace diversity), and community psychology (e.g., quality of life issues for children and minorities). His professional affiliations and networks include the Southern Management Association (SMA), the American Psychological Association (APA), and the American Educational Research Association (AERA).